# WEST'S LAW SCHOOL ADVISORY BOARD

CURTIS J. BERGER
Professor of Law, Columbia University

JESSE H. CHOPER
Professor of Law,
University of California, Berkeley

DAVID P. CURRIE
Professor of Law, University of Chicago

YALE KAMISAR
Professor of Law, University of Michigan

MARY KAY KANE
Dean and Professor of Law, University of California,
Hastings College of the Law

WAYNE R. LaFAVE
Professor of Law, University of Illinois

ARTHUR R. MILLER
Professor of Law, Harvard University

GRANT S. NELSON
Professor of Law, University of California, Los Angeles

JAMES J. WHITE
Professor of Law, University of Michigan

CHARLES ALAN WRIGHT
Charles Alan Wright Chair in Federal Courts
The University of Texas

# LABOR AND EMPLOYMENT ARBITRATION
## IN A NUTSHELL

By

DENNIS R. NOLAN
Webster Professor of Labor Law
University of South Carolina

**WEST GROUP**

**ST. PAUL, MINN.**
**1998**

*Nutshell Series, In a Nutshell*, the Nutshell Logo and the West Group symbol are registered trademarks used herein under license. Registered in the U.S. Patent and Trademark Office.

COPYRIGHT © 1998 By WEST GROUP
610 Opperman Drive
P.O. Box 64526
St. Paul, MN 55164-0526
1-800-328-9352

All rights reserved
Printed in the United States of America

**Library of Congress Cataloging-in-Publication Data**

Nolan, Dennis R., 1945–
    Labor & employment arbitration in a nutshell / by Dennis R. Nolan.
      p.   cm. — (Nutshell series)
    Includes index.
    ISBN 0-314-21160-8 (pbk.)
    1. Arbitration, Industrial—United States.  I. Title.
II. Series.
KF3425.N638  1998
344.7301'89143—dc21                             98-10054
                                                                                       CIP

**ISBN 0-314-21160-8**

*In Memory of*
Joseph L. Nolan, 1910–1990

*And for*
Fran,
To Whom I Owe All

\*

# PREFACE

This is a new book, but it does have a predecessor. In 1979, I published *Labor Arbitration Law and Practice in a Nutshell*. Despite good intentions of a timely second edition, other commitments intervened. By the time I returned to the topic, in 1997, I found that much had changed: the legal rules governing labor arbitration; the astounding growth of the new and related field of individual employment arbitration; and, not least, my own understanding of the topic. I wrote in 1979 from the point of view of a sincere but inexperienced academic. I write in 1997 from the view of an experienced arbitration practitioner—without, I hope, any loss of my original sincerity.

Because of these changes, a simple update was no longer possible. Any revision would have to be so thorough as to constitute a virtually new book. That is what I have done. A reader comparing the two works will find many similar section headings but few sentences, and hardly any paragraphs, without significant changes. More importantly, there is a wealth of new information. That is why the new book is so much longer than the old. That is also why there is a new title.

This book is not intended as a substitute for classroom instruction in labor arbitration, still less for

*PREFACE*

practical experience in the field. Nor is it intended to (or could it) take the place of the detailed treatises on labor arbitration already available to the practitioner and scholar. Its purpose is much narrower, to provide students and practitioners alike a simple but comprehensive description of the origin, development, and practice of labor and employment arbitration in America. Ideally this overview will serve as an introduction to more thorough study in other forms.

Even this limited purpose requires a good bit of detail. While trying to strike a balance between simplicity and comprehensiveness, I may have erred too much in the latter direction. If so, I apologize to the reader who looks for a shorter treatment. Nevertheless, I found it necessary to present the major issues in arbitration law at length to permit a full exploration of their importance and of the conflicting opinions on them. I have made every effort to be fair, but inevitably some personal beliefs have made their way into the text. The attentive reader should be able to identify these easily, and evaluate them accordingly.

Every book is the product of many people; no author writes in complete isolation from others. This one, so long in gestation, owes more debts than most. Among those who contributed to the book are students in my classes over the years, for helping me clarify issues; research assistants, who found even the most obscure cases and texts and boldly correct-

*PREFACE*

ed my mistakes; academic and arbitral colleagues who provided advice gladly and frankly; deans who provided needed financial and time support; and a family that tolerated the hours lost to "the book."

Several people deserve individual recognition. First, Dean Roger Abrams of Rutgers Law School, a classmate, friend, and able scholar and arbitrator, offered extensive comments on the predecessor book and worked with me on a score of articles and chapters. He taught me much, and this book is the better for it.

Second, one of the major intervening projects between the predecessor Nutshell and this one was *Labor Arbitration: A Coursebook*, written with Laura Cooper and published by West in 1994. Again, I learned much from working with Laura, in good part because she forced me to examine and defend almost every assertion I made. I am also indebted to her because I have cribbed shamelessly from our joint product. The student using that textbook will find echoes here.

Third, my latest research assistant, Jeff Dunleavy, has gone beyond the bounds of duty to make this work accurate and readable. In addition to the usual researching tasks, he served as my Everyman, letting me know time and again how my words in draft appeared to a reader unfamiliar with the subject.

*PREFACE*

Finally, I thank the American Arbitration Association for permission to reprint its copyrighted publications in the Appendices.

DENNIS R. NOLAN

Columbia, South Carolina
April, 1998

# OUTLINE

|  | Page |
|---|---|
| DEDICATION | III |
| PREFACE | V |

**Chapter I. The Development of Labor and Employment Arbitration** ......... 1
- A. Definition of the Concept .................... 1
- B. Origins and Development ................... 3
- C. The Arbitration Profession ................. 7

**Chapter II. Arbitration Procedure** ......... 10
- A. Contractual Requirements .................. 10
  1. In General ................................. 10
  2. The Submission Agreement ............ 12
  3. The Arbitration Clause ................. 13
- B. Initiating Arbitration ......................... 16
  1. The Demand for Arbitration .......... 16
  2. The Reply ................................... 17
- C. Types of Arbitration Systems .............. 18
  1. The Single Permanent Arbitrator System .................................... 18
  2. The Permanent Panel System ........ 21
  3. The Temporary Arbitrator System ... 22
- D. Selecting the Arbitrator ..................... 23
  1. The Arbitration Profession ............ 23
  2. Methods of Selection .................... 25

## OUTLINE

| | Page |
|---|---|
| **Chapter II. Arbitration Procedure**—Continued | |
|     3. Learning About An Arbitrator | 28 |
|     4. Appointment | 33 |
| E.   Advocates in Arbitration | 34 |
| F.   Preparing for Arbitration | 35 |
|     1. The Grievance Procedure | 35 |
|     2. Discovery | 38 |
|     3. Preparing the Evidence | 41 |
| G.   The Arbitration Hearing | 42 |
|     1. Time and Place | 42 |
|     2. Record of the Hearing | 43 |
|     3. Swearing Witnesses | 43 |
|     4. Order of Presentation | 44 |
| H.   Post–Hearing Procedure | 48 |
|     1. Briefs | 48 |
|     2. The Award; Finality | 49 |
|     3. Costs | 51 |
| I.   Summary Evaluation of Labor and Employment Arbitration: Time and Expense | 52 |
| **Chapter III. Variations on Traditional Labor Arbitration** | 55 |
| A.   Expedited Arbitration | 55 |
|     1. Early Experiments | 56 |
|     2. Current Expedited Arbitration Programs | 59 |
| B.   Compulsory Arbitration | 60 |
| C.   Advisory Arbitration and Fact–Finding | 65 |
| D.   Interest Arbitration | 68 |
|     1. In General | 68 |
|     2. The Private Sector | 69 |

*OUTLINE*

|  | Page |
|---|---|
| **Chapter III. Variations on Traditional Labor Arbitration**—Continued | |
| 3. The Public Sector | 74 |
| 4. Criteria | 75 |
| 5. Final–Offer Arbitration | 79 |

**Chapter IV. Application of Arbitration to New Situations** ............ 83
A. The Public Sector ............ 83
   1. The Federal Government ............ 83
   2. State and Local Governments ............ 87
B. Higher Education ............ 89
C. Professional Sports ............ 91
D. Airlines ............ 94
E. Individual Employment Arbitration ............ 97

**Chapter V. The Legal Status of Labor and Employment Arbitration** ............ 101
A. At Common Law ............ 101
B. Statutes Before the Taft–Hartley Act ............ 103
   1. Early State Laws on Labor Arbitration ............ 103
   2. Federal Legislation for Railway Labor Disputes ............ 104
   3. Other Federal Laws Before 1947 ............ 105
   4. Modern State Arbitration Laws ............ 107
C. Section 301 of the Taft–Hartley Act ............ 110
   1. The Language of Section 301 ............ 110
   2. The *Lincoln Mills* Case ............ 111
   3. An Introduction to the Relationship Between the Arbitrator and the Courts: The Steelworkers Trilogy ............ 113

## OUTLINE

Page

**Chapter V. The Legal Status of Labor and Employment Arbitration—Continued**
    4. Section 301 and the Norris–LaGuardia Act: *Boys Markets* and Later Developments .................... 121
D. Section 301's Preemptive Effect .............. 129

**Chapter VI. The Relationships Between Arbitrators, the NLRB, and the Courts** .................... 133
A. Arbitrability .................... 133
    1. Substantive Arbitrability .................... 134
    2. Procedural Arbitrability .................... 146
B. Arbitrators and External Law .................... 147
    1. The Theories .................... 151
    2. The Application .................... 154
C. The NLRB and the Arbitration Process .... 156
    1. Introduction .................... 156
    2. Post–Arbitration Deferral .................... 158
    3. Pre–Arbitration Deferral .................... 161
D. Court Deferral .................... 164
    1. Labor Cases .................... 164
    2. Statutory Cases in the Collective Bargaining Context .................... 165
    3. Statutory Cases in the Individual Employment Context .................... 171

**Chapter VII. Judicial Review of Arbitration Awards** .................... 180
A. Introduction .................... 180
B. Failure of the Award to "Draw Its Essence" From the Collective Agreement .... 183

*OUTLINE*

Page

**Chapter VII. Judicial Review of Arbitration Awards**—Continued

| | | |
|---|---|---|
| C. | Lack of Jurisdiction or Authority for the Award | 185 |
| D. | Party Misconduct, Arbitral Partiality, and Procedural Unfairness | 190 |
| | 1. Party Misconduct | 191 |
| | 2. Arbitral Partiality | 191 |
| | 3. Procedural Unfairness | 193 |
| E. | Gross Error or Irrationality | 196 |
| F. | Violation of Law or Public Policy | 197 |
| | 1. Introduction | 197 |
| | 2. Public Safety and Criminal Law Cases | 201 |
| | 3. Sexual Harassment Cases | 203 |
| G. | Incompleteness, Ambiguity, or Inconsistency | 206 |
| H. | Individual Challenges: The Duty of Fair Representation | 208 |
| I. | Judicial Review of Individual Employment Arbitration Decisions | 212 |
| J. | Administrative and Judicial Review of Federal Sector Arbitration Decisions | 214 |

**Chapter VIII. The "Common Law" of the Arbitration Process** — 217

| | | |
|---|---|---|
| A. | Some Problems of Due Process and Individual Rights | 217 |
| | 1. Notice | 219 |
| | 2. Separate Representation and Third–Party Intervention | 221 |
| | 3. Self–Incrimination | 224 |
| | 4. Search and Seizure | 226 |

XIII

## *OUTLINE*

**Chapter VIII. The "Common Law" of the Arbitration Process**—Continued

    5. Confrontation and Cross-Examination ............................................. 229
    6. Surprise: Changed Issues, Arguments or Evidence ......................................... 231
    7. Ex Parte Hearings ..................................... 234
    8. The Agreed Case ...................................... 235
B.  The Burden of Proof ..................................... 237
    1. The Burden of Producing Evidence .... 238
    2. The Burden of Persuasion .................. 239
    3. The Quantum of Proof ........................ 240
C.  Some Problems of Evidence ......................... 242
    1. The Applicability of Evidentiary Rules to Arbitration ............................. 242
    2. Hearsay .................................................. 245
    3. The Plain Meaning Rule and Extrinsic Evidence ........................................ 246
    4. Past Practice ......................................... 250
    5. Past Employee Conduct ...................... 255
    6. Medical Evidence .................................. 259
D.  The Arbitration Award and Opinion ......... 261
    1. Form and Content ................................. 261
    2. Time Limitations .................................. 262
    3. Arbitration Panels ................................ 264
    4. The Opinion ........................................... 265
    5. Publication ............................................. 267
    6. Termination of the Arbitrator's Authority ................................................... 269
    7. Interpretation, Modification or Correction of the Award by the Arbitrator ........................................................ 271

*OUTLINE*

| | Page |
|---|---|
| **Chapter VIII. The "Common Law" of the Arbitration Process**—Continued | |
| 8. Actions to Enforce or Vacate an Arbitrator's Award | 272 |
| E. Remedies | 274 |
| 1. In General | 274 |
| 2. Discharge Cases | 276 |
| 3. Monetary Awards in Non–Discharge Cases | 277 |
| 4. Calculation of the Amount of Damages | 278 |
| 5. Punitive Damages | 281 |
| 6. Rights Without Remedies | 282 |
| **Chapter IX. The Process of Contractual Interpretation** | 284 |
| A. The Role of Arbitral Precedent: Stare Decisis, Res Judicata, and Collateral Estoppel in Labor and Employment Arbitration | 285 |
| 1. Legal Concepts of Precedent | 285 |
| 2. Judicial Application of the Legal Concepts in Labor and Employment Arbitration | 287 |
| 3. Arbitral Approaches | 288 |
| 4. Persuasive Authority | 290 |
| B. The Arbitration Clause and Its Meaning: Arbitrability From the Arbitrator's Point of View | 293 |
| 1. Substantive Arbitrability | 293 |
| 2. Procedural Arbitrability | 299 |

XV

# OUTLINE

| | Page |
|---|---|
| **Chapter IX. The Process of Contractual Interpretation**—Continued | |
| C. Principles of Interpretation | 304 |
|    1. If the Relevant Language is Clear and Unambiguous, the Arbitrator Should Apply It Without Recourse to Other Indications of Intent | 305 |
|    2. The Sounds of Silence: Interpretation Without Specific Language | 306 |
|    3. Arbitrators Should Avoid Interpretations that Would Bring the Contract Into Conflict With Positive Law | 308 |
|    4. Specific Language Controls General Language | 309 |
|    5. Arbitrators Should Construe Ambiguous Language in Context | 309 |
|    6. Arbitrators Should Give Words Their Normal Meaning Absent Proof that the Parties Intended Some Other Meaning | 310 |
|    7. Arbitrators Should Construe Ambiguous Language Against the Drafter | 311 |
|    8. Arbitrators Should Avoid Interpretations that Would Create a Forfeiture | 312 |
|    9. Arbitrators Should Avoid Interpretations that Would Produce Harsh, Absurd or Nonsensical Results, if Another Interpretation Would Lead to Just and Reasonable Results | 313 |

*OUTLINE*

Page

**Chapter X. The Subject Matter of Labor and Employment Arbitration** ......... 314
A. Discipline and Discharge ..................... 314
   1. The Just Cause Principle .................. 315
   2. Common Reasons for Discipline and Requirements for Just Cause ......... 319
   3. Off–Duty Conduct ........................ 321
B. Management Rights ............................ 323
C. Seniority ............................................. 324
D. Wages and Hours ................................ 327
   1. Wage Disputes ............................. 327
   2. Hours Disputes ............................ 330
E. Fringe Benefits ................................... 331
F. Subcontracting ................................... 335
G. Union Security ................................... 337
H. Occupational Safety and Health ............ 340

**Appendices**
A. AAA Labor Arbitration Rules ............... 346
B. AAA Expedited Labor Arbitration Procedures ............................................. 363
C. AAA National Rules for the Resolution of Employment Disputes ...................... 367
D. AAA Excelleration Program ................. 389
E. AAA Forms ........................................ 394
F. FMCS Procedures for Arbitration Services .................................................. 404
G. FMCS Expedited Arbitration Rules ....... 420
H. FMCS Forms ...................................... 423
I. Code of Professional Responsibility for Arbitrators of Labor–Management Disputes .............................................. 426
J. The Federal Arbitration Act ................. 452

## OUTLINE

| | Page |
|---|---|
| **App.** | |
| K. Uniform Arbitration Act | 461 |
| L. A Due Process Protocol for Mediation and Arbitration of Statutory Disputes Arising Out of the Employment Relationship | 470 |
| INDEX | 479 |

# TABLE OF CASES

**References are to Pages**

Action Distributing Co. v. Teamsters Local 1038, 977 F.2d 1021 (6th Cir.1992), *287*

Aldens, Inc., 58 LA 1213 (John P. McGury, 1972), *227, 228*

Alexander v. Gardner–Denver Co., 415 U.S. 36, 94 S.Ct. 1011, 39 L.Ed.2d 147 (1974), *166, 170, 171, 172, 173, 178*

Allen v. Allied Plant Maintenance Co. of Tennessee, Inc., 881 F.2d 291 (6th Cir.1989), *236*

Allendale Nursing Home, Inc. v. Local 1115 Joint Bd., 377 F.Supp. 1208 (S.D.N.Y.1974), *193*

Allis–Chalmers Corp. v. Lueck, 471 U.S. 202, 105 S.Ct. 1904, 85 L.Ed.2d 206 (1985), *130, 131, 132*

Allis–Chalmers Manufacturing Co., 39 LA 1213 (Russell Smith, 1962), *336*

Amalgamated Ass'n of St. Elec. Ry. & Motor Coach Emp. of America, Division 998 v. Wisconsin Employment Relations Bd., 340 U.S. 383, 71 S.Ct. 359, 95 L.Ed. 364 (1951), *63*

Amanda Bent Bolt Co. v. UAW Local 1549, 451 F.2d 1277 (6th Cir.1971), *187*

American International Aluminum Corp., 68–2 ARB ¶ 8591 (John F. Sembower, 1968), *225*

American Nat. Can Co., 293 NLRB No. 110, 293 NLRB 901 (N.L.R.B.1989), enforcement granted N.L.R.B. v. American Nat. Can Co., Foster–Forbes Glass Div., 924 F.2d 518 (4th Cir.1991), *163*

American Nat. Can Co. v. United Steelworkers of America, 120 F.3d 886 (8th Cir.1997), *288*

American Postal Workers Union, AFL–CIO v. United States Postal Service, 52 F.3d 359, 311 U.S.App.D.C. 210 (D.C.Cir. 1995), *191*

## TABLE OF CASES

American Postal Workers Union, AFL–CIO v. United States Postal Service, 789 F.2d 1, 252 U.S.App.D.C. 169 (D.C.Cir. 1986), *184, 201*

Ampco–Pittsburgh Corp., 80 LA 472 (Steven Briggs, 1982), *331*

Anchor Hocking Corp., 81 LA 502 (Roger Abrams, 1983), *331*

Arizona Portland Cement Co., a Div. of California Portland Cement Co., a Div. of Calmag and Local 296, Independent Workers of North Amereica, 302 NLRB No. 5, 302 NLRB 36 (N.L.R.B.1991), *146*

Atkinson v. Sinclair Refining Co., 370 U.S. 238, 82 S.Ct. 1318, 8 L.Ed.2d 462 (1962), *129, 165*

AT & T Technologies, Inc. v. Communications Workers of America, 475 U.S. 643, 106 S.Ct. 1415, 89 L.Ed.2d 648 (1986), *135, 138*

Austin v. Owens–Brockway Glass Container, Inc., 78 F.3d 875 (4th Cir.1996), cert. denied ___ U.S. ___, 117 S.Ct. 432, 136 L.Ed.2d 330 (1996), *178*

Avco Corp. v. IAM Lodge 735, 390 U.S. 557, 88 S.Ct. 1235, 20 L.Ed.2d 126 (1968), *123*

Barrentine v. Arkansas–Best Freight System, Inc., 450 U.S. 728, 101 S.Ct. 1437, 67 L.Ed.2d 641 (1981), *170*

Becton v. Detroit Terminal of Consol. Freightways, 687 F.2d 140 (6th Cir.1982), cert. denied 460 U.S. 1040, 103 S.Ct. 1432, 75 L.Ed.2d 791 (1983), *169*

Bell Aerospace Co. Division of Textron, Inc. v. UAW Local 516, 500 F.2d 921 (2nd Cir.1974), *192, 194, 207*

Benson v. Communication Workers of America, 866 F.Supp. 910 (E.D.Va.1994), *219, 220*

Black v. Cutter Laboratories, 43 Cal.2d 788, 278 P.2d 905 (Cal. 1955), cert. dismissed 351 U.S. 292, 76 S.Ct. 824, 100 L.Ed. 1188 (1956), *198*

Blake v. U.S.M. Corp., Bailey Div., 94 LRRM 2509 (D.N.H.1977), *219*

Boston Printing Pressmen's Union v. Potter Press, 141 F.Supp. 553 (D.C.Mass.1956), affirmed 241 F.2d 787 (1st Cir.1957), cert. denied 355 U.S. 817, 78 S.Ct. 21, 2 L.Ed.2d 34 (1957), *73*

Botany Industries, Inc. v. New York Joint Bd., Amalgamated Clothing Workers of America, 375 F.Supp. 485 (S.D.N.Y. 1974), vacated Robb v. New York Joint Bd., Amalgamated Clothing Workers of America, 506 F.2d 1246 (2nd Cir.1974), *198*

## TABLE OF CASES

Bowen v. United States Postal Service, 459 U.S. 212, 103 S.Ct. 588, 74 L.Ed.2d 402 (1983), *212*

Boys Markets, Inc. v. Retail Clerks Union, Local 770, 398 U.S. 235, 90 S.Ct. 1583, 26 L.Ed.2d 199 (1970), *73, 122, 123, 124, 126, 128, 129*

Brisentine v. Stone & Webster Engineering Corp., 117 F.3d 519 (11th Cir.1997), *175, 178, 179*

Buffalo Forge Co. v. United Steelworkers of America, AFL–CIO, 428 U.S. 397, 96 S.Ct. 3141, 49 L.Ed.2d 1022 (1976), *73, 74, 125, 126, 127, 128*

Carbon Fuel Co. v. United Mine Workers of America, 444 U.S. 212, 100 S.Ct. 410, 62 L.Ed.2d 394 (1979), *129*

Carey v. Westinghouse Elec. Corp., 375 U.S. 261, 84 S.Ct. 401, 11 L.Ed.2d 320 (1964), *157, 159, 166, 223*

Carpenters Local No. 824 (AFL–CIO) v. Brunswick Corp., 342 F.2d 792 (6th Cir.1965), *146*

Cedar Coal Co. v. United Mine Workers of America, 560 F.2d 1153 (4th Cir.1977), cert. denied International Union, United Mine Workers of America v. Cedar Coal Co., 434 U.S. 1047, 98 S.Ct. 893, 54 L.Ed.2d 798 (1978), *128, 129*

Centel Business Systems, 90 LA 172 (Hy Fish, 1987), *302*

Champion International, 96 LA 325 (Gordon Statham, 1991), *322*

Charles Dowd Box Co. v. Courtney, 368 U.S. 502, 82 S.Ct. 519, 7 L.Ed.2d 483 (1962), *113, 122, 123*

Chas. Wolff Packing Co. v. Court of Industrial Relations of State of Kansas, 262 U.S. 522, 43 S.Ct. 630, 67 L.Ed. 1103 (1923), *61*

Chisolm v. Kidder, Peabody Asset Management, Inc., 966 F.Supp. 218 (S.D.N.Y.1997), *213*

Chrysler Motors Corp. v. International Union, Allied Indus. Workers of America, AFL–CIO, 959 F.2d 685 (7th Cir.1992), cert. denied Chrysler Corp. v. International Union, Allied Indus. Workers of America, AFL–CIO, 506 U.S. 908, 113 S.Ct. 304, 121 L.Ed.2d 227 (1992), *205*

**City of (see name of city)**

Clark v. Hein–Werner Corp., 8 Wis.2d 264, 99 N.W.2d 132 (Wis.1959), cert. denied Local 1377 of International Association of Machinists, AFL–CIO v. Hein–Werner Corp., 362 U.S. 962, 80 S.Ct. 878, 4 L.Ed.2d 877 (1960), *220*

Cole v. Burns Intern. Sec. Services, 105 F.3d 1465, 323 U.S.App. D.C. 133 (D.C.Cir.1997), *106, 175, 214*

## TABLE OF CASES

Collyer Insulated Wire, Gulf & Western Systems Co., 192 NLRB No. 150, 192 NLRB 837 (N.L.R.B.1971), *161, 162*

Colt Industries Operating Corp., 73 LA 1087 (William Belshaw, 1979), *329*

Columbia Broadcasting System, Inc. v. American Recording & Broadcasting Ass'n, 414 F.2d 1326 (2nd Cir.1969), *224*

Commodity Warehousing Corp., 60 LA 1260 (1973), *227*

Communications Workers of America, AFL–CIO v. New York Tel. Co., 327 F.2d 94 (2nd Cir.1964), *138*

Communication Workers of America v. Southeastern Elec. Co-op. of Durant, Okl., 882 F.2d 467 (10th Cir.1989), *206*

Cone Mills Corp., 298 NLRB No. 70, 298 NLRB 661 (N.L.R.B. 1990), *160*

Connecticut Light & Power Co. v. Local 420, Intern. Broth. of Elec. Workers, AFL–CIO, 718 F.2d 14 (2nd Cir.1983), *288*

Coordinating Committee Steel Companies v. United Steelworkers of America, 436 F.Supp. 208 (W.D.Pa.1977), *74*

Cornelius v. Nutt, 472 U.S. 648, 105 S.Ct. 2882, 86 L.Ed.2d 515 (1985), *214, 215*

Crittenton Hospital, 85 LA 177 (George T. Roumell, 1985), *232*

Darr v. N.L.R.B., 801 F.2d 1404, 255 U.S.App.D.C. 365 (D.C.Cir. 1986), *160, 161*

Dean Witter Reynolds, Inc. v. Deislinger, 289 Ark. 248, 711 S.W.2d 771 (Ark.1986), *242*

Delta Air Lines, Inc. v. Air Line Pilots Ass'n, Intern., 861 F.2d 665 (11th Cir.1988), cert. denied Air Line Pilots Ass'n, Intern. v. Delta Air Lines, Inc., 493 U.S. 871, 110 S.Ct. 201, 107 L.Ed.2d 154 (1989), *200, 201, 202*

Delta Queen Steamboat Co. v. District 2 Marine Engineers Beneficial Ass'n, AFL–CIO, 889 F.2d 599 (5th Cir.1989), cert. denied District 2 Marine Engineers Beneficial Ass'n v. Delta Queen Steamboat Co., 498 U.S. 853, 111 S.Ct. 148, 112 L.Ed.2d 114 (1990), *184*

Devine v. Pastore, 732 F.2d 213, 235 U.S.App.D.C. 327 (D.C.Cir. 1984), *215*

Devine v. White, 711 F.2d 1082, 229 U.S.App.D.C. 154 (D.C.Cir. 1983), *216*

DiRussa v. Dean Witter Reynolds Inc., 121 F.3d 818 (2nd Cir. 1997), cert. denied ___ U.S. ___, 118 S.Ct. 695 (1998), *213*

Dorchy v. State of Kansas, 264 U.S. 286, 44 S.Ct. 323, 68 L.Ed. 686 (1924), *61*

## TABLE OF CASES

Douglas v. Veterans Admin., 5 M.S.P.B. 313, 5 M.S.P.R. 280 (M.S.P.B.1981), *215*

Drake Bakeries, Inc. v. Local 50, Am. Bakery and Confectionery Workers Intern., AFL–CIO, 370 U.S. 254, 82 S.Ct. 1346, 8 L.Ed.2d 474 (1962), *164*

Dreis & Krump Mfg. Co. v. International Ass'n of Machinists and Aerospace Workers, Dist. No. 8, 802 F.2d 247 (7th Cir.1986), *182, 273*

Dresser Industries, 96 LA 1063 (Samuel J. Nicholas, 1991), *303*

EG & G Mound Applied Technologies, 98 LA 923 (Langdon Bell, 1992), *320*

E.I. DuPont de Nemours and Co. v. Grasselli Employees Independent Ass'n of East Chicago, Inc., 790 F.2d 611 (7th Cir.1986), cert. denied 479 U.S. 853, 107 S.Ct. 186, 93 L.Ed.2d 120 (1986), *199*

El Mundo Broadcasting Corp. v. United Steelworkers of America, AFL–CIO CLC, 116 F.3d 7 (1st Cir.1997), *147*

Enterprise Wire Co., 46 LA 359 (1966), *315*

Ethyl Corp. v. United Steelworkers of America, AFL–CIO–CLC, 768 F.2d 180 (7th Cir.1985), *184*

Evans Products Co., 70 LA 526 (David Feller, 1978), *154*

Fon du Lac, City of, 69–2 ARB ¶ 8520 (Robert Moberly, 1969), *327*

Ford Motor Co., 19 LA 237 (1952), *252*

Ford Motor Co., Opinion A–132 (1944), *321*

Gardner v. Broderick, 392 U.S. 273, 88 S.Ct. 1913, 20 L.Ed.2d 1082 (1968), *224*

Gateway Coal Co. v. United Mine Workers of America, 414 U.S. 368, 94 S.Ct. 629, 38 L.Ed.2d 583 (1974), *125, 342, 343*

General American Transp. Corp., 228 NLRB No. 102, 228 NLRB 808 (N.L.R.B.1977), *162, 163*

George Day Const. Co., Inc. v. United Broth. of Carpenters and Joiners of America, Local 354, 722 F.2d 1471 (9th Cir.1984), *207*

Gilmer v. Interstate/Johnson Lane Corp., 500 U.S. 20, 111 S.Ct. 1647, 114 L.Ed.2d 26 (1991), *98, 170, 171, 172, 173, 174, 175, 177, 178, 266, 269*

## TABLE OF CASES

Glass, Molders, Pottery, Plastics and Allied Workers Intern. Union, AFL–CIO, CLC, Local 182B v. Excelsior Foundry Co., 56 F.3d 844 (7th Cir.1995), *272*

Goodyear Tire and Rubber Co., 80–2 ARB ¶ 8468 (Gordon Knight, 1980), *330*

Great Scott Supermarkets, Inc. v. Teamsters Local Union No. 337, 363 F.Supp. 1351 (E.D.Mich.1973), *39*

Grief Brothers Cooperage Corp., 42 LA 555 (1964), *315*

Gulf South Beverages, Inc., 87 LA 688 (1986), *302*


Hammontree v. N.L.R.B., 925 F.2d 1486, 288 U.S.App.D.C. 266 (D.C.Cir.1991), *163*

Hanford Atomic Metal Trades Council, AFL–CIO v. General Elec. Co., 353 F.2d 302 (9th Cir.1965), *207*

Hartford Provision Co., 89 LA 590 (Howard Sacks, 1987), *338*

Harvey Aluminum (Inc.) v. United Steelworkers of America, AFL–CIO, 263 F.Supp. 488 (C.D.Cal.1967), *194*

Hercules, Inc., AAA Case No. 31 300 00129 91 (Robert Williams, 1992), *290*

Hercules, Inc., 91 LA 521 (Dennis R. Nolan, 1988), *261*

Hill v. Norfolk and Western Ry. Co., 814 F.2d 1192 (7th Cir. 1987), *182, 183*

Hines v. Anchor Motor Freight, Inc., 424 U.S. 554, 96 S.Ct. 1048, 47 L.Ed.2d 231 (1976), *210, 211*

H. K. Porter Co. v. United Saw, File and Steel Products Workers of America, Federal Labor Union No. 22254, AFL–CIO, 333 F.2d 596 (3rd Cir.1964), *189*

Holodnak v. Avco Corp., Avco–Lycoming Division, Stratford, Connecticut, 381 F.Supp. 191 (D.Conn.1974), affirmed 514 F.2d 285 (2nd Cir.1975), cert. denied 423 U.S. 892, 96 S.Ct. 188, 46 L.Ed.2d 123 (1975), *211, 217*

Hoteles Condado Beach, La Concha and Convention Center v. Union De Tronquistas Local 901, 763 F.2d 34 (1st Cir.1985), *195*

Howard Johnson Co., Inc. v. Detroit Local Joint Executive Bd., Hotel and Restaurant Emp. and Bartenders Intern. Union, AFL–CIO, 417 U.S. 249, 94 S.Ct. 2236, 41 L.Ed.2d 46 (1974), *144*

Huey v. Department of Health and Human Services, 782 F.2d 1575 (Fed.Cir.1986), *215*

## TABLE OF CASES

Humphrey v. Moore, 375 U.S. 335, 84 S.Ct. 363, 11 L.Ed.2d 370 (1964), *220*

Independent Petroleum Workers of America, Inc. v. American Oil Co., 324 F.2d 903 (7th Cir.1963), affirmed 379 U.S. 130, 85 S.Ct. 271, 13 L.Ed.2d 333 (1964), *136*

International Ass'n of Heat and Frost Insulators, Local No. 12 v. Insulation Quality Enterprises, Ltd., 675 F.Supp. 1398 (E.D.N.Y.1988), *193*

International Ass'n of Machinists, Dist. No. 15, Local No. 402 v. Cutler–Hammer, Inc., 271 A.D. 917, 67 N.Y.S.2d 317 (N.Y.A.D. 1 Dept.1947), affirmed 297 N.Y. 519, 74 N.E.2d 464 (N.Y.1947), *114, 116*

International Broth. of Elec. Workers, Local Union No. 278 v. Jetero Corp., 496 F.2d 661 (5th Cir.1974), *185*

International Broth. of Firemen and Oilers, Local 100, 95 LA 189 (Nicholas Duda, 1990), *339*

International Broth. of Firemen and Oilers, Local 261 v. Great Northern Paper Co., 118 LRRM 2317 (D.Me.1984), affirmed 765 F.2d 295 (1st Cir.1985), *191*

International Paper Co., Southern Kraft Division, Bastrop Mill, 69 LA 857 (F. Jay Taylor, 1977), *154*

International Union of Petroleum and Indus. Workers v. Western Indus. Maintenance, Inc., 707 F.2d 425 (9th Cir.1983), *207*

International Woodworkers of America, United States AFL–CIO v. Weyerhaeuser Co., 7 F.3d 133 (8th Cir.1993), cert. denied 511 U.S. 1128, 114 S.Ct. 2135, 128 L.Ed.2d 865 (1994), *195*

Interscience Encyclopedia Inc., 55 LA 210 (Benjamin Roberts, 1970), *141, 145*

Iowa Elec. Light and Power Co. v. Local Union 204 of Intern. Broth. of Elec. Workers (AFL–CIO), 834 F.2d 1424 (8th Cir.1987), *200, 201*

Jacksonville Bulk Terminals, Inc. v. International Longshoremen's Ass'n, 457 U.S. 702, 102 S.Ct. 2672, 73 L.Ed.2d 327 (1982), *127*

John Wiley & Sons, Inc. v. Livingston, 376 U.S. 543, 84 S.Ct. 909, 11 L.Ed.2d 898 (1964), *118, 135, 141, 142, 143, 144, 145, 146, 299*

J.W. Wells Lumber Co., 42 LA 678 (Robert Howlett, 1964), *338*

## TABLE OF CASES

Kaiser Permanente (Sunset Medical Office), 99 LA 490 (Martin Henner, 1992), *320*

Kidd v. Equitable Life Assur. Soc. of United States, 32 F.3d 516 (11th Cir.1994), *176*

King Company, 89 LA 681 (1987), *218, 225*

Lingle v. Norge Div. of Magic Chef, Inc., 486 U.S. 399, 108 S.Ct. 1877, 100 L.Ed.2d 410 (1988), *130, 131, 132*

Litton Financial Printing Div., a Div. of Litton Business Systems, Inc. v. N.L.R.B., 501 U.S. 190, 111 S.Ct. 2215, 115 L.Ed.2d 177 (1991), *142, 143*

Livadas v. Bradshaw, 512 U.S. 107, 114 S.Ct. 2068, 129 L.Ed.2d 93 (1994), *131, 178*

Local 416, Sheetmetal Workers Intern. Ass'n (AFL–CIO) v. Helgesteel Corp., 335 F.Supp. 812 (W.D.Wis.1971), reversed 507 F.2d 1053 (7th Cir.1974), *281*

Local 174, Teamsters, Chauffeurs, Warehousemen and Helpers of America v. Lucas Flour Co., 369 U.S. 95, 82 S.Ct. 571, 7 L.Ed.2d 593 (1962), *113, 122, 124, 129*

Local 369, Bakery and Confectionery Workers Intern. Union of America, AFL–CIO v. Cotton Baking Co., Inc., 514 F.2d 1235 (5th Cir.1975), cert. denied Cotton Baking Co., Inc. v. Local 369, Bakery & Confectionery Workers Intern. Union of America, AFL–CIO, 423 U.S. 1055, 96 S.Ct. 786, 46 L.Ed.2d 644 (1976), *277*

Local Union No. 998, Intern. Union, United Auto., Aircraft and Agr. Implement Workers of America, AFL–CIO v. B. & T. Metals Co., 315 F.2d 432 (6th Cir.1963), *143*

Local Union No. 251 v. Narragansett Imp. Co., 503 F.2d 309 (1st Cir.1974), *193*

Martin v. Dana Corp., 114 F.3d 421 (3rd Cir.1997), withdrawn 114 F.3d 428 (3rd Cir.1997), *179*

McDonald v. City of West Branch, Mich., 466 U.S. 284, 104 S.Ct. 1799, 80 L.Ed.2d 302 (1984), *170*

McKesson Corp. v. Local 150 IBT, 969 F.2d 831 (9th Cir.1992), *263*

Merrill Lynch, Pierce, Fenner & Smith, Inc. v. Bobker, 808 F.2d 930 (2nd Cir.1986), *213*

Methodist Hospital, 94 LA 616 (Mario Bognanno, 1990), *301*

Miller Brewing Co. v. Brewery Workers Local Union No. 9, AFL–CIO, 739 F.2d 1159 (7th Cir.1984), *273*

*TABLE OF CASES*

Missouri Portland Cement Co., 291 NLRB No. 146, 291 NLRB 1043 (N.L.R.B.1988), *146*

Mitsubishi Motors Corp. v. Soler Chrysler–Plymouth, Inc., 473 U.S. 614, 105 S.Ct. 3346, 87 L.Ed.2d 444 (1985), *173*

Monarch Tile, Inc., 101 LA 585 (Hartwell Hooper, 1993), *289*

Monsanto Chemical Co., 130 NLRB No. 119, 130 NLRB 1097 (N.L.R.B.1961), *159*

Morelite Const. Corp. (Div. of Morelite Elec. Service, Inc.) v. New York City Dist. Council Carpenters Ben. Funds, 748 F.2d 79 (2nd Cir.1984), *191, 192*

Muschany v. United States, 324 U.S. 49, 65 S.Ct. 442, 89 L.Ed. 744 (1945), *199*

Nashville Gas Co., 96 LA 897 (Dennis R. Nolan, 1991), *302*

Nashville Newspaper Printing Pressmen's Union, Local 50 v. Newspaper Printing Corp., 399 F.Supp. 593 (M.D.Tenn.1974), affirmed 518 F.2d 351 (6th Cir.1975), *73*

National Labor Relations Bd. v. Truitt Mfg. Co., 351 U.S. 149, 76 S.Ct. 753, 100 L.Ed. 1027 (1956), *39*

National Radio Company, Inc. v. Local No. 231, International Union of Electrical, Radio & Machine Workers, AFL–CIO, 198 NLRB No. 1, 198 NLRB 527 (N.L.R.B.1972), *162, 163*

National Steel & Shipbuilding Co., 40 LA 625 (Edgar Jones, 1963), *223*

Newark Stereotypers' Union No. 18 v. Newark Morning Ledger Co., 397 F.2d 594 (3rd Cir.1968), cert. denied 393 U.S. 954, 89 S.Ct. 378, 21 L.Ed.2d 365 (1968), *194*

Newsday, Inc. v. Long Island Typographical Union, No. 915, CWA, AFL–CIO, 915 F.2d 840 (2nd Cir.1990), cert. denied Long Island Typographical Union No. 915, CWA, AFL–CIO v. Newsday, Inc., 499 U.S. 922, 111 S.Ct. 1314, 113 L.Ed.2d 247 (1991), *204*

Nicolet Industries, Inc. (Eli Rock, 1978), *324*

N. L. R. B. v. Burns Intern. Sec. Services, Inc., 406 U.S. 272, 92 S.Ct. 1571, 32 L.Ed.2d 61 (1972), *143, 144*

N. L. R. B. v. C & C Plywood Corp., 385 U.S. 421, 87 S.Ct. 559, 17 L.Ed.2d 486 (1967), *158, 159*

Nolde Bros., Inc. v. Local No. 358, Bakery and Confectionery Workers Union, AFL–CIO, 430 U.S. 243, 97 S.Ct. 1067, 51 L.Ed.2d 300 (1977), *141, 142*

North American Rayon Corp., 95 LA 748 (1990), *289*

## TABLE OF CASES

Northwest Airlines, Inc. v. Air Line Pilots Ass'n, Intern., 808 F.2d 76, 257 U.S.App.D.C. 181 (D.C.Cir.1987), cert. denied 486 U.S. 1014, 108 S.Ct. 1751, 100 L.Ed.2d 213 (1988), *202*

NRM Corp., 51 LA 177 (Edwin Teple, 1968), *225*

Olin Corp., 268 NLRB No. 86, 268 NLRB 573 (N.L.R.B.1984), *159, 160, 161*

Outboard Marine Corp., 54 LA 112 (Louis Kesselman, 1969), *332*

Owens v. Texaco, Inc., 857 F.2d 262 (5th Cir.1988), cert. denied 490 U.S. 1046, 109 S.Ct. 1954, 104 L.Ed.2d 423 (1989), *170*

Philadelphia Marine Trade Ass'n v. International Longshoremen's Ass'n, Local 1291, 368 F.2d 932 (3rd Cir.1966), reversed International Longshoremen's Ass'n, Local 1291 v. Philadelphia Marine Trade Ass'n, 389 U.S. 64, 88 S.Ct. 201, 19 L.Ed.2d 236 (1967), *274*

Polk Bros., Inc. v. Chicago Truck Drivers, Helpers and Warehouse Workers Union (Independent), 973 F.2d 593 (7th Cir. 1992), *187, 188*

Port Chester Nursing Home, 269 NLRB No. 24, 269 NLRB 150 (N.L.R.B.1984), *163*

Procter & Gamble Independent Union of Port Ivory, N. Y. v. Procter & Gamble Mfg. Co., 312 F.2d 181 (2nd Cir.1962), cert. denied 374 U.S. 830, 83 S.Ct. 1872, 10 L.Ed.2d 1053 (1963), *143*

Prudential Ins. Co. of America v. Lai, 42 F.3d 1299 (9th Cir. 1994), cert. denied 516 U.S. 812, 116 S.Ct. 61, 133 L.Ed.2d 24 (1995), *176*

Pryner v. Tractor Supply Co., 109 F.3d 354 (7th Cir.1997), *178*

Publishers' Ass'n of New York City v. Newspaper & Mail Deliverers' Union of N.Y. and Vicinity, 280 A.D. 500, 114 N.Y.S.2d 401 (N.Y.A.D. 1 Dept.1952), *281*

Raytheon Co., 140 NLRB No. 84, 140 NLRB 883 (N.L.R.B.1963), *159*

Reichhold Chemicals, Inc., 66 LA 745 (Paul Jackson, 1976), *334*

Renteria v. Prudential Ins. Co. of America, 113 F.3d 1104 (9th Cir.1997), *176*

Riceland Foods, Inc. v. United Broth. of Carpenters and Joiners of America, AFL–CIO–CLC, Local 2381, 737 F.2d 758 (8th Cir.1984), affirmed 749 F.2d 1260 (8th Cir.1984), cert. denied 471 U.S. 1102, 105 S.Ct. 2327, 85 L.Ed.2d 845 (1985), *184*

## TABLE OF CASES

Roadmaster Corp. v. Production and Maintenance Employees' Local 504, Laborers' Intern. Union of North America, AFL-CIO, 851 F.2d 886 (7th Cir.1988), *190*

Rodriguez de Quijas v. Shearson/American Exp., Inc., 490 U.S. 477, 109 S.Ct. 1917, 104 L.Ed.2d 526 (1989), *173*

Rosenbloom v. Mecom, 478 So.2d 1375 (La.App. 4 Cir.1985), *287*

Roy Robinson Cheverolet, 228 NLRB No. 103, 228 NLRB 828 (N.L.R.B.1977), *162*

Saint Mary Home, Inc. v. SEIU District 1199, 155 LRRM 2457 (2nd Cir.1997), *203*

San Antonio, City of, 90 LA 159 (J. Earl Williams, 1987), *224*

School Dist. of Spooner v. Northwest United Educators, 136 Wis.2d 263, 401 N.W.2d 578 (Wis.1987), *192*

Selb Mfg. Co. v. International Ass'n of Machinists, Dist. No. 9, 305 F.2d 177 (8th Cir.1962), *275*

Shearson/American Exp., Inc. v. McMahon, 482 U.S. 220, 107 S.Ct. 2332, 96 L.Ed.2d 185 (1987), *173*

Sheet Metal Workers Intern. Ass'n Local Union No. 420 v. Kinney Air Conditioning Co., 756 F.2d 742 (9th Cir.1985), *194, 208*

Sinclair Refining Co. v. Atkinson, 370 U.S. 195, 82 S.Ct. 1328, 8 L.Ed.2d 440 (1962), *122, 123*

Smith v. Evening News Ass'n, 371 U.S. 195, 83 S.Ct. 267, 9 L.Ed.2d 246 (1962), *157*

Smith v. Hussmann Refrigerator Co., 619 F.2d 1229 (8th Cir. 1980), cert. denied Local 13889, United Steelworkers of America v. Smith, 449 U.S. 839, 101 S.Ct. 116, 66 L.Ed.2d 46 (1980), *222*

Southern Bell Telephone & Telegraph Co., 25 LA 270 (1955), *225*

Spielberg Mfg. Co., 112 NLRB 1080 (N.L.R.B.1955), *158, 159, 160, 162, 266*

Standard Tankers (Bahamas) Co., Ltd. v. Motor Tank Vessel, Akti, 438 F.Supp. 153 (E.D.N.C.1977), *193*

Stead Motors of Walnut Creek v. Automotive Machinists Lodge No. 1173, Intern. Ass'n of Machinists and Aerospace Workers, 886 F.2d 1200 (9th Cir.1989), cert. denied 495 U.S. 946, 110 S.Ct. 2205, 109 L.Ed.2d 531 (1990), *200, 202*

Steele v. Louisville & N.R. Co., 323 U.S. 192, 65 S.Ct. 226, 89 L.Ed. 173 (1944), *208*

Stroehmann Bakeries, Inc. v. Local 776, Intern. Broth. of Teamsters, 969 F.2d 1436 (3rd Cir.1992), cert. denied Local 776,

## TABLE OF CASES

Intern. Broth. of Teamsters v. Stroehmann Bakeries, Inc., 506 U.S. 1022, 113 S.Ct. 660, 121 L.Ed.2d 585 (1992), *206*

Suburban Motor Freight, Inc., 247 NLRB No. 2, 247 NLRB 146 (N.L.R.B.1980), *159*

Superior Forwarding Co., 282 NLRB No. 121, 282 NLRB 806 (N.L.R.B.1987), *163*

Swift Industries, Inc. v. Botany Industries, Inc., 466 F.2d 1125 (3rd Cir.1972), *196*


Taylor v. N.L.R.B., 786 F.2d 1516 (11th Cir.1986), cert. denied 493 U.S. 891, 110 S.Ct. 237, 107 L.Ed.2d 187 (1989), *160, 161*

Teamsters Local 757 v. Borden, Inc., 78 LRRM 2398 (S.D.N.Y. 1971), *40*

Teamsters Local Union 560 v. Bergen–Hudson Roofing Supply Co., 159 N.J.Super. 313, 387 A.2d 1246 (N.J.Super.Ch.1978), *192, 193*

Textile Workers Union of America v. Lincoln Mills of Ala., 353 U.S. 448, 77 S.Ct. 912, 1 L.Ed.2d 972 (1957), *106, 112, 113, 126*

Textile Workers Union of America, AFL–CIO, Local Union No. 1386 v. American Thread Co., 291 F.2d 894 (4th Cir.1961), *186, 195*

Thompson v. International Ass'n of Machinists, 258 F.Supp. 235 (E.D.Va.1966), *219*

Torrington Co. v. Metal Products Workers Union Local 1645, UAW, AFL–CIO, 362 F.2d 677 (2nd Cir.1966), *188, 189*

Trailways Lines, Inc. v. Trailways, Inc. Joint Council, 817 F.2d 1333 (8th Cir.1987), *183*

Trailways Lines, Inc. v. Trailways, Inc. Joint Council, 807 F.2d 1416 (8th Cir.1986), *288*

Trident Technical College v. Lucas & Stubbs, Ltd., 286 S.C. 98, 333 S.E.2d 781 (S.C.1985), cert. denied George A. Creed & Son, Inc. v. Trident Technical College, 474 U.S. 1060, 106 S.Ct. 803, 88 L.Ed.2d 779 (1986), *194*


Uniformed Sanitation Men Ass'n v. Commissioner of Sanitation of City of New York, 392 U.S. 280, 88 S.Ct. 1917, 20 L.Ed.2d 1089 (1968), *224*

Union Local 1296, Intern. Ass'n of Firefighters v. City of Kennewick, 86 Wash.2d 156, 542 P.2d 1252 (Wash.1975), *192*

## TABLE OF CASES

United Auto., Aerospace, and Agr. Implement Workers of America (UAW) Local 985, AFL–CIO v. W. M. Chace Co., 262 F.Supp. 114 (E.D.Mich.1966), *197*

United Food & Commercial Workers Intern. Union, AFL–CIO, CLC v. SIPCO, Inc., 142 LRRM 2256 (S.D.Iowa 1992), affirmed 8 F.3d 10 (8th Cir.1993), *195*

United Ins. Co. of America v. Insurance Workers Intern. Union, AFL–CIO, 315 F.Supp. 1133 (E.D.Pa.1970), *136*

United Paperworkers Intern. Union, AFL–CIO v. Misco, Inc., 484 U.S. 29, 108 S.Ct. 364, 98 L.Ed.2d 286 (1987), *194, 200, 202, 204, 205*

United Shoe Workers of America, Local 127, AFL–CIO v. Brooks Shoe Mfg. Co., 298 F.2d 277 (3rd Cir.1962), *281*

United States Gypsum Co., 56 LA 363 (Rolf Valtin, 1971), *145*

United States Postal Service v. American Postal Workers Union, AFL–CIO, 736 F.2d 822 (1st Cir.1984), *200, 202*

United States Postal Service v. National Ass'n of Letter Carriers, 839 F.2d 146 (3rd Cir.1988), *203*

United States Postal Service v. National Ass'n of Letter Carriers, AFL–CIO, 810 F.2d 1239, 258 U.S.App.D.C. 260 (D.C.Cir. 1987), cert. dismissed 485 U.S. 680, 108 S.Ct. 1589, 99 L.Ed.2d 770 (1988), *199*

United Steelworkers of America v. American Mfg. Co., 363 U.S. 564, 80 S.Ct. 1343, 4 L.Ed.2d 1403 (1960), *115, 116, 134*

United Steelworkers of America v. Enterprise Wheel & Car Corp., 363 U.S. 593, 80 S.Ct. 1358, 4 L.Ed.2d 1424 (1960), *118, 134, 147, 180, 181, 183, 190, 191, 196, 198, 199, 210, 211*

United Steelworkers of America v. Warrior & Gulf Nav. Co., 363 U.S. 574, 80 S.Ct. 1347, 4 L.Ed.2d 1409 (1960), *116, 118, 120, 134, 136, 185*

United Steelworkers of America, AFL–CIO v. United States Gypsum Co., 492 F.2d 713 (5th Cir.1974), cert. denied United States Gypsum Co. v. United Steelworkers of America, 419 U.S. 998, 95 S.Ct. 312, 42 L.Ed.2d 271 (1974), *145*

United Steelworkers of America, AFL–CIO–CLC v. Rawson, 495 U.S. 362, 110 S.Ct. 1904, 109 L.Ed.2d 362 (1990), *211*

United Technologies Corp., 268 NLRB No. 83, 268 NLRB 557 (N.L.R.B.1984), *163*

Vaca v. Sipes, 386 U.S. 171, 87 S.Ct. 903, 17 L.Ed.2d 842 (1967), *208, 211*

## TABLE OF CASES

Varner v. National Super Markets, Inc., 94 F.3d 1209 (8th Cir.1996), *178*

Vynior's Case, 77 Eng.Rep. 595 (K.B.1609), *101*

Wall Street Associates, L.P. v. Becker Paribas Inc., 27 F.3d 845 (2nd Cir.1994), *213*

Washington–Baltimore Newspaper Guild, Local 35 v. Washington Post Co., 442 F.2d 1234, 143 U.S.App.D.C. 210 (D.C.Cir. 1971), *39*

West Rock Lodge No. 2120, Intern. Ass'n of Machinists and Aerospace Workers, AFL–CIO v. Geometric Tool Co., Division of United–Greenfield Corp., 406 F.2d 284 (2nd Cir.1968), *109, 195, 263*

Westvaco, Virginia Folding Box Division, 91 LA 707 (Dennis R. Nolan, 1988), *233*

Worthington Foods, Inc., 89 LA 1069 (Bruce McIntosh, 1987), *324*

W.R. Grace and Co. v. Local Union 759, Intern. Union of United Rubber, Cork, Linoleum and Plastic Workers of America, 461 U.S. 757, 103 S.Ct. 2177, 76 L.Ed.2d 298 (1983), *149, 151, 198, 200, 287*

# TABLE OF STATUTES

**References are to Pages**

Age Discrimination in Employment Act, 29 U.S.C.A. Sec. 621 et seq., *98, 172, 176, 213*

Americans with Disabilities Act, *178*

Arbitration Act of 1888, *104*

Civil Rights Act of 1964, Title VII, *150, 166, 167, 169, 174, 176*

Civil Service Reform Act of 1978, 5 U.S.C.A. Sec. 7101 et seq., *64, 84, 85, 86, 214, 215*

Clayton Antitrust Act of 1914, 29 U.S.C.A. Sec. 52 et seq., *121*

Erdman Act of 1898, *104*

Fair Labor Standards Act, *149, 154, 170*

Federal Arbitration Act of 1947, Sec. 1 et seq., *40, 50, 105, 106, 107, 109, 172, 173, 175, 182, 190, 191, 193, 212, 213, 269*

Labor–Management Relations Act of 1947 (Taft–Hartley Act), 29 U.S.C.A. Sec. 185 et seq., *40, 65, 67, 73, 89, 103, 106, 107, 108, 110, 111, 112, 115, 121, 122, 123, 126, 129, 130, 131, 132, 139, 143, 144, 156, 159, 164, 166, 208, 209, 210, 212, 235, 263, 266, 269, 281, 342, 343*

Model Employment Termination Act of 1991, *109, 110*

National Labor Relations Act, Sec. 7 et seq., *39, 64, 131, 156, 157, 161, 162, 163, 190*

Newlands Act of 1913, *104*

Norris–LaGuardia Act of 1932, 29 U.S.C.A. Sec. 101 et seq., *73, 112, 121, 122, 123, 126, 128*

Occupational Safety and Health Act, *153*

Postal Reorganization Act of 1970, *64*

Railway Labor Act of 1926, 45 U.S.C.A. Sec. 151 et seq., *63, 65, 66, 94, 104, 105, 317*

Transportation Act of 1920, 40 U.S.C.A. Sec. 361, *104*

Uniform Arbitration Act, *40, 50, 51, 107, 109, 110, 182, 190, 262, 271, 275*

## TABLE OF STATUTES

United States Arbitration Act of 1925, *105*
Wagner Act, *61*
Wisconsin Municipal Employment Relations Act, *76*
Wrongful Discharge from Employment Act, *109*

# LABOR AND EMPLOYMENT ARBITRATION
## IN A NUTSHELL

*

# CHAPTER I

# THE DEVELOPMENT OF LABOR AND EMPLOYMENT ARBITRATION

## A. DEFINITION OF THE CONCEPT

Arbitration is a procedure in which parties to a dispute voluntarily agree to be bound by the decision of an impartial person outside of the normal judicial process. That impartial person, the arbitrator, is expected to decide the matter on the basis of evidence and arguments presented by the parties. Arbitration thus resembles a judicial proceeding in form, but is usually conducted with less formality and ordinarily does not involve government officials.

Labor arbitration is simply the arbitration of a dispute between an employer and the union representing its employees involving some aspect of the employment relationship. Those disputes are of two types: (1) "interest" disputes, involving disagreements over the terms to be included in a contract (called a "collective bargaining agreement") between the employer and the union representing its employees; and (2) "rights" or "grievance" disputes, involving disagreements over the meaning or application of terms already contained in a collective bargaining agreement. Unless otherwise stated, the discussion of labor arbitration in this book concerns grievance arbitration. Interest arbitration will be treated in a separate section below.

Employment arbitration, the newest and fastest-growing type of workplace arbitration, has no role for unions. Instead, an employer and an individual employee agree in some fashion to arbitrate their disputes. The agreement may appear in an initial employment contract, in an employer's policy accepted by the employee, or (as in the case of stockbrokers) in professional licensing regulations. "Agreement" in this context does not necessarily suggest a formal bargain. Rather, an employer may require job applicants to sign an arbitration provision in order to get a job, or may unilaterally announce an arbitration plan covering present employees; an employee who continues to work after such an announcement may be held to have accepted the new terms. In contrast to labor arbitration, employment arbitration agreements often cover statutory disputes as well as contractual disputes. Rarely do parties use arbitration to set the initial terms of employment.

Arbitration is similar to other forms of alternative dispute resolution but remains distinct. Its distinctive factor is the involvement of a third party with power to resolve the dispute. Negotiation between two parties avoids litigation, but it is not arbitration. Joint fact-finding, in which each party appoints a fact-finder to investigate a dispute and report back to the principals, helps to resolve many grievances and may simplify any later arbitration. The Teamsters union commonly uses joint committees to process grievances with employers, referring only the most intractable matters to arbitration. Some alternative dispute resolution processes use third parties without giving them decision-making power. An outsider may serve as a fact-finder, with or without the power to make recommendations, or as a mediator empowered only to help the parties find common ground. Without the authority to make a binding decision, however, the third party is not an arbitrator.

## B. ORIGINS AND DEVELOPMENT

Arbitration's logic and simplicity have commended that process to men and women from the earliest times. Mythology tells us, for example, that Venus, Juno and Pallas Athene agreed to allow Paris to decide their dispute over which of them was the most beautiful. Primitive societies have long favored resolution of disputes by impartial arbitration, frequently to the exclusion of any formal legal process. The arbitration process appears in the Norse sagas, in early Jewish law, among American Indian tribes and in the early Christian community (in I Corinthians VI:5, Paul urges Christians to submit their disputes to arbitration rather than to the courts). For the same reasons, arbitration was widely accepted as an adjunct to the formal law of the Romans and was the preferred means of settlement of commercial disputes of the Middle Ages.

It is thus hardly surprising that as industrialization led to an increase in labor disputes, arbitration was suggested as a remedy. For a long time the term "arbitration" had meanings far removed from the quasi-judicial process we know today. Originally demands for arbitration were really calls for employers to negotiate with unions claiming to represent their employees. Later "arbitration" came to mean something akin to what is now known as "mediation"—that is, the use of an impartial person to help the parties communicate and reach their own agreement. Still later, after several industries had appointed permanent "impartial chairmen," the term began to take on its modern meaning. Even then, the impartial chairmen most frequently engaged in "consensus arbitration," a mixture of mediation and quasi-judicial arbitration. Indeed, only in the last generation or so, with the decline in the percentage of "impartial chairmen" and a vast increase in the use of *ad hoc* arbitrators, have parties treated the arbitrator as a judge rather than a peacemaker.

As early as 1786, the Chamber of Commerce of New York organized an arbitration tribunal to resolve a dispute over seamen's wages. There were a few other labor arbitrations in those early years, but it was not a common phenomenon until the second half of the Nineteenth Century. Private tribunals for the settlement of labor disputes were organized in England in the 1860's and in the 1870's arbitrations were held in the Pittsburgh iron trade and in the Massachusetts shoe industry.

The labor arbitration process was familiar enough by the 1880's to be recognized in the laws of a number of states. Indeed, given the nearly universal hostility of the state and federal courts to arbitration, statutes were essential if arbitration agreements were to be anything more than scraps of paper. Typically these laws simply authorized the courts to appoint local boards of arbitration upon the joint request of employers and employees. These laws are discussed in detail below.

The first important step toward modern arbitration was the settlement of the 1902 strike in the nation's anthracite coal fields. A presidential commission produced a detailed award in 1903 and established a permanent "Anthracite Board of Conciliation" to interpret and apply the award. A neutral arbitrator known as an umpire decided disputes the Board could not resolve. A few years later, large segments of the clothing industry turned to arbitration to avoid crippling, sometimes violent strikes. Louis Brandeis, later a justice of the United States Supreme Court, helped negotiate a "Protocol of Peace" that ended a strike against New York's cloak and suit manufacturers in 1910. For the next ten years, he chaired the Board of Arbitration created by the Protocol. In 1911, a strike at Chicago suit manufacturer Hart, Schaffner & Marx ended with a similar agreement. The two Chicago negotiators (one of them was the famous criminal defense lawyer, Clarence Darrow) named themselves the agreement's arbitrators. Those arbitration plans and others modeled after them survived for many decades.

By the time General Motors and the United Automobile Workers agreed in 1937 to arbitrate grievances, labor arbitration was well known; by the time the same parties substantially revised their arbitration procedure in 1940, it was all but universal in the unionized sector of the American economy. Compulsory arbitration of major disputes by the War Labor Board (WLB) during World War II simply expanded the use of what was already an established process. Grievance arbitration has expanded to the point where today nearly every collective bargaining agreement includes an arbitration provision.

Labor arbitration naturally rises and falls with the fate of labor unions. Union membership in the United States has been declining, gradually but steadily, since 1975. It is now down about a quarter from that peak. The drop in union density (the percentage of the workforce belonging to unions) has been longer and steeper, from almost 35% in 1954 to about 15% in 1996. Although there is no central registry of labor arbitrations, the available evidence [reports of the two main arbitration agencies, the American Arbitration Association (AAA) and the Federal Mediation and Conciliation Service (FMCS)] indicates that the number of arbitration awards peaked in the early 1980s, then fell by a third before leveling off in the early 1990s. Some of that apparent decline may merely represent a shift of business from arbitration agencies to private arbitration panels, but clearly the use of arbitration has declined overall. The substantial growth in public-sector unionism and the resulting growth in public-sector labor arbitration only moderated the overall decline.

Recently, however, the development of individual employment arbitration has added a small but growing stream to the arbitration flow. As employment arbitration agreements become more popular, as they surely will if the federal courts continue to interpret them as waivers of statutory rights, nonunion arbitrations may replace some of the typical arbitrator's workload that has been lost due to the decline of unionization.

## C. THE ARBITRATION PROFESSION

As labor arbitration became more common, the need for experienced, professional arbitrators became more pressing. Labor and management soon realized that intelligence and objectivity alone did not make a person a good arbitrator. An understanding of industrial relations was essential. Familiarity with collective agreements was highly desirable. The ability to conduct a hearing to find out the facts of the case and the bases for the parties positions proved invaluable. Finally, a talent for writing an arbitration award that could explain the instant decision and guide the parties in their future conduct proved extremely useful. There was a limit to the amount of time volunteers could donate to settle labor disputes. There were few Louis Brandeises and Clarence Darrows, and they could not handle every conflict.

The obvious answer was to create a new profession of frequent (if not full-time) arbitrators who would provide the needed skills and be paid, like any other professionals, for their services. A few experts began to fill that role between the World Wars, among them William Leiserson and George Taylor. Leiserson was among the first to treat labor arbitration as a quasi-judicial process, viewing his function as that of a private judge. Taylor, in contrast, took a broader view of the arbitrator's responsibilities, arguing as strenuously for a "mediator" model as Leiserson did for a "judicial" model. Their differences set the stage for a conceptual conflict lasting for another 30 years and ending with the triumph of the Leiserson approach in the 1960s.

World War II's compulsory arbitration rules introduced many newcomers to the arbitration process. Publication of arbitration awards, which began with the *War Labor Reports* and continued in 1946 with the Bureau of National Affairs' *Labor Arbitration Reports,* enhanced the perception of a common endeavor. It was natural for arbitrators the seek out each other's companionship and advice and, eventually, to think of themselves as forming a new and unique profession. Two of the most common elements of professionalization are a professional association and a code of ethics. In 1947, a small group of WLB alumni, with the assistance of the Department of Labor's Conciliation Service, formed the National Academy of Arbitrators (NAA). The new Academy worked with the AAA and the FMCS to produce a "Code of Ethics and Procedural Standards for Labor–Management Arbitration" in 1951. Substantially revised in 1974 and now known as the "Code of Professional Responsibility for Arbitrators of Labor–Management Disputes," the Code (reprinted in Appendix F) remains the authoritative guide to ethical arbitral conduct.

# CHAPTER II
# ARBITRATION PROCEDURE
## A. CONTRACTUAL REQUIREMENTS

### 1. In General

The most important fact to keep in mind about arbitration is that it is a *contractual* process. With the exception of mandatory arbitration laws covering railroad and airline employees and some public employees, labor arbitration and employment arbitration occur only because disputing parties have agreed to it. In a union-management relationship, the arbitration agreement normally is a clause in a broader current collective bargaining agreement, although sometimes parties without a general arbitration agreement will refer a specific dispute to arbitration.

In a nonunion employment setting, the arbitration agreement may be in the employee's initial employment contract, if there is one. Because most private-sector employees are employed "at will" (that is, without an express contract or other restriction on termination, so that either party may end the relationship at any time), arbitration agreements typically appear in other documents. An employer may spell out the arbitration arrangement in a job application signed by new employees, in an employee handbook given to new or current employees, or in a separate document. Express or even tacit acceptance of the employer's plan may result in the creation of a limited common law contract.

In one important category of employment, the arbitration agreement is between the employee and a licensing authority rather than between the employee and employer. A person wishing to work as a stockbroker or in certain other jobs may have to obtain a license to trade on a given stock exchange. As part of the application for a license, the employee must promise to arbitrate any disputes with the employer. This requirement was designed to ensure speedy and simple resolution of financial disputes, such as those arising out of the broker's handling of client accounts. In the 1990's, however, arbitration of employment disputes became increasingly important. In 1997, stock exchange authorities finally dropped employment disputes from the mandatory arbitration provision, but employers may still impose it as a condition of employment.

As the creation of the parties, arbitration can take any form those parties wish to give it; there is no single model the parties must adopt. On the other hand, there are very few useful models. The vast majority of parties prefer to use a familiar and effective model. The parties may either spell out their arbitration procedure in their own words or incorporate an established procedure by reference. This section will discuss some of the problems involved in drafting an appropriate submission agreement or arbitration clause.

## 2. The Submission Agreement

Even without a contract clause mandating a certain arbitration procedure, parties may agree to submit a particular dispute to arbitration. This is not a frequent occurrence, but it does happen from time to time. In such cases they initiate arbitration by signing a "submission agreement." This is simply a document stating the nature of the dispute and affirming the parties' intentions to arbitrate the matter and to abide by the arbitrator's award. (One example is the AAA form reproduced in Appendix E, Form 2.)

The submission agreement constitutes a contract to arbitrate; it therefore establishes the extent of the arbitrator's authority. At the same time, it informs the arbitrator of the issues in dispute, the positions of the parties on those issues, and the relief sought. A carefully drafted submission agreement will also describe the desired procedure—whether there is to be a single arbitrator or a panel, when, where, and how hearings are to take place, and so on. Because those details are more commonly found in arbitration clauses, they are discussed below in that context. The ideal submission agreement would be as detailed as an arbitration clause. Because parties usually use submission agreements only for a specific pending case, they seldom spend much time drafting the submission.

## 3. The Arbitration Clause

The arbitration clause is simply a contractual provision requiring parties to use arbitration to settle disputes about the agreement's interpretation or application. The clause should also define the agreed arbitration process so that the parties can easily use it when a disputes arises, without confusion over the process itself. To be sufficiently complete, the arbitration clause should answer at least the following questions.[1] In practice, arbitration clauses are seldom this detailed.

WHAT _____

___ is to be arbitrated?

___ are the duties and obligations of each party?

HOW _____

___ is arbitration initiated?

___ are arbitrators appointed and vacancies filled?

___ are time and place for hearings fixed?

___ are hearings opened? Closed? Reopened?

___ are costs controlled?

WHEN _____

___ are arbitrators appointed?

___ must hearings begin?

[1]. The following list is from American Arbitration Association, *Labor Arbitration Procedures and Techniques* 7 (Undated).

___ must the award be rendered?

WHERE _____

___ are notice, documents and correspondence to be sent?

___ shall hearings be held?

___ is the award to be delivered?

WHO _____

___ administers the Arbitration?

___ keeps the records and makes technical preparations?

___ gives notice of hearings and other matters?

___ appoints the arbitrators if the parties cannot agree?

___ fills vacancies on arbitration boards when necessary?

___ grants adjournments?

The parties commonly will address other questions as well, particularly those involving pre-arbitration steps such as a grievance process during which the parties can evaluate the evidence and formulate their positions.

Drafting a clause answering those questions is not especially difficult. There are many books and articles providing sample terms and useful advice. The following pages deal with some of the major issues to be considered while drafting and negotiating an arbitration clause. If the parties are primarily interested in making arbitration a reality and are relatively unconcerned with the details of the procedure, the easiest path is to incorporate rules tested by the experience of others. Another collective bargaining agreement might provide a suitable reference point, but because each contract reflects its drafters' peculiar situation, a more objective model is preferable. The American Arbitration Association (AAA), a private, non-profit organization dedicated to the improvement and expansion of the arbitration process, has developed several sets of rules for different situations: *Labor Arbitration Rules*, *National Rules for the Resolution of Employment Disputes*, *Expedited Labor Arbitration Procedures*, and more. (See Appendices A–D.) The parties may well want to modify some of these rules to reflect their own beliefs, desires or circumstances, but they could simply adopt the AAA Rules by reference. The AAA recommends a simple clause like the following:

> Any dispute, claim or grievance arising out of or relating to the interpretation or the application of this agreement shall be submitted to arbitration under the Voluntary Labor Arbitration Rules of the American Arbitration Association. the parties further agree to accept the arbitrator's award as final and binding upon them.

Because the AAA rules are relatively precise and objective, this book will frequently use them as a model.

## B. INITIATING ARBITRATION

### 1. The Demand for Arbitration

If the parties do not use a separate submission agreement, a party to an arbitration agreement initiates the process by making a "demand" for arbitration. The demand is a formal request, usually in writing, made by one party to the other for arbitration of a particular dispute pursuant to the arbitration clause of their agreement. If the agreement provides for use of a designating agency such as the AAA, the FMCS, or a state or local government agency, the party seeking arbitration uses the demand to notify the appropriate group. (See Appendix E, Form 1, for the AAA labor arbitration demand form).

The demand must comply with any procedural requirements established in the arbitration clause. There may be time limits, for example, or an obligation that the moving party seek settlement through an internal procedure before going to arbitration. Failure to abide by these requirements might result in loss of arbitration rights on that issue (in the technical term, the issue might not be "arbitrable"). Because arbitration is the creation of an agreement, that agreement's procedural requirements must be satisfied before arbitration is required or appropriate.

To be complete, the demand should include the following items:

(a) names and addresses of both parties (if the demand is also submitted to a designating agency; the parties presumably already have this information).

(b) the effective dates of the arbitration agreement and the text of the arbitration clause.

(c) a brief statement of the issue or issues to be arbitrated and the relief sought. Because the demand simply phrases the issue, it is not an appropriate place for argument or evidence.

(d) the dated signature of the person authorized to demand arbitration.

## 2. The Reply

The responding party may submit a reply to the demand, briefly setting forth its position on the claim of the demanding party. Unless the arbitration clause provides otherwise, though, replies are neither essential nor common. In the absence of a reply, the parties and arbitration agency presume that the other party denies the claim. Only in individual employment arbitration cases is a reply normal. In AAA employment arbitration cases, the AAA will seek a reply as a matter of course [Appendix C, Rule 4.a.(ii)].

The arbitrator will read the demand and any reply before the arbitration hearing. Because the arbitrator often has no other knowledge of the dispute before evidence is presented, these two documents will guide rulings during the hearing. Because the arbitrator's authority is limited to the questions presented, the demand and reply may also mark the boundaries of the award. The demand and reply should therefore frame the issues and relief sought with as much precision as possible.

## C. TYPES OF ARBITRATION SYSTEMS

Arbitrators can be temporary or permanent and they may serve singly or as part of a panel. The three most common arbitration systems are the single permanent arbitrator, the permanent panel, and the temporary or "ad hoc" arbitrator (who may sit singly or as the impartial member of a tripartite panel).

### 1. The Single Permanent Arbitrator System

As the name suggests, the single permanent arbitrator system uses one arbitrator, sometimes called the "Impartial Chairman" or "Umpire." This method offers the parties several significant advantages. The permanent arbitrator (who is, in reality, only "permanent" for a stated period or for as long as both parties wish) possesses greater familiarity with the parties, their contract and processes, and their expectations about the arbitrator's role. This familiarity speeds hearings and decisions and gives the parties greater confidence in those decisions. A permanent arbitrator may also be in a better position to spot the parties' true concerns, if for some reason they cannot or do not express them at the hearing. A permanent arbitrator is also more likely to issue consistent decisions.

There are some disadvantages to this approach. One or both parties may find that their chosen arbitrator does not meet their expectations, and then may find dismissal difficult or awkward. The ready availability of a permanent arbitrator may tempt the parties to take their grievance procedure less seriously than they should and to arbitrate cases they should resolve themselves. It can be extremely difficult to find an experienced arbitrator with the talents and personality necessary to handle successfully the close, continuous relationship created by this system. Finally, there is a risk that an umpire who is too familiar with the parties and their past disputes might go beyond the contract to impose a resolution he or she deems "good" for the parties.

One common variation is the permanent tripartite board. Parties may choose the tripartite form to make sure their true positions (which may differ from their public positions) are forcefully presented to the neutral. This is possible because each side usually selects one partisan member of the panel, the third member being selected by agreement. When the board meets in executive session, the partisan arbitrators may be more candid than the parties' advocates were in the open session. The partisan arbitrators may also guide the neutral away from disastrous decisions.

Some parties once thought that the tripartite panel's majority-vote requirement lent greater weight to arbitration awards. Perhaps it did when party-selected arbitrators were expected to be somewhat independent. Today, though, the openly partisan nature of the parties' representatives on the panel (in some cases, a party's advocate may even serve as the partisan arbitrator) means that all participants realize that the neutral arbitrator has exclusive power to decide the case.

Moreover, tripartite panels present some special difficulties. During the hearing, a partisan arbitrator may use tactics not available to an advocate—asking leading questions, for example, or seeking hearsay or irrelevant evidence. The majority-vote requirement may make *any* decision hard to reach and may force the neutral to compromise in order to obtain the needed second vote. The neutral arbitrator may wish to order reinstatement without back pay in a discharge case, for instance, but, if neither party is willing to compromise, may have to order back pay or sustain the discharge. The partisan access to the neutral parties provided by a tripartite board poses a risk of an "informed" award, that is, a decision privately agreed upon by the parties but which they cannot recognize in public for political or other reasons. A dissenting opinion from the dissatisfied party may even undercut the award's authority and provide a rallying point for future grievances on the same issue.

The permanent arbitrator system was especially common in labor arbitration's early days. As employers and unions gained confidence in their own abilities, they had less need for an umpire's broad authority. As a result, the permanent arbitrator system is relatively rare today, confined mostly to relationships that began the practice many years ago. Few new collective bargaining relationships adopt this model, and individual arbitration plans never do. Similarly, tripartite boards seem less useful now that parties know better how to present their positions in the open hearing. Accordingly, many parties with contractual tripartite board arrangements waive them in practice.

## 2. The Permanent Panel System

Use of a permanent arbitration panel attempts to balance the advantages and disadvantages of the single permanent and temporary arbitrator systems. After selecting a small group of arbitrators, the parties simply use them in turn as disputes arise. Panel members eventually gain the familiarity with the parties and the enterprise fostered by the umpire system, but having several arbitrators offers the parties some variety. Moreover, no single member of a panel will have or seek the degree of control formerly exercised by permanent umpires.

Many large businesses with a steady stream of cases (the postal service, public utilities, and so on) find the permanent panel system efficient. It is also the most common plan for individual employment arbitration schemes that do not adopt a designating agency's procedures.

## 3. The Temporary Arbitrator System

Most collective bargaining agreements and individual employment arbitration plans call for temporary or *"ad hoc"* arbitrators. This system permits the parties to look for special qualifications for specialized questions (for example, industrial engineers for time-study disputes and lawyers for statutory issues) and to change neutrals easily if experience creates dissatisfaction with an arbitrator. While the temporary system does not preclude frequent or even exclusive re-selection of an arbitrator who satisfies both parties, it avoids some of the disadvantages of permanent systems.

The temporary arbitration system's disadvantages are almost the exact opposite of the permanent arbitrator system's advantages. *Ad hoc* arbitrators will lack familiarity with the parties and their processes, will not be as consistent as a single arbitrator (although most give some deference to prior decisions on the same issue), and may lack the necessary experience to deal with particular cases. Given these possibilities, a losing party in one case might seek to relitigate a similar issue before a new arbitrator in hope of a better outcome. That would hardly encourage stable labor relations.

The temporary arbitrator procedure is not as open-ended as it may seem, because the arbitration agreement usually specifies the source for choosing the arbitrator. The most common source is a large panel of qualified persons maintained by the AAA or FMCS. This system thus functions somewhat like an extremely large permanent panel with two main differences: someone else chooses the panel, and, instead of an automatic appointment of the next arbitrator in line, the parties must make a conscious selection from a subpanel for each new case.

## D. SELECTING THE ARBITRATOR

### 1. The Arbitration Profession

When arbitration was new, there were no professional arbitrators. Parties were free to choose (and usually did choose) any local person both sides deemed fair. A minister, retired judge, respected government official, even a trusted advocate for labor or management—any of these would do. It did not take long for them to learn that fairness was not a sufficient qualification for a satisfactory arbitrator. Knowledge of labor-management relations (and, preferably, of the particular industry and parties), skill at absorbing and evaluating evidence, talent for conducting an orderly hearing, and other factors became as important as fairness. The necessary skills changed, especially as arbitrated disputes shifted from "interests" to "rights"—that is, from determining the appropriate wage level to interpreting an increasingly detailed contract. The modern model of an arbitrator as a private judge succeeded the earlier model of an arbitrator as a consensus-seeking mediator.

As the demands changed, so did arbitrators. In short, they professionalized, coming to view themselves as highly skilled and highly trained technical experts rather than as amateur counselors. One sign of the change was the emergence of full-time arbitrators, people who earned a living doing what an earlier generation had done gratuitously. A second change was the formation in 1947 of a professional association, the National Academy of Arbitrators (NAA), with the attendant code of ethics and educational efforts. Several thousand people hold themselves out as competent labor and employment arbitrators. About 650 of these are members of the NAA, but that small percentage handles a large majority of arbitration cases.

The most thorough study to date of the arbitration profession [Mario F. Bognanno and Charles C. Coleman, editors, Labor Arbitration in America: The Profession and Practice (Praeger, 1992)] reported that most arbitrators are white (97%), male (91%), and senior (averaging 59 years of age). About half are lawyers and another fifth hold a doctorate, typically in industrial relations or economics. About an eighth are full-time arbitrators; the rest hold other jobs as teachers (of law and business administration, especially), government officials, or lawyers. The AAA and FMCS bar from their arbitration panels advocates for labor or management, so virtually all labor arbitrators are officially neutral, at least in terms of their jobs. There has been one partial reversal of the trend toward strict occupational neutrality. The emergence of individual employment arbitration has spawned new panels that sometimes include advocates.

By the 1950s or 1960s, arbitrating parties needed to choose among many possible arbitrators. This made the arbitrator-selection process all the more complicated. Today that is one of the important duties of a party's advocate. This section describes the available methods of selection and the ways an advocate can learn enough to make a wise selection of an arbitrator.

## 2. Methods of Selection

Methods of selecting an arbitrator vary with the type of arbitration system. In unionized settings, labor and management pick permanent arbitrators and permanent panels after very careful investigation. The pool from which they choose their permanent arbitrators often comes from the AAA or FMCS. A permanent arbitrator requires both parties' whole-hearted confidence. A permanent panel, in contrast, might be large enough for each party to include some favorites who are only marginally acceptable to the other, in return for allowing the other party the same liberty.

Permanent panels selected by employers for their individual employment arbitration plans present a special ethical concern. The employee appealing to arbitration may have equal say with the employer when selecting the arbitrator from the panel, but the employer has already screened the panel. No matter how fair the subsequent selection process, the employer's creation of the panel will already have limited the employee's options. The easiest way to avoid the appearance of bias is for an employer's arbitration plan to use a neutrally-selected panel such as that of the AAA.

Most temporary arbitrator systems specify that the parties will select the arbitrator from a panel of names submitted by an arbitration agency. The AAA and FMCS and several state agencies maintain lists of persons qualified by education and experience to serve as arbitrators. Upon request the agency will furnish the parties with a panel of names (usually 5 or 7 in total) drawn from this list (Appendix E, Form 3). The parties choose one person from the panel and then determine whether the chosen arbitrator is available for appointment.

The two most common methods for choosing one name from the panel are alternate striking and ranking. In the former case, the parties agree which is to strike first and then alternately eliminate the least desirable names until only one is left. Both tactical and practical reasons demand some thought to the striking process at the time the parties draft the arbitration clause. Each party would like an arbitrator whose judgment, competence and prejudices it trusts, and most practitioners in the field believe that it is possible to rank each panel member with some accuracy from most to least desirable. Sophisticated negotiators therefore try to gain every possible edge in the selection process. Better knowledge of the arbitrators is one such edge (the next subsection discusses ways to obtain such knowledge). Effective striking is another.

Advocates commonly believe that the last strike is the most important one, for it is essentially the same as having the sole strike in a panel of two names. Starting with an odd number of possibilities, the party who strikes first gives to the other the even strikes, and thus the last one. A careful negotiator will therefore suggest an arbitration clause giving the other party the first strike.

Careful drafting of striking provisions is also essential to avoid confusion and tangential disputes. If the contract is silent, an impasse could develop over such a small matter as which party is to make the first strike. Using some such phrase as "by lot" merely poses other questions. What method is meant by "lot?" A coin toss? Drawing straws? Who is to toss the coin or draw the straw? Does the one who "wins" the toss or draw win the choice of strikes or win the first strike?

The second selection method eliminates some of these difficulties. Each party strikes any arbitrator deemed totally unacceptable and ranks the rest from 1 to X, from most to least acceptable. The parties or the designating agency then add the rankings of those arbitrators not eliminated by either party; the person with the lowest total is selected. If no person is left after the eliminations (a problem that could be prevented by limiting the number of strikes each party may make) the parties may ask the designating agency for another list, or may allow the designating agency to make an appointment directly.

Even this method is not without some problems. What happens, for example, if two persons are tied for the lowest total ranking—if the employer ranks arbitrator A first and arbitrator B second, while the union or individual employee does the opposite? The easiest way to prevent such difficulties is to incorporate by reference the rules of the AAA or FMCS, both of which provide for an appointment by the agency if the parties cannot agree upon a choice (Appendix A, Rule 12; Appendix F, § 1404.12). Neither agency likes to select an arbitrator, for doing so deprives the arbitrator of the credibility and respect that come with joint selection. In some cases, though, there is simply no better way.

Direct appointment by an administrative agency may also be useful for expedited arbitration plans. Allowing the agency to make the appointment speeds up the process by eliminating one step. Both agencies now have rules allowing direct appointment in expedited cases [Appendix B, Rule E2; Appendix D, Rule 2; Appendix G, § 1404.18(c)].

### 3. Learning About An Arbitrator

How does a party know whether an arbitrator is "good" or "bad?" Such a judgment involves several factors, and these can be approached in different ways. The careful advocate will want to know about the arbitrator's:

**(a) *Educational Background*.** Most legally-trained advocates prefer legally-trained arbitrators, believing that they will be more analytical, while many nonlawyer advocates prefer nonlawyer arbitrators. Technical issues might call for a specialist in accounting, occupational health and safety, engineering, or some other discipline.

**(b) *Work Experience*.** With a few exceptions, parties doubt the impartiality of persons identified with management or labor, even if they have no connection with the parties to the immediate case. Not only are management representatives likely to suspect that a union official is prejudiced (and vice-versa), they are equally likely to regard a person with substantial experience on "their" side as untrustworthy. This is a bit subtle, but worth explaining because it helps to illustrate the careful attention serious practitioners give to the selection process.

Suppose that Doe, who was for many years a personnel manager for a large manufacturing company, becomes an arbitrator after retirement. A union business agent could be expected to believe that Doe has been indoctrinated for too long in the management way of thinking. But a management representative might be equally suspicious, believing that in order to establish credibility with union representatives Doe will have to bend over backward for unions in arbitration cases.

Arbitrators unanimously reject suggestions that they would be so mercenary—indeed, most would say that the surest way to *lose* business is to make awards based on such political factors—but that is nevertheless what many representatives on both sides believe. Arbitration is at least partially a game of odds, so parties use any hunch they believe will improve those odds. In any event, most parties do favor arbitrators whose recent work experience has been neutral. Full-time arbitrators, academics, and government officials are thus in the greatest demand. On the other hand, parties almost always want arbitrators who are familiar with employment relations, contracts, and the arbitration process. Some experience working for one side or the other is therefore desirable, provided that more recent jobs have washed away the taint of bias.

**(c) *Arbitration Experience*.** Parties rely heavily on the length of an arbitrator's experience in arbitration, with the result that a few well-established arbitrators handle an extraordinary percentage of all arbitrations. The strong preference for experience produces some unintended consequences. Parties often believe there is a shortage of qualified arbitrators and complain that their chosen arbitrators often have no available dates for many months. There is in fact no real shortage of potential arbitrators, but if the parties insist on using only those people they already know and trust, the pool will be a small one. Moreover, the few generally acceptable arbitrators may then have to use time as an allocation mechanism. Despite the difficulty parties may have in scheduling an established arbitrator, it is still extremely difficult for a new person to gain a foothold in the business.

Apart from the usual benefits of experience, one reason the parties rely so heavily on experienced arbitrators is because it is easier to predict whether they will be "good" or "bad" for a particular case. An experienced arbitrator may have decided scores of discharge cases, for example. Those decisions may well give a strong hint of how the arbitrator will react to the facts of a pending case.

How then do the parties learn what they need to know about an arbitrator? Designating agencies and the reporting services such as the Bureau of National Affairs (BNA), Commerce Clearing House (CCH), and the Labor Relations Press (LRP) provide basic biographical data about potential arbitrators. Because arbitrators submit that information, parties have to take it with a grain of salt. The main professional association, the NAA, only selects members with substantial experience (a bare minimum of 50 cases in the previous five years) and with favorable recommendations from parties and other arbitrators. NAA membership is no guarantee of quality, and non-membership is no indication of lack of quality, but selection is nevertheless a very favorable recommendation in a field with few other screening mechanisms. As a result, many arbitration agreements limit selection to NAA members.

The BNA, CCH and LRP publish a large number of arbitration awards, though nowhere near all of them. Because arbitration is a private procedure, it is unethical for an arbitrator to release an award for publication without the parties' consent. Moreover, many arbitrators choose not to submit their awards to publishers, and publishers can print only a few of those they do receive. Review of awards (and of arbitrators' biographies) became easier with the growth of computerized data bases. BNA has its own service, for example, available through both WESTLAW and LEXIS.

Reported cases give some indication of an arbitrator's experience, but again caution is required. Many highly experienced arbitrators do not submit cases for publication and some novices submit all of their decisions. Moreover, publishers use their own editorial judgment when deciding which cases to publish. Published awards may therefore not accurately reflect any given arbitrator's decisional history.

Finally, there are very few published decisions from individual employment arbitration cases. Because many employment arbitrators do not do labor arbitration, finding examples of their work may be especially difficult. The problem is especially severe for an individual grievant. Employers are "repeat players" with better contacts and greater investigatory resources. They will eventually learn about the available arbitrators. Individual employees, on the other hand, may find it almost impossible to evaluate the relative merits of the panel members. Even if an individual hires a lawyer, the average lawyer

Sec. D    *SELECTING THE ARBITRATOR*    33

will not have access to as much information as will the typical employer or management lawyer.

To many advocates, an arbitrator's leanings are more important than arbitral experience. There are many sources for opinions on such matters. One's own knowledge, and that of other established advocates, are important sources. Many law firms, business associations, and unions keeps files on arbitrators they have used. Many advocates are willing as a matter of professional courtesy to evaluate arbitrators for others on "their" side.

One for-profit management-side firm, R.C. Simpson, Inc., publishes information about arbitrators and their decisions in its "Arbitrators Qualifications Reports" service (AQR or, colloquially, "Simpson's"). The reports consist of basic biographical information, box scores of management and union wins and losses, and brief evaluations submitted by management advocates. The biographical information is already available, box scores are of little use without knowing the details of the cases, and advocates' evaluations are likely to be colored by whether the reporting advocate won or lost the case. Accordingly, experienced representatives use the Simpson's cautiously.

### 4. Appointment

If the parties use an arbitration agency, the agency will make the formal appointment after receiving their rankings. The AAA goes one step further than the FMCS and requires the selected arbitrator to execute an oath of impartiality (Appendix E, Form 4.) Many parties (over 40%, by one count) select arbitrators by mutual agreement without the assistance of arbitration agencies. In such cases one or both will inform the selected arbitrator of the appointment.

## E. ADVOCATES IN ARBITRATION

Like arbitrators, arbitration advocates have professionalized since the procedure's early days. When arbitration first began, union negotiators from the shop floor and any available management representatives often faced each other in arbitration as they had in their previous struggles. Gradually, both unions and employers developed trained cadres of arbitration advocates, often the same people who negotiated the agreement being arbitrated. On the union side, this usually meant business representatives assigned to a given geographic area or (in the case of very large bargaining units) to a specific employer. On the management side, it meant executives from the industrial relations department (now more commonly termed "human resources").

Even though nonlawyer advocates may be as qualified as lawyers to handle arbitrations, there is a distinct trend toward using lawyers. This follows from the increasing complexity of arbitrated issues (now often including statutory issues and greater potential liability) and from the increasing formalization of the arbitration process. One FMCS study found lawyers representing a quarter of unions and a third of employers. Other studies show higher rates of legal representation. Naturally, the exact figure will vary with local customs, the size and budget of the arbitrating entities, the issue to be arbitrated, and other factors. Because most individual employment arbitrations involve statutory issues and the possibility of greater monetary remedies, the use of lawyers is far more common than in labor arbitration.

There have been several studies on the effect of lawyer-advocates. One notable finding is that a party using a lawyer gains a statistical advantage—but only if the other side does not use a lawyer. If both do, there is no significant change in the percentage of cases won by labor or management. There may well be some difference in the *quality* of the arbitration decisions, however, at least in complicated or statutory cases. Legal training can help an advocate define issues more clearly and marshal evidence more effectively. Better advocacy might then mean better decisions.

## F. PREPARING FOR ARBITRATION

### 1. The Grievance Procedure

In a broad sense everything that happens between the parties beginning with the alleged breach of the agreement is in preparation for arbitration. More specifically, serious preparation begins with a grievance procedure, if the agreement specifies one. (The term includes any pre-arbitration steps toward resolving the dispute. All collective bargaining agreements provide grievance procedures, as do virtually all individual employment arbitration agreements, although the latter may not use that term.) Even if the grievance procedure does not produce a settlement, it will facilitate arbitration by forcing each party to organize its own arguments and evidence and to confront those of the other side. That should help to weed out irrelevancies and inaccuracies so that, at least in theory, the arbitration hearing will consist of relevant and relatively accurate testimony.

Contractual grievance procedures will frequently define the term "grievance." If not, the parties have little reason to interpret the term narrowly unless their contract allows all grievances to be taken to arbitration. (In that case the employer may try to limit the subjects covered by the grievance procedure to avoid the risks of arbitration). Both sides usually realize that it is better to air complaints in a procedure designed to correct problems than to let them fester in private.

Most collective bargaining agreements provide for a multi-step grievance procedure, with three or four steps being most common. The first step is usually between the grievant and the grievant's immediate supervisor, in the hope that they can dispose of most questions at that level. If the grievant remains dissatisfied, the grievant (or, more likely, the grievant's union representative) may take the matter to successively higher levels of the company hierarchy, for example, to the second-level supervisor, then to the human resources manager, then to the plant manager. If the employee had union representation at the first step, it was probably by the local union representative, the shop steward. At successive steps the grievant's representative might be the local union's business agent, the plant grievance committee, or the International Representative. In short, the grievance climbs both the union and employer hierarchies as it progresses.

Almost all collective bargaining agreements give the union control over the employee's grievance at some stage. Thus the union may drop or settle the dispute, or at least decline to take it to arbitration, even without the initial grievant's consent. Among other benefits, the multi-step procedure encourages resolution of disputes by forcing different persons with different interests to concentrate on the issue. The system achieves its purpose well, for most grievances are resolved at an early stage and never progress to arbitration.

Arbitration agreements commonly require grievants to write and sign their grievances at some early step, usually step 2. A written complaint helps to focus the grievance on a specific problem, while employers favor the signature requirement to deter frivolous grievances by making some employee take responsibility. There are usually exceptions for matters of concern to the union as an entity or to a large group of employees so that the union alone can process such grievances.

Contracts also commonly impose time limitations for filing and processing grievances. These limitations eliminate "stale" grievances and help to assure prompt resolution of fresh ones. Even when the agreement does not specify a time limit, an arbitrator may imply a standard of reasonableness. (Of course the parties are free to waive any limitations when they believe it wise to do so.) The agreement may penalize dilatory processing of the grievance, for example, by stating that the employer's last response will settle the grievance if the union does not carry it to the next step within a certain period. Rigid adherence to such limitations may frustrate the purpose of the grievance procedure by preventing resolution of the merits of serious complaints. It is therefore often to the advantage of both parties to waive minor lapses.

Grievance processes in individual employment arbitration arrangements tend to be a bit less formal. Even there, however, the grievant will usually have to submit a written grievance within a stated period and carry it up the management hierarchy before seeking arbitration. One advantage of employment arbitration to the individual is that, unlike labor arbitration, the individual "owns" the grievance at every step.

## 2. Discovery

One of arbitration's vaunted advantages over litigation is its simplicity. That simplicity (like the associated advantages of speed and economy) stems from arbitration's avoidance of formalities and procedural steps common to court suits. Chief among the avoided practices is the process of discovery. A major suit can involve reams of interrogatories and scores of depositions, among other tactics. Most arbitrations have neither. Still, if the arbitration hearing is to proceed efficiently, there must be some advance disclosure of relevant evidence. Without the exchange of evidence, neither party would know the other's case, and the hearing would be a form of trial by ambush.

The most common mechanism for exchanging information before arbitration is the grievance process. Some collective bargaining agreements require full disclosure. A few even bar previously undisclosed evidence from later use in arbitration. Some individual arbitration arrangements also require exchange of evidence.

Many contracts, however, are silent on the point. When that is the case, other legal rules may fill the gaps. The National Labor Relations Act, for instance, obliges employers to provide information needed by unions for performance of their collective bargaining duties, *NLRB v. Truitt Manufacturing Company* (S.Ct.1956). Those duties include grievance processing. Despite some early cases stating that "subpoenas are not available in private arbitration proceedings," *Washington-Baltimore Newspaper Guild, Local 35 v. Washington Post Co.* (D.C.Cir.1971) (dicta), most courts now find that arbitrators may issue subpoenas, *e.g.*, *Great Scott*

*Supermarkets v. Teamsters Local 337* (E.D.Mich. 1973).

Section 301 of the Labor–Management Relations Act of 1947, 29 U.S.C.A. § 185, (West 1978 & Supp. 1997) [referred to in this book as the Taft–Hartley Act] authorizes federal courts to enforce arbitration agreements. The Supreme Court has repeatedly held that an arbitrator has the power to resolve procedural questions. That apparently includes issuing subpoenas, *Teamsters Local 757 v. Borden, Inc.* (S.D.N.Y.1971). Whether or not it does, other statutory authorities are clear. The Uniform Arbitration Act, for example, expressly authorizes subpoenas (Appendix K, § 7), as does the FAA (Appendix J, § 7). The same authorities allow arbitrators to require depositions or other forms of disclosure.

If the parties have adopted the AAA's rules, the arbitrator's authority is contractual as well as statutory (Appendix A, Rule 28; see Appendix E., Form 6 for a sample AAA subpoena). The AAA's employment arbitration rules specifically address the topic of discovery, stating (Appendix C, Rule 7) that the arbitrator

> shall have authority to order such discovery, by way of deposition, interrogatory, document production, or otherwise, as the arbitrator considers necessary to a full and fair exploration of the issues in dispute, consistent with the expedited nature of arbitration.

Rules 22 and 23 reiterate the power. FMCS rules are less specific. The only relevant provision (Appendix F, § 1404.13) simply states that "the conduct of the proceeding is under the arbitrator's jurisdiction and control."

## 3. Preparing the Evidence

The preparation required for arbitration is similar to that required for any administrative or judicial proceeding. Each party should first attempt to learn all it can about the incident giving rise to the grievance. Each should study the applicable contract provisions and gather any evidence bearing upon interpretation of those provisions, such as minutes of negotiations and records of prior grievances and arbitrations. The parties should also investigate any relevant past practice in the plant, company, or industry.

Once a party has gathered all the available evidence, the next step is to organize the information. This will involve a detailed outline of the party's arguments, fleshed out by relevant evidence. It should also include an equally detailed outline of the *other* party's arguments and evidence. Only by analyzing what the other party might argue can one know what evidence to present, and in what order. Analysis of the other party's case is also essential to prepare for cross-examination of the other's witnesses. A party planning to use documentary evidence should prepare it for maximum impact. Charts and graphs make statistical data more comprehensible, for example, and sketches or photographs might illuminate a verbal description. On issues where there is no serious disagreement, the parties should consider using stipulations to conserve time and avoid confusion at the hearing (see Appendix E, Form 7).

No advocate should overlook the necessity of preparing witnesses. This does not mean telling witnesses what to say; it simply means helping them to express clearly and forcefully what they know. At a minimum, the advocate should lead the witness through the planned direct examination several times so that the questions will come as no surprise. Prudence dictates that the advocate should prepare the witness for cross-examination as well, by full discussion or perhaps by role-playing. The result should be simple, concise testimony that will hold up even under rigorous challenge.

## G. THE ARBITRATION HEARING

### 1. Time and Place

According to the AAA Rules, "The Arbitrator shall fix the time and place for each hearing" (Appendix A, Rule 19). In practice, it is far more common for the parties to have a settled place for arbitrations—usually a neutral location such as a hotel, courtroom, or hearing room of an impartial agency, although it may be a company or union conference room. It is also common for the parties to agree upon a few potential dates, then determine whether the arbitrator is available on one of those dates. More often still, the parties ask for the arbitrator's available dates and then select one that fits their needs. If the parties use an arbitration agency like the AAA, the agency's representative will communicate with the parties and arbitrator to set the place and time. The arbitration agency will then formally notify the parties and the arbitrator of the hearing (see Appendix E, Form 5).

### 2. Record of the Hearing

Most parties take extensive notes during arbitration hearings. One or both of the parties may want a more accurate record, however, and may arrange for a court reporter. If so, the court reporter will produce a transcript for the parties' use in preparing briefs and the arbitrator's use in drafting the award. If there is no official transcript, the record of the hearing will consist of the arbitrator's notes or tape recording.

Occasionally just one party wants a transcript. If a transcript requested by one party is to be the official record of the hearing, that party must make it available both to the arbitrator and to the other party for inspection (Appendix A, Rule 21).

### 3. Swearing Witnesses

The parties may agree whether witnesses are to be sworn, or may leave this decision up to the arbitrator. Under AAA Rule 24 (Appendix A), "The Arbitrator may require witnesses to testify under oath administered by any duly qualified person, and if required by law or requested by either party, shall do so." Such oaths may have little legal impact (prosecutions for perjury during an arbitration are unheard of) but they may add dignity to the hearing and impress witnesses with the importance of telling the truth.

There may be some question as to whether the arbitrator has the authority to swear witnesses. Few statutes specifically grant arbitrators that power, so unless the arbitrator has other authority (as by being a notary public of the state in which the hearing occurs) it may be necessary to call in an appropriate official. (Court reporters are usually notaries, so they may have authority to administer oaths even if the arbitrator does not.) Alternatively the arbitrator may proceed even without formal authority; the psychological impact should be the same in either case.

### 4. Order of Presentation

As with other formal proceedings, arbitrations usually begin with preliminary matters such as introduction of the parties and arbitrator, acceptance of joint exhibits, stipulations about undisputed facts, and an attempt to agree on the issues to be decided. Formulating the issues is important if not essential before presenting evidence. Mutual agreement on the issue is the best course, but often the arbitrator must define the issue if the parties are unable to agree on the wording. A stipulated issue is helpful in determining the relevance of offered

Sec. G  *THE ARBITRATION HEARING*  45

evidence. It also delineates the arbitrator's power, for one of the few grounds for reversal of an award is a decision that goes beyond the scope of the stipulated issue. Occasionally the arbitrator cannot even determine the real issues before hearing the parties' evidence. When that happens, the arbitrator may simply reserve that question for later determination.

The hearing proper is finally ready to begin. The arbitrator's next step is to invite the parties to make opening statements. Now an interesting question arises: who is to go first? In civil and criminal trials the party bearing the burden of proof (the plaintiff or the prosecutor as the case might be) also bears the burden of going forward. That is also true in most individual employment arbitrations, which usually substitute for litigation.

The procedure is not always the same in labor arbitration. In non-discipline cases, the initiating party (almost always the union) bears both the burden of proof and the burden of going forward. In discipline and discharge cases, in contrast, the uniform understanding is that the employer bears both burdens even though the union is the initiating party. It is not clear why this should be. Some have suggested that it is because the employer is likely to have the critical information, but certainly this is equally true of many non-discipline cases. Others suggest that the labor arbitration practice represents an attempt to help unions and grievants win more cases. Still others say that it is simply a matter of custom—that the former dean of the Yale Law School, Harry Shulman, did it that way when he was permanent umpire at Ford Motor Company in the 1940's and others have just followed his lead.

In rare circumstances, an arbitrator may separate the burden of proof from the burden of going forward. For example, in an individual employment arbitration where the grievant does not know the employer's explanation for the discharge, it may be more efficient for the employer to proceed first. Nevertheless, the grievant retains the ultimate burden of proof.

After the party with the burden of going forward makes its opening statement, the other party may respond. Often the responding party will reserve its opening until the first party completes its case, both to respond to the actual arguments and to avoid tipping its hand. In their opening statements the parties should briefly identify the issues, indicate what they intend to prove, and (at least for the initiating party) specify the relief sought.

Thereafter the arbitration hearing normally proceeds like a trial:

(a) Presentation of witnesses by the party going first, with opportunity for cross-examination after the direct examination.

(b) Presentation of witnesses by the other party, with like opportunity for cross-examination.

(c) Rebuttal witnesses, if appropriate.

(d) Summation by both parties.

Although judicial rules of evidence do not strictly apply in most arbitrations, the principles embodied in those rules are useful in guiding the decision-making process and in guaranteeing an orderly hearing. A party seeking to offer documentary and other evidence should be prepared to identify and authenticate it through a knowledgeable witness and should prepare copies for the arbitrator and for the other party.

At some point in the hearing it may be appropriate for the arbitrator and the parties to leave the hearing room to examine evidence that cannot be brought into it—a machine in an automation case or a work process in a staffing dispute, for example. If the parties foresee the necessity of such an examination, they should plan for it in advance, scheduling the inspection for the appropriate point in the hearing.

This describes the customary hearing procedure. Because it is only customary, the parties or arbitrator may alter it. Every case, though, should retain some clear structure to avoid confusion. Because parties using arbitration want a simple and quick form of dispute resolution, they (and their chosen arbitrator) should be careful to avoid a degree of formality that would prevent a complete airing of the dispute. Arbitration has therapeutic values beyond the mere fact of a decision. An overly technical application of procedural rules may make that therapy ineffective.

## H. POST-HEARING PROCEDURE

### 1. Briefs

The parties may choose to submit written briefs in lieu of or in addition to closing arguments. (Some expedited arbitration plans prohibit briefs.) A post-hearing brief is merely a summary of the submitting party's evidence and arguments. Only evidence submitted at the hearing is admissible, so neither party should attempt to introduce new evidence in its brief. As a general rule, a party should not raise new issues in the brief, either. Briefs are particularly helpful to the arbitrator in complicated cases, when the evidence involves technical or mathematical evidence, and when conflicts of testimony are critical. In most other cases, they add little. If the parties choose to submit briefs, they and the arbitrator will agree on a briefing schedule. Only after receipt of the briefs will the record be closed. (If the parties do not submit briefs, the arbitrator will close the hearing after their closing statements.) Reply briefs are extremely rare in arbitration, because the hearing should have revealed all the important issues, evidence, and arguments.

Once the arbitrator closes the hearing, it may be reopened only "for good cause shown" (Appendix A, Rule 32; Appendix C, Rule 27). Reopening is appropriate only when these principles are met:

- The request to reopen the hearing precedes the arbitrator's final award.

- The proffered evidence was not available with due diligence at the time of the hearing.
- The proffered evidence is pertinent and likely to affect the outcome of the case.
- Admission of the new evidence does not improperly prejudice the other party.

If the arbitrator reopens the hearing to receive new evidence, the other party must of course have the opportunity to challenge or rebut it.

## 2. The Award; Finality

Unless the parties agree otherwise, AAA Labor Arbitration Rules oblige the arbitrator to render the award within 30 days of the closing of the hearing (plus five days for mailing if briefs are filed) (Appendix A, Rule 37). The AAA's Employment Dispute Rules allow a flat 30 days (Appendix C, Rule 32.a.). FMCS regulations allow 60 days [Appendix F, § 1404.14(a)]. Expedited Arbitration Rules allow less time: Appendix B, Rule E9 and Appendix G, § 1404.19(d) (seven days). Usually the award will be accompanied by an opinion setting forth the reasons for the award. The term "award" is often used loosely, to include both the award proper (the statement of the holding and remedy, if any) and the opinion (the arbitrator's explanation of the decision).

The arbitrator's award is, in the common contractual phrase, "final and binding" on the parties. If the arbitration agreement does not state the award's finality, the applicable rules are likely to do so. The AAA's suggested contract clause incorporates the AAA's rules and adds that "the parties further agree to accept the arbitrator's award as final and binding on them" (Appendix A, Introduction). The AAA's employment arbitration rules include the finality provision in the rules themselves (Appendix C, Rule 32.g.).

Unless state law or the relevant contract provides otherwise, the authority of the arbitrator ends with the issuance of the award. (This is known as the doctrine of "functus officio," a Latin term meaning "a task completed.") With few exceptions, an arbitrator may change the award only if both parties agree to reopen the proceeding and restore the arbitrator's power. The Uniform Arbitration Act allows an arbitrator to change an award on the request of a single party only for clarification and for correction of arithmetical and descriptive errors and imperfections in matters of form (Appendix K, Section 9). So do the AAA's Employment Dispute Rules (Appendix C, Rule 33). In other cases, absent joint agreement, a dissatisfied party seeking some other change has no recourse but to challenge the award in court.

Even the courts have very little power to change an award. The FAA allows vacation or modification only for extreme reasons (corruption, fraud, "undue means," "evident partiality,") or for relatively minor corrections ("evident material miscalculation," "evident material mistake" in a description, and imperfection "in matter of form not affecting the merits of the controversy") (Appendix J, Sections 10 and 11). The Uniform Arbitration Act is similar (Appendix K, Sections 12 and 13).

## 3. Costs

Arbitration was originally supposed to be an inexpensive alternative to a law suit. It may still be less expensive, but as the procedure has become more formal in recent years, often involving lawyers and a court reporter as well as an arbitrator, costs have increased remarkably. A party contemplating arbitration should weigh potential gains against the following considerations:

(a) The time and expenses of participants. If a party chooses to be represented by an attorney, costs rise significantly. Investigation of the facts, presentation of exhibits and writing of briefs may cost a considerable amount.

(b) Cost of the stenographic record.

(c) Fee and expenses of the arbitrator.

(d) Administrative fee of the arbitration association.

(e) Rental of the hearing room.

Parties may be able to economize on several items, as by dispensing with briefs and transcript and holding the hearing in a location owned by one of the parties. Other expenses are usually shared equally (administrative costs and the arbitrator's fee and expenses) or are borne exclusively by the party incurring them (one's own time, expenses, and attorney's fees). Some contracts vary the normal practice by requiring the losing party to pay the arbitrator's fees and expenses. In some individual employment arbitration arrangements, the arbitrator has the power to award costs (including legal expenses) in favor of either party (Appendix C, Rule 32.c). Those provisions import into arbitration the practice under many anti-discrimination statutes; the adaptation is fitting because many of the issues in individual arbitration are in fact statutory.

## I. SUMMARY EVALUATION OF LABOR AND EMPLOYMENT ARBITRATION: TIME AND EXPENSE

The main reasons for choosing arbitration over litigation are that it is faster and cheaper. Is it, really? There is little comparative evidence, but the available evidence on arbitration provides a good basis for evaluating the process. The following information comes from the FMCS's report on fiscal year 1996. It covers only FMCS cases, but other arbitrations are not likely to differ in any consistent way.

First, as to time. The average time between the filing of a grievance and the arbitrator's award was about 307 days. A third of that time, however, was occupied by the parties' internal grievance procedure, and selecting the arbitrator took another 58 days. It took, again on average, almost three months from the time of appointment to the hearing date, presumably because of the difficulty coordinating participants' schedules. Finally, from the hearing to the award took about 74 days. When the parties opt for post-hearing briefs (which they usually do), it takes 41 days for them to submit their briefs to the arbitrator. The only portion of the time exclusively under the arbitrator's control, from receipt of briefs to issuance of the award, took just over a month. In sum, the entire arbitration process, from the request for a panel (the equivalent of filing a lawsuit) to issuance of the award (the equivalent of a judgment), took an average of less than seven months. Few court cases are that quick.

Next, as to costs. The average FMCS case cost less than $2,600 for the arbitrator's fee and expenses. Arbitrators' fees ranged from about $250 to $1,000 per day, averaging about $570. The average case took about four days for the hearing, travel, and "study" (the term used for the time spent deciding the case and writing the opinion and award). Expenses averaged under $250, but can be far higher if the parties bring an arbitrator in from out of town.

Parties can minimize costs by simplifying their own process to save the arbitrator's time. The parties can also reduce costs by using a less expensive arbitrator, but that poses a trade-off between saving money and having a reliable and experienced neutral. Except for minor cases, parties normally seek only arbitrators they know and trust. That usually means a well-established, and thus costly, person. Except for minor disputes, choosing an arbitrator on the basis of cost may well be penny-wise and pound-foolish.

Arbitration costs more than a court filing fee, but parties to an arbitration have more control over other expenses than do parties to a law suit. As noted above, by avoiding lawyers and transcripts, and by holding the hearing at one of the parties' offices, the parties can hold their out-of-pocket expenses close to the arbitrator's charges, or about $1,300 for each side. Trials require lawyers, of course, and thus are seldom so inexpensive. Even if the parties use lawyers, arbitration's simplicity and speed mean the lawyers' fees are likely to be lower than they would be if the parties were in court.

## CHAPTER III

# VARIATIONS ON TRADITIONAL LABOR ARBITRATION

One of labor arbitration's greatest strengths is its flexibility. It has changed over time to meet the needs of particular industries, companies and unions, to address new issues, and to respond to pressures from the public and from legislatures. This chapter surveys some of the most significant variations on the traditional labor arbitration system discussed in the preceding pages.

### A. EXPEDITED ARBITRATION

"Expedited arbitration" may be a tautology. Arbitration from its inception was to be "expedited" (at least in comparison with litigation), so expedited arbitration should be the norm rather than the variation. Nevertheless, as arbitration proceedings became formalized, the time from filing a grievance to receipt of the arbitrator's award lengthened considerably. Some parties have sought ways to speed things up.

Particular expedited arbitration systems vary, but they have in common four ways to minimize delays: (a) some form of automatic selection of the arbitrator; (b) a very short period during which the arbitration must take place; (c) a prohibition on transcripts and post-hearing briefs; and (d) a requirement that the the arbitrator issue the award promptly after the close of the hearing. Many also prohibit the use of lawyers. Two good examples of expedited arbitration programs are the AAA's Expedited Labor Arbitration Rules and its recent "Excelleration" program (Appendices B and D). Even the FMCS has developed an expedited arbitration program (Appendix K).

## 1. Early Experiments

The steel industry was the first major part of the economy to adopt an expedited arbitration system. Both management and labor came to realize that a large backlog of grievances was undermining the strength of their contract's grievance and arbitration provisions. In 1971 a joint study commission recommended, and negotiators for both sides adopted, a plan for quick decisions on the simpler sort of grievances, chiefly discipline cases turning on factual questions.

The new plan established a special panel of arbitrators for each plant. The total number of participating arbitrators was about 200, most of them new to the business and thus more likely than experienced arbitrators to be readily available. Assignments were to be made in rotation from the plant panel, to avoid disagreements over selection. If the chosen arbitrator could not hear the case within 10 days, the next panel member took the case. The arbitrator was to render a bench decision at the close of the hearing or provide a short written decision within 48 hours. Hearings were informal and neither party used an attorney. Decisions were nonprecedential—that is, the decision established no principle that would affect later cases. That eased fears that novice arbitrators would make serious mistakes.

The new system worked relatively well. The pattern and quality of decisions did not differ substantially from traditional arbitration, and there were several indirect benefits: expedited cases decreased the regular arbitration case load and gave those immediately affected (particularly grievants and their immediate supervisors) a better attitude toward arbitration. Perhaps the best indication of the experiment's success was that the parties adopted it in subsequent collective bargaining agreements. The Steelworkers even included similar plans in their agreements for aluminum and container company workers.

In the early 1970s, the United States Postal Service faced the same problems with its arbitration system that the steel industry had faced a few years earlier. The Postal Service is one of the largest employers in the nation, with some 600,000 employees. Almost ninety percent are unionized. The size of the operation and several systemic labor relations problems produce an enormous number of grievances, about 40,000 of which were appealed all the way to arbitration during the 1978 agreement. The resulting backlog of grievances (about 19,000 cases at one point) seriously delayed arbitration awards. That in turn led to the loss of evidence, the departure of critical witnesses, and a weakening of confidence in arbitration.

To solve these problems, the Postal Service and the major postal unions adopted an expedited arbitration system for certain types of disciplinary cases in their 1973 national agreement. The Postal Service's procedure resembled the steel industry's. The parties selected a panel of some 150 arbitrators from the AAA and FMCS lists and divided the panel into 30 regional groups. The Postal Service administers its own program to avoid delays. As arbitrations come up, the administrator selects the arbitrator from the appropriate list. Proceedings are informal, without briefs or transcripts. The arbitrator may render a bench award but more often will issue a brief written award shortly after the hearing. (The contract calls for a decision within 48 hours, although only a third of the expedited arbitrators met that goal.) In either case the decision carries no precedential force and may not even be cited in subsequent arbitrations. If the case raises complicated issues or involves a fundamental principle, either party can remand it to the regular grievance-arbitration process.

As with the steel industry, the Postal Service and its unions continued the program in later agreements and even expanded its use. By 1977, the parties used the expedited process for many non-discipline cases turning on factual determinations. There has been one major modification of the original plan. Because many issues that seem at first glance to be local actually raise issues of regional or national concern, the parties established a screening committee to decide which cases should receive expedited treatment.

## 2. Current Expedited Arbitration Programs

Expedited arbitration is now easily available to any parties wishing to use it. The American Arbitration Association has for years published Expedited Labor Arbitration Procedures (Appendix B) that parties can incorporate in their collective bargaining agreements or adopt on a case-by-case basis. These rules contain the four key elements of an expedited system mentioned earlier: selection of an arbitrator by the agency, prompt scheduling of the hearing (both in Rule E2), a ban on transcripts and briefs (Rules E6 and E8), and issuance of the award shortly after the hearing (Rule E9).

In 1996, the AAA adopted an even simpler expedited arbitration plan, which it called the EXCEL-LERATION program (Appendix D). The most novel elements of the program were the creation of a special panel of arbitrators who agreed to be available for quick appointments, extremely short time limits, and the option of decisions made on written submissions without a hearing. The rules prohibit transcripts and post-hearing briefs. Arbitrators are to hear and determine cases within just 15 days of the parties' submission of the case to the AAA (Rule 2). The award is due within 24 hours of the hearing (Rule 10). The arbitrator is to try to complete the hearing within three hours (Rule 7). The written-submission option is found in Rule 8.

In 1997, the FMCS first proposed its own expedited arbitration system (Appendix G). Like the others described above, the FMCS system uses a specially-created panel, this one of novice arbitrators (§ 1404.20), and prohibits transcripts and briefs [§ 1404.19(c)]. The time limits are a bit longer than the AAA's EXCELLERATION program. The arbitrator is to schedule a hearing within 30 days of the appointment and render a decision within seven days of the hearing (§ 1404.19).

## B. COMPULSORY ARBITRATION

At first glance, compulsory arbitration of negotiation disputes seems to be a simple alternative to strikes and lockouts. However, compulsion simply does not work in many cases—unions may still strike if dissatisfied with the arbitration award, and sanctions are seldom applied and less often effective. Moreover, there are strong theoretical objections to the concept. Briefly, these are that compulsory arbitration is repugnant to the principle of voluntarism on which our labor relations system rests and that it weakens the incentive of the parties to reach their own agreement (the so-called "narcotic effect"). With few and usually temporary exceptions, labor and management strenuously reject compulsion.

Nevertheless, outsiders (and occasionally a party that lacks the strength to gain its objectives through negotiations) recommend that the state or federal government should impose compulsory arbitration. Governments have responded to those suggestions in several circumstances. Some of the earliest attempts to establish compulsory arbitration systems came with state statutes long before the federal government adopted the Wagner Act, the first federal law governing labor relations throughout the economy. The Supreme Court quickly struck these down as unconstitutional takings of property, *Chas. Wolff Packing Co. v. Court of Industrial Relations* (S.Ct.1923); *Dorchy v. Kansas* (S.Ct. 1924).

During wartime, governments usually regard strikes and lockouts as intolerable interferences with the war effort. Almost inevitably they try to prevent these disruptions by wage controls or compulsory arbitration. During World War I, for example, President Wilson decided that all labor disputes should be arbitrated, but he never sought legislation making arbitration compulsory. Instead, by executive fiat, he created labor adjustment agencies for specific industries, some of which had the power to set employment terms. In 1918, President Wilson appointed a central body, the National War Labor Board (NWLB). Although the NWLB had authority to resolve labor disputes, it had no enforcement powers.

The next attempt came during World War II. President Roosevelt's Executive Order 9017 of 1942 established the War Labor Board (WLB). The WLB had more power than its World War I predecessor, especially after Congress granted it statutory authority. Section 3 of the Executive Order provided that, once the Board took jurisdiction of a case, it should "finally determine the dispute and for this purpose [it] may use mediation, voluntary arbitration or arbitration under the rules established by the Board." Disputes were often assigned to a single hearing officer or to a tripartite panel which submitted a recommended decision to the Board; the Board's decision was final and binding.

The WLB's impact was three-fold. First, it arbitrated thousands of cases directly. Second, it routinely included in its decisions a grievance arbitration clause. This forced parties to arbitrate disputes arising during the term of the contract or WLB decision. The omnipresence of grievance clauses encouraged non-governmental arbitration, and the parties' experiences were sufficiently favorable that most of them continued the practice after the War. Third, the WLB created a corps of experienced professionals labor arbitrators, many of whom formed the leadership of the arbitration community for the next four decades.

During the Korean War and the Vietnam War, Congress limited itself to imposing wage controls rather than full-scale arbitration programs.

Apart from these wartime experiences, the only early federal compulsory arbitration program covered the railroad industry. The Railway Labor Act (RLA) provides for compulsory arbitration of grievances (but not for negotiation disputes) before the National Railroad Adjustment Board (NRAB). The NRAB consists of four bipartite divisions that decide cases on the basis of paper records and briefs. An outside "referee" appointed by the National Mediation Board decides cases on which a division deadlocks. That remains the law today, although many parties (especially in the airline industry, also regulated by the RLA) use their own system boards of adjustment or "public law boards" rather than the NRAB. Congress enacted several laws commanding arbitration of specific railway negotiation disputes, notably to resolve disputes over crew size and the use of firemen on diesel trains. Many commentators have recommended compulsory arbitration to resolve private sector labor disputes affecting the national economy or creating emergencies in particular areas, but Congress has ignored the suggestions.

After World War II, the initiative in compulsory arbitration shifted back to the states. Several states adopted compulsory arbitration laws governing labor disputes in public utilities. Like the earlier state statutes, these were struck down by the Supreme Court, e.g., *Amalgamated Association of Street, Electric Railway and Motor Coach Employees of America Division 998 v. Wisconsin Employment Relations Board* (S.Ct.1951). This time the basis of the decision was preemption of state action by the National Labor Relations Act.

Several states have adopted compulsory arbitration in an area over which unconstitutional taking and preemption arguments have no sway—that is, in disputes involving employees of state and local governments. The federal government has done the same with regard to one group of its own employees, postal workers. Under the Postal Reorganization Act of 1970, Pub. L. No. 91–373, 84 Stat. 719 [codified in scattered volumes of U.S.C.A. (West)], unresolved negotiation disputes are presented to an arbitration panel empowered to establish contract terms. This provision was first used in 1978 and successfully averted a threatened postal strike. Other unionized federal employees have a form of compulsory arbitration over grievances as a result of the Civil Service Reform Act of 1978, Pub. L. No. 95–454, 92 Stat. 111 [codified in scattered sections of 5 U.S.C.A. (West 1996)].

State compulsory arbitration statutes usually cover critical employee groups like police and fire fighters. Many also cover other groups like teachers, and some cover all unionized state employees. Most state statutes provide for *ad hoc* impartial arbitrators, frequently sitting on a tripartite board. Almost all require the parties to use dispute-resolution methods such as mediation and fact-finding before arbitrating their contract disputes. To ensure that the parties make every effort to settle before arbitrating, some public-sector bargaining laws give a labor relations agency power to refuse arbitration. Some also require the parties to share the costs of arbitration.

Judicial review of compulsory arbitration awards is always available, but sometimes it is limited to constitutional or scope-of-authority issues. More often, review is available on the same standards applied to administrative actions generally; that is, the awards are to be upheld unless they exceed statutory authorization, are constitutionally infirm, or are arbitrary, capricious, or unreasonable. Because the statutes governing public-sector employment are stricter than laws covering the private sector, state courts have more leeway in reviewing arbitration awards. Some state courts have struck down mandatory-arbitration laws as unconstitutional delegations of government power to a private individual, but most courts have upheld statutes providing or implying reasonable criteria for the arbitration award.

## C. ADVISORY ARBITRATION AND FACT–FINDING

Advisory arbitration and fact-finding are similar methods of bringing impartial expert opinions to bear on collective bargaining disputes without surrendering the right of each party to reject that advice. Few parties in the private sector use these processes, although the RLA and the Taft–Hartley Act of 1947 provide for fact-finding panels in certain cases of unresolved negotiation disputes. These panels have occasionally helped resolve bargaining impasses, but not so regularly that other parties have adopted them.

In contrast, some public sector parties have used advisory arbitration for grievances as a compromise between no arbitration and binding arbitration. In some cases, advisory arbitration avoids state constitutional bans on delegating state authority to private individuals. The theory behind advisory arbitration is that an impartial ruling will convince the parties where the truth lies and thus facilitate a settlement. Some unions criticize advisory arbitration as inadequate because the employer retains the power to reject the decision. On the other hand, some employers dislike it because it seems to be a foot in the door, a step toward binding arbitration.

The unions' worry has not been borne out in practice. Public employers accept most advisory awards in full and very seldom completely reject awards, either because the opinions are in fact convincing or because political pressures make rejection difficult. The employers' fear, that advisory arbitration leads to binding arbitration, is more realistic, for many contracts and statutes do change in that direction. This does not necessarily prove that advisory arbitration is bad from an employer's point of view; to the contrary, it could simply indicate that the parties were satisfied enough to want to strengthen the procedure.

Fact-finding in public sector negotiation disputes grew out of the private sector experience with RLA and Taft–Hartley Act fact-finding panels. Some 20 states now have fact-finding procedures in their public sector labor relations laws. These laws vary in detail but fall into two categories, fact-finding without recommendations and fact-finding with recommendations.

Fact-finding without recommendations rests on the notion that proclamation of the factual truth by a respected neutral will assist parties who had not known the real facts to settle their dispute. The notion is dubious for several reasons. There is seldom just one set of "true" facts; usually there are many, and choosing among them requires a subjective decision. Moreover, the parties are almost certain to know the relevant facts (or at least the facts they are willing to admit are relevant) before fact-finding. The public may not know those facts, but will not be likely to learn them from fact-finding: most fact-finding reports receive little publicity and many others are far too complicated to create a consensus strong enough to influence the parties. For these reasons, one scholar claims that fact-finding without recommendations "is about as useful as a martini without gin."

Fact-finding with recommendations looks a bit like ordinary interest arbitration, with one crucial difference: the parties are free to reject the recommendations. In fact, there is little difference between fact-finding with recommendations and advisory arbitration. Under this system, the fact-finder examines the factual data submitted by the parties, the bargaining history, and the relevant labor market, then formulates recommendations with an eye toward persuasion, voluntary agreement, and acceptability. The fact-finder has somewhat more flexibility than an arbitrator because the recommendations need not rest solely on the basis of the strength of the competing cases. The fact-finder may draft recommendations to respond to political reality rather than to weigh the objective merits of the dispute. Like an arbitrator, the fact-finder considers strictly factual issues such as comparable wages in the locality. Unlike an arbitrator, the fact-finder also has to resolve broader questions of public policy.

Where fact-finding has been in effect for some time, the parties seem reasonably satisfied with it. One danger in the process is that unions might come to view the fact-finder's recommendations as a floor and then engage in further bargaining to raise that floor. This would in turn cause the parties to withhold their best offers in negotiations before fact-finding begins, and thus decrease the possibility of a voluntary settlement. To date this does not seem to have happened in many places.

## D. INTEREST ARBITRATION

### 1. In General

Interest arbitration has much in common with two of the topics previously discussed, compulsory arbitration and fact-finding. All of these deal primarily with resolution of negotiation disputes, but interest arbitration is broader than either of the others because it is both voluntary and binding.

Although interest arbitration remains far less common than grievance arbitration, it arose long before grievance arbitration. Logically this had to be so, because grievance arbitration presupposes a written agreement and a mature bargaining relationship, neither of which was common until relatively recent times. By contrast, interest arbitration could be used even in the newest of relationships, particularly when the dispute was over a single issue such as wages. Thus arbitration settled wage disputes in urban transit systems and coal mines as early as the turn of the century.

Interest arbitration decreased in popularity as contracts became more complex, for parties had less confidence in a neutral's ability to decide difficult questions of policy and procedure than to choose between two proposed wage scales. Interest arbitration fell victim to collective bargaining's success in another sense. As the parties became more skilled in collective bargaining, they had less need of a third party's advice.

## 2. The Private Sector

Only a few major employers and unions have used interest arbitration more than once or twice. Two that did use it for many years were the Amalgamated Transit Union (ATU) and several transit companies, and the newspaper industry. Early in their collective bargaining relationship the ATU and the local transit companies recognized that the public suffered if they could not settle their disputes short of a work stoppage. They therefore chose interest arbitration to avoid that problem. Today transit industry interest arbitration covers the full range of bargaining issues. The parties use a tripartite board which settles many issues voluntarily in executive session, almost as if it were an extension of negotiations rather than as an alternative to them.

Public agencies have almost completely taken over the transit industry in the last three decades, but the arbitration system remained largely intact because federal legislation conditioned federal aid on the preservation of transit employees' collective bargaining rights. Critics of interest arbitration claim that it may become addictive and that parties may negotiate less seriously if arbitration is always available in lieu of a strike or lockout, but this has not happened in transit negotiations, most of which settle far short of arbitration.

Large segments of the newspaper industry also used interest arbitration for many years. The first "International Arbitration Agreement" with the International Typographical Union was signed in 1901. Contracts between the International Printing Pressmen and the American Newspaper Publishers Association also provided for interest arbitration, with appeals of local arbitration awards to yet another arbitration body, the International Arbitration Board, composed of three representatives each from labor and management and one neutral. Most of these arrangements have disappeared as competitive pressures and a veritable technological revolution forced newspapers to cut labor costs and eliminate whole skill groups.

By far the most significant private sector adoption of interest arbitration was the 1974 Experimental Negotiating Agreement (ENA) between the United Steelworkers of America and the major steel producers. Unusual economic pressures forced the parties into this experiment. Several times after World War II, contract negotiations broke down and the resulting strikes deprived many customer industries of the steel they needed. As a result, many customers built up large reserves of steel before the contract expiration date. This created a boom-and-bust cycle: demand for steel boomed just before the expiration date and plummeted when the parties signed a new contract. This variation of demand prevented steady production at an optimum rate and cost the industry many millions of dollars. Other customers shifted purchases to foreign producers who could guarantee delivery. Finally, there was a strong risk of government intervention in steel strikes, a prospect neither party welcomed.

Both labor and management suffered from these problems. In 1973 they decided to try a new approach. The ENA provided that the parties would turn over to an arbitration panel any unresolved national issues at their next negotiating round. The panel was to consist of five members, one each from labor and management and three mutually selected neutrals, two of whom had to be thoroughly familiar with steel production and industrial relations. The panel's decision would bind both parties for the term of the next agreement.

Although outsiders warmly praised the ENA, it was highly controversial within the union. Many union members viewed it, quite accurately, as a waiver of the employees' best weapon. One dissident group even sued (unsuccessfully) in federal court to block the arrangement. Nevertheless, because the potential gains from the ENA were so large, because certain key items such as union security clauses were exempted from arbitration, and because each local union was free to strike on matters peculiar to the plant, the Steelworkers' leadership overcame objections and renewed the ENA in the 1977 contract.

In fact, some ENA supporters doubted its practical utility. Some industry observers even believed that the parties reached agreement in 1974, 1977, and 1980 partly because they feared what an interest arbitrator might decide. Severe internal and external pressures forced the parties to let the ENA lapse in 1980. Since then, neither steel nor any other major industry has adopted interest arbitration.

One unanswered question about private sector interest arbitration is whether agreements to arbitrate negotiation disputes are specifically enforceable. The Supreme Court held in *Boys Markets, Inc. v. Retail Clerks Union, Local 770* (S.Ct.1970), that federal courts could bar strikes in violation of contractual prohibitions. Six years later, in *Buffalo Forge Co. v. United Steelworkers of America* (S.Ct. 1976), the Court limited the reach of *Boys Markets*, holding that an anti-strike injunction was appropriate only if the dispute was "over" an arbitrable issue. A negotiation impasse subject to an interest arbitration agreement might seem an obvious arbitrable issue, but *Boys Markets* was a narrow exception to the strong anti-injunction policies of the Norris–LaGuardia Act. The Supreme Court justified it only because of Congress's expressed preference (in the Taft–Hartley Act) for grievance arbitration. The exception may therefore not include novelties like interest arbitration.

The Supreme Court has not yet addressed the issue, and the lower federal courts have sharply divided on this question. The earlier cases, such as *Boston Printing Pressmen's Union v. Potter Press* (D.Mass.1956), held that injunctions were not available. Cases decided after *Boys Markets* held the opposite. See, *e.g., Nashville Newspaper Printing Pressmen's Union, Local 50 v. Newspaper Printing Corp.* (M.D.Tenn.1974).

The only case to address the enforceability of the steel industry's ENA did not provide a conclusive answer but took an ominously narrow approach. The decision is unclear, but it seemed to deny an injunction because the dispute involved issues that were only arguably within the scope of the ENA which did not explicitly require arbitration of disputes over the coverage of the ENA itself. That being so, said the district court, *Buffalo Forge* prohibits an injunction. *Coordinating Committee Steel Companies v. United Steelworkers of America* (W.D.Pa.1977).

## 3. The Public Sector

Interest arbitration is a more recent phenomenon in the public sector, but it is already better established there than in the private sector. The primary reason for its legislative popularity is a widespread belief that society cannot tolerate strikes or lockouts by government employees. While perhaps true of public-safety employees such as police and firefighters, it is hard to imagine why a strike by government janitors would endanger the public any more than a strike by their private-sector counterparts. Collective bargaining without the right to strike, many union advocates argue, is no more than "collective begging." Many legislatures therefore enacted compulsory arbitration laws to provide an alternative to work stoppages.

Much of the preceding discussion on compulsory arbitration in the public sector applies as well to interest arbitration. The reasons for and against interest arbitration are the same, as are the bases for state constitutional challenge (chiefly as an impermissible delegation of power) and the court responses thereto (varied, but generally allowing arbitration if decisional standards are expressed or implied). Most states with public-sector interest arbitration laws encourage settlement by requiring parties to use mediation or fact-finding, or both, before arbitrating. For the same reason, most states provide mediation assistance out of general funds but require the parties to bear at least part of the cost of arbitration.

Beyond those generalities, state laws vary widely in the administration of the statutes, the processes for selecting arbitrators (although most use the tripartite board approach), the range of issues that may go to arbitration, and the methods that arbitrators may use. Most state statutes specify some criteria to be used by interest arbitrators (see subsection 4 below) and a few have adopted the "final-offer" form (subsection 5), but in other respects interest arbitration closely resembles grievance arbitration. As one might expect, this variety of approaches has produced a wide range of results. One of the most notable results is that Pennsylvania, where the statute makes arbitration easily available and does not require the exhaustion of intermediate bargaining steps, has a lower settlement rate than other states where arbitration is less freely available.

## 4. Criteria

The hardest part of designing or operating an interest arbitration system is selecting the controlling criteria. In grievance arbitration there is, in rough terms, only a single criterion: what did the parties intend in their agreement? In interest arbitration no single factor controls. In wage determinations, for example, comparability (wages paid to comparable employees elsewhere) will give some guidance, but so will the employer's ability to pay, recent changes in the cost of living, productivity changes, and many other things. Moreover, each of the potentially relevant factors is complicated and debatable. Is comparability of teachers' salaries to be determined by salaries in neighboring districts, by the county, state, or national averages, or by levels in certain districts that are themselves comparable? How are the employer's resources to be measured? What percentage of productivity savings should be devoted to wage increases and what percentage to tax decreases?

Notwithstanding these uncertainties, many contracts and statutes attempt to list criteria the arbitrator must apply. Some of these statements are very general, while others are quite specific. Typical of the latter is the Wisconsin Municipal Employment Relations Act, W.S.A. § 111.70(4)(cm) (West 1988). This section directs the arbitration panel to base its opinions on the following factors:

(a) The lawful authority of the municipal employer.

(b) Stipulations of the parties.

(c) The interests and welfare of the public and the financial ability of the unit of government to meet the costs of the proposed settlement.

(d) Comparison of the wages, hours and conditions of employment of the municipal employees involved in the arbitration proceeding with the wages, hours and conditions of employment of other employees performing similar services.

(e) Comparison of the wages, hours and conditions of employment of the municipal employees involved in the arbitration proceeding with the wages, hours and conditions of employment of other employees generally in public employment in the same community and in comparable communities.

(f) Comparison of the wages, hours and conditions of employment of the municipal employees involved in the arbitration proceeding with the wages, hours and conditions of employment of other employees in private employment in the same community and in comparable communities.

(g) The average consumer prices for goods and services, commonly known as the cost-of-living.

(h) The overall compensation presently received by the municipal employees, including direct wage compensation, vacations, holidays and excused time, insurance and pensions, medical and hospitalization benefits, the continuity and stability of employment, and all other benefits received.

(i) Changes in any of the foregoing circumstances during the pendency of the arbitration proceedings.

(j) Such other factors, not confined to the foregoing, which are normally or traditionally taken into consideration in the determination of wages, hours and conditions of employment through voluntary collective bargaining, mediation, fact-finding, arbitration or otherwise between the parties, in the public service or in private employment.

A moment's reflection will show that such an extensive list neither limits the arbitrator's discretion nor eases the arbitrator's burden. The most difficult problem is not in *identifying* the relevant criteria, but in *ranking* them, for inevitably some will conflict with others. An arbitrator may well face a situation where comparability demands a substantial wage increase but the employer's ability to pay leaves little room for improvement.

Related to this problem is the difficulty of weighing a mass of contradictory, inconclusive, or incomplete evidence. Rarely do the parties agree on "comparable wages" or on the magnitude of changes in the cost of living. It is far more common for them to have conflicting but equally well-documented positions. The arbitrator's unenviable task is to choose between them.

Each commentator has preferred additions to or subtractions from that type of list, but one broad factor suggested by Professor Tim Bornstein is especially important because it operates whether stated or not. Arbitrators, says Bornstein, should and do give substantial weight to the wishes and aspirations of employees, the employer, and (in public sector cases) the community. Stated another way, the arbitration award should be **acceptable**—that is, not so far outside the range of the parties' reasonable expectations as to be foredoomed to rejection.

Clearly the interest arbitrator's role is not simply judicial. The arbitrator must not simply try to determine what the parties "would have agreed on" had they bargained successfully, for their very presence shows that they could not agree. Rather, the arbitrator's task is legislative, to mandate a "fair" agreement based upon all of the relevant considerations.

## 5. Final–Offer Arbitration

How then does the arbitrator "legislate" a "fair" settlement? There is a natural tendency to regard the final positions of the parties as setting the parameters of a "fair" decision. For example, the arbitrator could reasonably assume that the parties expect the award to set wages above the employer's last offer but below the union's final offer. Moreover, there is a similar tendency to feel that the truth lies "somewhere in the middle." To put it less kindly, there is a strong attraction to a "split-the-difference" approach.

Of course the best answer may not be midway between the parties' last positions. Furthermore, a "split-the-difference" mentality makes voluntary settlement less likely. If the arbitrator is likely to improve upon each party's last offer, no sensible party would offer its true "bottom line" figure to the other side lest the arbitrator go beyond that figure. Both sides have an incentive to offer an exaggerated figure, making the chance of a voluntary settlement remote.

These fears are real, if not realistic. To avoid this problem, a few states and municipalities have adopted a procedure termed final-offer arbitration. As the term implies, this involves arbitration of negotiation disputes where the arbitrator chooses between the parties' final offers. (The "high-low" arbitration of baseball players' salaries discussed below is a private-sector example of final-offer arbitration.) Final-offer arbitration presumes that each party will moderate and refine its positions to make its final offer as attractive as possible to the neutral. By doing so, the parties may find their final positions so close as to permit settlement. Even if the parties do not settle, the process of developing an attractive final offer should narrow the number and scope of the issues going to the arbitrator.

The theory is appealing, but final-offer arbitration also has some distinct disadvantages. Arbitrators resent the lack of flexibility and fear having to choose between two unacceptable positions. Moreover, drafting a final offer requires a sophistication about arbitral standards many negotiators lack. "Political" factors may force one or both parties to include unfair or unjustified proposals in their final offers, with the attendant risk that the arbitrator might incorporate them in the final award.

There are several types of final-offer systems. The two most notable are the Wisconsin system and the Michigan system. In Wisconsin, a single arbitrator receives the final offers five days before the hearing and at its close must select one party's entire "package." In Michigan, a tripartite panel receives the final offers at any time up to the close of the hearing and selects between them on an issue-by-issue basis. Studies of these two models indicate that the Wisconsin system produces more settlements while the Michigan system compels arbitrators to engage in mediation during the hearing (resulting in a combination of mediation and arbitration, termed "med-arb"). Both systems help weak unions by reducing disparities between comparable communities. At least in Wisconsin, neither management nor labor has benefitted disproportionately, for each wins about half of the arbitrations. Neither system has had the feared "narcotic effect" on the parties' collective bargaining efforts, for relatively few negotiations result in arbitration.

Overall, final-offer arbitration accomplishes its objective of encouraging settlements. One study, by Temple University's Walter Gershenfeld, found that approximately 30 percent of public-sector negotiations in states with conventional arbitration laws went to arbitration, as opposed to 6–16 percent in states with some form of final-offer arbitration. Oddly, though, two of the states with the lowest arbitration rates, Iowa and Massachusetts, have different forms of final-offer arbitration, issue-by-issue and "package," respectively.

One very interesting use of a final-offer approach in the private sector was described in 1985 by Arbitrator Dallas Jones of Michigan. In a number of cases in which he found a discharge to be without just cause, he remanded the remedial issues to the parties with directions for them to submit final offers to him if they could not agree. In every case for eight years, the parties reached an agreement.

# CHAPTER IV

# APPLICATION OF ARBITRATION TO NEW SITUATIONS

Another aspect of arbitration's flexibility has been its application to situations far removed from its traditional industrial origins. The first four sections of this chapter describe arbitration's use in new occupational fields (the public sector, higher education, professional sports, and airlines). The last section explores the most important recent application, the extension of arbitration to individual employment disputes in nonunion settings, particularly for use in resolving statutory claims.

## A. THE PUBLIC SECTOR

### 1. The Federal Government

Collective bargaining is a relatively recent development in the federal government, and arbitration as a means of dispute settlement is just as new. The first major step toward labor arbitration in the federal sector came in 1962, when President Kennedy issued Executive Order 10988. Although immediately hailed as a "Magna Carta" for public employees, the Executive Order was but a pale reflection of the private sector collective bargaining system.

Among other limitations (chief among them the exclusion of wages and other monetary items from the scope of bargaining), the Order allowed only advisory arbitration of contract disputes.

In 1969 President Nixon issued Executive Order 11491, which constituted a major revision of federal labor relations. The new executive order governed federal sector labor relations until 1978, when Congress passed the Civil Service Reform Act of 1978, Pub. L. No. 95–454, 92 Stat. 1111 [codified in scattered sections of 5 U.S.C.A. (West 1996)] [referred to in this book as the CSRA]. That Act finally established a statutory scheme of labor relations for the federal government. For instant purposes, the most important part of the new law is Title VII, 5 U.S.C.A. § 7101 *et seq.* For ease of reference, citations herein are to the appropriate sections of the Code.

The CSRA provides for both interest arbitration and grievance arbitration. In the event of a negotiation impasse, the Federal Services Impasses Panel (FSIP) will consider the matter on request of either party. Alternatively, the parties may, if the FSIP approves, adopt a binding arbitration procedure of their own. If the FSIP considers the matter itself and is unable to bring about a settlement, it may "take whatever action is necessary and not inconsistent with this chapter to resolve the impasse." The FSIP's action "shall be binding on such parties during the term of the agreement, unless the parties agree otherwise." 5 U.S.C.A. § 7119.

The CSRA is even more explicit about grievance arbitration. Unless the parties agree otherwise, all collective bargaining agreements must establish a system of binding arbitration for the resolution of grievances. There are a few statutory exceptions (e.g., disputes over examination, certification, or appointment, or involving retirement or insurance plans), but the clear intention is to make arbitration the normal method of resolving disputes. 5 U.S.C.A. § 7121.

A party dissatisfied with a grievance arbitration award may file an exception with the Federal Labor Relations Authority (FLRA), which can modify or overturn an award it finds contrary to any law, rule or regulation or deficient "on other grounds similar to those applied by Federal courts in private sector labor-management relations." If no party files an exception within 30 days, the award becomes final and binding. 5 U.S.C.A. § 7122.

Grievance arbitration agreements are now almost universal in the federal government. By one recent count, 90% of the government's collective bargaining agreements contained provisions for arbitration of at least some disputes. There has been a good deal of criticism, however, particularly from unions. One major complaint concerns the relatively limited subject matter in federal-sector arbitration. The CSRA excludes many important terms of employment, among them wages, hours, overtime pay, holidays, vacations, pensions and insurance, from bargaining, leaving them subject to statute rather than contract. As a result, disputes over such matters are not arbitrable.

A second problem concerns the wide scope of administrative and judicial review. To get FLRA review, either party need only request it. The FLRA has broader authority over challenges to awards than would a court over a private-sector dispute. In addition to the usual grounds for review, the FLRA must ensure that the award complies with all federal rules and regulations. The federal courts have interpreted that requirement as meaning the award must also follow administrative agency and court precedent.

In addition to the FLRA, another federal-sector body, the Merit Systems Protection Board, or MSPB, has jurisdiction over some personnel matters. The MSPB deals with suspensions of more than 14 days, removals from the federal service, and "adverse actions" for unacceptable performance. If the employee chooses to arbitrate one of those issues rather than appeal the agency's decision to the MSPB, the arbitrator must follow MSPB rules. Both the FLRA and MSPB apply the CSRA but their interpretations do not always agree. That means the federal-sector arbitrator may have to choose between two equally authoritative administrative interpretations of the statute.

Federal-sector grievances thus often involve consideration of statutes, regulations, and decisions, as well as the usual factual and documentary items. According to Jean McKee, the former Chairman of the FLRA, in 1991 the FLRA was reviewed a fifth of the federal-sector arbitration decisions and reversed or modified a fifth of those reviewed. That means that about four percent of federal-sector awards are changed on appeal to the FLRA. Although small, that figure is far higher than in the private sector. Private-sector parties take only a fraction of one percent of their awards to court, and the courts are less willing than the FLRA to tamper with awards. A party appealing a federal-sector arbitration award is thus at least ten times, and perhaps a hundred times, more likely to be successful than a comparable private-sector appellant.

In sum, the federal-sector arbitrator has far less discretion and faces many more pitfalls than the private-sector arbitrator. The complexity of federal-sector cases and the ready availability of administrative review make federal-sector work unappealing for many arbitrators.

## 2. State and Local Governments

State and local governments vary widely in their use of labor arbitration. Some states still prohibit collective bargaining with public employees. A few permit bargaining but do not regard negotiated agreements as binding; in such a situation either party could refuse to proceed with an arbitration or to abide by an award. In still other states, courts have held contractual arbitration agreements, even when authorized by statute, unconstitutional as a prohibited delegation of governmental power to a private individual. Notwithstanding these exceptions, in most states public-sector labor arbitration is both legal and common. Moreover, some states have led the way in development of new forms of arbitration, in particular the compulsory, expedited, final-offer and interest arbitration variations discussed in the previous chapter.

It is impossible to describe completely all the varieties of arbitration practiced by state and local governments, and it would probably be useless to try because of the rapidity of changes in this area. Nevertheless, a few general comments are in order.

First, most public-sector grievance arbitration agreements are similar to those found in the private sector. Discipline and discharge cases, seniority disputes, subcontracting grievances, and most others are argued and decided much as they would be in the private sector. The main differences in the public sector are that bargaining laws often limit the permissible scope of arbitration and that arbitrators must pay more attention to relevant laws and regulations.

Second, state courts are more willing to review public-sector than private-sector awards. Some state statutes expressly grant the courts more power in this respect. Even when the statute does not, the courts often choose to be more active, perhaps because they feel a special responsibility for the proper operation of government activity.

Third, as mentioned in the previous chapter, states and localities frequently mandate arbitration as an alternative to strikes and lockouts. Compulsory arbitration is virtually unknown in the private sector—even the national emergency procedures set forth in the Taft–Hartley Act only require mediation. In the public sector, however, it is common.

Fourth, interest arbitration is far more common in state and local government labor relations than elsewhere in the economy. It is almost unknown in the private sector.

Finally, a few state governments were among the earliest employers to offer arbitration even to their nonunion employees. Florida, for example, has long permitted its employees, including those covered by collective bargaining agreements, to use an internal dispute-resolution system culminating in arbitration by a neutral outsider.

## B. HIGHER EDUCATION

Arbitration provisions covering colleges and universities do not differ markedly from those in other types of employment situations except in their exclusions. Appointment, retention, promotion, and tenure disputes constitute the bulk of faculty grievances, but many contracts exclude questions of "academic judgment" from arbitration. Definition of that term varies, but it usually includes both setting the appropriate criteria for personnel decisions and applying those criteria to individual cases. Thus an arbitrator could decide whether the employer followed contractual procedures (or institutional rules incorporated in the contract), and in some cases may decide whether the institution used academic judgment at all, but usually could not second-guess the relevant committee's or administrator's evaluation of the candidate's teaching or research. That much of the peer-review information is confidential only adds to the problems for grievants, their representatives, and arbitrators.

An arbitrator hearing a faculty personnel case will face a serious problem in determining the applicable standards. A few higher-education collective bargaining agreements spell out the requirements for retention, promotion and so on, but most are either so general as to be of little help (like the college or university rules themselves, these contracts are likely to refer generally to "teaching, research, and service"). University policy and past practice can flesh out such contracts, but even these leave decision makers a lot of discretion.

In all personnel decisions, an employer must meet a standard of reasonableness. An arbitrator may judge a decision on that basis just as a reviewing court would do when hearing a challenge to an administrative agency decision. In practice, a reasonableness standard merely requires a rational explanation for the employer's decision. That decision will stand unless the grievant can show that it was arbitrary, capricious, discriminatory, illegal, or otherwise in violation of the contract. Needless to say, it is hard for a grievant to meet such a burden of proof. The heavy deference arbitrators give to peer judgments moderates any unfairness in the burden of proof. If the grievant's academic peers agree with the administration's decision, the grievant has little chance for success. If the peer reviewers favored the application, however, the college or university may have a difficult time explaining why it did not accept their evaluation.

## C. PROFESSIONAL SPORTS

Collective bargaining was not a major force in professional sports until recently. As a result, arbitration too is relatively new in this area. Arbitration systems vary from sport to sport, but almost all of the systems differ from those in other industries in two important respects: first, arbitration agreements in professional sports are far more likely to cover salary disputes, an aspect of interest arbitration; and second, the agreements exempt more subjects from arbitration.

Labor relations in major league baseball are more advanced than in other sports, but the experience there is instructive. Until the 1960s, club owners had almost total control of the terms and conditions of employment. When the players' union negotiated its first contract in the 1960s, one of its key demands was a system of impartial arbitration of grievances. Initially it could not achieve that objective and had to settle instead for a grievance system that ended with "arbitration" before the commissioner of baseball, who was selected and paid by the same club owners with whom the union was in dispute. One players' representative was fond of describing this system as "partial arbitration," a *double entendre* of some accuracy.

Eventually the club owners chose as their new commissioner Bowie Kuhn, an attorney who had represented the owners in the 1968 negotiations. Clearly Kuhn could not claim to be an objective interpreter of the contract he helped to draft. The parties therefore selected baseball's first impartial arbitrator to handle the remaining cases under that contract. In the 1970 contract the parties formally adopted impartial arbitration (in the form of a tripartite panel) for disputes, although the commissioner retained the last word on matters involving the integrity of the game.

Athletes' unions have generally refrained from negotiating actual salaries, preferring to leave the precise amount above a stated minimum to agreement between the player and the club. Unresolved salary disputes seriously impair a team's performance, however, so baseball players and owners alike searched for a method to settle such disputes promptly. The parties settled on an approach called "high-low" arbitration, a variant form of the final offer interest arbitration discussed in the previous chapter.

Under the high-low system, the player and the team submit their last salary offers to an arbitrator who must choose either the high or the low figure. The arbitration involves no other issues, and the arbitrator renders no opinion. Like other forms of final-offer arbitration, the object is to encourage settlement by maximizing the all-or-nothing risk of an arbitrator's decision. According to one arbitrator who has served in baseball salary disputes, the "high-low" system results in a battle of statistics. The parties shower the arbitrator with information about batting averages, runs batted in, earned run averages, and so on.

How then does the arbitrator decide? In a recent speech to the National Academy of Arbitrators, baseball arbitrator John LaRocca suggested that arbitrators focus on the "player's true value," or PTV, rather than on the parties' offers, and then chooses the figure that is closest to the PTV. An earlier study by James Dworkin found a noticeable bias toward the player in baseball arbitration awards. Arbitrators tended to favor the employee's offer even when it was somewhat above the midpoint set by the PTV.

Baseball arbitrations have dealt with broader issues as well, among them well-publicized disputes over the "reserve" system limiting the player's ability to contract with the team of his choice, the cancellation of individual player contracts, and the renewal or option year before a player can become a "free agent" for negotiating purposes.

Arbitration provisions are narrower in other sports. In professional football, the Commissioner used to decide almost all disputes. Arbitration has assumed a greater role over the years. One important and almost unique component, in fact almost the only arbitrable issue in football for several years, has been the arbitration of "injury grievances." For obvious reasons, the risk of being unable to play because of work-related injuries is greater in football than in most other sports. Workers compensation, typically providing only a small income-replacement figure, is little comfort to the disabled player, so the parties agreed to arbitrate the compensation due the player. Beginning in 1977, football arbitrators gained some authority to interpret provisions in the collective bargaining agreement.

## D. AIRLINES

Since 1936, the Railway Labor Act has covered airlines, apparently because the first head of the Airline Pilots Association believed the RLA's compulsory mediation provisions would help his fledgling union. Title II of that Act authorized creation of a bipartite National Air Transportation Adjustment Board (NATAB), paralleling the railroads' adjustment board, for compulsory arbitration of grievance disputes. Instead of pressuring the National Mediation Board to establish a working NATAB, however, the parties set up their own "system boards of adjustment" for each airline. These boards are tripartite, with three, five, or seven members, and have jurisdiction over all the airline's unionized employees.

While the industry was highly regulated, the labor relations climate was relatively friendly. Each carrier simply passed on labor costs to the consumer, confident that its competitors would face the same costs. The result was an extraordinarily generous package of wages and benefits for almost all airline employees. There were few grievances, and the system boards usually resolved those without even using a neutral. With the advent of deregulation in 1978, established airlines found themselves facing nimbler upstarts with markedly lower labor costs. The new competition forced the major employers to squeeze their own labor costs, at the price of rockier labor relations. One consequence was a vast increase in the number of arbitrated grievances.

Airline arbitrations sometimes present all the difficulties common to tripartite boards. Scheduling hearings is harder, routine procedural matters become a topic in caucus discussions, questioning of witnesses becomes a round-robin affair, executive sessions delay the final decision, costs increase substantially because each party has to pay its own arbitrators as well as its advocates and witnesses, and so on. On the other hand, the boards offer some advantages. Partisan arbitrators may be able to help advocates ask the right questions and can help the neutral understand technical issues. They also may bring an "institutional memory" to the hearing, helping the neutral avoid unintended results. The benefits must outweigh the costs, for the parties could switch to a single-arbitrator system but have not done so.

Airlines have presented arbitrators with a nearly unique issue, that of merging seniority lists. Throughout the history of the airline industry, airlines have purchased or merged with one another. This causes a great deal of pain for employees who have built up seniority. If the acquiring airline's employees had their way, all the newcomers would enter at the bottom of the seniority list, a process known as "end-tailing." Crediting the acquired airline's employees with full seniority for all their service (known as "dove-tailing") might allow many of them to displace others who had earned expectations of job security and route preference. In an extreme case, a small group of very senior pilots or flight attendants at an acquired airline could suddenly become the most senior people at a different airline, much to the chagrin of those they displace. Matters become more complicated when the merger eliminates jobs and when the employees are represented by different unions. The usual standard, that the combined seniority list be "fair and equitable," does not provide much guidance.

Arbitrators have responded with a variety of integration plans. Some have dove-tailed the groups according to length of service. Others have used a ratio-rank system. For example, if Airline A has twice the number of pilots as acquired Airline B, then two of the first three positions on the new seniority list would go to A's pilots and the third to a pilot from B, even if another of B's pilots had more seniority than the junior A pilot.

These matters all involve labor arbitration between employers and unionized employees. One airline, Trans World, was a leader in developing a system of individual employment arbitration for nonunion employees. TWA introduced the system in the 1950s, largely to discourage unionization of its agent and clerical work force. Initially the neutral arbitrator held no hearing, ruling instead on the documents compiled at earlier stages of the grievance process. Not until 1969 did Trans World's arbitrators sit at adversarial hearings in discharge cases.

## E. INDIVIDUAL EMPLOYMENT ARBITRATION

By far the most important development in arbitration in the last quarter-century has been the growth of individual employment arbitration—a term indicating arbitration agreements between an employer and its nonunion employees. Until recently, there was no reason for private-sector employers (or most of their nonunion employees) to seek arbitration agreements. Apart from a few executives, entertainers, and sports figures who had the leverage to negotiate employment contracts, employment was "at will." Either party could terminate the relationship at any time for any legal reason with no liability. An arbitration agreement would be pointless without some substantive terms to arbitrate. Worse, from an employer's perspective, was the risk that an arbitration agreement might destroy the at-will nature of the employment relationship.

Over the last 25 years, however, state courts chipped away at the employment-at-will doctrine. Almost all state courts now recognize exceptions for discharges violating public policy and for contracts implied from employee handbooks or other documents. Some allow common-law actions for wrongful discharge or for violation of the implied covenant of good faith and fair dealing. More importantly, statutes have given nonunion employees protection their predecessors could gain only from collective bargaining agreements—for example, protection from discrimination on the basis of age, sex, or race.

Until 1991, the accepted legal rule was that an arbitration agreement did not bar an employee from suing under state common law or under state or federal statutes. In that year, though, the Supreme Court decided *Gilmer v. Interstate/Johnson Lane Corp.* (S.Ct.1991). Chapter V, Section D, discusses that case in detail. For the moment, its significance is simply that the Supreme Court enforced a stockbroker's promise in his application for registration with a stock exchange to arbitrate any disputes with his employer. The Court found that the agreement applied to Gilmer's claim that his employer had discharged him in violation of the Age Discrimination in Employment Act.

Lower federal courts have given *Gilmer* a broad reading, finding that it applies to arbitration agreements in employment contracts, to common law actions, and to suits brought under other antidiscrimination laws. Within a few years, more and more employers decided that individual arbitration agreements promised them more benefits than simply trying to maintain the at-will relationship. Many began to impose arbitration agreements on their employees.

Those employer-promulgated arbitration programs raised legal problems, discussed below in Chapters VI and VII, and practical problems. The practical problems concerned the design of a suitable arbitration program. When unions and employers draft and use an arbitration clause, they are both familiar with the options and relatively equal in bargaining power. Accordingly, the arbitration arrangement is likely to be fair in design and operation. When an employer unilaterally adopts an arbitration plan, that balance is missing. Some employers might be tempted to stack the deck, for example by selecting the arbitrator, by limiting the employee's procedural rights, or by restricting the available remedies.

To avoid unfairness in the developing field, several groups worked to establish minimal criteria for individual employment arbitration. The most important was a broadly-based, blue-ribbon committee that produced "A Due Process Protocol for Mediation and Arbitration of Statutory Disputes Arising Out of the Employment Relationship" (Appendix L) in 1995. The committee dodged the question of whether mandatory pre-dispute arbitration agreements were proper, but unanimously agreed that any employment arbitration plan should contain at least these elements:

- Freedom to choose one's representative.
- Access to relevant information, including reasonable discovery.
- Development of a new panel of impartial arbitrators skilled in conducting hearings and knowledgeable in the statutory issues at stake.
- Selection of arbitrators from a panel drawn from the roster of a designating agency.
- Power for the arbitrator to award whatever relief would be available under the law.

Arbitration agencies quickly agreed to comply with the Protocol's provisions. The AAA, for example, appropriately revised its employment arbitration rules (Appendix C). The rules now encourage mediation, allow necessary discovery "consistent with the expedited nature of arbitration" (Rule 7), establish qualifications for arbitrators (Rule 11), and enunciate the arbitrator's remedial authority (Rule 32).

# CHAPTER V

# THE LEGAL STATUS OF LABOR AND EMPLOYMENT ARBITRATION

## A. AT COMMON LAW

Until very recent times courts in the United States have not been receptive to labor arbitration. Their critical attitude stemmed from jurisdictional jealousy and doctrinal difficulties, both factors far removed from the merits and demerits of labor arbitration itself.

The primary problem was the jealousy of courts of equity to all forms of arbitration. Early courts viewed agreements to arbitrate as attempts to "oust them from their jurisdiction," a concern perhaps aggravated by the feared loss of litigants' fees. The courts held the upper hand, though, and therefore refused to enforce arbitration agreements by injunctions. The courts dressed up their concerns with bald statements, as in *Vynior's Case* (K.B. 1609), that no one person has the power to make an irrevocable grant of authority to an arbitrator. The rationale is question-begging, to say the least, and it ignores the fact that such grants of authority occur only in *bilateral* contracts.

Nevertheless, the undeniable effect of the courts' hostility was to permit a party to withdraw from an arbitration agreement at any time until the arbitrator rendered the award. A party injured by the other's repudiation of an arbitration clause could still sue at law for breach of contract, but proving actual damages was difficult: how could a plaintiff demonstrate the amount he or she would have received from an arbitration that never occurred? Nominal damages hardly served to deter breaches.

When the arbitration clause was part of a collective bargaining agreement, doctrinal concerns supported the courts' turf-protection worries. One doctrinal problem was that a party to the contract, the union, was an unincorporated association. In many jurisdictions, therefore, a union could not sue or be sued as an entity. Individuals might be able to sue in their own names, but that proved clumsy at best.

A second and more serious difficulty involved the very nature of collective agreements. Strictly speaking, they are not contracts at all, for only in individual contracts of employment, express or implied, is there an exchange of "consideration," the indication that the agreement was a true bargain rather than a mere statement of intentions. An individual employment contract involved an exchange of an offer of work for a promise to perform the work. A collective agreement did not.

In Great Britain, the courts still treat collective agreements as non-binding. In the United States, some courts gave labor agreements practical effect by treating them as stating a "custom" or "usage" incorporated in each individual contract of employment, by treating the union as an "agent" of its members, or by regarding individual employees as third party beneficiaries of the contract between the union and the employer. Even those courts, however, regarded executory agreements to arbitrate as revocable at any time by either party.

Because of these difficulties, statutes were necessary to make effective arbitration possible. There were several of these, beginning in the nineteenth century.

## B. STATUTES BEFORE THE TAFT–HARTLEY ACT

### 1. Early State Laws on Labor Arbitration

By 1886, at least eight states had adopted statutes providing either for *ad hoc* labor arbitration boards, usually appointed by district courts, or for permanent, full-time state boards of arbitration. The idea caught on, and sixteen more states enacted legislation by 1901. For all the good intentions, there were pitifully few arbitrations in those early years. Only four states had more than ten cases before 1904. Except in Massachusetts, most of the cases involved mediation rather than arbitration as we know it today.

## 2. Federal Legislation for Railway Labor Disputes

Early federal legislation for the settlement of railway labor disputes was no more effective than the early state statutes. Congress passed the Arbitration Act of 1888, Ch. 1063, 25 Stat. 501, which provided for mediation and voluntary arbitration before neutral *ad hoc* arbitration boards, but there was not a single arbitration during the ten years the Act was in force. The Erdman Act of 1898, Ch. 370, 30 Stat. 424, also provided for mediation and for voluntary arbitration. It specified that the arbitration board would consist of one representative of each side and a third person selected by those representatives. (If the representatives could not agree on a neutral arbitrator, federal officials would appoint one.) It took eight years for the first Erdman Act arbitration to occur, and there were only a dozen in all by 1912. The Newlands Act of 1913, Ch. 6, 38 Stat. 103, established a new government agency to deal with railway disputes, the Board of Mediation and Conciliation. In its thirteen year existence the Board helped to settle twenty-one cases by arbitration.

After the failure of the Transportation Act of 1920, Ch. 91, 41 Stat. 456 [codified as amended at 40 U.S.C.A. § 361 (West 1986)], which set up a tripartite Railway Labor Board with arbitration authority but no enforcement power, Congress finally passed the Railway Labor Act of 1926, Ch. 317, 44

Stat. 577 (referred to in this book as the RLA). Congress amended the RLA, most importantly in 1934, Ch. 691, 48 Stat. 1185 [codified as further amended at 45 U.S.C.A. §§ 151–63, 181–88 (West 1986)]. The RLA still governs the settlement of labor disputes in that industry.

As described in Chapter III, grievance disputes go before one of four divisions of the National Railway Adjustment Board (NRAB), each of which consists of equal numbers of labor and management representatives. In the case of a tie vote, the decision is left to a neutral referee. RLA dispute resolution procedures have been used in tens of thousands of cases. Neither side has been completely satisfied with NRAB procedures—employers complain of too many union victories and unions complain of lengthy procedural delays—but they do seem to be a substantial improvement over those provided in earlier laws.

## 3. Other Federal Laws Before 1947

Chapter III mentioned the pioneering role of World War II's War Labor Board. One other early federal statute deserves mention. In 1925 Congress passed the United States Arbitration Act (USAA, renamed the Federal Arbitration Act, or FAA, in 1947; see Appendix J), which made arbitration agreements in contracts involving interstate or international commerce enforceable in federal courts.

FAA § 1 excludes "contracts of employment of seamen, railroad employees, or any other class of workers engaged in foreign or interstate commerce." There is still some dispute over the reach of the exclusion. Does it apply only to employment contracts in the transportation industry (its main advocate was a union leader from that field), or does it also apply to employment contracts of employees engaged in "interstate commerce" as the courts now interpret that phrase? Either way, does it also apply to collective bargaining agreements, which many courts did not regard as contracts at all?

Lower federal court decisions on the question are in conflict, and the Supreme Court has not resolved the issue. Dissenting in *Textile Workers Union v. Lincoln Mills of Alabama* (S.Ct.1957), Justice Frankfurter construed the majority's opinion as a silent rejection of the applicability of this act to labor disputes, but his view has not been widely accepted. By providing alternate grounds for federal court action (namely § 301 of the Taft–Hartley Act), however, *Lincoln Mills* made use of the FAA unnecessary in most union-management situations.

Some courts, including the Supreme Court, dodged the question by using the FAA by way of analogy whenever its direct application might be questionable. The best judicial explication of the controversy is Judge Harry Edwards's recent opinion in *Cole v. Burns International Security Services* (D.C.Cir.1997), a case involving an individual contract of employment. Judge Edwards held that § 1 excluded only contracts of employees engaged in transportation. By reading the exclusion narrowly, the D.C. Circuit gave the FAA a much greater role in the field of employment arbitration (and perhaps in labor arbitration as well).

## 4. Modern State Arbitration Laws

There have been two major attempts to draft a uniform state arbitration act that would gain wide acceptance. The first attempt, in 1925, was a complete failure. The proposal was withdrawn after adoption by a few states. The second attempt produced the Uniform Arbitration Act (UAA, Appendix K). The National Conference of Commissioners on Uniform State Laws (NCCUSL) approved the draft in 1955 and recommended enactment in all states. Most states have adopted the UAA, although often with significant amendments. Some state laws specifically exclude individual or collective employment contracts from the UAA's coverage. Because the federal courts use § 301 to enforce arbitration clauses in collective bargaining agreements and are now giving the FAA greater reach in individual employment disputes, state law exclusions (or the absence of state laws) will have less importance.

Most of the major industrial states do have arbitration statutes expressly applicable to labor disputes. Some of these merely charge a state agency to "promote" arbitration and others were designed primarily for commercial disputes, but many are detailed laws clearly envisioning labor arbitration. Among the states having comprehensive laws are

California, Illinois, Massachusetts, Michigan, New Jersey, New York, and Ohio. Most of these statutes follow similar lines. They generally provide for state court enforcement of labor arbitration agreements and supervision of the process, a formal hearing, issuance of subpoenas, and judicial review and enforcement of awards.

The relationship between state statutes governing labor arbitration and federal labor relations law is far from settled. As will be seen in the following pages, federal law recognizes that state statutes and courts are relevant to labor arbitration under the Taft–Hartley Act, but state laws must be consistent with the federal policy. The difficulty in applying this general rule of accommodation is that almost any provision of state law affecting arbitration can be interpreted by one party as interfering with federal policy. A grant of subpoena power to arbitrators might be viewed as a means of improving the quality or quantity of evidence on which the arbitrator will make his decision, but the recipient of the subpoena might just as easily regard it as an unwarranted intrusion into matters best left to collective bargaining, an intrusion that actually hinders arbitration agreements by making them less attractive to potential subpoena recipients.

There has been little litigation on this question, but the few courts that have dealt with the issue seem to treat state laws as valid *prima facie*, that is, until clearly shown to be in conflict with some aspect of federal policy. In one notable case, a federal appeals court held that a state law requiring arbitration awards to be issued within a stated time could not be used to challenge a late award. *West Rock Lodge No. 2120, IAM v. Geometric Tool Co.* (2d Cir.1968).

The role of state arbitration laws remains an important issue despite the ingenuity of the federal courts in finding ways to enforce arbitration agreements. At the very least, state laws could provide ancillary support for the arbitration system, for example by specifying arbitral powers not mentioned by the FAA. The NCCUSL is considering that topic among many others in its current work to redraft the UAA.

One other state law development is significant. As state courts chipped away at the employment-at-will doctrine, employers and some employee advocates began to think that a wrongful termination statute was a better way to address the legal nature of the employment relationship. Only one state, Montana, passed such a law, the Wrongful Discharge from Employment Act, Montana Code §§ 39–2–901 to –914 (1987). (Puerto Rico and the Virgin Islands also have wrongful termination laws.) Section 39–2–914 authorizes enforcement of arbitration agreements covering claims of wrongful termination and even imposes some financial sanctions to encourage employment arbitration.

In 1991, the NCCUSL issued its Model Employment Termination Act, or META, drafted under the leadership of the University of Michigan law professor Theodore St. Antoine. (The Commissioners termed the draft a "model" act rather than a "uniform" act to indicate a less enthusiastic endorsement.) META would make arbitration the preferred remedy for wrongful-termination claims, leaving the details to be supplied by the UAA, if the parties have an arbitration agreement, or by state regulations, if they do not. No state has adopted META, however, and none appears likely to do so soon.

## C. SECTION 301 OF THE TAFT–HARTLEY ACT

### 1. The Language of Section 301

In the Taft–Hartley Act, Congress stated its preference for arbitration by declaring in § 203 (d) that "[f]inal adjustment by a method agreed upon by the parties" is "the desirable method for settlement of grievance disputes." Of far greater importance for labor arbitration is § 301 of that Act. Because § 301 has been so important, it is essential to examine it in some detail. The first two subsections, the most important for our purposes, read:

> Sec. 301 (a) Suits for violation of contracts between an employer and a labor organization representing employees in an industry affecting commerce as defined in this Act, or between any such labor organizations, may be brought in any district court of the United States having jurisdiction of the parties, without respect to the amount

> (b) Any labor organization which represents employees in an industry affecting commerce as defined in this Act and any employer whose activities affect commerce as defined in this Act shall be bound by the acts of its agents. Any such labor organization may sue or be sued as an entity and in behalf of the employees whom it represents in the courts of the United States. Any money judgment against a labor organization in a district court of the United States shall be enforceable only against the organization as an entity and against its assets, and shall not be enforceable against any individual member or his assets.

Some of the effects of this section should be clear from the language. Among other things, it eliminated hindrances to enforcement of arbitration agreements by allowing a union to sue and be sued as an entity and by clearly stating that collective bargaining agreements are enforceable contracts. Other effects became clear only after many years of litigation.

## 2. The *Lincoln Mills* Case

After Congress's enactment of § 301 there was a great deal of debate over whether that section gave federal courts authority to compel or stay arbitration or to enforce or vacate arbitration awards. If the federal courts had such power, they would have to decide what substantive law to apply. The primary question at issue in *Textile Workers Union v. Lincoln Mills of Alabama* (S.Ct.1957), an action to force a reluctant employer to abide by a promise to arbitrate certain grievances, was whether § 301 was simply *jurisdictional* or *substantive* as well. If it was simply jurisdictional, the federal courts would have to apply state law to the collective bargaining agreement. If it was substantive, the federal courts would have to discover or create a federal common law of the collective agreement.

In an opinion by Justice Douglas, the Supreme Court left no doubt where it stood on this issue. It held, first, that Congress authorized specific performance of promises to arbitrate grievances, and second, that "the substantive law to apply in suits under § 301 (a) is federal law, which the courts must fashion from the policy of our national labor laws." State law may be relevant in the fashioning of that law, the Court said, but "any state law applied ... will be absorbed as federal law and will not be an independent source of private rights." Finally, the Court rejected the argument that the anti-injunction policy of the Norris–LaGuardia Act, 29 U.S.C.A. § 101 (1988), prohibited specific enforcement of arbitration agreements, because "the failure to arbitrate was not a part-and-parcel of the abuses against which the Act was aimed." Norris–LaGuardia, in other words, was to be read in conjunction with the pro-arbitration policy of the Taft–Hartley Act, not in opposition to it.

Later cases expanded the impact of *Lincoln Mills*. In *Charles Dowd Box Co. v. Courtney* (S.Ct.1962), and *Local 174, Teamsters v. Lucas Flour Co.* (S.Ct. 1962) the Supreme Court held that state courts retained concurrent jurisdiction to enforce collective bargaining agreements but that in doing so they must apply federal law fashioned in light of *Lincoln Mills*. One other part of the *Lucas Flour* decision is at least tangentially relevant here. Operating on the assumption that arbitration is a *quid pro quo* for agreements not to strike, the Supreme Court held that a trial court should imply a no-strike promise in any dispute "which a collective bargaining agreement provides shall be settled exclusively and finally by compulsory arbitration." In other words, if the parties make a dispute subject to arbitration, the courts are to *assume* the union waived its right to strike over the matter. Other cases authorized federal courts to compel a successor employer to abide by an arbitration agreement made by its predecessor and to grant judgments where the right or duty to arbitrate is not clear.

## 3. An Introduction to the Relationship Between the Arbitrator and the Courts: The Steelworkers Trilogy

*(a) Introduction.* One of the knottiest issues in the federal law of labor and employment arbitration has been the relationship between the arbitrator and the courts. This subsection provides an introduction to the controversy. Chapter VI explores the topic in more detail.

In a 1960 trio of cases, collectively known as the *Steelworkers Trilogy,* the Supreme Court first addressed the problem of the relationship between arbitral and judicial processes. In what seemed to many observers to be an extraordinary exercise in judicial passivity, the Court, speaking again through Justice Douglas, clearly placed arbitration in the dominant position. To establish the primacy of arbitration under federal labor policy the Court had to overcome several decades of judicial hostility toward that procedure, and this may have caused Justice Douglas to overstate his case.

Typical of the earlier judicial attitude is a decision explicitly criticized in the *Trilogy, International Ass'n of Machinists v. Cutler–Hammer, Inc.* (N.Y. 1947). The contract at issue provided that "the Company agrees to meet with the Union early in July 1946 to discuss payment of a bonus for the first six months of 1946" and that the parties would arbitrate disputes as to the "meaning, performance, non-performance or application" of the contract's provisions. At one meeting, the parties discussed *whether* a bonus was to be paid. The union took the position that the contract meant that a bonus *must* be paid and that all there was to discuss was the amount of the bonus. When the employer refused to pay a bonus, the union demanded arbitration. When the employer denied the union's request, the union sought a court order to compel arbitration.

The New York Court of Appeals rejected the union's suit, stating that "if the meaning of the provision of the contract sought to be arbitrated is beyond dispute, there cannot be anything to arbitrate and the contract cannot be said to provide for arbitration." According to the court, the part of the contract that was "beyond dispute" meant that the employer agreed only to discuss a bonus. The union's demand for actual payment was therefore not within the scope of the arbitration clause. In sum, the New York court's approach was to require arbitration only if the contract was ambiguous—and to substitute its judgment for that of the arbitrator over whether a clause was ambiguous.

**(b) The Trilogy.** In the first two cases of the *Steelworkers Trilogy*, a union used § 301 to force reluctant employers into arbitration. *United Steelworkers v. American Mfg. Co.* (S.Ct.1960), involved a claim that the employer believed was not arbitrable. One Sparks, an employee of the respondent, left work due to an injury and sought workers' compensation benefits. The parties settled his claim on the basis of a permanent partial disability. Two weeks later, the union filed a grievance charging that Sparks was entitled to return to his job. The employer refused to arbitrate the grievance and the lower federal courts upheld its refusal. The district court applied an estoppel theory: because Sparks had settled the compensation case on the basis of a permanent disability, he could not work. The circuit court affirmed on a different ground, holding that the grievance was "a frivolous, patently baseless one, not subject to arbitration under the collective bargaining agreement."

The Supreme Court reversed, holding that the parties' agreement (which contained a standard arbitration clause providing arbitration for all disputes "as to the meaning, interpretation and application of the provisions of this agreement") was to submit *all* grievances to arbitration, "not merely those that a court may deem to be meritorious." The function of a court in such cases is very limited:

> It is confined to ascertaining whether the party seeking arbitration is making a claim which on its face is governed by the contract. Whether the moving party is right or wrong is a question of contract interpretation for the arbitrator.

This is so, said the Court, both because of the national labor policy favoring arbitration and because "[T]he processing of even frivolous claims may have therapeutic values of which those who are not a part of the plant environment may be quite unaware." Contrary decisions like *Cutler-Hammer*, wrote Justice Douglas, "could only have a crippling effect on grievance arbitration."

*United Steelworkers of America v. Warrior and Gulf Navigation Co.* (S.Ct.1960), involved a broader arbitration clause, covering "any local trouble of any kind." Unlike the arbitration agreement in *American Manufacturing*, however, this one stated that "matters which are strictly a function of management shall not be subject to arbitration." The union sought a court order forcing arbitration of its claim that the employer violated the agreement by contracting out certain work. The lower federal courts dismissed the complaint, agreeing with the employer that contracting out fell within the exception for "matters which are strictly a function of management."

Again the Supreme Court reversed, holding that there is no room under federal labor policy for the hostility toward arbitration the courts had shown in commercial cases. To the contrary, because arbitration in these cases is a substitute for labor strife rather than for litigation, the courts should read arbitration clauses in the manner most favorable to arbitration:

> An order to arbitrate the particular grievance should not be denied unless it may be said with positive assurance that the arbitration clause is not susceptible of an interpretation that covers the asserted dispute. Doubts should be resolved in favor of coverage.

Why should such matters of interpretation be left to arbitrators rather than the courts? Because the parties want them to be, answered Justice Douglas. The collective bargaining agreement is part of an attempt to establish a system of industrial self-government, the gaps in which "may be left to be filled in by reference to the practices of the particular industry and of the various shops covered by the agreement." The parties select a labor arbitrator for a presumed knowledge of "the common law of the shop" and an ability to bring to bear considerations which "may indeed be foreign to the competence of courts.... The ablest judge cannot be expected to bring the same experience and competence to bear upon the determination of a grievance, because he cannot be similarly informed."

Moreover, Justice Douglas went on, because a no-strike clause is the usual trade-off for an arbitration agreement, an absolute no-strike clause (as was present in this case) subjects "in a very real sense" everything management does to the arbitration clause. Any exceptions must be explicit, and the phrase "strictly a function of management" does not explicitly cover the practice of contracting out work.

*Warrior & Gulf* does not mean that all questions of arbitrability are for the courts to decide. The parties may authorize their arbitrator to decide issues of *"substantive arbitrability"*—that is, whether the arbitration agreement even applies to the dispute. In a later case, *John Wiley & Sons, Inc. v. Livingston* (S.Ct.1964), the Court held that issues of *"procedural arbitrability"*—that is, whether the party seeking arbitration has satisfied the procedural conditions established in the contract—are to be resolved by the arbitrator. *Warrior & Gulf* means only that (unless the parties specify otherwise) the courts are to resolve questions of substantive arbitrability—and should resolve them in favor of arbitration whenever possible.

The third case of the *Trilogy, United Steelworkers of America v. Enterprise Wheel & Car Corp.* (S.Ct. 1960), addressed the relationship between the arbitrator and the courts from a different perspective.

There the issue was not whether a court should specifically enforce an agreement to arbitrate, but whether it should enforce an arbitration award rendered pursuant to such an agreement. In other words, are the courts any freer to interpret the meaning of the contract after the arbitrator has spoken than before? The dispute involved an arbitration award requiring reinstatement of discharged employees with back pay even for a period following the termination date of the contract. The circuit court of appeals refused to enforce the portion of the award granting reinstatement and back pay beyond the contract termination date.

Once again the Supreme Court reversed, holding that judicial deference to arbitration was just as appropriate after the arbitrator issued the award. Allowing courts the final say on the merits of arbitration awards would undermine the federal policy favoring voluntary arbitration. This is not to say that the arbitrator has unlimited authority. The arbitrator, said Justice Douglas, "does not sit to dispense his own brand of industrial justice." Rather, the award is legitimate "only so long as it draws its essence from the collective bargaining agreement." The arbitrator may look for guidance from many sources, including "the effect upon productivity of a particular result, its consequence to the morale of the shop, his judgment whether tensions will be heightened or diminished." The arbitrator need not provide reasons for the award, and therefore "a mere ambiguity in the opinion accompanying an award, which permits the inference that the arbitrator may have exceeded his authority, is not a reason for refusing to enforce the award." Where it is clear that the arbitrator's words "manifest an infidelity to this obligation," however, the court must refuse to enforce the award. In this case, however, no such infidelity was evident. The court below therefore erred by substituting its judgment on the merits for that of the arbitrator.

*(c) Criticism of the* **Trilogy.** Justice Douglas' discovery of a federal policy heavily weighted in favor of arbitration, and his unbounded praise of arbitrators and the arbitration process, have not gone unchallenged. Justice Whittaker, dissenting in *Warrior & Gulf*, termed the assertions that federal policy grants arbitrators powers far beyond the contract and that a no-strike clause makes everything that management does subject to arbitration "an entirely new and strange doctrine," for which the Court cited no legislative or judicial authority.

A few years later, a distinguished arbitrator and federal judge, Paul Hays, endorsed Whittaker's criticisms and carried them even further. In his Storrs Lectures on Jurisprudence at Yale Law School, later published as *Labor Arbitration: A Dissenting View* (1966), Hays challenged the core of Douglas' position, that arbitrators are better qualified in this field than "the ablest judge." "No authority whatever is cited for any of these statements," said Hays, and "I know of no authority that would lend them support." The parties choose an arbitrator for an expected favorable verdict or for a perceived ability to interpret the written agreement, not because of any trust in the arbitrator's judgment about considerations not expressed in the contract. In other words, they choose arbitrators for the same skills a judge would use—and if this is so, there is no reason to give arbitration a position of such dominance.

Such criticisms have not done much to change the attitude of the courts. The Supreme Court still adheres to the *Trilogy* approach, albeit with less enthusiastic language. The lower federal courts maintain an ostensible fealty to the *Trilogy* doctrine, although in practice their loyalty is often qualified. One result of the Court's approach has been to enhance the finality of arbitrators' decisions by making review on the merits extremely difficult to obtain. Few awards are challenged in court and only a small percentage of those challenges are successful. For the most part, the Trilogy has kept arbitration disputes out of the courts.

## 4. Section 301 and the Norris–LaGuardia Act: *Boys Markets* and Later Developments

*(a) Revival of the Labor Injunction:* **Boys Markets**. If there has been a single preeminent rule of federal labor policy in the past half-century, it is that the federal courts should not use their injunction power to break strikes. The Clayton Antitrust Act of 1914, 29 U.S.C.A. § 52 (West 1973), and the Norris–LaGuardia Act of 1932, 29 U.S.C.A.

§§ 101–15 (West 1973), strictly limited the federal courts in this regard. It was inevitable that some newer but equally important policy would eventually come into conflict with the anti-injunction rule. That finally happened in *Boys Markets, Inc. v. Retail Clerks Union, Local 7701* (S.Ct.1970), where the anti-injunction rule finally bowed to the pro-arbitration policy enunciated in Taft-Hartley and confirmed in the *Trilogy*.

Several Supreme Court decisions in the years immediately following the *Trilogy* set the stage for that ruling. *Charles Dowd Box Co. v. Courtney* (S.Ct.1962), held that state courts had concurrent jurisdiction with federal courts over § 301 suits to enforce collective bargaining agreements. *Local 174, Teamsters v. Lucas Flour Co.* (S.Ct.1962), held that state courts using § 301 had to apply federal substantive law, though presumably they retained their own procedural and remedial law. A third 1962 case, *Sinclair Refining Co. v. Atkinson* (S.Ct.1962) held that federal courts could not enforce a no-strike pledge by injunction.

The catch to this division of authority was that the Norris–LaGuardia Act did not apply to state courts. Some states permitted anti-strike injunctions. In other words, it would be possible for state courts, exercising jurisdiction under a federal statute and applying federal substantive principles, to do something federal courts had been prohibited from doing for several decades, that is, enjoin strikes.

Sec. C  *SECTION 301 OF TAFT–HARTLEY*  123

This would have been clear enough but for one complicating problem. In *Avco Corp. v. IAM Lodge 735* (S.Ct.1968), the Supreme Court held that a union could remove to federal court an employer's state court suit for breach of a no-strike clause. Because of *Sinclair*, removal would eliminate the threat of an injunction. No sensible union would remain in state court. It was clearly inconsistent to hold that Congress intended § 301 to supplement rather than displace state court jurisdiction in these cases, which the Court did in *Dowd Box,* and yet allow a *de facto* displacement of state injunctive power by unlimited removal to federal courts which could not grant injunctive relief. Something had to give.

*Sinclair* gave. A new majority of the Court, stating that it was simply accommodating the Norris–LaGuardia Act to the new legislation favoring peaceful resolution of labor disputes, held in *Boys Markets* that in certain cases the federal courts could enjoin a strike in breach of a no-strike clause. The holding was narrow, applying only where the collective bargaining agreement contained a mandatory grievance adjustment or arbitration procedure, and not always even then. Quoting from the dissenting opinion in *Sinclair*, the Court adopted some rather severe limiting principles:

> A District Court entertaining an action under § 301 may not grant injunctive relief against concerted activity unless and until it decides that the case is one in which an injunction would be

appropriate despite the Norris–LaGuardia Act. When a strike is sought to be enjoined because it is over a grievance which both parties are contractually bound to arbitrate, the District Court may issue no injunctive order until it first holds that the contract does have that effect; and the employer should be ordered to arbitrate, as a condition of his obtaining an injunction against the strike. Beyond this, the District Court must, of course, consider whether issuance of an injunction would be warranted under ordinary principles of equity—whether breaches are occurring and will continue, or have been threatened and will be committed; whether they have caused or will cause irreparable injury to the employer; and whether the employer will suffer more from the denial of an injunction than will the union from its issuance.

To reiterate, *Boys Markets* sets forth three tests for an anti-strike injunction: the strike must be over a grievance the parties have promised to arbitrate; the employer as well as the union must be ordered to arbitrate; and the party seeking the injunction must satisfy traditional equity requirements. The last two of these are self-explanatory, but the first deserves some explanation.

The strike must be "over a grievance which both parties are contractually bound to arbitrate." Note that there is no requirement of an express no-strike clause. In *Lucas Flour*, the Court, over the bitter dissent of Justice Black, held that a broad mandatory arbitration clause implies a no-strike obligation. Twelve years later, in *Gateway Coal Co. v. UMW*, (S.Ct.1974), the Court allowed enforcement of such a "constructive no-strike agreement" by injunction.

**(b) Limiting the Boys Markets *Exception:* Buffalo Forge.** Note, too, that the strike must be "over" an arbitrable grievance. What if the strike itself, not the underlying cause, is the alleged violation of the contract subject to arbitration? That was precisely the issue in *Buffalo Forge Co. v. United Steelworkers* (S.Ct.1976). The union represented three groups of employees of the same employer in different bargaining units. While the union was negotiating a contract for one of these groups, its contracts for the other two contained mandatory arbitration and no-strike provisions. the first group (clerical and technical employees) struck when negotiations failed. After a few days the union ordered the others (production and maintenance workers) to honor the first group's picket lines.

The underlying cause of the contract-breaching work stoppage by the production and maintenance workers was the failure of negotiations involving the clerical and technical workers. The failed negotiations could hardly be the subject of a grievance under the existing contracts governing production and maintenance employees. Moreover, although the employer was willing to go to arbitration, the sympathy strike itself, not its motivating cause, would be the arbitrable issue.

In a 5–4 decision, the Supreme Court held that *Boys Markets* did not authorize injunctions against sympathy strikes. Speaking for the Court, Justice White said that the "driving force" of the earlier decision was the strong congressional preference for the private dispute settlement mechanisms agreed upon by the parties. Strikes over arbitrable issues would of course frustrate such arbitral processes and deprive the employer of the *quid pro quo* for its promise to arbitrate.

That was not the case in *Buffalo Forge,* said Justice White, for a strike over a non-arbitrable issue neither frustrates the arbitration process nor deprives the employer of the benefit of its bargain. As a result, there is no necessity in such cases to accommodate the Norris–LaGuardia Act to § 301. The sole admittedly arbitrable issue, the permissibility of the sympathy strike under the terms of the collective bargaining agreements, must itself be decided by the arbitrator before an injunction would be appropriate. (The union in *Buffalo Forge* did not refuse to go to arbitration. If it had refused, presumably it could have been required to arbitrate pursuant to *Lincoln Mills*, but an order to arbitrate would not prohibit a concurrent strike.)

**(c) Ramifications of the Buffalo Forge *Limitation.*** The attentive reader may perceive some inconsistency between *Boys Markets* and *Buffalo Forge*. The reasons for allowing any exceptions to the Norris–LaGuardia Act's prohibitions on strike injunctions—to promote the arbitration process and guarantee the employer its *quid* (uninterrupted production during the term of the agreement) for its *quo* (agreement to arbitrate disputes)—surely call for enjoining sympathy strikes as well as others. The facts of the case give no reason to believe the parties had intended their no-strike clause to exclude sympathy strikes, and the possibility of judicial error in granting injunctions is no greater where only one issue (the strike itself) is to be submitted to arbitration rather than two (the strike itself and the underlying cause).

Moreover, the possible ramifications of *Buffalo Forge* reach far beyond the sympathy strike situation. If injunctions are inappropriate unless the strike is over an arbitrable issue, then a wide range of strikes that are clearly in breach of an agreement may not be halted by the courts even while a grievance is pending before an arbitrator. Among these would be strikes over issues such as an employer's pricing, advertising or marketing practices, or over the employer's dealings with other companies or governments opposed by the union; strikes to change the terms of a contract during the contract term; and strikes over matters not even within the employer's power to control. However flagrantly such strikes might violate the union's own agreement, however seriously they might interfere with production, they may not be enjoined because of the *Buffalo Forge* decision.

A good example is *Jacksonville Bulk Terminals v. International Longshoremen's Association* (S.Ct.

1982). In apparent violation of a no-strike agreement and an arbitration clause, a union offended by the Soviet Union's war in Afghanistan refused to load ships bound for the Soviet Union. The Supreme Court held that the case did not come within the *Boys Markets* exception to the Norris–LaGuardia Act's ban on labor injunctions because, under *Buffalo Forge*, the underlying issue was plainly not arbitrable. The Court did say, however, that if an arbitrator found that the strike violated the agreement, the employer could obtain an injunction enforcing the award.

One last aspect of the sympathy strike problem should be mentioned. Suppose the grievance underlying the *primary* strike is arbitrable (unlike the *Buffalo Forge* situation, where the cause of the strike was the failure of contract negotiations, a non-arbitrable issue), but only under the contract of the primary union. This obviously falls somewhere between the *Boys Markets* and *Buffalo Forge* situations, and the courts have not had an easy time dealing with it.

In the leading case of *Cedar Coal Co. v. UMW Local 1759* (4th Cir.1977), the Court of Appeals faced just this problem. It struck a new balance, holding that when a sympathy strike's purpose and potential effect are to compel the primary strikers' employer to concede an arbitrable issue to the striking union, a federal court could enjoin the sympathy strike as well as the primary strike. The case involved two locals of the same international union, but the same employer, collective bargaining agreement, bargaining unit, and locality of employment. Whether the "object of the strike" test will be applied in different circumstances is impossible to predict. Indeed, the *Cedar Coal* court refused to apply its own test to a third local whose members were employed by a different employer.

Even if an employer may not be able to obtain a *Boys Markets* injunction because the strike is not "over" an arbitrable issue, there may be other remedies. Most collective bargaining agreements permit only a union to file a grievance and demand arbitration. If an employer is not bound to arbitrate complaints of union breaches, it may sue for damages in state or federal court under § 301. *Atkinson v. Sinclair Refining Co.* (S.Ct.1962). To tap the deep pockets of the international union, however, an employer must prove that the international had a contractual obligation to prevent the strike in question; there is no automatic liability on the international simply because local employees stage a wildcat strike. *Carbon Fuel Co. v. United Mine Workers of America* (S.Ct.1979).

## D. SECTION 301's PREEMPTIVE EFFECT

*Lucas Flour* held that Congress intended the new federal common law of the collective agreement to prevail over inconsistent state law. Later cases have held that the necessity of uniformity may bar employees from bringing some state contract, tort, or statutory actions.

The leading case on preemption of state actions is *Allis-Chalmers Corp. v. Lueck* (S.Ct.1985). Lueck was covered by a collective bargaining agreement that included both a disability benefits plan and an arbitration clause. He received benefits for an injury but later sued the employer and the insurance company for allegedly handling his insurance claim in bad faith. The Supreme Court held that "the interests in interpretive uniformity and predictability" require that collective bargaining agreements be subject to uniform federal interpretation. The test for § 301 preemption, said the Court, was whether the state law conferred rights independent of the collective agreement or was instead "inextricably intertwined with consideration of the terms of the labor contract." It concluded that a state court could not resolve Lueck's tort claim of bad faith without interpreting the collective agreement to find out what obligations it imposed.

Three years later, in *Lingle v. Norge Div. of Magic Chef, Inc.*, (S.Ct.1988), the Supreme Court revisited the topic. Lingle had sued her employer for allegedly retaliating against her for filing a workers' compensation claim. The lower courts found her state action preempted because it was "inextricably intertwined" with the collective bargaining agreement's provision requiring "just cause" for discipline. The Supreme Court reversed, holding that the issue was not the two actions' factual parallelism but rather whether resolving the state law claim required construing the collective bargaining agreement. The trial court could determine the

Sec. D   *301's PREEMPTIVE EFFECT*   131

retaliation claim without ever looking at the labor agreement, so § 301 did not preempt the action. Somewhat confusingly, the Court suggested that a trial court could use a labor contract to determine the proper damages payable in a state action without construing that agreement.

The Supreme Court's latest explanation of § 301's preemptive effect is *Livadas v. Bradshaw* (S.Ct.1994). Bradshaw, California's Labor Commissioner, ruled that California's wage-payment law barred him from enforcing the law on behalf of employees covered by a collective-bargaining agreement containing an arbitration clause. When Lividas filed a claim to collect a penalty because of her former employer's allegedly willful delay in paying her certain money, she received a form letter informing her of the state policy. She sued to have that policy declared preempted because it limited employees' rights under the National Labor Relations Act. Bradshaw responded that *Lueck* and *Lingle* barred California from enforcing its law when the employee could pursue an action under the arbitration clause.

The Supreme Court rejected Bradshaw's defense. Once again the Court emphasized the distinction between state law actions that depend on a collective agreement and state actions that are "independent." The issue was not whether the statutory and contractual claims arose from the same set of facts, but rather whether the state could decide the statutory question without interpreting the contract. Because California need not interpret the agreement to determine whether the employer's delay was "willful," there was no § 301 preemption. Addressing *Lingle*'s statement about using the collective agreement to fix the amount of damages, the Court stated that the mere need to "look to" the agreement for damage computation "is no reason to hold the state law claim defeated by § 301."

In both *Lueck* and *Lingle*, the Court warned that preemption determinations required a case-by-case analysis. To no one's surprise, the murky Supreme Court holdings have led to inconsistent preemption decisions.

# CHAPTER VI

# THE RELATIONSHIPS BETWEEN ARBITRATORS, THE NLRB, AND THE COURTS

Perhaps the most complex area of the law of labor arbitration involves the relationships between arbitrators, the National Labor Relations Board (NLRB), and the courts. Chapter V briefly mentioned some aspects of this problem, for example the deference courts give to arbitration awards and the notion of arbitrability. This chapter explores those topics in greater detail. It also deals with several new issues, among them the authority of arbitrators to apply external law in addition to, or in place of, contract terms, and the attitude of the NLRB toward labor arbitration.

## A. ARBITRABILITY

Arbitrability—that is, the question whether a particular dispute is properly subject to arbitration—has two aspects. The first, termed *substantive arbitrability*, involves claims that the subject matter is not arbitrable because there is no valid contract in force or because the contract or arbitration clause does not deal with the disputed issue. The second, termed *procedural arbitrability*, involves claims that the party seeking arbitration has not met the procedural requisites to arbitration such as time deadlines or exhaustion of an internal grievance procedure. Broadly speaking, the Supreme Court has decided that courts are responsible for substantive arbitrability determinations and arbitrators for procedural arbitrability issues.

## 1. Substantive Arbitrability

*(a) General.* The Supreme Court in the *Steelworkers Trilogy* severely restricted the role courts were to play in determinations of substantive arbitrability. When a party brings a case before the court seeking to force or block arbitration, the court is confined "to ascertaining whether the party seeking arbitration is making a claim which on its face is governed by the contract" *(American Mfg. Co.)*. In making even that determination, the court must order arbitration "unless it may be said with positive assurance that the arbitration clause is not susceptible of an interpretation that covers the dispute," resolving doubts in favor of coverage *(Warrior & Gulf Navigation Co.)*. Only an express exclusion or "the most forceful evidence" of a purpose to exclude a claim from arbitration can prevail against this pro-arbitration policy. Once the arbitrator renders an award, the courts may not tamper with it so long as it "draws its essence from the collective bargaining agreement" (which means the written contract and any additions to it by virtue of past practice) *(Enterprise Wheel & Car Corp.)*.

On the other hand, a court may not avoid determining substantive arbitrability by leaving the issue to the arbitrator. In *AT & T Technologies, Inc. v. Communications Workers of America* (S.Ct.1986), the Court of Appeals tried to dodge the arbitrability question because answering it would entangle the court in interpretation of the agreement's substantive provisions. The Supreme Court reversed. The parties are free to agree in their contract that the arbitrator rather than a court will determine arbitrability disputes, but unless they do so "clearly and unmistakably," the Court stated, "the question of whether the parties agreed to arbitrate is to be decided by the court, not the arbitrator."

Notwithstanding these strictures, many courts have found themselves dealing with questions of substantive arbitrability rather more deeply than the language of the *Trilogy* would seem to allow. Indeed, the Supreme Court itself authorized a broader judicial role by recognizing in *John Wiley & Sons v. Livingston* (S.Ct.1964), that at some point the demand for arbitration might be "so plainly unreasonable that the subject matter of the dispute must be regarded as non-arbitrable because it can be seen in advance that no award to the Union can receive judicial sanction." The problem is that making such a determination requires a court to review (and perhaps judge) the merits of the case. That is just what the *Trilogy* warned courts not to do.

Occasionally a court will find a particular claim inarbitrable simply because the contract is silent on the issue. That is what the Seventh Circuit did in *Independent Petroleum Workers of America, Inc. v. American Oil Co.* (7th Cir.1963). The union sought arbitration of a subcontracting dispute. The agreement contained a standard arbitration clause but no reference to subcontracting. According to the court of appeals, the bargaining history of the parties showed that the union had tried but failed to limit the company's right to contract out work. It therefore refused to order arbitration. That decision probably represents a minority position. Most courts, when faced with a broad arbitration clause and no other specific reference to the disputed issue, would order arbitration because the parties may have tacitly amended the agreement by their past practice or because they may have intended other clauses (such as those on union recognition and seniority) to cover the issue.

The courts have not welcomed the notion of implied exclusions. Thus in *Warrior & Gulf*, the Supreme Court refused to assume that the phrase "strictly a function of management" impliedly excluded subcontracting decisions from the scope of the arbitration clause. Similarly, a management rights clause giving the employer the "exclusive right" to make certain decisions will not bar arbitration of a grievance challenging one of those decisions. Only if the agreement stated that management's use of that authority is inarbitrable should a court refuse an order to compel arbitration, *United Ins. Co. v. Insurance Workers International Union* (E.D.Pa.1970). The attempted exclusion in that case, if that is what it was, was not explicit, and the employer did not show "the most forceful evidence" of an intent to exclude that subject.

Similarly, general language limiting arbitration, such as common prohibitions on arbitrators modifying or adding to the contract, affect only the arbitrator's "authority" to render a particular award, not the arbitrator's "jurisdiction" to hear the case. This attitude seems to stem from the therapeutic value of arbitration the Supreme Court recognized in *Trilogy*. The parties may benefit from the decision of an outsider, even where the contract gives the outsider only a single choice.

The tighter the parties make the language of the arbitration clause, the greater the chance that a court will refuse to order arbitration. The odds of refusal go up significantly, for example, where the contract provides for arbitration only if the union alleges violation of a specific clause; conversely, the odds go down significantly where the contract provides for arbitration of "any dispute." Of course the courts must enforce a specific contractual exclusion. In a case reaching the Second Circuit Court of Appeals, for example, the agreement said that "in no event" shall a dispute arising out of the promotion clause "be subject to arbitration." The union nevertheless sought to force arbitration of a promotion dispute. The court turned down the application: not even the strong presumption in favor of arbitration could overcome such clear language.

*Communications Workers v. New York Tel. Co.* (2d Cir.1964).

**(b) Arbitral Determinations of Substantive Arbitrability.** Suppose a court orders arbitration of a dispute where one party claims the matter is not arbitrable. May the arbitrator then decide the contrary? Some of the Supreme Court's language from the *Trilogy*'s and *AT & T Technologies* suggests that *only* a court may decide arbitrability, leaving nothing to the arbitrator (unless the parties "clearly and unmistakably" give that decision to the arbitrator).

However, both fairness to the parties and the *Trilogy*'s principles require that the arbitrator have authority to decide arbitrability issues. Fairness to the parties requires fidelity to their agreement. Labor arbitration is *voluntary*; thus some decision maker has to decide whether in fact the parties agreed to arbitrate the question in dispute. The *Trilogy* directs courts to make only a cursory investigation—to ask only whether the contract "on its face" governs the issue. To prohibit the arbitrator, too, from looking behind the contract's "face" would deprive the parties of the only other forum for determining their true intent. It would amount to a requirement that all decision makers are to make only a superficial determination of the parties' intentions—and a biased one at that, for they are told to resolve all doubts in favor of arbitration. No one would have the power to find out what the parties really meant. This would indeed be a strange way to effectuate the national policy expressed in § 203(d) of the Taft–Hartley Act favoring final adjustment of disputes "by a method agreed upon by the parties."

The principles of the *Trilogy* also require that the arbitrator be free to resolve questions of substantive arbitrability. Arbitration is favored, said the Court, because the parties voluntarily seek the arbitrator's knowledge of the "common law of the shop" and judgment to apply considerations not expressed in the contract. For these reasons, the arbitrator is better qualified to decide contract interpretation questions than the "ablest judge." It would be contradictory to bind an arbitrator by the superficial examination of a judge lacking that expertise.

In practice, arbitrators can and do decide the vast majority of substantive arbitrability challenges. Courts seldom review (and even more rarely overturn) arbitrators' determinations about the contract's coverage. A grievant may get to arbitration by presenting a *prima facie* case of arbitrability to a court. To prevail with the arbitrator, though, the grievant must prove the issue arbitrable by the preponderance of the evidence.

Finally, even when reluctant to rule a grievance inarbitrable, an arbitrator may achieve the same result by ruling against the grievant on the merits. That upholds the original intentions of the parties without sacrificing the therapeutic value of the arbitration process. The therapy is not without cost, for it may defeat the legitimate expectation of the parties that only certain matters would be arbitrable and may waste the parties's time and resources.

***(c) Post-expiration Arbitrability.*** Collective bargaining agreements occasionally expire while grievances are still pending. If a party seeks arbitration before the contract's expiration, the arbitrator will still have jurisdiction over the subject matter; the expiration would at most affect the available remedies. If the contract expires before the request for arbitration, however, there is some doubt whether the arbitrator may even hear the case. Even though the Supreme Court has dealt with these issues several times, most of the decisions involved a complicating factor that is best discussed separately: the presence of a successor employer. Those decisions thus did not resolve some fundamental issues. At stake is a clash between contract law, which normally will enforce an agreement only during its stated term, and the federal policy favoring arbitration.

The termination problem can occur in three situations: (1) where the grievance arose before, but the arbitration hearing would occur after, expiration; (2) where the grievance arose after, but rests on a right that arguably accrued or "vested" before, expiration; and (3) where the grievance arose after termination and depends on the continuance of rights of a non-accruing type established in the terminated contract.

Sec. A  ARBITRABILITY  141

The Supreme Court dealt with the first situation in *Wiley*. A unionized employer, Interscience Publishers, Inc., merged with John Wiley & Sons, a larger, nonunion firm. The union sought arbitration of several grievances, some of which sought continuation of the contract beyond the termination date. Wiley refused to arbitrate, but on appeal the Supreme Court ordered arbitration on all the grievances. In very broad dicta, the Court cited national labor policy as requiring some balance of protection for employees threatened by a sudden change in the employment relationship, and said that industrial strife would be avoided if employees' claims continued to be resolved by arbitration rather than by the parties' economic power. The Court recognized that expiration of the contract might affect some of the claims. Because that issue went to the merits of the dispute, the Court held that the arbitrator rather than a court should decide it. Ultimately the arbitrator found that the contract's expiration extinguished the employees' seniority rights, *Interscience Encyclopedia Inc.* (Benjamin Roberts, 1970).

The Supreme Court dealt with the second situation in *Nolde Bros. v. Local No. 358, Bakery & Confectionery Workers Union* (S.Ct.1977). The employer closed the plant after the contract expired, but the union sought arbitration of its demand for severance pay, claiming that the right accrued during the term of the contract. The Supreme Court noted that nothing in the contract actually *prohibited* arbitration of the claim and ordered the parties to go to arbitration. The dispute, "although arising *after* the expiration of the collective-bargaining contract, clearly arises *under* that contract." The Court cited the federal policy favoring arbitration and its *Wiley* decision, but relied heavily on the fact that the union's claim was based on an obligation "arguably created by the expired agreement."

Lower federal courts differed on the meaning of the *Nolde* decision. Some required a vested right or a pre-expiration event before finding arbitrability. Others simply applied the presumption of arbitrability regardless when the event occurred or whether the right vested. A few restricted the *Nolde* presumption to a limited time after expiration. The Supreme Court finally clarified its decision in *Litton Financial Printing Division v. NLRB* (S.Ct.1991). In a 5–4 decision, the Court opted for a narrow reading of *Nolde*. After the collective agreement expired, the employer ceased to make layoffs according to seniority. The Supreme Court adopted the NLRB's interpretation of *Nolde*, finding that:

> A postexpiration grievance can be said to arise under the contract only where it involves facts and occurrences that arose before expiration, where an action taken after expiration infringes a right that accrued or vested under the agreement, or where, under normal principles of contract interpretation, the disputed contractual right survives expiration of the remainder of the agreement.

In *Litton*, the asserted rights had not vested, so the employer did not have to arbitrate the layoffs. The dissenting justices argued that whether a contract right had vested was itself a question of interpretation for the arbitrator.

*Litton* effectively resolved the third situation. Some unions had argued that contractual rights such as protection from discharge except for just cause and a prohibition on lockouts continue even beyond the expiration of the contract. Most courts rejected that argument, pointing out that it would mean that an employer who once agreed to submit its managerial actions to arbitration did so for all time. *See, e.g., Procter & Gamble Independent Union of Port Ivory, N. Y. v. Procter & Gamble Mfg. Co.* (2d Cir.1962); *Local 998, U.A.W. v. B. & T. Metals Co.* (6th Cir.1963). After *Litton*, the range of arguably accrued rights seems quite narrow.

*(d) Successorship.* Can the arbitration agreement bind a successor party? There are two aspects of this problem, that of the successor employer and that of the successor union.

The Supreme Court has decided three major employer successorship cases. The first and last expressly address arbitration agreements. In *John Wiley & Sons*, an action under § 301, the Court held that a successor employer had to arbitrate grievances under its predecessor's collective bargaining agreement, so long as there is "substantial continuity in the business enterprise before and after a change." In *NLRB v. Burns International*

*Security Services, Inc.,* (S.Ct.1972), an unfair labor practice case, the Court held that a successor employer must bargain with the union representing its predecessor's employees if those employees constitute a majority of the new work force. More importantly for the current topic, it held that the successor must apply the terms of the predecessor's contract with that union. Finally, in *Howard Johnson Co. v. Detroit Local Joint Executive Board* (S.Ct.1974), another § 301 action, the Supreme Court held that a successor must arbitrate under the predecessor's contract only if there is "substantial continuity of identity in the business enterprise." (Only a small percentage of the new work force in that case had been in the previous bargaining unit).

These cases do not mesh neatly. In particular, the holding in *Burns* that a successor is not bound by its predecessor's contract seems to be at odds both with *Wiley*'s **holding** that the successor is bound by at least one part—the arbitration clause—of the predecessor's contract and with *Wiley*'s **implication** that the arbitrator could find the successor bound by *all* of the contract's terms. It is possible to distinguish the two cases (one was a merger, the other a sale; one was brought in court under § 301, the other before the NLRB) but the distinctions are not persuasive; in fact, the Supreme Court expressly rejected the latter distinction in *Howard Johnson*. It is likely that the Court will make further attempts to clarify successorship issues. Until then, two guidelines will have to do.

First, a successor employer normally must arbitrate under the predecessor's contract so long as there is substantial continuity of the business enterprise. Without substantial continuity—where, for example, new employees form a majority or the old employees are dispersed throughout the new employer's operations—the successor has no obligation to arbitrate under the predecessor's agreement.

Second, where the successor does arbitrate, the arbitrator may find that the agreement's substantive terms bind the successor as well as the predecessor. The courts will enforce such a holding.

The last point deserves some explanation. After the *Wiley* decision, the arbitrator selected by the parties held that Wiley was bound by the Interscience contract until its expiration or until a change of conditions occurred that altered or abolished the separate identity of the old bargaining unit, whichever came first. Several months after the merger, Wiley distributed the former Interscience employees among its own departments. That change ended the continuity of the employment relationship, the arbitrator held. Thereafter, the Interscience employees had no substantive rights under the predecessor's contract. *Interscience Encyclopedia, Inc.* (Benjamin Roberts, 1970). Another arbitrator reached a similar conclusion in *United States Gypsum Co.* (Rolf Valtin, 1971). A court of appeals enforced Arbitrator Valtin's award three years later: *United Steelworkers v. United States Gypsum Co.* (5th Cir.1974).

There is less to say on the problem of the successor union. A union decertified by employees in a bargaining unit retains the power to arbitrate the "unfinished business"—that is, cases that arose during the union's period as bargaining representative. *Missouri Portland Cement Co.* (N.L.R.B.1988). If the employees selected a successor union, however, the employer has no obligation to arbitrate with the new union: the advent of a new union terminates the old agreement; and without an agreement, there is no basis for imposing an obligation to arbitrate. *Arizona Portland Cement Co.* (N.L.R.B. 1991).

## 2. Procedural Arbitrability

The Supreme Court held in *Wiley* that arbitrators rather than courts are to decide questions of procedural arbitrability because those issues are likely to be inextricably tied up with the merits of the case. That explanation is hardly convincing. Procedural arbitrability questions are if anything *less* likely than substantive arbitrability questions to require interpretation of the contract's substantive terms.

Decisions on such questions receive the same deference from the courts as decisions on the merits. Thus courts have on numerous occasions rejected pleas to review an arbitrator's decision on timeliness, mootness, lack of specificity, and lack of a proper initiating party. *See, e.g., Carpenters Local No. 824 v. Brunswick Corp.* (6th Cir.1965). On the other hand, those decisions receive no more deference than other sorts of arbitral determinations. The same tests apply, such as the rule that the award must draw its essence from the collective bargaining agreement. In *El Mundo Broadcasting Corp. v. United Steelworkers of America* (1st Cir. 1997), an arbitrator determined that a promotion grievance was timely because the claim "is of a continuous nature" and "arises and is renewed from day to day." The Court of Appeals decided that the missed salary was not the allegedly wrongful act, but merely one of its consequences; the union should therefore have met the contractual time limits from the date of the challenged promotion. Having made its own interpretation of the facts and the contract, the court had no trouble in concluding that by "misstating the basic nature of the occurrence the arbitrator read the time provisions out of the contract, ignoring its 'essence.' "

Procedural arbitrability questions are thus merely a subset of the issues arbitrators routinely resolve. Chapter VII, Section A., below, covers that topic in more detail.

## B. ARBITRATORS AND EXTERNAL LAW

One of the most hotly debated issues within the arbitration community today is whether arbitrators may, should, or must rule on questions of law that arise in connection with contractual grievances. The Supreme Court held in *Enterprise Wheel* that an arbitrator would "exceed the scope of the submission" by deciding a case "*solely* upon the arbitrator's view of the requirements of enacted legislation," rather than on an interpretation of the agreement (emphasis added). The Court noted, though, that an arbitrator could look to the law "for help in determining the sense of the agreement." There is a lot of room between those boundaries.

There are three primary situations which force an arbitrator to grapple with this issue. In the first, and least problematic situation, a labor agreement and a statute may prohibit the same conduct, for example, discrimination on the basis of union membership or race. No one doubts that an arbitrator could use the relevant statute and case interpretation to determine "the sense of the agreement." That is especially appropriate where some portion of the agreement arguably violates the statute. Where the contract term is susceptible to two interpretations, one of which is consistent with the law and the other of which is in conflict with it, arbitrators may reasonably assume that the parties intended the lawful interpretation.

The second situation involves a legal issue that turns on a matter of contract interpretation. The most common case is a union's claim that an employer changed the terms of employment without bargaining. Because a union may waive its collective right to bargain over certain employer actions, the legal issue depends on the interpretation of the contract. If the arbitrator finds that the agreement authorized unilateral management action, there would be no violation of the law. Again, this presents no serious problem for arbitration theory, because the arbitrator is performing only the usual function of contract interpretation. That the arbitrator's decision on that issue may have legal consequences does not change the arbitrator's role. The next section of this chapter examines the NLRB's opinions in such cases.

Finally, the contract might appear to authorize or require some action arguably prohibited by law. A contract might specify the use of a seniority system challenged as being prohibited by civil rights laws. Another might call for wage increases in violation of wage and price controls (this was a frequent problem during the early 1970s when such controls were in effect). Still another might provide for piece rates that fall below the minimum wage established by the Fair Labor Standards Act. This is the only part of the "external law" question that has divided the arbitration community.

Often, however, the alleged conflict is not as clear as one party would have it seem. A good example is *W. R. Grace and Co. v. Local Union 759, International Union of the United Rubber, Cork, Linoleum and Plastic Workers of America* (S.Ct.1983) (*W. R. Grace*, for short). The EEOC charged the employer with discriminating against blacks and women. While that matter was pending, the employer hired strike replacements and gave the female replacements preference over returning male strikers. When the union sought to arbitrate that decision, the employer responded with a suit seeking to bar arbitration pending negotiation of a conciliation agreement with the EEOC. Before the district court acted, the EEOC and employer entered into a conciliation agreement providing that the company would maintain the proportion of female employees in the event of layoffs. Some layoffs followed. Men who would have been protected by the seniority clause filed grievances. The district court then sided with the employer, holding that Title VII authorized the employer to modify the seniority provisions to alleviate the effects of past discrimination.

The union appealed that ruling, but before the Court of Appeals decided the case, the employer laid off still more employees. Again, male employees filed grievances. Eventually the Court of Appeals reversed the district court. The employer reinstated the male employees, but the grievances proceeded over the issue of back pay. The first arbitrator to rule on the conflict agreed with the union that the contract entitled the grievant to an award, but held that it would be "inequitable" to penalize the company for complying with an outstanding court order. He therefore denied the grievance. The second arbitrator concluded that he did not have to follow the first award, that under the agreement he had power only to interpret the contract, and that the company violated the seniority clause. The company's good faith in following the court order and the conciliation agreement did not excuse its breach.

The company went back to court to overturn the second award. The Supreme Court, viewing the issue as limited to the enforceability of the second award, held that the award "drew its essence" from the agreement and therefore should have been enforced. The Court had no sympathy for the company's dilemma, which was, according to the Court, of its own making. The company "committed itself voluntarily to two conflicting contractual obligations"; by following a court order that proved erroneous, it incurred liability for breaching the contract. There was no conflict with public policy, because the second award did not require the company to violate the court order: it simply held that the grievants were entitled to damages.

What lessons does *W. R. Grace* teach? First, an arbitrator need not apply external law, at least when the contract does not require an illegal act. Second, an employer who makes inconsistent promises may have to bear the costs of damages for breaching one of them. And third (a matter explored in greater depth in Chapter VIII, Section A), an arbitrator is not required to follow a previous award, even if the first case involved the same parties, issue, and contract.

## 1. The Theories

Several of the nation's wisest arbitrators and legal scholars grappled during the 1960s and 1970s with the question of what arbitrators should do when faced with a potential conflict between the collective agreement and statutory or common law. Two papers presented at the 1967 annual meeting of the National Academy of Arbitrators marked the polar positions. Professor Bernard Meltzer of the University of Chicago argued that the key to the problem was to be found in the parties' intentions. They "typically call on an arbitrator to construe and not to destroy their agreement." Moreover, the arbitrators they choose often have no expertise in legal issues or in the statutory questions involved. Where there was an "irrepressible conflict" between the contract and the law, he concluded, the arbitrator "should respect the agreement and ignore the law."

At the opposite pole was Arbitrator Robert Howlett of Michigan. All contracts, he argued, incorporate all relevant law. Thus separating the two subjects may be impossible. An award that does not consider the law may result in costly error and do an injustice to a grievant. An arbitrator "who decides a dispute without consideration of legal issues disserves his management-union clients, and acts inconsistently with" NLRB and court decisions. Howlett contended that an arbitrator should "probe" to find a statutory issue even if neither party raises one.

The following year, Arbitrator Richard Mittenthal, reviewing the debate, charged that Howlett's incorporation theory was inaccurate, unnecessary, and contrary to both contract law doctrine and to the typical arbitration clause confining the arbitrator to interpreting and applying the collective agreement. When turning to the arbitrator's duties in the face of a conflict, Mittenthal recommended an intermediate position: the arbitrator should apply the law rather than the contract only when the grievance "would require conduct the law forbids or would enforce an illegal contract"; if so, the arbitrator should deny the grievance. Put differently, "although the arbitrator's award may permit conduct forbidden by law but sanctioned by contract, it should not require conduct forbidden by law even though sanctioned by contract."

If the arbitrator does rule on a legal question in the course of interpreting a contract, should that interpretation bind the parties? Some have argued that because such issues are outside the arbitrator's authority and expertise, a ruling on the legal issue should be viewed as advisory only, subject to *de novo* review if the parties seek enforcement or vacation of the award in court. Professor Theodore St. Antoine of the University of Michigan has challenged this view. Arguing that parties engage an arbitrator as their sole "contract reader," St. Antoine concludes that interpretations of the law made in that role are binding **as between the parties.** If the arbitrator reads the Occupational Safety and Health Act in a proper case as imposing a stricter obligation on the employer than the reviewing court would find the law to require, the arbitrator's opinion should govern.

## 2. The Application

What do these theories mean in practice? Consider two cases from the early years of this debate, *International Paper Co., Southern Kraft Division, Bastrop Mill* (F. Jay Taylor 1977), and *Evans Products Co.,* (David Feller, 1978).

In the first case, the contract allowed the senior qualified employee to transfer to an apprenticeship and denied the arbitrator power to "add to or subtract from or modify any of the terms of this agreement." Allegedly following its affirmative action plan (but refusing to give the union a copy of that plan), the company awarded an apprenticeship to a junior black employee. The arbitrator stated that he was obliged to "consider the obligations of the equal employment policies of this nation, and the many laws and executive orders which spell out that policy." Those policies, he concluded, made the company's choice of a remedy for past discrimination "exempt from contractual obligations." Failing to exempt that choice would place the company "in an impossible position," because the company might lose government contracts.

In the second case, Arbitrator Feller considered and rejected Arbitrator Taylor's approach. The agreement prohibited the company from discriminating "on the basis of age." Nevertheless, the company refused to hire a 17–year-old applicant, on the good-faith belief that Fair Labor Standards Act regulations barred any person under 18 from performing the job. The agreement also prohibited the arbitrator from making any decision "on matters not covered by specific provisions of this Agreement." In the face of that limitation, he found he could only decide the contractual issue, and on that issue he sustained the grievance. He found no problem in ordering the applicant's retroactive hiring, because any remedy he might order "is obviously subject to nullification by a court having authority to determine the disputed question of federal law."

It is an interesting irony that Arbitrator Taylor, who was willing to interpret and apply the law, is not a lawyer, while Arbitrator Feller, who declined to do so, is one of the most distinguished labor lawyers and scholars of the century. (He successfully argued the *Steelworkers Trilogy* for the United Steelworkers of America.)

One should not overestimate the significance of the external-law question. The debate about it is out of proportion with its actual occurrence. A study published in 1985 by Perry Zirkel found that external law played a significant role in only 5% of a sample of 100 published awards. (Because publishers disproportionately select complicated, controversial, and topical cases, that 5% figure undoubtedly and grossly overstates the frequency of legal issues in arbitration.) The whole debate, Professor Zirkel concluded, was "much ado about relatively little."

## C. THE NLRB AND THE ARBITRATION PROCESS

### 1. Introduction

The attitudes of the NLRB toward the arbitration process and, more importantly, toward the relationship between that process and the unfair labor practice provisions of the LMRA have undergone several major changes in recent years. The problem of overlapping jurisdiction occurs chiefly in two types of cases, namely those where the legality of an act depends solely upon the interpretation of the collective bargaining agreement, and those where the contract is at most only one element bearing upon the legality of the act.

Representative of the first type is the "unilateral change" problem. NLRA § 8(a)(5) obliges an employer to bargain with the union representing its employees over their "wages, hours and other terms and conditions of employment." By extension, this obligation applies to proposed changes in the terms of employment. Bargaining before every minor change can be costly and inconvenient, so one way an employer can fulfill this obligation is to bargain with the union for contractual authority to make certain changes during the contract term without further bargaining. For example, an employer might gain the right to adjust hours and work assignments in response to market change. If the union later challenges a certain change as outside the scope of that clause, the unfair labor practice charge may depend entirely on interpretation of the contract. Add a broad arbitration clause covering the issue and the result is a potential conflict of jurisdiction between the Board and the arbitrator.

The second type of case can be illustrated by a fairly common union security dispute. NLRA § 8(a)(3) prohibits discrimination against employees because of union membership or non-membership, except pursuant to a valid union security agreement. If an employer fires employee A for not joining the union, resolution of a § 8(a)(3) charge might depend in part upon an interpretation of the contract (whether the union security clause applied to A and if so, whether A complied with it) and in part on the legal question whether the union security clause was actually valid under § 8(a)(3). Here again there is a potential conflict of jurisdiction between the Board and an arbitrator.

In several cases in the 1960s, the Supreme Court took the view that the NLRA did not require either the Board or an arbitrator to yield to the other in cases of overlapping jurisdiction. *Smith v. Evening News Ass'n,* (S.Ct.1962); *Carey v. Westinghouse Electric Corp.* (S.Ct.1964). Each would remain dominant in its proper sphere—the Board over questions of law, the arbitrator over contract interpretation. Even if the Board's decision would ultimately govern in a hybrid case, the Court said in *Carey,* arbitration was desirable because it might resolve (or at least avoid fragmentation of) the dispute. The

Board can of course interpret a collective agreement when necessary to resolve an unfair labor practice claim, *NLRB v. C & C Plywood Corp.* (S.Ct.1967).

Those decisions left it to the Board to decide what deference, if any, to pay to arbitration awards and to the arbitration process. The Board *may* decide a case that has been or could be decided by an arbitrator, but *should* it do so? And if so, when?

## 2. Post–Arbitration Deferral

The Board's first attempts to answer those questions fortuitously involved the easier case for deference, that is, after an arbitrator had rendered an award on a contract-interpretation issue. In *Spielberg Mfg. Co.,* (N.L.R.B.1955), the employer had refused to reinstate four employees for alleged misconduct during a strike. An arbitration proceeding that would by today's standards seem dubious (the company attorney and the neutral arbitrator were close associates, the hearing was perfunctory, and the award conclusory) sustained the company's position. The discharged employees filed unfair labor practice charges and won before the Trial Examiner (now called an Administrative Law Judge). The Board used the case to announce a new policy of deferral to arbitration awards. Henceforth, it would accept arbitration awards as conclusive on legal issues before the Board as a way of encouraging the voluntary settlement of labor disputes, provided that (1) the proceedings were fair and regular; (2) all parties had agreed to be bound by the award;

and (3) the award was "not clearly repugnant to the purposes and policies" of the LMRA.

The Board fiddled with the requirements for deferral several times but has never departed from the central principle. In *Monsanto Chem. Co.* (N.L.R.B. 1961), and *Raytheon Co.* (N.L.R.B.1963), the Board added a fourth requirement, that the arbitrator actually consider the unfair labor practice issue. In *Suburban Motor Freight,* (N.L.R.B.1980), it placed the burden of proving the requirements for deferral on the party seeking deferral. In *Olin Corp.,* (N.L.R.B.1984), the Board reversed those two decisions, holding that the arbitrator would have "adequately considered" the unfair labor practice if the contractual and statutory issues were "factually parallel" and the parties presented the arbitrator "generally with the facts relevant to resolving the unfair labor practice." Explicating *Spielberg*'s "clearly repugnant" standard, the Board emphasized that an arbitrator's award need not be "totally consistent" with Board precedent: the Board would defer, it said, unless the award is "palpably wrong"—that is, unless the decision "is not susceptible to an interpretation consistent with the Act." Finally, *Olin* switched the burden of proof to the party seeking to avoid deferral.

The Supreme Court has not expressly ruled on the Board's deferral policy, but it has favorably acknowledged the practice both for representation issues *(Carey, supra)* and for unfair labor practice issues, *NLRB v. C & C Plywood Corp.* (S.Ct.1967).

The *Olin* elaboration of *Spielberg* has been more controversial. In one of the Board's early applications of the new policy, the Court of Appeals for the District of Columbia remanded the case to the Board for a better explanation of why the Board could defer to an award that is "doctrinally different from Board precedent," *Darr v. NLRB* (D.C.Cir. 1986). An arbitrator had ordered the reinstatement of a discharged union steward, but without back pay. The arbitrator recognized that the Board would have ordered full back pay, but failed to reconcile the contractual and legal matters. The Court of Appeals expressed "profound doubts" about the legitimacy of deferral to an award "merely because the award is roughly analogous to that which the Board would grant." In a lengthy opinion in the case four years later (and nearly 13 years after the discharge that started the action), the Board concluded that the award was indeed "clearly repugnant" to the Act, even under the *Olin* standard. *Cone Mills Corp.—White Oak Plant* (N.L.R.B. 1990).

Another court found unreasonable *Olin*'s policy of presuming that all arbitrations confront and decide every unfair labor practice issue. *Taylor v. NLRB* (11th Cir.1986). The "arbitration" in that case was actually a meeting of a bipartite Joint Area Grievance Committee, not a hearing before a neutral decision maker. There was absolutely no evidence that the Committee considered the unfair labor practice issue, yet the Board deferred to its decision. The Court of Appeals held that *Olin*'s presumption "gives away too much of the Board's responsibility under the NLRA" and "cannot be reconciled with the need to protect statutory rights." On remand, the Board accepted the Court of Appeals' decision as the "law of the case," found that the employer failed to show that the Joint Area Grievance Committee had considered the facts relevant to the unfair labor practice issue, and therefore declined to defer to that Committee's decision. Significantly, though, the Board did not modify the *Olin* opinion.

Despite the *Darr* and *Taylor* interruptions, *Olin* has drastically increased the rate of Board deferrals to arbitration awards. One study found that the NLRB had refused to defer in nearly 19% of cases before *Olin* but in only 3.8% after. Patricia A. Greenfield, *The NLRB's Deferral to Arbitration Before and After* Olin: *An Empirical Analysis*, 42 Industrial and Labor Relations Review 34 (1988).

## 3. Pre–Arbitration Deferral

In 1972 the Board announced a major expansion of its deferral policy. In *Collyer Insulated Wire* (1971) (3–2), it announced that it would defer to the arbitration process *before* the arbitration decision as well as after. That case involved a § 8(a)(5) charge in a "unilateral action" situation: the employer made certain wage adjustments that the union contended exceeded its power under the collective bargaining agreement. The Board dismissed the complaint but retained jurisdiction to review the arbitration process and award under the *Spielberg* criteria.

*Collyer* has had a topsy-turvy career. The two dissenters predicted extension of the deferral doctrine to wrongful-discharge cases. Later that year, their prediction came true in *National Radio Co.* (N.L.R.B.1972). Five years later, however, the Board took one step back, ruling that it would no longer defer in such cases because arbitration was not suited to resolving statutory issues that did not depend on contract interpretation, *General American Transportation Corp.* (N.L.R.B.1977). That decision turned on the vote of one member, Member Betty Murphy, who argued that the Board should defer only when the dispute is between the contracting parties and there was no claim of interference with individual employees' § 7 rights. The other four members divided evenly over the legality of pre-award deferral. As if to illustrate her distinction, Member Murphy switched sides in a companion case, *Roy Robinson, Inc.* (N.L.R.B.1977), which deferred to arbitration a complaint alleging unilateral employer action.

Member Murphy's concurrences in those cases point out an important distinction: different types of cases involve different criteria for decision, and while arbitration may be the most appropriate forum for some issues, it may not be for all. Unilateral action cases are the most obvious choices for deferral, for they frequently involve only a contract interpretation question. Discriminatory treatment cases may be less suitable for deferral because the statutory rights of a third party, the grieving employee, may be at stake. Representation and work-assignment disputes may well be the least suited for arbitral resolution. The Board applies different criteria to these cases than those used by most arbitrators and the arbitrator is unlikely to have all the necessary parties (the two or more unions claiming the work or the representation rights) participating in the hearing.

Whatever the merits of Member Murphy's distinction, they were not enough to convince new Board members. Seven years later, in *United Technologies Corp.* (N.L.R.B.1984), the Reagan Board reversed *General American* and returned to the *National Radio* doctrine, to which it adheres today. Though still controversial, the Board's pre-award deferral policy has withstood court challenges. See, for example, *Hammontree v. NLRB* (D.C.Cir.1991) (en banc). The only major areas in which the Board does not defer are charges that an employer has denied a union information necessary for processing grievances, *American National Can Co.* (N.L.R.B. 1989); allegations of retaliation for filing NLRB charges or giving testimony in connection with an NLRA proceeding, *Superior Forwarding Co.* (N.L.R.B.1987); and representation disputes, *Port Chester Nursing Home* (N.L.R.B.1984).

## D. COURT DEFERRAL

### 1. Labor Cases

The *Steelworkers Trilogy* demonstrated that the courts will enforce arbitration agreements. Section 301 gives the courts jurisdiction to redress any breach of a collective bargaining agreement, however, which raises an interesting question: does the availability of arbitration mean that the courts may not or should not deal with alleged contract breaches?

In *Drake Bakeries, Inc. v. Local 50, American Bakery Workers* (S.Ct.1962), the employer brought a court action for damages caused by a strike in breach of contract. The federal district court ordered a stay in the action pending arbitration. On appeal to the Supreme Court, the employer argued that the parties could not have intended to arbitrate so fundamental a matter as a union strike in breach of the contract, and that in any event the strike amounted to a repudiation of the contract and thus freed the employer from any obligation to arbitrate. The Court rejected both claims. If breach of the no-strike clause was so fundamental, it held, the parties would have expressly excluded that issue from the arbitration provisions; and the company itself recognized the continued vitality of the contract by suing for damages pursuant to it and by continuing to apply its other provisions.

*Drake Bakeries* thus announced a policy of judicial deferral to arbitration, at least in cases where the issue would be the same in either forum. That decision depended upon the availability of arbitration to resolve the issue, however. Unlike most collective bargaining agreements, this one allowed the employer as well as the union to file a grievance and seek arbitration. If the agreement does not require the employer to arbitrate claims against the union, litigation may be the only remedy available to the employer. The courts will not close their doors to a plaintiff in that situation. *Atkinson v. Sinclair Ref. Co.* (S.Ct.1962). Because arbitration is a voluntary process, courts will not force it on a party who never agreed to it.

## 2. Statutory Cases in the Collective Bargaining Context

The NLRB defers even some statutory questions to arbitration. Should (or must) the courts do the same? The first cases to raise that question came from unionized environments. Not until 1991 did an individual employment arbitration case presenting the same issue reach the Supreme Court. For the moment, at least, the rules differ between the two situations.

In employment discrimination cases the courts generally will not defer to arbitration, both because of a strong congressional desire to provide an additional remedy for employment discrimination and because certain distinctive aspects of arbitration make it a less appropriate forum for discrimination complaints than for other claims.

In *Alexander v. Gardner–Denver Co.* (S.Ct.1974), the plaintiff argued before an arbitrator that his dismissal violated the collective agreement's "just cause" and non-discrimination provisions. The arbitrator's opinion made no reference to the claim of racial discrimination but held that the petitioner had been discharged for just cause. Alexander later filed a race-discrimination suit in federal court under Title VII of the Civil Rights Act of 1964. The lower courts dismissed his action on the ground that, having chosen to arbitrate his grievance under the non-discrimination clause of the collective bargaining agreement, he was bound by the adverse result and thereby precluded from suing his employer under Title VII.

The Supreme Court unanimously reversed. The Court held that the arbitration did not foreclose Alexander's Title VII right to a trial. The Court first noted that Congress had clearly intended Title VII to provide "parallel or overlapping remedies against discrimination," analogizing to the overlap between arbitration and the LMRA found in *Carey v. Westinghouse Electric Corp.* (S.Ct.1964). As in that case, the procedures in discrimination cases were complementary rather than exclusive since "consideration of the claim by both forums may promote the policies underlying each."

The Court then rejected the argument that the arbitration clause and Alexander's use of the arbitration procedure constituted a waiver of Title VII rights. There can be no prospective waiver by the union of an individual's Title VII rights, it said, and "mere resort" by the individual to the arbitration procedure does not constitute a waiver. The Court recognized that an individual might make a "voluntary and knowing" express waiver as part of a formal settlement to a Title VII claim, but Alexander had not done so. The Court also stated that the preclusion argument advanced by the Company would not be proper in light of the different functions of arbitrator and judge. The arbitrator sits to apply the contract; unlike a judge, the arbitrator has no independent general authority to invoke public laws.

For the same reason, the Court declined to adopt a policy of deferral to arbitration awards. It held that the arbitrator's role is to effectuate the parties' intent, not the purposes of the Civil Rights laws. Arbitrators' specialized competence is in the law of the shop, not the law of the land. Many arbitrators are not even lawyers, let alone experts in this subject matter. Moreover, arbitration's fact-finding processes are inferior to judicial fact-finding: the record is not as complete, the rules of evidence do not apply, discovery and compulsory process may be limited or unavailable, arbitrators have no obligation to give reasons for their awards, and so on. Finally, if courts were to impose a strict deferral standard, they would tend to make arbitration more complex, expensive and time-consuming, and thus detract from its greatest advantages.

The Court also worried about a potential conflict of interest between the union (which usually has exclusive control over the decision to arbitrate) and the employee. The union might not use the same theories or insist on the same settlement terms as the employee would. "In arbitration, as in the collective-bargaining process, the interests of the individual employee may be subordinated to the collective interests of all employees in the bargaining unit."

The Court did not completely foreclose arbitration of discrimination cases. A court could admit the arbitration decision as evidence in the trial and accord it "such weight as the court deems appropriate." In a relatively famous footnote to that statement, the Court gave some indication of what it had in mind:

21. We adopt no standards as to the weight to be accorded an arbitral decision, since this must be determined in the court's discretion with regard to the facts and circumstances of each case. Relevant factors include the existence of provisions in the collective-bargaining agreement that conform substantially with Title VII, the degree of procedural fairness in the arbitral forum, adequacy of the record with respect to the issue of discrimination, and the special competence of particular arbitrators. Where an arbitral determination gives full consideration to an employee's Title VII rights, a court may properly accord it great weight. This is especially true where the issue is solely one of fact, specifically addressed by the parties and decided by the arbitrator on the

basis of an adequate record. But courts should ever be mindful that Congress, in enacting Title VII, thought it necessary to provide a judicial forum for the ultimate resolution of discriminatory employment claims. It is the duty of courts to assure the full availability of this forum.

That statement seems to indicate that arbitration could yet play an important role in the resolution of discrimination cases, but to date that has not happened, at least not in unionized environments. Parties to collective bargaining agreements have been noticeably cautious in amending arbitration provisions to comply with the standards of footnote 21, perhaps because they realize, as the Court did, that arbitration under such conditions would be nearly as formal, expensive and slow as a court suit. In some cases where parties have consciously tried to comply with those standards, the cases never reached federal court. Some involved the "voluntary and knowing" waiver that would preclude court action, and most resulted in awards favorable to the grievant, which could obviate a Title VII suit.

In a few other cases federal courts have given arbitral awards some weight as evidence. One court held that a favorable arbitration award might satisfy the employer's burden of proving a legitimate reason for a discharge, but it could not prevent a plaintiff from introducing evidence on the question, *Becton v. Detroit Terminal of Consolidated Freightways* (6th Cir.1982). Another court held that it was error for a trial court simply to ignore an arbitrator's finding, *Owens v. Texaco, Inc.* (5th Cir.1988). When employees do sue after losing in arbitration, they seldom prevail. One 1984 study found that employees litigated discrimination cases about 17% of the time after raising those issues in arbitration; they were successful in only 7% of the cases in which they sued. Michele Hoyman and Lamont Stallworth, *The Arbitration of Discrimination Grievances in the Aftermath of* Gardner–Denver, 39 Arbitration Journal 49 (September, 1984).

*Alexander* proved to be a landmark case. Later Supreme Court cases used it as a basis for denying arbitration any preclusive effect in other legal schemes. *Barrentine v. Arkansas–Best Freight System, Inc.* (S.Ct.1981), held that an adverse arbitration award did not bar employees from pursuing a claim under the Fair Labor Standards Act. *McDonald v. City of West Branch* (S.Ct.1984), held that an arbitrator's finding of just cause for a discharge did not prevent a civil rights claim against a municipal employer under 42 U.S.C.A. § 1983 (1994).

In sum, *Alexander* and its progeny clearly established that courts need not and should not defer to arbitration or to arbitration awards when an employee subject to a collective bargaining agreement's arbitration clause files a statutory claim. The recent *Gilmer* case, discussed in the next section, may prompt reexamination of that conclusion.

## 3. Statutory Cases in the Individual Employment Context

*(a) The* **Gilmer** *Decision.* In light of *Alexander* and similar later cases, there seemed little reason to believe that the Supreme Court would be any more receptive to arbitration of statutory claims in the nonunion context. *Gilmer v. Interstate/Johnson Lane Corp.* (S.Ct.1991), thus came as a great surprise to most observers. Stockbrokers and some other employees in the securities industry promised as part of their registration with a stock exchange to arbitrate disputes with their employers. The agreement appears on the Uniform Application for Securities Industry Registration or Transfer, also known as a "Form U–4." The relevant clause binds the applicant to arbitrate "any dispute, claim or controversy that may arise between me and my firm, or a customer or any other person, that is required to be arbitrated under the rules, constitutions, or by-laws" of the named organizations. Those rules, in turn, usually broadly and vaguely command arbitration of almost any dispute.

Because stock exchange registration is a requirement for many jobs in the industry, the arbitration agreement effectively becomes a condition of employment. The arbitration requirement originally served as a means of resolving financial disputes, for example disagreements between brokers and their employers over the allocation of costs and profits, or between customers and brokers over alleged misconduct. The language is broad enough to cover other claims, however, and that is what occurred in the *Gilmer* case.

Gilmer was a securities executive who was registered with the New York Stock Exchange (NYSE). When his employer terminated him in 1987, he sued under the Age Discrimination in Employment Act (ADEA), 29 U.S.C.A. § 621, *et seq.* (West 1985 & Supp. 1987). Interstate filed a motion to compel arbitration, relying on Gilmer's registration and the Federal Arbitration Act (FAA). The district court denied the motion, but the Court of Appeals reversed. By a vote of 7–2, the Supreme Court affirmed. Because Gilmer had promised to arbitrate such claims, the burden of proof was on him to show that Congress intended to preclude waiver of a judicial forum for ADEA actions. The Court found no evidence of such a congressional intent.

But what of *Alexander*? The Court used much of its opinion to distinguish that case. First, *Alexander* and related cases did not deal specifically with the enforcement of an arbitration agreement, but rather with the question of whether arbitration of contract-based claims precluded later judicial resolution of statutory claims. Employees had not agreed in their collective agreements to arbitrate statutory claims, so their arbitrators had no authority to resolve those issues. Second, the presence of the union as the contracting party created a tension between the individual's rights and those of the group. Third, the earlier cases were not decided under the FAA, which reflects a liberal policy favoring arbitration agreements.

The Court then had to address *Alexander*'s criticism of arbitration as procedurally inferior to the judicial process. Some of that criticism, the Court said, reflected an unjustifiable hostility to arbitration. As to the specific concerns, the Court found that the NYSE arbitration rules established a satisfactory procedure. There were ways to avoid biased panels, the rules allowed some discovery, arbitrators had to render written awards that are available to the public, and arbitrators have the power to award equitable relief.

Another significant factor in the Court's change of heart was the development of statutory arbitration in commercial cases. In the years after *Alexander*, the Supreme Court had enforced arbitration agreements covering such statutes as the Sherman Antitrust Act, the Securities Exchange Act of 1934, the Racketeer Influenced and Corrupt Organizations Act, and more. See, for example, *Mitsubishi Motors Corp. v. Soler Chrysler–Plymouth, Inc.* (S.Ct. 1985); *Shearson/American Express, Inc. v. McMahon* (S.Ct.1987); and *Rodriguez de Quijas v. Shearson/American Express, Inc.* (S.Ct.1989). Having become accustomed to arbitration of statutory issues in that context, the Court had no trouble extending the development to employment cases.

For the most part, lower federal courts have enthusiastically extended *Gilmer*. The doctrine applied, they held, with equal force to securities industry employees' claims of sex or race discrimination violating Title VII of the Civil Rights Act of 1964, to their claims of violations of more obscure federal statutes like a prohibition on use of polygraphs, and to pendant state claims. Next, they applied the doctrine to employees outside the securities industry—and that meant to people whose arbitration agreements were in their employment contracts. Finally, as the state courts jumped on the arbitration bandwagon, employees found themselves having to arbitrate state common law claims such as breach of contract and wrongful discharge.

Obviously a court should not rashly assume that an employee has given up the right to use a statutory procedure to remedy discrimination. Cases after *Gilmer* have concluded that an arbitration clause will bar litigation of a federal statutory claim only if three conditions are met:

> First, the employee must have agreed individually to the contract containing the arbitration clause—the union having agreed for the employee during collective bargaining does not count. Second, the agreement must authorize the arbitrator to resolve federal statutory claims—it is not enough that the arbitrator can resolve contract claims, even if the factual issues arising from those claims overlap with the statutory claim issues. Third, the agreement must give the employee the right to insist on arbitration if the federal statutory claim is not resolved to his satis-

faction in any grievance process. All three of those requirements were met in the *Gilmer* case.

*Brisentine v. Stone & Webster Engineering* (11th Cir.1997).

*(b) Special Legal Concerns.* Individual employment arbitration raises a number of unique legal concerns. The first was FAA § 1's exclusion of contracts for employment. As discussed above, in Chapter V, Section B., the federal courts seem to be interpreting that exclusion narrowly, thus allowing use of the FAA in individual employment arbitration cases. (*Gilmer* did not resolve that question because the plaintiff's promise was in his stock exchange registration rather than in his employment contract.) The decision of Judge Harry Edwards in *Cole v. Burns International Security Services* (D.C.Cir.1997), is likely to be extremely influential. After carefully reviewing the exemption's legislative history and policy, Judge Edwards concluded that it excluded only employment contracts in the transportation industry.

The second legal concern was the matter of consent. There is precious little "bargaining" about the typical individual arbitration agreement. Normally, employers simply require applicants for employment to sign the agreement, or suddenly announce it to current employees. One who does not wish to waive access to the courts has a simple but drastic alternative: find another job. Moreover, the arbitration agreements are often extremely broad. They seldom indicate which statutory rights employees are waiving. The Form U–4 signed by Gilmer, for example, referred only to New York Stock Exchange rules. The critical rule, should Gilmer ever have found it, provided for arbitration of any controversy "arising out of the employment or termination of such registered representative"—no reference to the ADEA, Title VII, or any other statutory or common law action.

Given those realities, is there an intelligent waiver? Most courts, for example *Kidd v. Equitable Life Assurance Society of the United States* (11th Cir. 1994), have had no problem finding a waiver. After all, employees are normally presumed to consent to documents they sign. The Ninth Circuit, however, has taken a strict stance. In two notable cases, it held that the general language of the stock exchange promise to arbitrate is not sufficiently clear to make the alleged waiver "knowing." See *Prudential Insurance Co. of America v. Lai* (9th Cir.1994), and *Renteria v. Prudential Insurance Co. of America* (9th Cir.1997). A prudent employer could avoid the risks posed by those decisions simply by making the waiver explicit, but that might cause more employees to object.

There has been some opposition to mandatory statutory arbitration from another quarter. The Equal Employment Opportunity Commission (EEOC) has taken the position that an employer may not discriminate against an applicant or employee for refusal to waive Title VII rights. The NLRB has moved toward a similar position. As a result, most well-drafted arbitration agreements limit only an employee's right to sue, but not the right to file a charge with an administrative agency.

The third area of legal concern has to do with the minimum procedural standards provided in the arbitration agreements. The Supreme Court accepted the NYSE procedures in *Gilmer* because they were fundamentally fair. A sham arbitration system, for example one making the employer the sole "arbitrator," would not fare so well. But what are the necessary minimum standards? There is no consensus yet among the courts, but the arbitration community is quickly reaching agreement. The key document is the "Due Process Protocol for Mediation and Arbitration of Statutory Disputes Arising Out of the Employment Relationship" (Appendix L), discussed in Chapter IV, Section E. The diverse blue-ribbon committee that drafted the Protocol unanimously agreed that *any* fair system of statutory arbitration would include the freedom to choose one's representative; access to relevant information, including reasonable discovery; selection of an independent, skilled arbitrator from a designating agency's roster; and power for the arbitrator to award whatever relief would be available under the law. Designating agencies adhere to the Protocol, and no doubt the courts will as well.

Criticisms of mandatory arbitration, particularly the arbitration procedures used in the securities industry, have not slowed the growth of individual employment arbitration. Facing some external pressure, the National Association of Securities Dealers exempted claims of discrimination and sexual harassment from the U–4 requirement in 1997, but some of the biggest firms have added arbitration agreements to their employees' contracts. Outside the securities industry, mandatory arbitration provisions have been growing exponentially.

*(c) The Possible Impact of* **Gilmer** *on* **Alexander.** The Supreme Court in *Gilmer* went far out of its way to distinguish rather than overrule *Alexander*. In a later case, *Livadas v. Bradshaw* (S.Ct. 1994), it reiterated that *Gilmer* was consistent with *Alexander*. That should have been enough to convince the lower courts that *Alexander* remains good law: in other words, that an arbitration clause in a collective bargaining agreement will not waive an individual employee's statutory rights. In 1996, however, the Court of Appeals for the Fourth Circuit affirmed a lower court's dismissal of an Americans with Disabilities Act claim because the plaintiff was subject to an arbitration clause in a collective agreement, *Austin v. Owens–Brockway Glass Container, Inc.* (4th Cir.1996).

To put it mildly, *Austin* has not been well received by other courts. Virtually every other court to consider the effect of *Gilmer* on *Alexander* reached the opposite conclusion, for example *Varner v. National Super Markets, Inc.* (8th Cir.1996), *Pryner v. Tractor Supply Co.* (7th Cir.1997), and *Brisentine v. Stone & Webster Engineering Corp.* (11th Cir.1997). Only the Third Circuit endorsed it, but even that panel decision has been withdrawn so that the court can consider the matter *en banc*: *Martin v. Dana Corp.* (3d Cir.1997) . The *Brisentine* decision held that a unionized employee's statutory claim would be subject to the collective bargaining agreement's arbitration clause only if the employee individually consented to the arbitration agreement, the arbitrator had the power to resolve statutory as well as contractual issues, and the employee had the right to insist on arbitration. Very few collective bargaining relationships provide those protections to employees.

# CHAPTER VII

# JUDICIAL REVIEW OF ARBITRATION AWARDS

## A. INTRODUCTION

Arbitration awards reach court in one of three ways: the prevailing party seeks judicial enforcement of the award against a losing party who refuses to comply with it, the losing party seeks to have the award set aside because of some alleged substantive or procedural error, or one of the parties (or a third party, such as an individual employee covered by collective bargaining agreement) invokes an arbitration award to buttress its case in a collateral judicial proceeding.

The Supreme Court announced the basic rules governing judicial review of arbitration awards in the last of the *Steelworkers Trilogy* cases, *United Steelworkers of America v. Enterprise Wheel & Car Corp.* (S.Ct.1960), discussed above in Chapter V, Section C.3. Justice Douglas wrote that "[t]he refusal of courts to review the merits of an arbitration award is the proper approach to arbitration under collective bargaining agreements.... The federal policy of settling labor disputes by arbitration would be undermined if courts had the final say on the merits of the awards." His opinion placed few limits on the arbitrator's power. The arbitrator is "confined to interpretation and application of the collective bargaining agreement; he does not sit to dispense his own brand of industrial justice." The award is legitimate "only so long as it draws its essence from the collective bargaining agreement. When the arbitrator's words manifest an infidelity to this obligation, courts have no choice but to refuse enforcement of the award."

These exemptions are narrower than they might appear. The award must "draw its essence" from the agreement, but the arbitrator may "look for guidance from many sources" and "a mere ambiguity in the opinion accompanying an award, which permits the inference that the arbitrator may have exceeded his authority, is not a reason for refusing to enforce the award." The problem is that the Supreme Court's phrases delineating the arbitrator's authority are impossibly vague. Nevertheless, the Court's central command was clear: absent very strong reasons to do otherwise, federal courts should enforce arbitration awards.

It is therefore not surprising that courts have hesitated to overrule arbitrators since the *Enterprise Wheel* decision. Indeed, relatively few arbitration awards are ever challenged in court because the futility of doing so is apparent. One study published in 1991 found that federal courts enforced awards approximately 70% of the time. Michael H. LeRoy and Peter Feuille, *The* Steelworkers

Trilogy *and Grievance Arbitration Appeals: How the Federal Courts Respond*, 13 Industrial Relations Law Journal 78, 102 (1991). Some courts, notably the Court of Appeals for the Seventh Circuit, impose sanctions on losing parties in arbitration appeals, for example, *Hill v. Norfolk and Western Railway Co.* (7th Cir.1987), and *Dreis & Krump Manufacturing Co. v. International Association of Machinists* (7th Cir.1986).

Nevertheless, courts have not abdicated their authority, nor should they. The FAA specifically authorizes vacation of arbitration awards on a number of grounds—corruption, fraud, undue means, evident partiality, procedural misconduct or other misbehavior, exceeding the contractual authority or failing to render a final award (Appendix J, § 10). FAA § 11 allows a court to modify an award to correct miscalculations or mistakes, to eliminate a portion of an award on a matter not submitted to the arbitrator, and to correct a matter of form not affecting the merits. The Uniform Arbitration Act (UAA), modeled after the FAA, states similar grounds for vacation and modification (Appendix K, §§ 12 and 13).

Those grounds add meaning to the Supreme Court's rather vacuous phrases. Still, it is all too easy for a judge who disagrees with an arbitrator's decision to conceal substantive disagreement with phrases like "exceeds his jurisdiction" or "fails to draw its essence from the collective bargaining agreement." See, for example, Judge Heaney's criticism of his colleagues in *Trailways Lines, Inc. v. Trailways, Inc. Joint Council* (8th Cir.1987) (dissenting from a decision to deny rehearing en banc): "The panel rejects the arbitrator's award claiming that it fails to draw its essence from the collective bargaining agreement. It is clear, however, that the panel did so because it disagrees with the arbitrator's construction [of the agreement]."

Successful challenges to arbitration awards since *Enterprise Wheel* usually fall into one or more of these categories: (1) failure of the award to "draw its essence" from the collective agreement; (2) lack of jurisdiction or authority for the award; (3) arbitral misconduct and procedural unfairness; (4) gross error or irrationality; (5) violation of law or public policy; (6) ambiguity, incompleteness or inconsistency; and (7) a union's breach of the duty of fair representation. Some special considerations apply to judicial review of individual employment arbitration awards and federal-sector arbitration awards. The last two subsections briefly survey those considerations.

## B. FAILURE OF THE AWARD TO "DRAW ITS ESSENCE" FROM THE COLLECTIVE AGREEMENT

The Supreme Court obviously intended its "essence" test to be a very narrow one. As one court interpreted it, the question is *whether* the arbitrator interpreted the contract, not whether the arbitrator interpreted it *correctly*. *Hill v. Norfolk and Western*

*Railway Co.* (7th Cir.1987); accord, *Ethyl Corp. v. United Steelworkers of America* (7th Cir.1985). Most courts apply the test in the proper spirit of restraint. In *American Postal Workers Union v. United States Postal Service* (D.C.Cir.1986) (hereafter, *APWU*), for example, an arbitrator relied on an arguably mistaken understanding of the Supreme Court's *Miranda* decision when deciding to reinstate a discharged employee. The Court of Appeals enforced the award, stating that an alleged mistake of law does not alter the "essence" standard of review.

That idea—that a court should enforce an arguably mistaken interpretation of federal law—is hard for most courts to swallow. Several courts have therefore criticized the *APWU* decision, and many expressly judge awards by a tougher standard.

A good example is *The Delta Queen Steamboat Co. v. District 2, Marine Engineers Beneficial Association* (5th Cir.1989). An agreement allowed the employer to discharge employees for "carelessness." An arbitrator found a ship's captain "grossly careless" in causing a near collision but nevertheless ordered reinstatement because the discipline imposed was disparately harsh. Evaluating the level of discipline imposed is a common part of an arbitrator's determination of "just cause." The Court of Appeals vacated the reinstatement order on the ground that once the arbitrator decided the carelessness question, his contractual authority was at an end. To the same effect, see *Riceland Foods, Inc.*

*v. United Brotherhood of Carpenters and Joiners of America, Local 2381* (8th Cir.1984).

## C. LACK OF JURISDICTION OR AUTHORITY FOR THE AWARD

By far the most common reason for setting aside an arbitrator's award is that the arbitrator was not authorized to make the award. This is obviously very close to the Supreme Court's "essence" standard: if a contract denies the arbitrator authority to rule on a certain matter, an award on that subject cannot draw its essence from the agreement.

This situation arises in a number of ways. The most obvious case occurs when the arbitrator ignores (in the words of *Warrior & Gulf*) an "express provision excluding a particular grievance from arbitration" or "the most forceful evidence of a purpose to exclude the claim from arbitration." This is, of course, the old question of "substantive arbitrability." Thus an arbitration clause covering a certain contract "and amendments thereto" will not allow an award based on wage rates contained in a subsequent agreement that was not an amendment of the initial contract. *IBEW Local 278 v. Jetero Corp.* (5th Cir.1974). Of course if the parties allow the arbitrator to decide the substantive arbitrability issue, the arbitrator's decision on that question is subject only to the same limited review appropriate for an arbitrator's award on the merits.

There are less obvious limitations on an arbitrator's substantive authority. One is that an arbitrator has jurisdiction only when there is a valid and binding arbitration agreement. If the alleged agreement has expired, has been obtained by fraud, or was not properly ratified, a court may hold that an arbitrator lacked authority to apply the terms of the document—or indeed, that there can be no arbitration at all. Another restriction comes from the submission agreement, for the parties can submit an issue to the arbitrator that is narrower than the scope of the arbitration clause. For example, a standard arbitration clause might provide for arbitration of any dispute over the "meaning, interpretation or application of this agreement" but the parties might ask the arbitrator simply to determine a factual issue, say whether or not Employee X lied on an application form. If so, the arbitrator has authority only to deal with the issue submitted. A court may properly set aside rulings on other issues. See, for example, *Textile Workers Union of America Local 1386 v. American Thread Co.* (4th Cir.1961).

An agreement may also limit an arbitrator's authority to issue a particular remedy. The concept of "just cause" has grown to include notions such as proportionality between the offense and the punishment, use of progressive discipline, and consistency in the application of discipline. Arbitrators frequently hold that although an employee engaged in some misconduct, the punishment levied by the employer was too severe. To prevent arbitral second guessing, employers occasionally bargain for and sometimes obtain contract clauses prohibiting arbitral modification of discipline. Courts readily set aside awards that disregard those prohibitions. See, for example, *Amanda Bent Bolt Co. v. UAW Local 1549* (6th Cir.1971).

An arbitrator is similarly bound to respect *procedural* limitations expressed in the collective bargaining agreement. As noted above, however, the courts regard these questions as peculiarly suited for an arbitrator's determination and will not readily overturn such a determination. Still, if a contract allows arbitration only if a party requests it within a certain period, an arbitrator must enforce that term. An arbitrator who ignored a procedural limitation would be acting beyond the scope of the authority granted by the parties. In practice, most arbitrators either respect such limitations or have recognized reasons (such as a waiver by the party opposing arbitration) for not applying them. One exception is *Polk Brothers, Inc. v. Chicago Truck Drivers, Helpers and Warehouse Workers Union* (7th Cir.1992). The arbitrator awarded a remedy extending beyond the contract's termination date. While recognizing the narrow scope of judicial review, the Court of Appeals concluded that, because the labor contract prohibited the arbitrator from modifying the agreement, the arbitrator had no authority to enforce the contract beyond its stated expiration date.

Finally, there is a broad category of arbitral error that is subject to judicial overreaching. Many contracts, like the one in *Polk Brothers*, provide that an arbitrator may not "alter, modify or add to" the agreement. The "agreement" typically referred to, however, may include more than the written collective bargaining agreement. Arbitrators routinely refer to "the common law of the shop," a practice enthusiastically endorsed by the Supreme Court in the *Steelworkers Trilogy*. Negotiating history may cast light on the meaning of an ambiguous clause, and a consistent practice of long duration might tacitly amend the contract. To one party or to a reviewing court, though, an arbitrator's decision premised on such evidence can look suspiciously like a modification of or an addition to the contract.

The most famous (and much-criticized) instance of a court trying to hold an arbitrator to the contract's written terms is *Torrington Co. v. Metal Products Workers Union Local 1645* (2d Cir.1966). For many years the employer had paid employees for one hour away from work on election day, but the parties never incorporated that practice in their contract. One year, before beginning contract negotiations, the employer announced that it would no longer pay for that hour. The contract ultimately signed was as silent on the point as its predecessors. When the employer refused to pay for the accustomed hour at the next election day, the union took the case to arbitration. The arbitrator ruled that the past practice could be terminated only by mutual agreement.

The federal district and appeals courts denied enforcement of the award, holding that it changed the contract and was thus outside the arbitrator's authority. Critics pointed out that the courts simply substituted their judgment on the merits for that of the arbitrator, for the award simply held that the past practice was, in fact, part of the contract. The parties, in other words, had amended the written agreement by their actions and the arbitrator merely gave force to that amendment.

A similar but more defensible decision is *H. K. Porter Co. v. United Saw File & Steel Products Workers* (3d Cir.1964). The contract in that case expressly limited eligibility for pensions to those employees who were at least 65 years old and had at least 25 years of service. Without the support of past practice, the arbitrator awarded a prorated pension to employees over 65 but with less than 25 years of service when the employer terminated them after a plant removal. The Court of Appeals held that the arbitrator had tried to administer "his own brand of industrial justice." It therefore revised the award to reflect the court's view of the parties' intentions.

As *Torrington* and *H. K. Porter Co.* indicate, judicial examination of the arbitrator's authority to make an award can easily slip into review of the merits of the cases—and that, in turn, to substitution of the judges' views for those of the arbitrators. Fortunately, these cases are exceptions. Few courts intrude so deeply into arbitral prerogatives.

If an arbitrator relies too heavily on extra-contractual authorities to the exclusion of the contract, a court is likely to overturn the award. Use of external sources is not an error, as the Supreme Court stated in *Enterprise Wheel*; it becomes a problem only if the arbitrator relies *solely* on that external authority. Rarely is an arbitrator rash enough to admit to such a sin, but courts sometimes infer it. In *Roadmaster Corp. v. Production and Maintenance Employees' Local 504* (7th Cir.1988) (*en banc*), an arbitrator held that the employer violated NLRA § 8(d)(2) by refusing to bargain with either of two competing unions. The Court of Appeals vacated the award because the arbitrator exceeded the scope of the submission by relying on the statute rather than on the contract.

## D. PARTY MISCONDUCT, ARBITRAL PARTIALITY, AND PROCEDURAL UNFAIRNESS

The FAA and UAA recognize the possibility that an arbitrator's bias could deny justice to a party. The terms used in those statutes blend into one another: corruption, fraud, "undue means," partiality. For analysis, the grounds can be divided into three parts: misconduct by a party, partiality by the arbitrator, and procedural unfairness. There are very few reported arbitration cases of this sort, which may be due in part to the difficulty of proving the charges. For a detailed summary of the cases in this area, see Perry A. Zirkel and Peter D. Winebrake, *Legal Boundaries for Partiality and Misconduct of Labor Arbitrators*, 1992 Detroit College of Law Review 679.

## 1. Party Misconduct

The first ground for reversal listed in the FAA concerns misconduct by one of the parties, namely obtaining an award by "corruption, fraud, or undue means" [Appendix J, § 10(a)]. Following the spirit of *Enterprise Wheel*, most courts interpret those terms very narrowly. In *International Brotherhood of Firemen and Oilers, Local 261 v. Great Northern Paper Co.* (D.Me.1984), the court rejected a losing party's assertion that an award was obtained by "undue means." The "means" cited by the union was an alleged misstatement of fact in a post-hearing brief. The Court interpreted that term as referring only to actions by a party "equivalent in gravity to corruption or fraud, such as a physical threat to an arbitrator or other improper influence," quoting *American Postal Workers Union v. United States Postal Service* (D.C.Cir.1995).

## 2. Arbitral Partiality

FAA § 10(b) authorizes vacation of an award for "evident partiality or corruption in the arbitrators." Actual corruption in labor and employment arbitration is virtually unheard of. That leaves "evident partiality" as the most common claim under § 10(b). A party asserting partiality bears a heavy burden. "Evident partiality" requires more than a mere "appearance" of bias but does not require proof of actual bias, *Morelite Construction Corp. v. New York City District Council Carpenters Benefit*

*Funds* (2d Cir.1984). In one well-publicized case, an arbitrator created an appearance of bias by drinking with a party's representative at the airport for an hour and a half after the hearing, but the Washington Supreme Court held that the relevant state statute did not permit vacation for that reason, *Union Local 1296, International Association of Firefighters v. City of Kennewick* (Wash. 1975). Consistently ruling against one party does not prove partiality, *Bell Aerospace Co. v. Local 516* (2d Cir. 1974).

Occasionally an arbitrator will have a personal or financial relationship with a party or a party's advocate that suggests partiality. Designating agency rules and the Code of Professional Responsibility for Arbitrators of Labor–Management Disputes (Appendix I, Section 2.B.) mandate strict neutrality and oblige arbitrators to disclose any potential sources of bias. Some fail to do so. In *Morelite*, for example, the arbitrator was the son of the president of the international union whose district organization was a party to the arbitration. The Court of Appeals held that the father-son relationship rose to the level of "evident partiality." More often, an arbitrator's view of what must be disclosed and that of a losing party will simply differ. An arbitrator's previous work as a lawyer for one of the parties, for example, may or may not be sufficient cause for disqualification. Compare *Teamsters Local 560 v. Bergen–Hudson Roofing Supply Co.* (N.J.Super.Ct.1978) (no) with *School District of Spooner v. Northwest United Educators* (Wis. 1987) (yes). However, an arbitrator need not disclose an affiliation that is trivial [*Standard Tankers (Bahamas) Co. v. Motor Tank Vessel, Akti* (E.D.N.C.1977)], obvious [*International Association of Heat and Frost Insulators Local No. 12 v. Insulation Quality Enterprises, Ltd.* (E.D.N.Y.1988)], or already known (*Bergen-Hudson*).

## 3. Procedural Unfairness

FAA § 10(c) allows a court to vacate an award because of the arbitrator's misconduct in refusing to postpone a hearing, refusing to hear pertinent evidence, or for "any other misbehavior by which the rights of any party have been prejudiced." An arbitrator has broad discretion in determining whether to postpone a hearing. An arbitrator may properly deny a postponement sought solely because one party wants to present more testimony, *Local Union No. 251 v. Narragansett Improvement Co.* (1st Cir.1974). In contrast, denying a postponement sought when a party's representative became ill and had to leave the hearing is reversible misconduct, *Allendale Nursing Home, Inc. v. Local 1115 Joint Board* (S.D.N.Y.1974).

Rarely will an evidentiary ruling cause an award to be set aside. The rules of evidence normally do not bind an arbitrator, and designating agency rules expressly allow arbitrators to determine relevance and materiality, so their rulings on such questions are seldom challenged. Labor arbitrators, many of whom are not lawyers, cannot be expected to "follow all the niceties observed by the federal courts," *Bell Aerospace*. Mere error in excluding certain evidence is no basis for vacation. According to the Supreme Court, the error must be "in bad faith or so gross as to amount to affirmative misconduct" before a court should void the award, *United Paperworkers International Union v. Misco, Inc.* (S.Ct. 1987).

Thus, allowing a party to bypass a step of the contractual grievance procedure and failing to convene a hearing within the contractually-specified time are not sufficient to justify vacation, *Sheet Metal Workers International Association, Local No. 420 v. Kinney Air Conditioning Co.* (9th Cir.1985). Even refusing to allow briefs or oral arguments does not create reversible error, *Trident Technical College v. Lucas & Stubbs, Ltd.* (S.C.1985). The ultimate question is whether the procedural error deprived a party of a fair hearing, *Newark Stereotypers' Union No. 18 v. Newark Morning Ledger Co.* (3d Cir.1968).

An erroneous and severely prejudicial admission or exclusion of evidence can taint the proceedings. In one such case, where the parties had not strictly applied evidentiary technicalities in the past, the arbitrator refused to allow introduction of certain evidence in rebuttal on the ground that it should have been presented as part of the case in chief. The district court vacated the award, stating that applying such a strict rule without first warning the parties denied them a fair hearing, *Harvey Alumi-*

*num Inc. v. United Steelworkers of America, AFL–CIO,* (C.D.Cal.1967). Another court overturned an award because the arbitrator relied on a previous award referred to in the hearing but never actually introduced into evidence, *Textile Workers Union of America, Local 1386 v. American Thread Co.* (4th Cir.1961). Refusing to give any weight in a discharge case to the transcript of the criminal trial for the conduct that led to the discharge was reversible error, *Hoteles Condado Beach v. Union De Tronquistas, Local 901* (1st Cir.1985).

Other errors that might provide grounds for judicial review include denial of opportunity for cross-examination or refusal of a reasonable request for a continuance. In one troubling recent case, a court overturned an award because the arbitrator relied on an ambiguous provision of the agreement that was not discussed in the hearing. The court held that the arbitrator should first have sought the parties' guidance on the provision's meaning. *International Woodworkers of America v. Weyerhaeuser Co.* (8th Cir.1993). Another court vacated an award because the arbitrator had *ex parte* contacts about the case with a nonparty and relied on information not in evidence, *United Food & Commercial Workers International Union v. SIPCO, Inc.* (S.D.Iowa 1992). A federal court will not set aside an award because of a breach of *state* procedural requirements, especially if those requirements interfere with the federal policy favoring the arbitration process. *West Rock Lodge No. 2120, I.A.M. v. Geometric Tool Co.* (2d Cir.1968).

## E. GROSS ERROR OR IRRATIONALITY

The Supreme Court plainly did not want judges reviewing arbitrators' decisions on the merits, but some lower courts have read into the *Enterprise Wheel* opinion an implied exception for cases of "gross" error. A judicial finding that an arbitrator with proper jurisdiction who conducted a fair hearing nevertheless reached the wrong result seems to be just what the Supreme Court tried to prevent, however. Courts engaging in such a review process have used a variety of terms to distinguish their cases from *Enterprise Wheel*. A few cases have relied on an admittedly erroneous assumption of fact by the arbitrator. Others have introduced a minimum standard of rationality. Sometimes courts state the standard in terms of a decision that an "honest intellect" or some "judge, or group of judges" could conceivably reach. Sometimes they state it negatively, as prohibiting a "capricious, unreasonable interpretation" and an award that is "wholly baseless and completely without reason." See, for example, *Swift Industries, Inc. v. Botany Industries, Inc.* (3d Cir.1972) ("completely irrational").

Strenuous language does not disguise the fact that those courts are simply reviewing the merits of the arbitrator's decision. In bargaining for arbitration the parties assumed that the arbitrator would be reasonable; setting aside an "irrational" decision would thus seem entirely consistent with their intentions. The difficulty, of course, comes in separating decisions that are only arguably wrong from those that are completely irrational. Finding irrationality is especially hard when one of the parties argued for just such an award and, having received it, does not regard it as irrational.

## F. VIOLATION OF LAW OR PUBLIC POLICY

### 1. Introduction

Chapter VI, Section B. examined the split in the arbitration community over the role of the arbitrator when the contract conflicts with external law. Many believe that the arbitrator should enforce the contract and ignore the law, and a few believe the opposite. All agree that the external law is relevant in some cases, for example if the parties incorporate it in their agreement, or if the arbitrator uses it to help find the contract's meaning. Whatever approach the *arbitrator* adopts, the function of the *courts* is clear: they will not enforce an arbitration order sustaining or commanding illegal conduct. As one court put it,

> [I]t is too plain for argument that no court will order a party to do something, if in order to comply with the court's directive, he must commit a crime. This is so despite any protestations that the party contracted to do what it is said that he should be ordered to do.

*UAW Local 985 v. W. M. Chace Co.,* (E.D.Mich. 1966). This attitude involves no conflict with the

*Enterprise Wheel* strictures on judicial review, for it involves only a determination of the lawfulness of enforcing an award, not a review of the arbitrator's interpretation of the contract. Similarly, if the contract itself is illegal, a court will not enforce an award implementing that contract, *Botany Industries, Inc. v. New York Joint Board* (S.D.N.Y.1974).

Beyond the few cases in which an arbitration award seems to direct a crime, there is a much broader field of judicial concern that goes by the title of "public policy." Forty years ago, for example, the California Supreme Court vacated an award because it offended the Court's understanding of public policy, not because it conflicted with any law. In *Black v. Cutter Laboratories* (Cal.1955), an employer had fired an employee ostensibly because he was a Communist. The arbitrator found that the real motive for the discharge was the employee's union activity. Because union activity was not just cause for discharge, the arbitrator ordered the employer to reinstate the grievant. No law barred employment of a Communist, but the California court, citing federal and state laws banning Communist party activity, held that those laws established a public policy sufficiently strong to void an arbitration order of reinstatement "in a plant which produces antibiotics used by both the military and civilians."

The modern use of the public policy doctrine to overturn arbitration awards starts with the Supreme Court's dictum in *W. R. Grace & Co. v. Local*

*759, International Union of the United Rubber, Cork, Linoleum and Plastic Workers of America* (S.Ct.1983): "a court may not enforce a collective-bargaining agreement that is contrary to public policy." The Supreme Court hedged that statement by warning that courts should not refuse to enforce an arbitrator's interpretation of a contract unless that interpretation would violate "some explicit public policy" that is "well defined and dominant," ascertained by " 'reference to the laws and legal precedents and not from general considerations of supposed public interests,' " (quoting from *Muschany v. United States* (S.Ct.1945)). Those general phrases provide a wide pathway for courts that are uncomfortable with *Enterprise Wheel*'s strictures on judicial review.

Must the public policy be found in "positive law," or will some lesser source suffice? In *E.I. DuPont de Nemours and Co. v. Grasselli Employees Independent Association of East Chicago, Inc.* (7th Cir.1986) (Easterbrook, J., concurring), Judge Frank Easterbrook suggested that a court should set aside an award only when the award violates some positive law or seeks to compel unlawful action. Otherwise, he suggested, the court would be interfering with the "real public policy" favoring enforcement of arbitration awards. See also *United States Postal Service v. National Association of Letter Carriers* (D.C.Cir.1987). Other courts take a more liberal view of the sort of public policy that would allow them to reverse an arbitrator, as the next sections show. The Court of Appeals for the First Circuit, for instance, expressly rejected the "positive law" test in *United States Postal Service v. American Postal Workers Union* (1st Cir.1984). The Supreme Court could have resolved the split in its latest "public policy" decision, *United Paperworkers International Union v. Misco* (S.Ct.1987), but instead contented itself with repeating the *W. R. Grace* phrases.

What must be the content of the public policy used to vacate an award? Many reviewing courts have taken the simplistic view that if public policy, from whatever source, opposes the employee's offense, an arbitrator's reinstatement award cannot stand. Two good examples discussed below are *Iowa Electric Light & Power v. Local Union 204, International Brotherhood of Electrical Workers* (8th Cir. 1987) and *Delta Air Lines v. Air Line Pilots Association International* (11th Cir.1988). Both courts vacated awards reinstating employees guilty of serious safety violations, because of the public policy favoring safety in dangerous workplaces.

A more sophisticated analysis would ask whether the asserted public policy prohibits the remedy the arbitrator selects. In those two cases, the employer would not have violated any public policy by deciding to retrain the employee or to discipline him short of discharge. If the employer could do so, how could an arbitration award relying on a contract signed by the employer violate public policy? The clearest discussion of this distinction is in *Stead Motors of Walnut Creek v. Automotive Machinists Lodge No. 1173, International Association of Ma-*

*chinists* (9th Cir.1989) (*en banc*, plurality opinion). See also *Grasselli*, 790 F.2d at 615–16, and *American Postal Workers Union v. United States Postal Service* (D.C.Cir.1986).

## 2. Public Safety and Criminal Law Cases

Here is a common scenario: an employee violates some safety rule with potentially serious consequences; the employer fires the employee; an arbitrator finds that the discharge was not for just cause, either because the employee was capable of rehabilitation, or because the employer did not impose a similar penalty on employees guilty of serious offenses, or because the employer violated the employee's procedural rights. What is a reviewing court to do? Clearly there is a public policy against violating safety rules, but does that make every reinstatement order unenforceable?

Two cases mentioned above, *Delta Air Lines* and *Iowa Electric*, so indicate. The courts overturned reinstatement orders, respectively, of a pilot who flew while drunk and a nuclear power plant mechanic who disabled a safety system in order to leave for lunch early. Both courts asserted that the public policy against safety violations barred reinstatement. In fact, public policy did not. In both cases, discipline short of discharge would have been consistent with the asserted public policy. The goal is safety, but there is no reason to believe that discharge is the only means to ensure that goal.

Other cases, relying on the distinction between a policy against the employee's conduct and a policy against reinstatement of offending employees, reached contrary conclusions. In almost direct contrast to the *Delta Air Lines* case is *Northwest Airlines, Inc. v. Air Line Pilots Association, International* (D.C.Cir.1987). An arbitrator had ordered reinstatement of a pilot discharged for violating the employer's rule against drinking within 24 hours before a flight, but only if and when the appropriate government agency, the Federal Aviation Agency, recertified the pilot. The Court of Appeals held that the reinstatement order was lawful and did not seek to force any illegal conduct; it thus did not violate public policy. See also *Stead Motors*, discussed above.

Reinstatement orders in cases of illegal conduct raise the same concerns—and produce the same judicial conflicts—as reinstatements in safety cases. Even though the Supreme Court in *Misco*, a case of alleged marijuana use and possession at work, cautioned that the public policy used to overturn an award must be well-defined and dominant, some lower federal courts have refused to permit arbitrators to reinstate law-breakers. *United States Postal Service v. American Postal Workers Union* (1st Cir. 1984), involved an employee discharged after conviction for embezzling postal funds. An arbitrator ordered reinstatement without back pay because the employee had intended to repay the money he embezzled and because he had seven years of service without discipline. The Court of Appeals held that the award violated the well-defined public policy against employing dishonest postal employees and would diminish public trust "in the entire federal government." It therefore denied enforcement of the award.

In almost diametrical contrast is *United States Postal Service v. National Association of Letter Carriers* (3d Cir.1988). An arbitrator reinstated a Postal Service employee who shot up his supervisor's car—fortunately while the supervisor was not in it. The arbitrator found that the employee was amenable to lesser discipline and showed no likelihood of committing further aggression. Analyzing the public policy exception, the Court of Appeals held that these decisions were within the arbitrator's authority and that no public policy required discharge in light of those findings. See also *Saint Mary Home v. SEIU District 1199* (2d Cir.1997), confirming an award reinstating an employee discharged after a drug conviction because the employer failed to identify an established public policy "that calls for a fixed disciplinary action of permanent dismissal in all cases where drug related conduct occurs in the workplace."

## 3. Sexual Harassment Cases

Each era has its special concerns. In the 1960s, the United States adopted laws to eliminate discrimination in employment; in the 1970s and early 1980s, it cracked down on workplace substance abuse. The most recent focus of public concern in the field of employment law is the belated legislative and judicial recognition in the last decade that many working women faced pervasive sexual harassment. As with earlier concerns, this one has produced conflicting judicial decisions. Sexual harassment is illegal and violates most employers' work rules—but does that mean that discharge is the only permissible penalty? Even if it is the employee's first offense, and there is no evidence progressive discipline would fail? Even if the employer has treated other employees more leniently in similar circumstances?

It is first essential to distinguish between the various reasons why an arbitrator might reinstate an employee charged with such a serious offense. If the arbitrator finds as a factual matter that the employee is not guilty of the charge, a reviewing court has no power to change that decision, as the Supreme Court made clear in *Misco*. More commonly, though, the arbitrator orders reinstatement because the penalty is too severe in light of the employee's seniority, good work record, or prospects for rehabilitation, or because the employer did not use progressive discipline. Some courts, apparently believing that discharge is the only proper response to sexual harassment, refuse to accept an arbitration award imposing any lesser penalty. In *Newsday, Inc. v. Long Island Typographical Union, No. 915* (2d Cir.1990), the Court of Appeals held that a reinstatement award based on the severity of the penalty violated the well-defined public policy against sexual harassment in the workplace.

Another court of appeal, in similar circumstances, enforced an award reinstating an employee who grabbed a coworker's breasts, *Chrysler Motors Corp. v. International Union, Allied Industrial Workers of America* (7th Cir.1992). The arbitrator determined that severe discipline short of discharge would deter future harassment while vindicating the employer's opposition to such conduct. The Seventh Circuit, traditionally a strong supporter of arbitration, recognized the importance of punishing sexual harassment but upheld the award, quoting the Supreme Court in *Misco*: "where it is contemplated that the arbitrator will determine remedies for contract violations he finds, courts have no authority to disagree with his honest judgment in that respect."

The split between the courts on this issue reflects the split over arbitration awards in other public policy cases. The controlling standard in both situations should be the same: courts should overturn only those awards that violate the law or order an employer to do so. An award that merely orders an employer to use progressive discipline or to mitigate a penalty does neither.

A third reason for ordering reinstatement is that the employer breached the employee's procedural rights. Arbitrators regard due process and equal protection as important elements of the "just cause" required for discharge. Roger I. Abrams and Dennis R. Nolan, *Toward a Theory of "Just Cause" in Employee Discipline Cases*, 85 Duke Law Journal 595, 612, 620–21 (1985). They often overturn otherwise valid discharges where the employer has denied the employee those protections.

Courts are sometimes bothered by awards ordering reinstatement because of the employer's procedural violations because they do nothing to redress what might have been a serious offense. In *Stroehmann Bakeries, Inc. v. Local 776, International Brotherhood of Teamsters* (3d Cir.1992), the arbitrator found the discharge improper because the employer had not given the employee a chance to respond to the allegations against him. The Court of Appeals granted the employer's motion to vacate the award on the ground that reinstating an alleged harasser without determining the merits of the case violated well-established public policies. In contrast, when the arbitrator in *Communication Workers of America v. Southeastern Electric Cooperative of Durant, Oklahoma* (10th Cir.1989), reinstated an employee who was treated more harshly than another guilty of a similar offense, the Court of Appeals enforced the award, despite the strong policy against sexual harassment.

## G. INCOMPLETENESS, AMBIGUITY, OR INCONSISTENCY

The last of the most common grounds for judicial review of private-sector labor arbitration awards is of a different nature, involving defects in the arbitration award itself. If the award is incomplete, for instance by not answering the issue posed, a court may be unable to enforce it. Given the alternatives of rewriting the award or resubmitting it to the arbitrator, most courts would deny enforcement and follow the latter option. Similarly, if the award is so ambiguous as to defy understanding, the appropriate action for the court to take would be resubmission to the arbitrator for clarification, as the Court of Appeals did in *Hanford Atomic Metal Trades Council v. General Electric Co.* (9th Cir.1965). A mere ambiguity in the opinion underlying the award, however, will not invalidate the award. *W. R. Grace*; *George Day Construction Co. v. United Brotherhood of Carpenters, Local 354* (9th Cir. 1984).

Finally, an award that is too ambiguous to make sense may not be in suitable shape for judicial enforcement. In *Bell Aerospace Co. v. UAW Local 516* (2d Cir.1974), none of the parties could offer a "clear and compelling interpretation of the award," so the court remanded for further arbitration. However, a simple inconsistency with a prior award in the same plant will not bar enforcement. Different readings of the same contract or conflicting actions required by different contracts can best be resolved by negotiation. This may leave one party in an awkward, expensive position, but the courts deem that preferable to judicial intervention in the parties' dispute resolution procedure.

Challenges on these grounds are rarely successful. Usually courts will make sense of the arbitrator's opinion, often by examining the nature of the award itself. *International Union of Petroleum*

*Workers v. Western Industrial Maintenance, Inc.* (9th Cir.1983); *Sheet Metal Workers International Association, Local Union No. 420 v. Kinney Air Conditioning Co.* (9th Cir.1985).

## H. INDIVIDUAL CHALLENGES: THE DUTY OF FAIR REPRESENTATION

Each of the previously discussed grounds for judicial review of labor arbitration awards presumes that a *party* to the collective bargaining agreement is attacking the award. Individual employees are not parties. The only way they can challenge an award is by first proving that their union's failure to represent them fairly so tainted the award as to destroy its claim to finality. This requires proof that the union breached the duty of fair representation (DFR) recognized in a long series of cases beginning with *Steele v. Louisville & Nashville Railroad* (S.Ct. 1944). Once the plaintiffs clear that hurdle, they must prove that the employer actually breached the agreement.

Cases in 1962 and 1965 held that employees could maintain a § 301 action against an employer's contract breaches provided they first attempted to exhaust contractual grievance and arbitration procedures. In *Vaca v. Sipes* (S.Ct.1967), the Supreme Court allowed an employee to sue his union in a § 301 action for breach of the DFR in its handling of a grievance. The employer in that case refused to reinstate one Owens for health reasons after he was hospitalized for heart disease. The union processed

Owens's grievance through the contractual steps, but, after receiving a negative report from a doctor selected by Owens, declined to take the case to arbitration.

The Supreme Court recognized that in some instances aggrieved employees could obtain court review of a union's grievance processing, but warned that allowing every grievant to force arbitration would undermine the collective bargaining relationship and overburden the arbitration process. Such an action under § 301 was appropriate, the Court wrote, only when the union's conduct was "arbitrary, discriminatory or in bad faith." A grievant who proved the union breached the DFR by refusing to arbitrate could then sue the employer directly, even if the contract included a mandatory arbitration clause. If the grievant prevailed over both the union and the employer, the union would be liable for any increase in the damages suffered by the employee as a result of its wrongful conduct, and the employer would be liable for the remainder.

That much is simply background for the current topic. If the union arbitrates the grievance, it could still breach the DFR. The union might conduct a sham arbitration, for example, or handle the case in a "perfunctory" way, to use the Supreme Court's term. The union would obviously be liable for damages for breaching the DFR, but can the "tainted" arbitration award stand? May an employer who breached the contract but acted in good faith stand behind a tainted award and claim the benefit of the finality established by *Enterprise Wheel*?

In *Hines v. Anchor Motor Freight Inc.* (S.Ct. 1976), the Supreme Court answered both of these questions in the negative. A joint area committee (JAC) composed of equal numbers of employer and union representatives upheld the discharge of several employees for falsifying expense vouchers. The employees filed a hybrid DFR/§ 301 action claiming that the union had breached its duty of fair representation by not properly investigating the case and that the employer had breached the contract because the employees were not guilty of the offense charged.

The lower courts dismissed the action against the employer because the JAC decision was final and binding. Treating the JAC as the equivalent of an arbitration board, the Supreme Court reversed, holding that a union's breach of the DFR

> relieves the employee of an express or implied requirement that disputes be settled through contractual procedures and, if it seriously undermines the integrity of the arbitral process, also removes the bar of the finality provision of the contract.

In other words, a "tainted" process provides no defense to an employer who unknowingly breaches the collective agreement. Although the question of what constitutes a union breach of the DFR was not at issue before the Court, it offered several comments on that subject, suggesting that the union's decisions must be made "honestly and in good faith and without invidious discrimination or arbitrary conduct," and cannot be "dishonest, in bad faith or discriminatory."

*Hines* seriously limited the finality that *Enterprise Wheel* gave to arbitration awards. Just how serious a blow to finality *Hines* is—or, in simpler terms, just how easy it will be for individual employees to overturn arbitration awards—depends on the breadth courts give to such terms as "arbitrary" and "bad faith." Most lower court cases after *Vaca* have required a showing of malice or hostility. Some courts interpreted those terms as encompassing simple negligence. In *Holodnak v. Avco Corp.,* (D.Conn.1974), the district court vacated an award and faulted the union attorney for overlooking some legal arguments and for not being sufficiently aggressive in protecting the grievant's rights.

The Supreme Court finally established the appropriate standard in *United Steelworkers of America v. Rawson* (S.Ct.1990), holding that the applicable terms—"arbitrary, capricious, or in bad faith"— required a showing of more than "mere negligence." If a plaintiff need not prove actual bad faith (else why would the Court include the words "arbitrary" and "capricious?"), this must mean that the governing standard is conduct that is "grossly negligent" or worse.

The consequences of a union breach of the DFR can be devastating. After *Vaca*, some commentators thought the Court's suggested allocation of damages made the union liable only for the plaintiff's legal fees and other costs. In a 5–4 decision, however, the Supreme Court held that the union was responsible for all back pay after the date that an untainted grievance and arbitration process would have reinstated the employee. *Bowen v. United States Postal Service* (S.Ct.1983).

## I. JUDICIAL REVIEW OF INDIVIDUAL EMPLOYMENT ARBITRATION DECISIONS

In most respects, judicial review of individual employment arbitration decisions parallels that of traditional labor arbitration cases. There are three significant differences. One is that because the use of arbitration in individual employment cases is new, so is the the review of those cases. The novelty of the issues leads to greater variety in judicial decisions. The second difference is that because most individual arbitration cases reach court under the FAA rather than § 301, the courts naturally hold more tightly to the FAA grounds for review. The only common addition to the FAA list of bases for judicial review is a doctrine termed the "manifest disregard" standard. That doctrine allows a court to vacate an award if the arbitrator "manifestly disregarded" the relevant law. The third difference is that individual employment arbitration cases usually involve statutory issues, as discussed in Chapter IV, Section E. and Chapter VI, Section D.3.

In *Chisolm v. Kidder, Peabody Asset Management, Inc.* (S.D.N.Y.1997), for instance, a National Association of Securities Dealers arbitration panel summarily dismissed Chisholm's claim that Kidder had constructively discharged him because of his age. Chisholm moved to vacate the award and to obtain trial of a statutory claim under the Age Discrimination in Employment Act. Viewing her authority as defined by the FAA, the judge stated that she could vacate the award only on the grounds stated in § 10 (none of which applied) or on the "manifest disregard" standard. Quoting from *Merrill Lynch, Pierce, Fenner & Smith v. Bobker* (2d Cir.1986), the judge found that "manifest disregard" means more than an error or misunderstanding of the law: rather, the arbitrator must have known of a governing legal principle and then ignored it. See also, *DiRussa v. Dean Witter Reynolds, Inc.* (2d Cir.1997) (arbitrators' unknowing error in not awarding attorney's fees to the prevailing party in an ADEA action does not amount to "manifest disregard" of the law).

Finding deliberate disregard for the law is difficult when arbitrators provide no reasons for their decisions, as is often the case in individual employment arbitration decisions. The party challenging the award must therefore show that "no proper basis for the award can be inferred from the facts of the case," *Chisolm*, quoting *Wall Street Associates v. Becker Paribas, Inc.* (2d Cir.1994). Applying that very high standard, the district court denied Chisholm's motion and granted the defendant's motion to confirm the award.

Recognizing the importance of statutory arbitration and the risk that arbitrators might not fully vindicate plaintiffs' statutory rights, some other courts have suggested a broader understanding of the "manifest disregard" standard. See, for example, Judge Harry Edwards' decision in *Cole v. Burns International Security Services* (D.C.Cir.1997).

## J. ADMINISTRATIVE AND JUDICIAL REVIEW OF FEDERAL SECTOR ARBITRATION DECISIONS

The last aspect of judicial (and in this case, administrative) review that deserves separate discussion concerns review of federal-sector arbitration cases. The controlling statute, the CSRA, permits the Federal Labor Relations Authority to review an arbitration award that is contrary to any law, rule, or regulation or that is deficient "on other grounds similar to those applied by Federal courts in private sector labor-management relations," 5 U.S.C.A. § 7122 (1996). In other words, the only distinctive element about review of federal-sector cases is the requirement that a mere error of law will justify intervention.

*Cornelius v. Nutt* (S.Ct.1985), provides a good illustration of the complexities facing federal-sector arbitrators. Two discharged federal employees of the General Services Agency (GSA) had a choice of appealing to the Merit Systems Protection Board

(MSPB) or challenging their discharges through the contractual grievance and arbitration procedure. They chose arbitration. To reverse the GSA's decision, the MSPB or the arbitrator would have to find that the GSA's procedures resulted in "harmful error," 5 U.S.C.A. § 7701(c)(2)(A) (West 1996). The arbitrator found that the GSA violated the agreement by not allowing them union representation during the investigatory interview, but that the error did not prejudice the employees. Because the procedural error was "harmful" to the union, however, the arbitrator reduced the discharges to suspensions. An MSPB regulation interpreted the harmful error rule as requiring substantial prejudice to the affected *employee*'s rights. The Supreme Court concluded that the award was improper because the arbitrator should have followed the MSPB's interpretation of the statute.

Similarly, when deciding whether to mitigate serious penalties, arbitrators must apply the twelve factors listed by the MSPB in *Douglas v. Veterans Administration* (M.S.P.B.1981). Some courts have even found that *Cornelius* obliges federal-sector arbitrators to follow the MSPB's *procedural* rules, for example, *Huey v. Department of Health and Human Services* (Fed.Cir.1986). When evaluating a penalty, federal-sector arbitrators, unlike their private-sector counterparts, may only determine whether the agency's choice was arbitrary or capricious. They may not make an independent judgment about the appropriate penalty. *Devine v. Pastore* (D.C.Cir. 1984).

These legal burdens have proved too much for some arbitrators. In *Devine v. White* (D.C.Cir.1983) (*per curiam*), the arbitrator made an initial error in applying the "harmful error" rule, so the Court of Appeals remanded for clarification. On remand, the arbitrator attempted to explain what he meant, but the Court found it

> difficult to fathom any coherent line of reasoning in his long and rambling opinion, which consists almost entirely of random quotes from other sources. In reading his opinion, we are hard-pressed to identify either a glimmer of reasoned consideration, to which we might defer, or a hint that his observations bear any significant relation to the real world.

The Court found itself forced to choose "between placing its stamp of approval on utter gibberish or conducting what would amount to de novo review on a hopelessly inadequate record." *Id.* at 1083–84. With strict and critical review like that, it is no wonder that many arbitrators prefer not to handle federal-sector cases.

# CHAPTER VIII

# THE "COMMON LAW" OF THE ARBITRATION PROCESS

This chapter explores the rules governing the conduct of labor and employment arbitrations—what might be called the "common law" of the arbitration process. Many of those rules are indeed matters of law, imposed and enforced by courts. Most, however, are matters of custom developed and applied by arbitrators and parties.

## A. SOME PROBLEMS OF DUE PROCESS AND INDIVIDUAL RIGHTS

Some commentators have suggested that arbitrators should recognize substantive and procedural constitutional rights. Public employers are subject to the Constitution, of course. So too may be a few highly-regulated private employers that function as an arm of government; see, for example, *Holodnak v. Avco Corp.* (D.Conn.1974). Because the Constitution restricts only governmental power, however, it has little direct effect on most private-sector employers. Arbitrators have been reluctant to add a wide range of limitations on management action in the guise of contractual interpretation. Only a few go as far as Arbitrator Joseph Bard in *King Company* (1987):

> Today, there can be little doubt that the Fifth Amendment of the Constitution creates a privilege against self-incrimination which is available outside of criminal court proceedings and serves to protect persons in all settings in which their freedom of action is curtailed in any significant way from being compelled to incriminate themselves.

Still, constitutional protections have had an undeniable if indirect impact on labor arbitration. Arbitrators occasionally refer to constitutional cases in determining whether certain employee actions constitute just cause for discharge, and they quite frequently use constitutional notions of "due process" in the course of their own rulings on procedural questions. As arbitrators resolve more statutory questions, courts will expect them to provide protections at least equal to those in the Constitution.

This section examines the ways arbitrators deal with issues corresponding to constitutional problems of criminal procedure. One of the primary areas of this overlap between private and public procedure, the duty of fair representation, was discussed in Chapter VII, Section H. So long as the union acts fairly (that is, without bad faith or discrimination), it can decide to drop or settle the grievance, thus depriving the employee of access to arbitration. Similarly, it may pursue the grievances of some employees to the detriment of others, *Benson v. Communication Workers of America* (E.D.Va. 1994). There are many other areas where such questions are likely to arise. The following pages deal with the most important of these.

## 1. Notice

The relationship between the individual employee and the labor arbitration process is marked by some confusion. Traditionally arbitrators and the courts have held that the employer and the union were the only parties to a collective bargaining agreement. Others, including individual grievants, have no role and no rights in arbitration except those granted by the contract or the union. *Blake v. U.S.M. Corp.* (D.N.H.1977). Some agreements do grant individual grievants a special role or enforceable rights, and the employee has long been able to demand fair representation from the union, but for the most part the grievant is at the mercy of the bargaining representative.

This traditional approach has some exceptions. The NLRB has indicated that it will not defer to an arbitration award where the employee's interests and those of the union diverge, unless the employee has notice of the time and place of the arbitration hearing, or unless fully represented the employee's interests. One federal district court specifically incorporated a notice requirement in the duty of fair representation where the employee was the only affected party, *Thompson v. IAM, Lodge 1049*

(E.D.Va.1966). Furthermore, failing to notify adversely affected employees of a union's grievance activities may be evidence of the union's breach of its duty of fair representation, *Benson v. Communication Workers of America* (E.D.Va.1994).

One state court even held that a union must notify all employees whose rights could be affected by the grievance. In *Clark v. Hein–Werner Corp.* (Wis.1959), the Wisconsin Supreme Court concluded that

> where the interests of two groups of employees are diametrically opposed to each other and the union espouses the cause of one in the arbitration, it follows as a matter of law that there has been no fair representation of the other group. This is true even though ... the union acts completely objectively and with the best of motives.

The *Clark* decision has been widely criticized for placing too much of a burden on unions. Five years later, the United States Supreme Court disagreed with the *Clark* holding. *Humphrey v. Moore* (S.Ct. 1964) expressly rejected the assertion that a union cannot fairly represent groups of employees with conflicting interests. The Court found no violation in a union action that favored one group of employees over another, so long as the union acted in good faith upon relevant considerations.

"Just cause" for discipline or discharge also includes a notice requirement. Arbitrators expect employers to have informed the employee of the charges. Normally they will not allow the employer to justify the discipline by citing new reasons, although after-acquired evidence of other offenses may be reason to impose separate discipline or to limit the remedy for an erroneous first discipline. Notice of the arbitration hearing, in contrast, may not be so crucial as notice of the charges. If the union is able to represent the grievant, the grievant need not even be present. Nevertheless, most arbitrators expect the grievant to be present.

## 2. Separate Representation and Third–Party Intervention

Naturally some employees wish to represent themselves or to select their own representative for an arbitration. The union's representation of the employee will in most cases fulfill the right to counsel and obviate the need for separate representation or for any direct participation by the employee. Indeed, most unions strenuously resist any direct intervention by separate counsel for the employee because of a belief that it would undercut the union's role as exclusive representative of the entire bargaining unit. Arbitrators have been reluctant to permit formal employee intervention against the wishes of the parties, because arbitration is the creature of the parties. Despite the formal rule, most arbitrators seek an accommodation when the employee wants separate representation, even warning the union of potential liability under the duty of fair representation. The Code of

Professional Responsibility recognizes that an arbitrator may have to rule on a request for separate representation but offers no guidance on how to decide: see Appendix I, § 2.C.1.a.

An employee may be entitled to separate representation and participation as a matter of law if the union will not provide fair representation. A few courts have held as much—see *Smith v. Hussmann Refrigerator Co.* (8th Cir.1980)—but such cases are rare and proving the union's unwillingness to represent the employee would be difficult. The NLRB has adopted a broader rule, that individuals should have the right to separate representation whenever their interests do not coincide with those of the union. The Board will not defer to an award where the union wrongly denied the employee the right to separate representation. The Board's position has had little effect because few arbitrations involve potential unfair labor practices and because both arbitrators and parties dislike the idea of a trilateral arbitration. In addition to the union's interest in maintaining its position as exclusive representative, there is a reasonable fear that employee intervention would lead to confusion and disruption.

Participation by other third parties is even rarer. Arbitrators occasionally encourage or permit attendance and even informal participation by employees who might be affected by the arbitration award. The AAA Rules specifically allow attendance by any person with a direct interest in the arbitration (Appendix A, Rule 22). A conflict between two unions and a single employer can present such a problem. This happens most often in work-assignment disputes where each union claims a contractual right to certain work. Separate arbitrations might lead to equally valid but directly conflicting awards. In just such a case, *Carey v. Westinghouse Electric Corp.* (S.Ct.1964), the Supreme Court held that the employer could not refuse to arbitrate simply because of that possibility.

Obviously a single arbitration involving both unions would minimize the problem. (It would not always eliminate it because the two contracts might in fact contain conflicting but equally valid provisions.) If one union rejects such a suggestion may the arbitrator nevertheless require, invite, or permit participation by another union? Arbitrators have differed on each of these possibilities and there have been few court rulings.

In *National Steel & Shipbuilding Co.* (Edgar Jones 1963), an arbitrator held that a dispute between two unions over assigned work was not arbitrable unless both unions participated in the arbitration. He then tried to force the reluctant second union into the arbitration with an "interpleader" order and invited the first union to enforce the order in court. The employer and unions all disliked the idea of trilateral arbitration and avoided it by allowing the unions to settle their dispute under the auspices of the AFL–CIO. Arbitrator Jones's activism pro. apted a lengthy debate between him and Professor Merton Bernstein. See *Jurisdictional Dis-*

*pute Arbitration: The Jostling Professors*, 14 UCLA Law Review 347 (1966) and the other articles cited therein. The Second Circuit Court of Appeals resolved one such dispute by ordering consolidation of two pending arbitrations, but other courts have not followed its lead. *Columbia Broadcasting System, Inc. v. American Recording and Broadcasting Association* (2d Cir.1969).

## 3. Self–Incrimination

Invocation of a claimed Fifth Amendment right against self-incrimination is most frequent where an employer has discharged an employee for conduct that may also be illegal. The employee's position in such a case is difficult and a reluctance to testify understandable. Some employees make the same claim in less compelling circumstances, where there is no question of criminal liability but where the employee simply resists testifying lest the testimony help the employer prove the charged offense. As a matter of law, the protection against self-incrimination may not even apply when a governmental agency acts in its capacity as an employer. Compare *City of San Antonio* (J. Earl Williams, 1987) (right against self-incrimination not applicable to employment disputes) with *Gardner v. Broderick* (S.Ct.1968) and *Uniformed Sanitation Men Association, Inc. v. Commissioner of Sanitation* (S.Ct.1968) (government may not discharge employees for invoking the privilege against self-incrimination).

As a practical matter, arbitrators cannot force a reluctant employee to testify. They may issue a subpoena but enforcing a subpoena requires court action. Arbitrators can and frequently do draw adverse conclusions from a failure to testify, though. That is why grievants invoke the Fifth Amendment: in criminal cases, a judge or jury may not lawfully draw a negative inference from the defendant's silence. Conversely, a private-sector employer may discipline an employee specifically for refusing to give evidence, as when the employee refuses to cooperate in an investigation of theft or drug use.

The ruling of Arbitrator Bard in the *King Company* decision cited at the beginning of this chapter is an aberration. Most arbitrators reject assertions that the constitutional right against self-incrimination applies to private-sector employment disputes. A few have recognized the desirable policy behind the Fifth Amendment and have therefore refused to draw any negative inferences from the grievant's failure to testify, *e.g.*, *American International Aluminum Corp.*, 68–2 ARB ¶ 8591 (John F. Sembower, 1968). Most arbitrators do draw negative inferences, *e.g.*, *NRM Corp.* (Edwin Teple, 1968). They are particularly likely to do so when the reluctant employee faces no risk of a subsequent criminal proceeding.

What does an "adverse inference" amount to? Silence alone does not prove guilt. Arbitrators therefore require other evidence, which the employee's failure to refute may bolster. In *Southern Bell*

*Telephone & Telegraph Co.* (1955), Arbitrator Whitley McCoy stated the proper balance:

> Inferences may be resorted to in aid of evidentiary facts; they cannot supply facts of which there is no evidence. Findings of fact must be based on credible evidence. The failure to deny or refute incredible evidence does not change the character of that evidence from incredible to credible. Testimony that is merely weak can gain strength from failure to deny; but testimony that is utterly incredible can never become credible that way.

In short, the employer must first present a *prima facie* case establishing just cause for the discipline. If the employee, after being warned of a possible adverse inference, refuses to testify, an arbitrator may use the refusal as evidence that the employer's case is correct. The adverse inference is useful only when the employee has other evidence disputing the employer's charge, of course; without any such evidence for the defense, the employer would prevail even without an adverse inference.

### 4. Search and Seizure

In the wake of court decisions excluding improperly obtained evidence from criminal trials, arbitrators have been asked on many occasions to do the same. Arbitrators have universally upheld the use of evidence obtained in searches pursuant to reasonable work rules, such as routine inspection of employees' handbags and lunch boxes on leaving the plant. With almost similar universality, they have accepted evidence obtained in searches of company property such as lockers, even if an employee has temporary exclusive use of that property. In addition, arbitrators have upheld discipline levied for refusal to permit such searches. Obviously a search pursuant to an established rule or practice will appear more legitimate than one that is merely an immediate reaction to a new problem.

On the other hand, arbitrators have divided sharply on the admissibility of evidence obtained in an *ad hoc* search of an employee's person or property. At bottom, the question in these cases is whether arbitrators should adopt the "exclusionary rule" created by the courts in criminal cases. Two cases illustrate the issue. In *Aldens, Inc.* (John P. McGury, 1972), a hospital's security guards searched the trunk of a car without proper cause. In the trunk, they found shoes apparently stolen by the grievant from his employer, a retail store. A judge suppressed the seized evidence and dismissed criminal charges. When the grievant challenged his discharge in arbitration, he asked the arbitrator to disregard that evidence. Arbitrator McGury applied the exclusionary rule because the employer sought to use the results of a violation by others of the grievant's constitutional rights, holding that "the rationale which supports the exclusionary rule generally, supports its application to the grievant in this set of circumstances."

In contrast, Arbitrator Lawrence Doppelt refused to suppress evidence from an illegal search in *Com-*

*modity Warehousing Corp.* (1973). Labor arbitrators, wrote Arbitrator Doppelt,

> should tread lightly when it comes to interpreting exclusionary rules of evidence based on criminal and constitutional law. The parties have chosen the arbitrator for his presumed expertise in matters pertaining to labor-management relations, not as an expert on rules of evidence in criminal cases.

He went on to doubt the wisdom of applying exclusionary rules at all in arbitration because of the different policies involved:

> Criminal law pertains to vindicating the rights of society against individuals who have broken society's laws.... Labor arbitration, on the other hand, vindicates the rights and responsibilities of employers, unions, and employees under a labor contract. It involves private disputes without any spectre of governmental excesses.

Finally, he concluded that the main issue in the arbitration case is whether the employer had cause to discharge the grievant, something he could not determine without knowing all the facts on which the employer relied. (Even with the challenged evidence, however, the arbitrator concluded that the employer failed to meet its burden of proof.)

Arbitrator McGury represents the minority position. In a later *Aldens* case, (1973), Arbitrator David Dolnick declined to follow the McGury decision, finding that he could not agree "with the concepts or with the reasons given for sustaining the motion to suppress."

## 5. Confrontation and Cross-Examination

A fundamental tenet of our criminal justice system is that defendants must have the opportunity to confront their accusers and cross-examine their testimony. The underlying basis of that principle, that the rigors of the adversarial process best enable the decision maker to judge the truth of a statement, is so compelling that it has had a considerable influence on civil law as well as criminal. It has also influenced arbitration. The problem comes up almost exclusively in one of four contexts: hearsay generally, and evidence coming from customers, fellow employees, or professional "spotters." Each of these deserves brief discussion.

*(a) **Hearsay.*** Hearsay will be dealt with in more detail below, along with other evidentiary questions. For the moment it is sufficient to note that arbitrators almost universally accept hearsay evidence when there is any sort of reasonable explanation why first-hand testimony is not feasible. At the same time, they moderate the risks by evaluating hearsay more critically than other sorts of evidence. Perhaps the most common statement from arbitrators on hearsay is the evidentiary ruling "I'll admit it for what it is worth," carrying the implication that it may not be worth very much.

*(b) **Customers, Co-workers and "Spotters."*** Employers are understandably reluctant to put any

of these three categories of witnesses on the stand even when their testimony is absolutely crucial. An employer may take disciplinary action against an employee following customer complaints but may feel that calling the customer to testify would discourage patronage or at least discourage such complaints. Calling an employee as a witness may lead to strife within the bargaining unit that neither party wants, and "spotters" (employees who pose as customers to watch for employee misconduct) lose their effectiveness once employees know who they are. Yet in each of these cases the disciplined employee certainly has good reason to want the opportunity to confront and cross-examine the witness.

Faced with these conflicting arguments, arbitrators tend to require the testimony of employee witnesses notwithstanding potential strife, but not the testimony of customers or spotters. In those latter cases, arbitrators have been known to suggest compromises such as private investigation by the arbitrator alone, acceptance of the proffered hearsay evidence subject to the right of the union representative to verify its accuracy privately with the witness, or testimony of the "spotter" behind a screen or by telephone. Contracts in industries where these types of cases are frequent sometimes spell out procedures to be used. Mutual agreement is obviously the best way to resolve the problem. Absent agreement, compromises along this line are preferable to simple acceptance or exclusion of new hearsay.

## 6. Surprise: Changed Issues, Arguments or Evidence

In theory, the grievance process weeds out weak cases and focuses the issues in those cases taken to arbitration. Usually it does so. Often, however, a party raises at the hearing or in a post-hearing brief an issue, argument or piece of evidence not considered in the grievance procedure. An employer who discharged employee A for drunkenness might later cite insubordination as the reason; a union that challenged subcontracting as a violation of the recognition clause might assert instead that it was prohibited by an agreed past practice; or either party might offer the testimony of a surprise witness unknown to the other party.

Resolution of these problems will differ depending upon several factors. One is the nature of the surprise. A party may try to change the direction of the case so significantly as to be arguing a new grievance. The only appropriate response in such a case is to remand the issue to the appropriate step of the grievance procedure. Doing otherwise would undercut the utility of the grievance procedure and would force the other party to respond to a new issue without adequate time to prepare.

A second factor is the wording of the particular contract. Some contracts expressly bar the introduction of new evidence or issues beyond some step of the grievance procedure; naturally the arbitrator must follow the parties' rules.

A third factor is the type of arbitration system. A permanent umpire may have more flexibility than an *ad hoc* arbitrator with no previous knowledge of the parties or continuing role in their relationship. Virtually all arbitrators agree that an employer may not introduce at the hearing a new reason to justify a discharge. Newly-discovered evidence of misconduct may affect the remedy or may support a new imposition of discipline, but it cannot change the basis for the original discipline.

Where the problem is simply that neither party has clearly defined the issues during the grievance procedure, arbitrators are likely to be more tolerant. What appears to one party to be a new issue might instead be a rephrasing or elaboration of the issue discussed in the grievance procedure. See *Crittenton Hospital* (George T. Roumell, 1985). The arbitrator's concern should be to conduct a fair hearing on the issues raised; this may require a recess or continuance to allow the surprised party to prepare for an issue it had not expected to meet, but should seldom require a substantive limitation on a party's arguments.

If the problem is one of new evidence rather than new issues or arguments, the same considerations should apply. Absent a contractual agreement or past practice to the contrary, an arbitrator should not bar a party from presenting newly-discovered evidence even though the better policy would be to disclose such evidence to the other party prior to the hearing. On the other hand, the surprised party should have whatever time is needed to evaluate and respond to the new evidence. This presumes both parties are acting in good faith. Where one party has deliberately withheld important evidence until the hearing, an arbitrator could properly bar its admission. Even then, some arbitrators would avoid questions of good faith and deal only with the "surprise" issue.

The equities change when a party raises the new argument or evidence after the hearing. On a party's request and for good cause, an arbitrator may reopen a hearing before issuing a decision (Appendix A, Rule 32). Good cause would include the discovery of new evidence not previously available. For a discussion of other requirements for reopening a hearing, see *Westvaco, Virginia Folding Box Division* (Dennis R. Nolan, 1988). An arbitrator should not accept new evidence that a party includes in a post-hearing brief. The problem with such evidence is that the other party has no opportunity to examine or reply to it.

A new argument in a brief presents a more difficult question. So long as the other party receives a copy of the brief and could, if it wished, submit a reply, many arbitrators would have no objection. Others would feel some obligation to ask the other party for comment, particularly if the new argument might be critical to the decision. Few would totally refuse to consider the new argument so long as it does not amount to an entirely new issue.

In fact, an arbitrator may, while reviewing the record, discover a possible basis for a decision that was not mentioned by either party. Is the arbitrator free to use that discovery, or should the arbitrator first ask the parties for their comments? Is the arbitrator free to develop a stronger case for one side than that party did for itself? There is no generally accepted answer to this dilemma. Common sense dictates that if the contract clause or theory "discovered" by the arbitrator is only an arguable solution, the arbitrator ought not rely on it without asking the parties for comments. On the other hand, most arbitrators do not feel that their role is limited by the imagination of counsel for the parties. Bad representation should not lead to a bad decision.

## 7. Ex Parte Hearings

Occasionally one party to an arbitration agreement refuses to participate in the hearing. Obviously the agreement to arbitrate would be worthless if a party could so easily stymie the process, so in some circumstances *ex parte* hearings and awards are permissible. AAA rule 27 (Appendix A) states the requirements for *ex parte* arbitration:

> Unless the law provides to the contrary, the arbitration may proceed in the absence of any party, who, after due notice, fails to be present or fails to obtain a postponement. An award shall not be made solely on the default of a party. The Arbitrator shall require the other party to submit

such evidence as may be required for the making of an award.

Similarly, the Code of Professional Responsibility authorizes arbitrators to conduct an *ex parte* hearing after determining that the absent party had adequate notice of the hearing (Appendix K, § 5.C.2.).

Rule 27 is not aimed at simple tardiness. The better course of action in that situation would be to delay or reschedule the hearing. Even when a party expressly refuses to participate, an *ex parte* hearing is not desirable. Nevertheless, it may be essential if the injured party is to receive the benefit of the arbitration agreement. If the contract provides a method of selecting an arbitrator if one party fails to participate, or if the parties have mutually selected an arbitrator before one of them withdraws, the arbitrator does not lose authority. Where there is no provision for arbitrator selection except by mutual agreement, one party cannot on its own appoint an arbitrator and conduct an *ex parte* hearing; the appropriate remedy in such a case would be a § 301 action to force the participation of the reluctant party.

## 8. The Agreed Case

"Agreed" cases are those in which the parties agree on the desired resolution but want the arbitrator to announce it as a decision. There are different reasons why they might prefer an agreed award to a settlement. In some instances, they may believe the award would carry more weight. In others, they might think the award would be more easily enforceable in court or in another arbitration. In still other instances, one or both may hesitate to admit to the agreed result. Union leaders might, for example, understand that a certain result is "right" but may not be able to sell it to the membership on their own authority. This happens from time to time with wage negotiations in weak companies. The union leadership may share management's fear that a sizeable wage increase would drive the company to bankruptcy but may be unable to face vocal elements within the union that are simply unwilling to credit such concerns. Or "political" reasons might force union leaders to challenge the discharge of a popular employee they believe to be guilty as charged. Or management and union leaders might want to get rid of a dissident employee. The union could then arbitrate the resulting discharge only to let the arbitrator know by one means or another that it would just as soon lose this one.

The reasons run the gamut from perfectly innocent to perfectly corrupt. All such cases pose ethical problems for the arbitrator. On the one hand, simple acceptance of the parties' wishes makes the hearing a sham. On the other hand, the main purpose of arbitration is to facilitate peaceful resolution of disputes. The last-mentioned type of case, a conspiracy to get rid of an employee, is clearly illegal. In *Allen v. Allied Plant Maintenance Company of Tennessee, Inc.* (6th Cir.1989), the company and union conspired to select an arbitrator likely to rule in favor of the employer. As a result, the court found that the union breached its duty of fair representation, set aside the arbitration award, and awarded damages against both parties.

Arbitrators differ in their reactions to requests for such "consent awards." In the wage example, many would have no problem so long as the agreement reached by the parties seemed to the arbitrator to be reasonable in the particular context. Individual grievance cases present more of a problem because the union's interests might conflict with the grievant's. Applicable agency rules allow consent awards in settlement of disputes in both labor arbitration and individual employment arbitration [Appendix A, Rule 39; Appendix C, Rule 32(e)].

The Code of Professional Responsibility (Appendix I, § 2.I.1.) recognizes the ambivalent nature of consent awards by authorizing them only where the arbitrator is sure the result is fair. The arbitrator must first take all necessary steps to understand the case. If the matter involves an individual grievant, the arbitrator should also be sure the grievant understands the agreed result.

## B. THE BURDEN OF PROOF

The term "burden of proof" actually comprises several distinct burdens: the burden of producing evidence, the burden of persuasion, and the burden of establishing a sufficient quantum of proof.

## 1. The Burden of Producing Evidence

Logic and custom dictate that in arbitration as in court the moving party must produce some evidence to support its position. In legal terms, the moving party is expected to establish a *prima facie* case, that is, sufficient evidence to convince the trier of fact of the rightness of the party's cause if the other offers no refutation. Once the moving party does so, the burden of producing evidence shifts to the other party, which must refute the *prima facie* case or lose the dispute. If the moving party cannot establish a *prima facie* case, it will lose the dispute even if the other party remains mute.

The burden of producing evidence may shift from one party to the other as the issue under discussion changes. For example, a union claiming a seniority violation would have the initial burden of proceeding. If the employer asserts an affirmative defense such as a legal obligation to favor certain groups, the employer would then have the burden of producing evidence on that point. Similarly, a union asserting reasons to mitigate a disciplinary penalty (long seniority, provocation, condonation, diminished responsibility, and the like) must present evidence to support its assertions.

Arbitration custom has established one major exception to this rule. In labor arbitration cases involving discipline of an employee, arbitrators require the employer to proceed first and show the justification for the discipline imposed. It is not clear how or why this exception arose. The most common explanations are that in such cases management's actions precipitated the grievance and that the employer is likely to have a greater knowledge of the pertinent facts and records. Especially with regard to discharges, one also hears the suggestion that management should properly bear the burden because of the serious harm erroneously imposed discipline can cause the employee. The trouble with these explanations is that they are equally true of many other kinds of cases (layoffs and automation, for example) where the arbitrator would never think of asking the employer to proceed first. One pragmatic explanation is that arbitrators developed the rule to help unions win more cases. A more prosaic story is simply that an early arbitrator—Dean Harry Shulman of Yale Law School is the one mentioned most frequently—did it that way, and everyone else soon followed.

The advent of individual employment arbitration forced a modification of that practice. Because employment arbitration commonly serves as an alternative forum for resolving statutory claims, the parties stand in the same position they would in court. That means that the grievant is essentially a plaintiff, with the plaintiff's usual burden of proceeding.

## 2. The Burden of Persuasion

The question of which party is to present its case first would hardly be worth arguing if the parties did not see it as reflecting the burden of persuasion. If the evidence presented is equally balanced, which side prevails? The perception of the parties is for the most part correct. Although some arbitrators hesitate to state which side must carry the burden of persuasion, most place it on the same party bearing the burden of going forward—the union in contract cases and the employer in discipline cases.

Like the burden of presenting evidence, the burden of persuasion shifts with the issue. A party arguing an affirmative defense, or asserting mitigating or aggravating circumstances must prove its point, even if it was not the party with the initial burden of presenting evidence. Again, the grievant in an individual employment arbitration case raising statutory issues bears the burden of proof, even if the dispute is over discipline or discharge.

## 3. The Quantum of Proof

The burdens of presenting evidence and of persuading the decision-maker are relatively non-controversial. The more difficult question is the proper quantum of proof required. Some arbitrators dislike the entire topic, describing it as a legalism that has no place in arbitration. Even those arbitrators, however, use some implicit standard of proof. The ultimate question is *how much* proof the party with the burden of proof must provide. There are three possible levels, proof beyond a reasonable doubt, proof by "clear and convincing" evidence, and proof by a preponderance of the evidence.

The first of these, proof beyond a reasonable doubt, is the standard applied in criminal trials. As one might expect, arbitrators use it only in the most serious cases, usually discharges for offenses constituting criminal conduct or demonstrating moral turpitude. The explanation for imposing such a strict standard is that discharge for such reasons will brand an employee for life just as severely as would a criminal conviction for the same charges.

Most arbitrators reject the criminal law analogy. They note that because of the liberal application of evidentiary rules in arbitration no one could fairly regard an arbitrator's upholding of a discharge as being as conclusive of the facts as a criminal conviction. Courts reserve the "beyond a reasonable doubt" standard for criminal cases, using the modest "preponderance of the evidence" standard in civil cases, even where the commission of a crime is an issue or the civil sanction exceeds the analogous criminal penalty. An employer suing an employee for damages for theft, for example, would only have to prove the theft by a preponderance of the evidence. There is no strong reason to require the higher standard in arbitration—which, after all, is simply a non-governmental form of civil litigation.

While usually rejecting the criminal law standard, arbitrators recognize a distinction in different reasons for discharge. They tend to impose the middle standard, proof by "clear and convincing" evidence, in discharge cases alleging criminal or immoral conduct. Just how much evidence it takes to meet the "clear and convincing" test is of course hard to pin down.

The least severe standard, proof by a preponderance of the evidence, is the most popular. In addition to those cases explicitly using it, many that contain no discussion of the appropriate standard seem to apply this one. It has the virtue of being the easiest to use, for the arbitrator need only ask which case seems the stronger, or which version of the facts is more likely to be true.

Once again, individual arbitration cases are a bit different. The quantum of proof in those cases is the same as in the civil litigation they replace: a simple preponderance of the evidence.

## C. SOME PROBLEMS OF EVIDENCE

### 1. The Applicability of Evidentiary Rules to Arbitration

AAA Rule 28 (Appendix A) states that "The Arbitrator shall be the judge of the relevance and materiality of the evidence offered and conformity to legal rules of evidence shall not be necessary." Courts also recognize the difference between arbitral and judicial proceedings. They uniformly hold that an arbitrator may exclude evidence that a court would admit, *e.g.*, *Dean Witter Reynolds, Inc. v. Deislinger* (Ark.1986). Admission of evidence a court would exclude is just as permissible. There are many reasons why evidentiary rules are not strictly applied in labor arbitration. First, arbitration is supposed to be a simple, informal procedure. Most parties would even prefer to avoid using lawyers at all. Rigid adherence to technical rules would obviously conflict with the parties' intentions.

Second, many of the legal rules of evidence were developed to protect lay juries from prejudicial or unreliable testimony or exhibits. Those rules are not necessary when the decision maker (a judge, an administrative tribunal, an arbitrator) is experienced and skillful. To the contrary, most arbitrators are eager to learn all they can about the situation before them. They fear hearing too little evidence, not too much. Evidence that would not be admissible in court may nevertheless assist them. If the evidence turns out to be useless, redundant, or unreliable, they can always ignore it.

Third, many arbitrators believe that there is a "therapeutic value" to testimony—that is, that parties and witnesses benefit when people get something "off their chests," even if that something has no probative value to the issues in the arbitration.

Fourth, as a practical matter, a court is unlikely to overturn an award no matter how liberal the evidentiary rulings, as least so long as the award does not rest on obviously irrelevant or erroneous evidence. Refusal to hear relevant evidence, on the other hand, may provide a reason for a court to overturn an award. See Appendix J, § 10(a)(3) and Appendix K, § 12(a)(4).

To recognize that legal rules of evidence are not binding in arbitration is not to say that they are irrelevant. They are in fact useful in several different ways. AAA Rule 28, quoted above, recognizes that arbitrators must make judgments about materiality and relevance and should not allow introduction of obviously immaterial, irrelevant or redundant testimony. The rules of evidence developed over centuries of litigation may help decide those issues.

Even if the arbitrator decides to admit questionable evidence, the rules of evidence may help decide how much weight to give it. The reasons courts distrust hearsay evidence, for example, (likelihood of errors in reporting and the impossibility of cross-examination), should warn the arbitrator not to place too much reliance upon it. Even if the advocate believes the arbitrator will overrule the hearsay objection, making the objection allows the advocate to point out the unreliability of the evidence.

Finally, the arbitrator has an obligation to conduct an orderly proceeding that will lead to a fair resolution of the issues. Implicit in that obligation is a duty not to allow the proceeding to wander too far afield, drag on interminably, or be influenced by prejudicial or unreliable testimony. The rules of evidence, flexibly applied, can help to fulfill those obligations without unduly curtailing the rights of the parties to establish their cases.

The following sections deal with the major evidentiary issues in labor arbitration.

## 2. Hearsay

Hearsay is second-hand evidence, *i.e.*, evidence not of what the witness knows but of what the witness heard another say. In the words of Federal Rules of Evidence rule 801(c), it is "a statement, other than one made by the declarant while testifying at the trial or hearing, offered in evidence to prove the truth of the matter asserted." Courts exclude hearsay in jury trials because of the risk of inaccuracy in the repetition and because there is no opportunity to cross-examine the person making the original statement. Statements offered for some reason other than to prove the truth of the statement—for example, to show why a person reacted in a certain way—do not fall within the hearsay rule. Statements initially falling within the rule may nevertheless be admissible because of the rule's many exceptions. Some of the exceptions recognize an unusual degree of reliability, for example, business records and testimony from a previous hearing or another suit. Other exceptions recognize a particular need for the testimony, for example, declarations of a dying person.

Arbitrators generally accept hearsay, although they frequently qualify the admission with the statement that the arbitrator will consider it only "for what it's worth." In addition to the generally liberal application of evidentiary rules in arbitration and the absence of an easily misled jury, admission of hearsay in arbitration can be explained by the desire of all concerned for simple proceedings. It would be hard to keep the process informal and speedy without hearsay. The parties would need more witnesses, would have to prepare their cases more carefully, and would more often need to engage attorneys.

Because arbitrators understand hearsay's slippery nature, they often require non-hearsay corroboration on important points. They also give hearsay little weight when the opposing party presents contradictory evidence that is subject to cross-examination.

AAA Rule 29 (Appendix A) expressly allows admission of affidavits, even though affidavits are usually hearsay. Rule 29 cautions that the arbitrator shall give an affidavit "only such weight as seems proper after consideration of any objection made to its admission." Affidavits are especially helpful when the witness is unavailable or would be available only at great expense. Usually there is a fully satisfactory non-hearsay alternative even in those cases. A deposition at a convenient time can permit cross-examination even if the witness cannot attend the arbitration hearing. A telephone conference call can permit a witness to participate without travel expenses or costly fees.

## 3. The Plain Meaning Rule and Extrinsic Evidence

The arbitrator's job is to interpret and apply the parties' agreement. Often the most difficult part of that job is the first step of determining just what their agreement is. Contracts in complex, continuing relationships can never anticipate all possible contingencies. Of necessity, then, parties resort to general language or intentionally or accidentally fail to address some matters. The arbitrator then must determine what their generalities or their silence means.

Until recently, courts interpreting contracts used the so-called "plain meaning rule." This simply held that an interpreter of an agreement was to apply the usual meaning to words that seemed unambiguous, without resorting to "extrinsic" evidence (evidence of the parties' intentions other than the agreement itself). The meaning of a term might vary, however, depending on the rest of the document. One subset of the plain meaning rule is the "parol evidence rule" that bars evidence of prior or contemporaneous oral agreements and prior written agreements to vary the terms of an integrated and complete written agreement. (The plain meaning rule is broader than the parol evidence rule because it would also bar subsequent evidence such as the parties' administration of their agreement.) At bottom, both rules reflect a belief that words have fixed meanings apparent to all.

The plain meaning rule is less sweeping than may at first appear. If the questioned terms are ambiguous, extrinsic evidence is clearly admissible to help the interpreter determine their meaning. General language is inherently ambiguous, as is a contract's silence on the matter at hand. The rule does not bar evidence that the parties later amended their agreement, whether they did so in writing, orally, or through their practices. Finally, the less extreme form of the rule would admit extrinsic evidence to prove the existence of an ambiguity.

Twentieth-century contracts scholars, legislators, and judges have come to doubt the assumption that words have unvarying meanings. Instead, they recognize the inherent slipperiness of words—in particular, how the meaning of contract terms depends on context. The Uniform Commercial Code (§ 2–202) and the Restatement Second of Contracts (§ 212) thus reject the plain meaning rule, the former by allowing evidence of course of dealing, trade usage, and course of performance, the latter by allowing interpretation "in light of the circumstances." Strict application of the rule makes even less sense in labor relations because of the peculiar circumstances of labor negotiations (including drafting by non-lawyers acting under great pressure) and because of constant "practical interpretation" through the course of permanent relationships.

Contract law has thus advanced beyond the plain meaning rule. Nevertheless, some arbitrators still use it. The best examination of its use in arbitration is in Professor Carlton Snow's article, *Contract Interpretation: The Plain Meaning Rule in Labor Arbitration*, 55 Fordham Law Review 681 (1987). The parties are often responsible for its lingering force, because many collective bargaining contracts and some individual employment contracts contain their own exclusionary rule, stating that the writing contains all agreements between the parties and permitting only those modifications that are in writing and signed by both parties. The plain meaning rule is thus closely related to the jurisdiction of the arbitrator: a party asserting the rule claims, in effect, that the arbitrator has power only to interpret the written contract.

The key to resolving disputes over the plain meaning rule is to remember that the arbitrator is to interpret the agreement according to the parties' intentions. If the written agreement does not accurately reflect their intentions, the arbitrator must follow the true agreement rather than the inaccurate one. At a minimum, that requires the arbitrator to hear all evidence as to whether the contract is ambiguous. That will usually and quickly slide into an interpretation of the words themselves: plausible evidence about a variant interpretation will establish sufficient ambiguity to allow the arbitrator to use the evidence to resolve the main question. At that point, the interpretation the parties gave their agreement through their practices will carry great weight.

In short, the best way for an arbitrator to interpret a labor or employment agreement is to hear and weigh all relevant evidence about the parties' intended meaning. A rule that keeps such relevant information away from the arbitrator disserves the parties themselves.

## 4. Past Practice

Justice Douglas stated in the *Steelworkers Trilogy* that

> The labor arbitrator's source of law is not confined to the express provisions of the contract, as the industrial common law—the practices of the industry and the shop—is equally a part of the collective bargaining agreement although not expressed in it.

Justice Douglas was referring in part to binding past practices—that is, ways of doing things that effectively have become part of the parties' agreement. Parties can by their practices clarify, supplement, or in some cases even change those terms. The three aspects of past practice that are worth discussing here are the requirements for creating a binding past practice, for using such a practice, and for ending a practice.

*(a) Creating a Past Practice.* Arbitrators agree that a party asserting a binding past practice bears the burden of proving the existence of that practice. A party does so by showing that both parties regarded some action as the normal, proper and exclusive response to a particular situation. Several factors bear on that determination. The most important is *mutuality*, either express or implied. (Mutuality can be implied, for example, by a party's continued failure to object to a course of conduct that is open and repeated.) Almost any

form of objection may disprove mutuality, such as reprimands to employees engaging in the asserted practice or complaints from union representatives to a responsible company official.

Second, the asserted practice should be *clear and consistent*. Ambiguity about the content of a practice reveals lack of any understanding that certain conduct was the normal and proper response to a particular situation. Inconsistency demonstrates that there was not a single past practice.

Third, the practice should be of some significant *frequency and duration*. A single prior incident might constitute a past practice if the circumstances giving rise to it are unlikely to recur and the other party did not object to the conduct, but cases of this sort are rare. Most arbitrators insist on several instances of the conduct in question, and give weight to the conduct in proportion to its frequency and duration.

Finally, most arbitrators require the party asserting the practice to show that it was *not a simple gratuity*. They would not, in other words, force an employer to continue some act of good will that was never intended to become a binding term. A cash bonus, paid only by special order of the Board of Directors after a year of particularly high profits would not become a binding past practice without more, but an annual gift of a Thanksgiving turkey might.

Simply doing something a certain way thus does not amount to a binding past practice. As Arbitrator

Harry Shulman wrote long ago in *Ford Motor Co.* (1952),

> ... there are other practices which are not the result of joint determination at all. They may be mere happenstance, that is, methods that developed without design or deliberation. Or they may be choices by Management in the exercise of managerial discretion as to convenient methods at the time. In such cases there is no thought of obligation or commitment for the future. Such practices are merely present ways, not prescribed ways, of doing things....

A contrary holding would place past practice on a par with written agreement and create the anomaly that, while the parties expend great energy and time in negotiating the details of the Agreement, they unknowingly and unintentionally commit themselves to unstated and perhaps more important matters which in the future may be found to have been past practice.

*(b) Using a Past Practice.* Once a party proves the existence of a consistent past practice, the arbitrator must decide what effect it is to have. The best way to resolve that issue is through the contract itself. Arbitrators naturally will honor a clear statement that all past practices constituting a benefit to employees are to be deemed incorporated in the contract, just as they would honor a comparably clear statement that no past practice is binding unless spelled out in the contract. Vague language is of little help, however. Several arbitrators have

held that a broad management rights clause or a statement that the written document constitutes the "entire agreement" between the parties will not negate a practice that the parties intended to be binding.

Absent a contract provision barring the use of past practices, arbitrators can use them in several different ways. The most widely accepted use is to *clarify ambiguous language*. Almost as common is the use of a past practice to *implement general language* such as "just cause" for discharge or "relatively equal ability" for promotion.

More controversial is the use of a past practice to *supplement a silent contract*. Some arbitrators believe that parties intend their written agreements to be complete and exclusive, so that neither party should be burdened with any implied obligations. At the opposite pole are those who regard all past practices not in conflict with the contract to be incorporated in it, sub silentio. The latter view is well expressed by the quote from Justice Douglas at the beginning of this section.

Most difficult of all is the use of a past practice to *contradict apparently unambiguous contract language*. Traditional contract law frowns upon such use of past practice, and many arbitrators take the same position. After all, why would the parties settle on certain language if they did not intend to follow it?

While the traditional approach stands as a caution against ignoring carefully expressed agreements, it should not constitute a rigid barrier. Even traditional contract law recognizes that parties may amend their agreements by their actions (at least where the Statute of Frauds is not applicable). There is no reason to treat labor and employment agreements more strictly than other contracts in this respect. Traditional contract law also assumes the existence of clear and unambiguous language, used in the normal fashion by persons who were completely conscious of what they were doing. In the collective bargaining context those assumptions may not be valid. Much of the drafting of labor agreements is done in very pressured circumstances by persons with no special gift with the English language. Contracts often use even simple words in peculiar or inconsistent ways.

These factors suggest that even apparently clear language in collective bargaining agreements may be inherently ambiguous. If so, arbitrators should not take such language at face value. A better approach to the use of evidence of a past practice conflicting with contract language is to ask which type of evidence provides the strongest indication of the parties' intentions. In most cases that will be the contract, but where the practice is a better indication, the arbitrator should not ignore it.

*(c) Terminating a Past Practice.* Once a past practice has become part of the labor or employment agreement, it can be terminated only as other parts of that agreement can be terminated. Usually this requires mutual consent. It is important to

note that the parties can express their consent to terminating a practice in the same ways they consent to establishing a practice—in writing, words, actions, or even by inaction. Additionally, many arbitrators would allow unilateral termination in some circumstances. If a particular practice arose as a result of a certain manufacturing process, a legitimate change in that process might justify a unilateral change in the practice. The size of a work crew might become a binding practice for instance, but introduction of a new machine might make it possible to reduce crew size with no extra burden on the remaining crew members; many arbitrators would find the reduction (and thus the ending of the practice) permissible.

### 5. Past Employee Conduct

Parties to a disciplinary grievance sometimes seek to introduce evidence of the employee's previous conduct or misconduct. Whether that evidence is admissible is primarily a question of relevancy. Certain past conduct may be highly relevant to the grievance and therefore readily admissible. Other conduct may show nothing about the merits of the current grievance; most arbitrators would therefore exclude it as irrelevant or would give it little weight. Admissibility thus depends on the nature and time of the conduct offered as evidence, and on the specific question for which the party offers it.

In any event, an arbitrator will consider only evidence of past misconduct involving proved offenses of which the employee had notice. To admit evidence of other sorts of past misconduct would force the grievant to defend against stale charges that might serve only to prejudice the current case. Evidence of satisfactory past conduct is more liberally accepted, although only to prove the employee's character as an employee and to evaluate the appropriateness of the penalty.

An employer may offer evidence of previous misconduct (a) to justify the degree of penalty imposed, as when the employer shows that progressive discipline has not corrected some recurring problem; (b) to suggest the likelihood that the employee actually committed the charged offense; or (c) to undermine the witness's credibility.

Evidence offered for the first purpose, to justify the degree of penalty imposed, is usually admissible. Whether it will have any impact depends on the relationship between the offenses and the period of time involved. Evidence of serious absenteeism in recent months may explain a discharge because of absenteeism, for example, but the same record would hardly be relevant if it was several years old with no sign of recurrence. Evidence of previous insubordination proves nothing about an absenteeism problem, but might well indicate that the employee is generally unsatisfactory or does not respond to corrective discipline. Evidence of prior misconduct is generally as relevant to the appropriate remedy as evidence of previous good conduct.

Evidence offered for the second purpose, to show that the employee committed the charged offense, is more dubious. That an employee misused sick leave or disobeyed orders months or years before normally would prove little about a later alleged offense. The criminal law is an inexact analogy, but it does provide a good basis for comparison on this matter. Courts use past convictions to determine the appropriate penalty, not to determine guilt. (One exception, in both criminal trials and arbitration, is when the previous conduct proves a tendency or reveals a particular method of committing an offense like the one at issue.) In the criminal law context, that distinction reflects the belief that a judge is less likely than a jury to be prejudiced by such information. It may also reflect a belief that the sentence should fit the individual as well as the crime while the determination of guilt should rest solely upon the facts presented. The distinction makes little sense in arbitration, because the arbitrator is both judge and jury and must receive evidence on all matters before making a decision on any. Then, too, the arbitrator normally sits in review of management's decision and does not have the broad discretion possessed by a sentencing judge.

These differences between arbitration and the criminal law do not fully explain the fact that many arbitrators not only admit evidence of past misconduct but often treat it as having significant probative value on the question of guilt. To the extent the evidence is at all relevant on the question of guilt, its weight depends on proximity in time and on any "functional relationship" between the offenses. If the employer satisfies those tests, many arbitrators would assume that an employee who previously ignored orders or reported to work intoxicated would be likely to do so again. All arbitrators would require corroborating evidence of the new offense. Past misconduct, in other words, may be relevant but not conclusive evidence of current guilt.

Finally, employers frequently offer evidence of past misconduct to undermine a witness' credibility. The most obvious example would be the use of previous disciplines to refute an employee's claim to have an excellent work record. A second example is the use of prior criminal convictions notwithstanding pleas of not guilty to suggest that the employee's current denial is unreliable.

The only non-disciplinary occasion for using an employee's previous misconduct is in a promotion case where the employer passes over the senior employee because of a bad work record. Most of these disputes turn on the wording of the particular contract. If the agreement does not state whether past conduct is relevant to promotion decisions, arbitrators differ in their rulings. Some deny the admissibility of instances of past misconduct because it does not bear on the grievant's ability to perform the work in the higher classification. An employee with a poor attendance record might nevertheless be excellent at the job. If the employer disqualifies the employee because of the attendance problems, some arbitrators would exclude that evidence. Others would admit it, particularly if the employer proved the job in question required steady attendance.

## 6. Medical Evidence

Medical evidence can be relevant to many types of grievances: in disciplinary cases involving alleged drug use, insurance fraud, or abuse of sick leave, or in explanation of misconduct because of mental illness; in non-disciplinary terminations for inability to perform one's job; in denials of promotions or transfers because of medical requirements; and, most recently, in cases of alleged violations of statutory or contractual prohibitions against discrimination because of disabilities.

Because medical experts are often unavailable to testify (or would be available only at substantial cost), much medical evidence is in the form of documents—excuses for absences, physical examination reports, prescriptions, test results, and notes of office visits. As indicated above, arbitrators usually accept those documents despite their hearsay nature but may give them less weight than testimony subject to cross-examination. When a doctor's evaluation is likely to prove critical, however, parties should consider using alternatives like depositions and telephone conference calls rather than relying solely on documents.

Medical-clearance requirements imposed by employers usually present no significant problem so long as the requirements are reasonably related to the job in question. Employers have a legal obligation to provide a safe workplace; with that obligation goes the right to determine whether employees can perform their jobs without endangering themselves or others. Arbitrators routinely uphold medical clearance requirements, concentrating instead on whether the procedure used was fair and the ultimate decision reasonable.

The more difficult problem for the arbitrator is to evaluate conflicting medical testimony. There is no simple way to do this. The arbitrator's role in such cases is like that of a lay jury presented with conflicting expert testimony of any sort. Like a jury, the arbitrator must decide between the experts using critical analysis of the evidence, perception of the relative credibility of the witnesses, and certain helpful presumptions. The most important presumption is that an employer may rely on its medical advisors where there is no reason to doubt their accuracy or good faith—provided the employer acts in complete good faith and offers the employee a fair opportunity to counter the evidence of the employer's advisors. Another helpful presumption is that an employee who has performed certain work for a long time without problem should be able to continue doing so. With the consent of the parties, the arbitrator could choose a doctor to evaluate the medical testimony, but this rarely happens.

If the issue is still in doubt after application of these presumptions, common sense dictates a few additional rules-of-thumb. Testimony is better than documents; a doctor who has examined the grievant is in a better position to evaluate the matter than one who has not; a specialist in the appropriate area is likely to be more expert than a primary-care physician; a doctor who has considered the requirements of the job is more persuasive than one who has not; and recent examinations are better than old ones. See *Hercules, Inc.* (Dennis R. Nolan 1988).

Drug testing disputes are becoming more common and more complex. Medical evidence can be critical in evaluating the test results. For example, a doctor or other scientific expert is more likely than a lay person to know how reliable the test is, what besides illegal drugs might have caused a positive result, and whether the positive result proves actual impairment.

## D. THE ARBITRATION AWARD AND OPINION

### 1. Form and Content

The object of arbitration is to resolve the dispute. To do this effectively, the arbitrator must render an award—that is, a statement of the arbitrator's conclusions. The award need not be in any particular form but normally must be a written statement answering the questions posed by the parties [Appendix C, Rule 32(b); Appendix K, § 8(a)]. That much is necessary to ensure finality and to end the dispute. Courts cannot enforce incomplete awards, and the NLRB may not defer to awards that fail to address the unfair labor practice claim.

Although the award must be complete, it need not be detailed. It is perfectly proper for the arbitrator to state the controlling principle and remand to the parties the details of implementation (for example, the calculation of the amount of back pay due the grievant or the identity of the employees harmed by an erroneous overtime assignment).

## 2. Time Limitations

The arbitrator must comply with contractual time limits for the award [Appendix K, § 8(b)]. If the arbitration agreement does not specify a time limit, the designating agency's rules might; the AAA, for example, allows 30 days from the closing of the hearings for both labor arbitration and individual employment arbitration [Appendix A, Rule 37; Appendix C, Rule 32(a)], while the FMCS allows 60 days (Appendix F, § 1404.14). Expedited rules naturally allow less time—just seven days in the case of the AAA's Expedited Labor Arbitration Procedures (Appendix B, Rule E9). The Uniform Arbitration Act allows a court to fix a time on the application of a party if the agreement does not specify one [Appendix K, § 8(b)]. Some state statutes specify a deadline.

Failure to meet a contractual or statutory deadline may have little practical effect. The FMCS rules expressly state that it does not: tardiness does not invalidate the arbitration process or the arbitrator's award [Appendix F, § 1404.14(a)]. The United States Court of Appeals for the Ninth Circuit reached the same conclusion in *McKesson Corp. v. Local 150, IBT* (9th Cir.1992). A party to a labor arbitration would have to rely on § 301, and no federal court has held that § 301 incorporates state time limits. One held the opposite, that a state limitation may not frustrate an otherwise fair arbitration. *West Rock Lodge No. 2120, IAM v. Geometric Tool Co.* (2d Cir.1968).

In a case of extreme delay with resulting harm to a party, a federal court could apply a version of the equitable doctrine of laches, but even that is unlikely unless the other party is responsible for the delay. The parties themselves could provide that an arbitrator would lose authority after a certain time, but even in the interest of speed such a provision might prove unwise. An unexpected illness or other good cause might delay the award by a few days and the losing party would simply have an excuse for not abiding by the award when it did come in. That would force the prevailing party to litigate, to use economic pressure, or to repeat the arbitration process. The most a court would do in the case of long-overdue award is remove the arbitrator and select a replacement.

This is not to minimize the importance of prompt decisions. To the contrary, if arbitration is to be more desirable than other forms of dispute resolution it must provide quick decisions. Market pressures are the best guarantor of satisfactory performance. Parties can weigh each arbitrator's record for timely awards when making a new selection. If promptness really matters to them, they will soon drive the tardy arbitrators out of the profession. Notwithstanding stated time limits and the policy favoring prompt awards, late awards are a regrettable fact of life, not at all uncommon in this business.

## 3. Arbitration Panels

When the arbitration is conducted before a panel of arbitrators, a majority vote is essential for a valid award (Appendix A, Rule 25; Appendix K, § 4). While in many cases this makes good sense, in some cases it may prevent a decision. The problem is most likely to arise in labor arbitration where two of the arbitrators are in fact representatives of the parties. The neutral arbitrator may want to render an award falling between the parties' positions but may be unable to convince either side to budge. This may prevent the arbitrator from making any award. That in turn would force the parties to use their economic weapons and would destroy the value of the arbitration agreement. Alternatively, it could force the arbitrator to move to one pole or the other and render a decision that would further outrage the losing party.

For example, a neutral arbitrator might find discipline warranted but believe that discharge was too severe a penalty. The neutral arbitrator might want to order reinstatement without back pay, but unless one of the parties is willing to compromise, there will not be a majority vote for the proposed award. To prevent such deadlocks, some agreements have abandoned the tripartite approach in favor of the single arbitrator. Others authorize the neutral arbitrator to issue a binding award if there is no majority.

## 4. The Opinion

Commercial arbitration requires an award (a statement of the arbitrator's conclusion) but usually not an opinion (an explanation of the arbitrator's reasons for reaching the conclusion in the award). In those cases the parties are usually more interested in ending the dispute than in knowing why the arbitrator reached a certain result. Moreover, the parties may never have to deal with one another again, so they have little need of guidance for the future.

In contrast, the parties in the typical labor arbitration have to deal with one another for the foreseeable future, usually under the same or a very similar contract. An explanation of the arbitrator's interpretation is therefore quite useful. Accordingly, written opinions have been the norm in labor arbitration for decades, even though the controlling rules do not require one. See, for example, AAA Rule 38 (Appendix A) and the Code of Professional Responsibility (Appendix I, § 6.C.1.a.). The AAA's Expedited Labor Arbitration Procedures allow the arbitrator to determine whether an opinion is necessary but provide that any opinion "shall be in summary form" (Appendix B, Rule E10).

What are the benefits to the parties of an arbitrator's opinion? First, by stating the reasons for an award an opinion demonstrates that the award was in fact a reasoned one. This in turn contributes to the willingness of the parties to accept and abide by the award. Second, a written opinion provides guidance to the parties in dealing with similar issues. An arbitrator who provides such guidance in a persuasive manner may save the parties from needless future grievances and arbitrations. Third, a reasoned opinion may obviate appeals to other forums. The NLRB will defer to arbitration awards under its *Spielberg* doctrine only if it finds that the award is not repugnant to the LMRA. Without an opinion it may be difficult to determine whether that condition has been met. Similarly, a court would be less likely to overturn an award backed by a careful opinion, and failure to provide such an opinion might encourage appeals to courts by losing parties.

Individual employment arbitration falls between the commercial and labor arbitration poles. If the courts are to defer to the arbitrator's interpretation of a statute, they need some evidence that the result was rational. On the other hand, requiring a full opinion where the employment relationship has ended might delay the process or substantially increase its cost. Thus the Supreme Court in the *Gilmer* case (discussed in Chapter VI, Section 3) accepted the New York Stock Exchange's arbitration rules requiring only a brief statement of the case. The AAA's National Rules for the Resolution of Employment Disputes do not require an opinion (Appendix C, Rule 32).

A cynic could suggest several distinct reasons why an arbitrator would *want* to write an opinion. Arbitrators are normally paid for their time; writing an opinion will therefore justify a larger fee. Moreover, experienced arbitrators are more likely to be selected by parties than inexperienced arbitrators, and one of the main indications of experience is the number of published opinions. An arbitrator might also want to impress other arbitrators. One way to do so is to publish well-reasoned decisions.

For all of these reasons, formal opinions are generally expected and provided.

## 5. Publication

Arbitration is a confidential process. An arbitrator may not ethically disclose the result to anyone without the parties' approval. (Code of Professional Responsibility, § 2.C.). At the same time, however, arbitrators' opinions can provide needed guidance for other parties and arbitrators. Earlier awards are not binding on later arbitrators, but they can help them make consistent decisions. Without publication of awards, it would be virtually impossible to develop a "common law" of labor arbitration. Each case would take place in a vacuum. From the earliest days of arbitration, therefore, some arbitration awards have been published. Apart from publications limited to specific industries (notably the steel industry) and those of the AAA, the most important are those of the Bureau of National Affairs (BNA), Commerce Clearing House (CCH), and the Labor Relations Press (LRP). Some of these are available on computer through the WestLaw and Lexis systems. The DNA on-line service includes many awards not selected for publication in hard copy.

Reconciling confidentiality and the desirability of publication has been difficult. The AAA asks the parties if they have any objection; if they do not express an objection, the AAA is free to publish. The FMCS used to obtain awards and make them available to publishers, but it stopped that practice long ago. Publishers other than the AAA have therefore had to rely on parties or arbitrators to submit awards to them for consideration. Parties seldom bother to do so, so that puts the burden on arbitrators.

The Code of Professional Responsibility formerly required the arbitrator to obtain the parties' express approval before submitting any award for publication. When arbitrators raised the issue before issuing the award, parties sometimes felt pressured to agree. Rather than offend the parties, many arbitrators simply decided not to submit awards for publication. Asking for permission after the award proved time consuming and frustrating, because many parties with no objection just did not bother to reply.

To deal with the dilemma, the National Academy of Arbitrators proposed amending the Code to allow a simpler process. The other sponsors of the Code, the AAA and FMCS, quickly agreed. Current § 2.C.1.c. allows an arbitrator to state when issuing the award that failure to answer the inquiry within 30 days "will be considered an implied consent to publish." That process seems to work, for the publishers suffer from no lack of awards.

## 6. Termination of the Arbitrator's Authority

The arbitrator can render a binding award only while he or she has jurisdiction. That jurisdiction can end in a number of ways:

*(a) By the Withdrawal of One of the Parties.* Under common law rules an agreement to arbitrate was purely executory. Either party could terminate it at any time until the arbitrator rendered an award. Terminating the arbitration might breach the contract, but damages, being difficult if not impossible to ascertain, were likely to be nominal. Section 301 changed that rule for labor arbitration cases, and the Supreme Court's treatment of the FAA in the *Gilmer* case seems to have ended it in individual arbitration cases, too. Courts now routinely enforce agreements to arbitrate.

*(b) By Expiration of Time Limits.* Time limitations established in the collective bargaining

agreement, the submission agreement, or in a separate understanding are valid and enforceable. Arbitration, after all, is purely a contractual process. If a party agrees to arbitrate only for a specified period, that limitation is as binding as any other part of the arbitration agreement. The arbitrator's authority thus expires automatically when the contract specifies. Courts do interpret arbitration agreements broadly and exclusions narrowly, though. Thus borderline cases are likely to be sent to arbitration. If a dispute arises during the agreement's term but the contract expires before the hearing occurs, a court is likely to hold that the arbitrator retains jurisdiction. Similarly, an arbitrator normally has jurisdiction to hear disputes over rights that accrued during the contract term, even if the contract expired before the grievance was filed.

*(c) By Rendition of a Final Award.* Under the doctrine of *functus officio* an arbitrator's power ceases once the arbitrator completes the assigned task of rendering a final award. At common law, the arbitrator lacked authority to take any action after rendering the award—reopening the hearing, changing the award, or even interpreting it.

*(d) By Operation of Law.* State statutes and common law occasionally provide a few automatic terminations. The most obvious of these is the death or disability of the arbitrator; less obvious (and perhaps irrelevant in labor arbitration cases today because of the continuing nature of corporate

and labor organizations) is the death or disability of one of the parties.

## 7. Interpretation, Modification or Correction of the Award by the Arbitrator

As mentioned above, the common law doctrine of *functus officio* held that an arbitrator's power expired with the rendering of a final award. The arbitrator had no legal authority thereafter to interpret, modify or correct that award. Much of that common law rule remains in effect today. The Code of Professional Responsibility states that "No clarification or interpretation of an award is permissible without the consent of both parties" (Appendix I, § 6.D.1.).

*Functus officio* is actually a narrow doctrine. It does not even apply until there is a complete and final award. An arbitrator may therefore issue a tentative or partial award, or retain jurisdiction to resolve remedial disputes such as the amount of back pay, without running afoul of the doctrine. If the parties jointly ask for an interpretation or supplementation, they grant the arbitrator new authority. Applicable statutes or rules may allow the arbitrator to make some changes. UAA § 9 (Appendix K) allows an arbitrator to modify or correct the award on the application of a party in case of "an evident miscalculation of figures or an evident mistake in the description of any person, thing or property," or if the award is imperfect "in a matter of form, not affecting the merits of the controversy." The AAA's Employment Arbitration Rules now allow correction of clerical, computational, or similar errors on the request of one party within 21 days of the decision (Appendix C, Rule 33). The rule does not allow an arbitrator to revisit the merits of the dispute. Finally, a court may in appropriate cases remand an award to an arbitrator for clarification or correction. Despite these exceptions, the "hard core" of the doctrine, that an arbitrator may not change or interpret an award in a way affecting the merits of the case without the consent of both parties, remains good law.

There are good policy reasons behind this rule, but there is at least one good argument against it: *functus officio* forces a party to litigate to correct even the most obvious mistakes or to obtain the simplest of clarifications if the other party is obstinate. As a result, there has been serious criticism of the doctrine in recent years, some by distinguished federal judges. The most thorough judicial discussion of the doctrine is in Judge Richard Posner's opinion in *Glass Molders, Pottery, Plastics and Allied Workers Union, Local 182B v. Excelsior Foundry Co.* (7th Cir.1995).

## 8. Actions to Enforce or Vacate an Arbitrator's Award

Chapter VII discussed the general principles of judicial review at length, so they need not be repeated here. Nevertheless, a few practical aspects of the review process bear mention at this point.

First, it should be noted that actions to enforce or vacate an arbitration award are exceedingly rare in labor and employment cases because the parties generally wish to avoid formal legal proceedings and because of the evident futility of challenging an arbitrator's award after the *Steelworkers Trilogy.* It is not in the long-term interest of either party to undercut arbitration's finality.

Second, a dissatisfied party who believes that a court would not uphold the award has two options. Which option the party takes will depend on the strategy appropriate to the facts of the case. A party can take the offensive and bring an action in equity to vacate the award. Challenging an arbitration award poses certain risks. Besides incurring transaction costs and possibly damaging the employment relationship, the challenger might face sanctions for frivolous litigation. The grounds for judicial review are so narrow that skeptical courts might view anything other than an extremely strong case as frivolous. In *Miller Brewing Co. v. Brewery Workers Local Union No. 9* (7th Cir.1984), the Court of Appeals warned that it would award an injured party attorney's fees if the other baselessly challenged an award. In later cases, for example, *Dreis & Krump Manufacturing Co. v. International Association of Machinists and Aerospace Workers, District No. 8* (7th Cir.1986), it carried out that threat, with a vengeance: rules "designed to discourage groundless litigation are being and will continue to be enforced in this court to the hilt.... Lawyers practicing in the Seventh Circuit, take heed!"

Not all circuit courts have been so ready to impose sanctions in labor arbitration cases. In individual arbitration cases posing statutory issues, the arbitrator has the same remedial authority a judge would have. In civil rights matters, that usually allows an award of attorney's fees. A court would therefore have the same power to award attorney's fees for the costs of an appeal of the arbitrator's award. That would make such an appeal especially risky.

Alternatively, a dissatisfied party may refuse to comply with the award. If the other party takes no further action, the recalcitrant will win by default. It should hardly be necessary to note that actions of that sort do little to foster good labor relations. If the prevailing party obtains court enforcement of the award, disobedience would be foolhardy. The violator would be guilty of civil or criminal contempt of court and face severe sanctions. In one noteworthy case, a court of appeals affirmed a fine of $100,000 per day levied by a district court against a union in such a situation. *Philadelphia Marine Trade Association v. International Longshoremen's Association, Local 1291* (3d Cir.1966).

## E. REMEDIES

### 1. In General

An arbitrator's broad authority extends to remedies as well as to interpretation. As Justice Douglas put it in Enterprise Wheel,

When an arbitrator is commissioned to interpret and apply the collective bargaining agreement, he is to bring his informed judgment to bear in order to reach a fair solution of a problem. This is especially true when it comes to formulating remedies. There the need is for flexibility in meeting a wide variety of situations. The draftsmen may never have thought of what specific remedy should be awarded to meet a particular contingency.

An arbitrator dealing with a statutory claim has the same remedial powers a judge would have [Appendix C, Rule 32(c); Appendix L, § C.5.]. In fact, the arbitrator's authority may even be greater than a judge's: the UAA states that "the fact that the relief was such that it could not or would not be granted by a court of law or equity is not ground for vacating or refusing to confirm the award." [Appendix K, § 12(a)(5)].

Arbitrators have not hesitated to exercise this power to the fullest. One arbitrator, after finding that the employer breached the contract in transferring work, ordered it at great expense to reverse the earlier decision, return the work and the equipment used to perform it from Arkansas and Colorado to St. Louis, recall laid off employees, and reinstate them with full back pay. A federal court enforced the award in full: *Selb Manufacturing Co. v. IAM, District No. 9* (8th Cir.1962).

The arbitrator's power comes solely from the contract. Parties who fear an inappropriate remedy can easily prevent it. Some contracts simply prohibit certain types of remedies; others specify the remedy to be applied in the event of a certain breach; and still others limit the arbitrator's role to a determination of whether there has in fact been a breach, leaving the selection of a remedy to the parties themselves.

## 2. Discharge Cases

If an arbitrator finds that a discharge was not for just cause, the typical remedy is reinstatement with full seniority and back pay. This is not always the case, however. An arbitrator must consider the alleged misdeeds, the severity of the penalty imposed, and the procedure followed. It is quite common to trim the remedy to find some middle ground.

If an employee did in fact commit the charged offense but the arbitrator believes that discharge was too harsh a penalty, the arbitrator might order conditional reinstatement (thus creating a form of probationary employment) or reinstatement with reduced or no back pay. The arbitrator might believe, for example, that repeated tardiness would justify only a week's suspension and order reinstatement with back pay for the time off work less one week. Or if the union unjustifiably delayed in bringing the case to arbitration, the arbitrator might order reinstatement less pay for the length of the delay.

Arbitrators will generally insist on even-handed administration of discipline—that is, that the employer impose like penalties for like offenses. At the same time, they recognize that there are many valid reasons for distinguishing between employees. If a large number of employees participate in a wildcat strike, for example, discharge of all might not be practical and most arbitrators would therefore uphold discharge of the leaders of the strike but not others. All that the employer must show is that its basis for selection was fair and reasonable.

## 3. Monetary Awards in Non–Discharge Cases

Monetary awards are also the appropriate remedy in many non-disciplinary cases. In general, however, the grievant must show actual loss. In labor arbitration cases, the union may receive only compensatory damages; with rare exceptions discussed below, punitive damages are not available. General damages and punitive damages are more common in individual employment arbitrations because the statutes at issue expressly authorize those remedies. An arbitrator should award no damages when the harm, if any, is too speculative to calculate.

It is sometimes necessary to make rough approximations of the amount of damage. So long as the arbitrator does so in good faith and with some basis in the record, a court will not overturn the award. In *Local 369, Bakery and Confectionery Workers v. Cotton Baking Co.* (5th Cir.1975), the employer wrongly failed to use bargaining unit employees for certain bargaining unit work. The bargaining unit thus lost work but it was impossible to know which workers lost wages. The arbitrator ordered monetary damages to the union in the amount of one year's wages for the job in question, and the Court of Appeals upheld his award.

A few cases awarded monetary damages against unions, usually for breach of a no-strike agreement. This should not be surprising, for such agreements would be useless if the injured employer could not receive compensation. Usually, though, the arbitration agreement allows only unions to file grievances. An employer injured by a union's breach thus has to proceed in court. Normally an employer seeking monetary damages in arbitration will have to prove that the union authorized, participated in, or ratified an illegal strike. When the contract obliges the union to use its best efforts to stop a wildcat strike, however, failure to do so will expose the union to substantial damages.

## 4. Calculation of the Amount of Damages

It is often difficult to determine how much harm the grievant suffered from the other party's breach. The arbitrator need not calculate the exact amount due, so long as the award provides some formula the parties can apply. Usually a general order to reinstate a discharged employee "with full back pay" will suffice, for the parties can calculate the wage rate times the number of lost hours. It is usually safe for an arbitrator to remand the calculation to the parties. That is what the parties commonly expect, so they seldom bother to present evidence on the amount of back pay due the grievant.

There may be situations where a simple remand would not work. If the parties do not have a good relationship, they may quarrel as much over the remedy as over the merits of the case. It may therefore be necessary for the arbitrator to resolve a dispute over the exact amount of back pay due. When the arbitrator thinks that is a possibility, the appropriate action is to render a partial award limited to the merits of the case and the principles controlling the remedy, and to retain jurisdiction to resolve any remaining questions about implementation of the award.

A wrongly discharged employee is entitled to compensation for the harm caused by the employer. Employees are expected to mitigate damages pending the arbitrator's decision. That means seeking work. The normal award will therefore provide back pay less any alternative earnings the employee had following the erroneous discharge. If the employee fails to make a reasonable search for work, or fails to accept available work, the arbitrator may deduct the amount the employee would have earned by exercising due diligence.

There is no simple rule about unemployment compensation. Some arbitrators ignore it entirely, while others (noting that it is the employer, not the employee, who pays for unemployment compensation) will deduct it from the amount of back pay due. The proper decision on unemployment compensation will therefore turn on the particular state law. An employee who cannot work after the discharge is not entitled to back pay when that period of lost income is not attributable to the discharge.

"Back pay" includes vacation pay and holiday pay. In addition, a "make-whole" remedy includes benefits other than wages. An employee who would have been covered by a health plan, would be entitled to reimbursement for medical expenses during the time away from work. Similarly, the employer must make up missed contributions for retirement plans.

Problems of calculation are much greater when the employer seeks damages from the union, for there is typically no simple hourly rate to be applied. Among the standards applied in wrongful strike situations are (a) the average daily "overhead cost," or expenses incident to maintenance of the plant; (b) overhead cost plus the amount of overtime pay needed to catch up on lost production; (c) fair rental value of idle machinery; and (d) loss of profits.

Arbitrators differ over whether they should award interest on back pay awards. Some regard interest as a form of punitive damages, an attitude reinforced by arbitration awards that use interest to punish aggravated or "bad faith" breaches. Other arbitrators believe that parties do not authorize unusual remedies like the award of interest. Properly considered, interest is a form of compensation, not punishment. Interest compensates the injured party for the time-value of money: one loses the value of money for the period of the delay. That is why courts and government agencies routinely award interest in similar situations. There is no reason arbitrators should not do the same.

## 5. Punitive Damages

Arbitrators asked to award punitive damages confront a dilemma of arbitration theory. Punishment and retribution are concepts foreign to the purpose of arbitration—the amicable settlement of disputes. In some cases, though, punitive damages seem be the only incentive the arbitrator can impose to assure future obedience to the contract. The courts have been similarly ambivalent. One early, muchcriticized decision refused to enforce an award of punitive damages, holding that an arbitrator could only award damages a court could award in a contract case. *Publishers' Association of New York City v. Newspaper and Mail Deliverers' Union of New York and Vicinity* (N.Y.1952). Other cases have simply interpreted § 301 to be remedial, not punitive, *e.g., United Shoe Workers, Local 127 v. Brooks Shoe Manufacturing Co.* (3d Cir.1962).

Nevertheless some arbitrators have awarded punitive damages in cases of willful or malicious violations, or where it is impossible to determine the actual damage caused by a serious breach. Some federal courts have enforced such awards, *e.g., Local 416 Sheetmetal Workers International Associa-*

*tion v. Helgesteel Corp.* (W.D.Wis.1971) (relying on broad arbitral power discussed in the *Trilogy*).

In many cases the difference between true compensatory relief and a punitive award may be slender indeed. This is especially true when there has been some harm but the amount is intangible. A rough estimate might be labeled compensatory when it is in reality only an amount selected to punish the wrongdoer.

There is only one area of arbitration in which punitive damages are indisputably proper. Many individual employment arbitrations simply provide an alternative forum for statutory claims. If the underlying claim rests on a statute authorizing punitive damages, the arbitrator may award them just as a judge or jury could.

## 6. Rights Without Remedies

There are a number of situations in which an arbitrator finds a violation but issues no remedy. The most common of these is where the breach is *de minimis* (about trifles), as where a supervisor performs a few minutes of work that should be assigned to a bargaining unit member. Arbitrators should be cautious about applying that doctrine. While the law does not concern itself about trifles, collective bargaining (and, perforce, labor arbitration) does. A minor event may involve a principle of some magnitude (preserving a rigid seniority system or guaranteeing that work will be kept in the bargaining unit, for example). And there is always the therapeutic value of arbitration, a value that would disappear in any case dismissed as trifling. At the very least, the arbitrator should order compliance with the contract, even if no grievant merits a monetary award.

The same is true of cases where the harm is not measurable *(e.g.,* where the employer ignores its obligation to notify the union before taking certain action) or where there is no accurate information as to which employee is entitled to damages *(e.g.,* where at some time during a shift the employer should have called in another employee, but it is uncertain which of many would have been called or available). Even in these cases the arbitrator should issue some remedy such as a cease-and-desist order rather than simply dismiss the grievance. In a few cases parties ask only for a declaration of rights; a monetary award would obviously not be appropriate in such a case.

# CHAPTER IX

# THE PROCESS OF CONTRACTUAL INTERPRETATION

Contract interpretation is the heart of the arbitrator's job. Collective bargaining agreements and individual contracts of employment are contracts, of course. Many of the general rules of contract law and many of the usual principles of contract interpretation apply to those documents as well as to others. However, there are some special elements that arise in the interpretation of labor and employment agreements. This chapter explores the rules governing contract interpretation in labor and employment arbitration. It begins with the subject of precedent: in particular, the legal topics of stare decisis, res judicata, and collateral estoppel. Section B examines issues of substantive and procedural arbitrability. Those issues are interpretive matters because the arbitrator must decide whether the agreement allows the arbitration of the pending matter. Finally, Section C discusses the most important principles of contract interpretation.

## A. THE ROLE OF ARBITRAL PRECEDENT: STARE DECISIS, RES JUDICATA, AND COLLATERAL ESTOPPEL IN LABOR AND EMPLOYMENT ARBITRATION

To understand the influence previous arbitration awards have on a new case, one must first understand three closely related legal concepts, *stare decisis* (literally, "to stand decided"), *res judicata* (literally, "an issue adjudged"), and *collateral estoppel*. Readers seeking a more detailed examination of arbitral precedent should examine Dean Timothy Heinsz's recent article, *Grieve It Again: Of Stare Decisis, Res Judicata, and Collateral Estoppel in Labor Arbitration*, 38 Boston College Law Review 275 (1997), on which this Section relies.

### 1. Legal Concepts of Precedent

*Stare decisis* is simply the application of a previous decision's reasoning to a new case involving similar issues but different parties. Common law courts have adopted the principle of stare decisis to maintain decisional consistency within a jurisdiction. Thus the lower courts of a state must apply the holdings of superior appellate courts. Because labor and employment arbitrators are independent of one another, stare decisis does not apply in arbitration. Every arbitrator is free to accept or reject another arbitrator's principles and practices.

Nevertheless, every dispute resolution mechanism strives toward predictability. The knowledge that neutrals will apply recognized principles serves that goal. Moreover, parties to arbitrations have long accepted certain principles and practices and therefore expect their arbitrators to apply them. As a result, there is a strong tendency among arbitrators to follow at least the most established customs. In a word, arbitral precedent is *persuasive* if not controlling. Subsection 4 examines this phenomenon.

*Res judicata* is better known today as "claim preclusion." This legal doctrine bars a party from relitigating a claim that was (or could have been) raised in a prior case that led to a final judgment if the later action involves the same or closely related parties. A party who lost a case at trial in California, for example, could not raise the same claim in New York.

*Collateral estoppel* is better known today as issue preclusion. This legal doctrine bars a party from relitigating an issue decided in a prior case against that party (or a closely related party) if the forum provided a full and fair opportunity to litigate the issue.

The main difference between the latter two doctrines is that res judicata rests on the finality of judgments while collateral estoppel enforces the prior proceeding's fact finding process. A second difference is that collateral estoppel requires an actual decision on the issue in the first proceeding, while res judicata requires only that the other party had an opportunity to raise the claim.

## 2. Judicial Application of the Legal Concepts in Labor and Employment Arbitration

Some courts have applied res judicata and collateral estoppel in litigation arising out of labor arbitration decisions. A good example is *Action Distributing Co. v. Teamsters Local 1038* (6th Cir.1992), in which the court held that a previous award between the parties barred later court action on any issue that could have been raised in the first arbitration. See also *Rosenbloom v. Mecom* (La.App.1985), holding that an arbitration award rendered by National Football League Commissioner Pete Rozelle barred the plaintiff's cause of action over the same issue, but not his claims on other issues.

It is not clear that those principles bind arbitrators to the same extent as they bind the courts. Flexibility is an essential and welcome attribute of the arbitration process. Strict application of preclusion doctrines would severely limit that flexibility. It would also run afoul of the Supreme Court's direction in the *Steelworkers Trilogy* that federal courts should enforce every arbitration award that draws its essence from the agreement.

The Supreme Court demonstrated that rule in *W. R. Grace & Co. v. Local 759, United Rubber Workers* (S.Ct.1983). A second arbitrator declined to follow the first arbitrator's award in a seniority dispute. The Supreme Court focused only on the enforceability of the second award, concluding that the second arbitrator's decision to ignore the first holding was itself a matter of contract interpretation. Because the second arbitrator's decision drew its essence from the contract, the federal court should have enforced it. In arbitration, then, res judicata is a matter of contract interpretation, not a binding legal principle. At most, the second arbitrator must "consider" the previous award, not follow it. *Trailways Lines, Inc. v. Trailways, Inc. Joint Council* (8th Cir.1986). Factual differences between the earlier and later situations may naturally justify different results, *American National Can Co. v. United Steelworkers of America, Local 3628* (8th Cir.1997).

Inconsistent awards obviously pose a potentially serious problem for the parties. Courts have simply decided to leave that potential problem to the good sense of the arbitrators and parties, rather than constrict the arbitration process. Some courts find that approach intolerable, however. In *Connecticut Light & Power Co. v. Local 420, International Brotherhood of Electrical Workers* (2d Cir.1983), for example, the court held that in such cases the reviewing court should simply "select that interpretation which most nearly conforms to the intent of the parties."

## 3. Arbitral Approaches

Arbitrators differ in their respect for previous awards. All recognize that if the contract specifies the authority of previous awards, arbitrators must accept that determination. Some agreements expressly make previous awards binding; a few expressly state that previous awards (especially awards under expedited proceedings) are not binding. Most arbitration agreements, though, are silent on the question.

Faced with a silent contract, most arbitrators take one of two possible approaches. The majority approach, which Dean Heinsz terms the "incorporation theory," is to treat previous awards as becoming part of the agreement until changed by the parties. The typical agreement provides that awards are "final and binding." They would hardly be so if a later arbitrator could change them. The presumption that the parties intended awards to control their future contractual disputes is strongest when the parties have renegotiated the agreement without changing the first award's interpretation. Failing to give the first award binding effect would put the parties "right back where they were when the dispute first arose," with resolution despite the time and expense of two arbitrations. *Monarch Tile, Inc.* (Hartwell Hooper 1993). Worse, the possibility of turning a loss into a win would only encourage the first losing party to try again.

Even under the incorporation theory, an arbitrator could sometimes decline to follow an earlier award between the same parties over the same issue. In *North American Rayon Corp.* (1990), Arbitrator Jack Clarke summed up the situations where that would be permissible:

(1) the prior decision was an instance of bad judgment, (2) conditions existing at the time of

the prior decision and of the grievance being arbitrated are significantly different, (3) there was not a full and fair hearing at the time of the earlier decision, and (4) the prior decision was made without the benefit of some important facts or considerations.

The minority approach, termed by Dean Heinsz the "independent judgment principle," asserts that the parties want their arbitrators to decide each case regardless of other arbitrators' opinions. In *Hercules, Inc.*, (Robert Williams 1992), the arbitrator rejected Arbitrator Clarke's incorporation theory. Arbitrator Williams declined to follow two previous awards that he regarded as incorrect, stating that "erroneous awards promote instability, not stability."

## 4. Persuasive Authority

Past arbitration awards are not legally binding on an arbitrator no matter how similar they might be to the instant situation, parties and issues. They may carry some influence, however. The purpose of this subsection is to explore the nature and extent of this influence.

Many commentators deplore the very notion of arbitral precedent. To them it smacks of rigid legalism, of a slavish adherence to past decisions that becomes an end in itself to the detriment of flexibility, informality and even justice. They fear that if the doctrine gains a foothold, it will develop into an exaggerated form of stare decisis, with far less justification for its existence in arbitration than in the courts of law.

Notwithstanding this criticism, most arbitrators and parties do make some use of past awards. The body of published awards represents the accumulated experience and wisdom of thousands of arbitrators, and careful use of that accumulation can assist the parties and the arbitrator alike. Frequent interpretation of contract language enables parties to use such language in their agreements with reasonable assurance that in the future the language will mean what it meant in the past. This helps to stabilize employment relations and to discourage frivolous grievances. The body of precedent also guides arbitrators in later cases by providing statements of prevailing rules, standards and meanings. The arbitrator who looks to a settled course of arbitral precedent for guidance will find the job easier, may benefit from views not presented at the hearing, and should be confident that the opinion will not come as a terrible shock to either party.

The usefulness of any prior award will of course depend on its inherent logic and fairness and on the similarity of its terms and facts to those of the later case. Precedential force is always a matter of degree controlled by those factors. Keeping this in mind, it is possible to distinguish between "authoritative" awards, which possess a high degree of influence on later cases, and "persuasive" awards, which are helpful but not in any sense controlling.

The most authoritative award is one in which the parties, contract language, issues, and facts are similar to the later case, and in which the arbitrator rendered a clear and logical interpretation. Few arbitrators would depart from such a precedent, even when they might have reached a different result had they heard the first case. Where there are conflicting awards, awards with no supporting opinions, or mere dicta in opinions on other issues, there is no such precedent. The arbitrator is free to blaze a new path.

Authoritativeness decreases when any of those factors is missing. A change in parties, for example, undercuts the authoritative nature of earlier awards even if the language and facts are identical. If a company and union borrow some or all of a contract recently negotiated by other parties, an arbitration decision in a dispute in the first plant would not necessarily control a case arising at the second, for each pair of parties might have adopted the language with different intentions. Where one of the parties is the same, as in the case of a new employer signing a master contract previously negotiated by the union with other employers, the newcomer might well be bound by existing arbitral construction of that contract. The very purpose of a master contract is to guarantee similarity in the terms and conditions of employment; most arbitrators would therefore be very hesitant to force inconsistent results on different employers.

A prior award also carries less weight if the challenging party can show that it was clearly erroneous or that applying it to the new case would be unfair. If the earlier opinion reveals flagrant bias or bad judgment, no arbitrator would feel compelled to follow it. If the prior award was made without the benefit of crucial facts, its authority is suspect. If conditions have changed so substantially that continued adherence would be unreasonable, a different ruling might be expected. Absent such an unusual claim, most arbitrators hesitate to upset a well-established rule where the parties themselves have not chosen to do so.

All other awards are more or less persuasive, but not authoritative. A settled course of arbitral decision on a recurring issue, such as whether certain conduct constitutes just cause for discharge, is likely to influence arbitrators, although the weight of the precedent may stem more from the inherent logic of the position than from its frequent repetition. In less settled areas, the weight of a particular opinion will depend on the similarity of language and situation and on the logic and equity of the opinion.

## B. THE ARBITRATION CLAUSE AND ITS MEANING: ARBITRABILITY FROM THE ARBITRATOR'S POINT OF VIEW

### 1. Substantive Arbitrability

A "standard" arbitration clause covers disputes over the "interpretation or application" of the collective or individual contract of employment. A "broad" arbitration clause usually applies to "any dispute." Standard clauses usually (and broad clauses often) contain an additional sentence like the following: "The arbitrator shall have no authority to add to, subtract from, or modify the provisions of this agreement." The following discussion of substantive arbitrability assumes the existence of a standard clause with no specific inclusions or exclusions, both because standard clauses are more common and because they produce more substantive arbitrability disputes.

As noted above, the Supreme Court has consistently held that questions of substantive arbitrability are for the courts to determine, even if the judge's only function is the superficial investigation of whether a particular dispute is "on its face" subject to the arbitration clause. As also noted above, though, arbitrators do in fact decide substantive arbitrability issues. Some contracts specify that arbitrability questions are for the arbitrator. In other cases, the parties as a matter of choice raise arbitrability questions in arbitration rather than litigation. In still other cases, arbitrators may rule anew on arbitrability after a court has determined that the contract "on its face" provides for arbitration of the dispute.

Thus it is important to know how arbitrators react to claims that a particular issue is not arbitrable. For purposes of this discussion, the realm of labor relations issues arguably subject to arbitration can be divided into three categories: (a) issues involving the type and number of jobs and employees covered by the agreement; (b) issues involving the level or amount of contract wages or benefits; and (c) issues involving the range of subjects with which the agreement concerns itself.

**(a) *Issues Involving the Type and Number of Jobs and Employees Covered by the Agreement.*** This category includes the most fundamental aspect of the employment relationship, the connection between work and workers. Arbitrators generally find those issues arbitrable, for the whole employment agreement would be illusory if an employer could separate workers from their work without having to demonstrate a strong justification.

Subcontracting, for example, could eliminate the bargaining unit if carried to an extreme. On the other hand, some subcontracting decisions produce no measurable effects on the bargaining unit. For example, the subcontracting at issue might be trivial or might concern work the bargaining unit employees are not capable of performing. In the absence of an express contractual restriction on subcontracting, the union must show at least that subcontracting impairs substantial rights established elsewhere in the agreement. (In order to prevail on the merits, the union might also have to show that the employer took the challenged actions chiefly to avoid those other obligations.)

The obvious example of an arbitrable subcontracting issue even without a specific subcontracting clause is the total subcontracting of all bargaining unit work to a non-union plant. Less obvious but still arbitrable cases include subcontracting simply to avoid paying contractual wages or overtime, or to escape union work rules. By contrast, subcontracting of major construction work never previously performed by bargaining unit members would not impair the wages or benefits clauses of the collective bargaining agreement and would not be arbitrable in the absence of a specific requirement to that effect.

Arbitrators also usually interpret a standard arbitration clause to cover disputes over whether certain employees are within the bargaining unit (even though the National Labor Relations Board has legal jurisdiction over representation disputes) and disputes over whether certain jobs constitute bargaining unit work. Both types of cases involve interpretation of the recognition clause. It would be difficult in most such cases to argue that the recognition clause was so clear as to make the dispute inarbitrable.

Termination disputes are the most difficult cases in this category. The vast majority of collective bargaining agreements contain some limitation on discharges, usually of the "just cause" variety. If a contract does *not* contain such a clause, is the employer free to discharge at will? As with the subcontracting cases, allegations of employer intent to evade other contract provisions, such as seniority, vacation pay, or pension obligations, raise clearly arbitrable issues. Absent such an allegation, arbitrators differ on arbitrability. Some take the view that termination is so fundamental an issue that limitations on management action in this regard are implied in *all* collective bargaining agreements. That assumption is a two-edged sword, however: if just cause is such a fundamental issue, wouldn't the parties mention it? If they did not, the contractual silence may have been intentional, and thus the arbitrator has no business amending the agreement.

**(b) *Issues Involving the Level or Amount of Contract Wages or Benefits.*** This category includes two types of cases calling for different presumptions about arbitrability. The first type, grievances demanding a change in the general structure of wages or benefits, or in the standards used to determine them, is generally not arbitrable. Arbitrators have no authority to rewrite the terms of a contract. One exception to this general statement involves "wage-reopener" provisions. These are clauses that allow a party to reopen negotiations at a certain time for the limited purpose of adjusting wage levels. Some wage-reopeners call for arbitration if the parties are unable to agree on the new wages.

The second type is quite different. When the question is the *application* rather than the *creation* of a wage structure, most arbitrators will take jurisdiction. Looked at differently, this type of dispute is a standard, garden-variety interpretation question and there is no reason to deny arbitrability.

***(c) Issues Involving the Range of Subjects with Which the Contract Concerns Itself.*** Falling within this category are matters that are normally the subject of negotiation such as hours, job descriptions, and seniority. As a general rule the *existence* of such rights is not arbitrable, but once established by negotiation their *application* is subject to arbitration.

For example, an arbitrator is unlikely to rule on the merits of a union demand for seniority rights where none existed previously, or on the merits of a claim for extension of existing seniority rights to cover new types of decisions. However, if the grievance alleges that the employer improperly calculated an individual's seniority or did not follow negotiated seniority rules, the dispute will almost certainly be held arbitrable.

The same principle applies in another area. Absent some specific contractual limitation, complaints about changes in the *job process*, such as introduction or discontinuance of product lines or mechanization of a job formerly done by hand, will not be arbitrable. A simple change in the speed at which some task is to be performed or the addition of duties to an existing job may well be arbitrable, however.

Similarly, while most arbitrators would not take jurisdiction over a grievance seeking to create a new benefit such as severance pay, most would find arbitrable a grievant's claim that the employer must respect some "vested" benefit such as vacation pay. Arbitrators will not create new rights because the typical contract limits their authority to interpreting the existing agreement.

**(d) *Summary*.** Arbitrators will usually find arbitrable grievances involving (i) the interpretation or application of terms included in the collective bargaining agreement; (ii) alleged violations of a definite and clear past practice; and, less certainly, (iii) items that, if held not to be arbitrable, might impair or negate a substantial right established in the agreement. Arbitrators will generally find inarbitrable (i) disputes over subjects not covered in the collective bargaining agreement or in a definite and clear past practice, if the parties' silence on the point seems to be deliberate; and (ii) complaints over impasses in matters subject to negotiation.

## 2. Procedural Arbitrability

Although the Supreme Court gave the federal courts ultimate authority over questions of substantive arbitrability, it left procedural arbitrability issues in the hands of the arbitrator: "Once it is determined ... that the parties are obligated to submit the subject matter of a dispute to arbitration, 'procedural' questions which grow out of the dispute and bear on its final disposition should be left to the arbitrator." *John Wiley & Sons, Inc. v. Livingston* (S.Ct.1964). That division of labor, said the Court, "best accords with the usual purposes of an arbitration clause and with the policy behind federal labor law to regard procedural disagreements not as separate disputes but as aspects of the dispute which called the grievance procedures into play." The number of procedural defects a party may cite to deny a grievance's arbitrability is almost endless, but discussion of the two most common should illustrate arbitrators' reactions to such claims.

**(a) *Time Limitations.*** Many contracts establish precise time limits on the filing or processing of a grievance and on the demand for and completion of arbitration. Other contracts have more flexible provisions. There is good reason to believe that a rule of reasonableness, akin to the equitable doctrine of laches, applies to all agreements.

A breach of a clear time limitation usually makes a grievance inarbitrable, however strong the case might be on the merits. In part this simply represents the will of the parties, who must have meant "ten days" if they said "ten days." In part, it also recognizes that an effective dispute resolution procedure requires quick and efficient processing of grievances. An arbitrator who ignores agreed time limits weakens the very process those rules were created to protect.

But "the law abhors forfeitures," as the legal maxim goes, and so do arbitrators. As a result, they eagerly look for reasons to find a dispute arbitrable despite a late filing or processing. Some exceptions are obvious, for example fraud. If one party deliberately gets the other to delay action until the time limitation passes, and then refuses to proceed with the grievance process, it may lose its right to insist on application of the contractual limits. A similarly obvious exception involves an express or implied waiver. If the parties have routinely ignored the contractual time limits, or have routinely granted extensions of time to one another, that practice may amount to an implied waiver of the right to demand strict application of the deadlines.

A less obvious exception is the "continuing violation" theory. Some (but by no means all) arbitrators believe that alleged breaches with continuous or recurring effects give rise to a new grievance with every application. For example, if an employer erroneously placed an employee in a low pay grade, the continuing violation theory would allow a grievance after any payday, even long after the original error. Other arbitrators doubt the fairness of the theory. Taken broadly, it would make all wage grievances arbitrable no matter how long the individual or union waited to file a grievance.

Time limits pose several interpretive problems. The biggest is in deciding the event that "triggers" the obligation to file a grievance. Does the clock start running as soon as the employer breaches the agreement, when the grievant or union first learns about it, or when they *should* have learned of it? If the agreement is silent, is a grievance timely even years after the alleged violation?

In *Methodist Hospital* (Mario Bognanno 1990), the employer unilaterally raised the wage rates of casual employees to the level of regular employees in May of 1998. Two months later, it reinstated a differential by raising wages for regular employees. The arbitrator found that the union knew of the May adjustment and should have known of the July change, but failed to grieve until the following year. Arbitrator Bognanno ruled that the union's knowledge or "constructive" knowledge (that is, facts of which a party should have been aware) triggered the contract's 30–day filing period. Because wage grievances create a new injury with each paycheck, however, the arbitrator applied the continuing violation theory and allowed the grievance. Nevertheless, he noted that delays in bringing a grievance may limit the appropriate remedy.

The continuing violation theory is less powerful when the alleged breach seems to be a one-time error (such as an erroneous layoff), even if that error produces lasting effects. See, for example, *Centel Business Systems* (Hy Fish 1987). Most employer policies are intended to have a continuing effect. Must the union file a grievance immediately, or may it wait until the employer first applies the policy? Arbitrator John Caraway ruled that a grievance is timely "at any time during the continuance of an ongoing policy," *Gulf South Beverages, Inc.* (1986). Other arbitrators disagree. A union *need* not wait for a specific application if it could object to the employer's authority to adopt the questioned policy or to the facial validity of the policy. In such a case, the clock might start running when the employer first announces the policy. *Nashville Gas Co.* (Dennis R. Nolan 1991). Of course, the union would be free to challenge the application of the policy in a given case, even if it has lost the right to challenge the policy's validity.

A common law doctrine known as *laches* bars assertion of a claim after an unreasonable delay, especially if the other party has changed its position in the meantime. In effect, the doctrine imposes a waiver on the tardy party. Arbitrators split over the applicability of the doctrine to labor and employment arbitration. Some hold that a party injured by an alleged breach must act within a reasonable time even if the contract imposes no time limitations. Others believe that a party should be free to raise an alleged breach at any time, unless the contract provides otherwise.

In *Dresser Industries* (Samuel J. Nicholas 1991), an arbitrator found timely a grievance over elimination of certain jobs and shifting of work outside the bargaining unit, even though the union waited ten years to file. The issue, Arbitrator Nicholas found, remained "open" throughout the decade. Like many other arbitrators, he hesitated to allow a "technical procedural defect" to "foreclose the review of a matter on its merits where the alleged flaw is [neither] acceded to nor acquiesced in by the opposing party and when no real prejudice is done to the subject party."

*(b) Changed Issues.* Suppose a union files a grievance alleging that the employer improperly assigned work to non-unit personnel, but at the arbitration hearing argues instead that those per-

sons are actually members of the unit who deserve the higher pay the contract provides. May the arbitrator decide the new issue?

Most arbitrators would not do so, absent a stipulation by both parties. Normally the arbitrator may decide only those issues raised in the grievance process. To do otherwise would give the grieving party unfair advantage over the other, because it will come prepared to argue an issue that may be a complete surprise to the other. Moreover, allowing a party to introduce a new issue at the hearing would weaken the grievance procedure itself. That in turn would give the parties an incentive to withhold until the hearing matters they might have been able to settle during the grievance procedure. The grievance form filled out on the shop floor need not read like a legal pleading, but each party is entitled to know before the arbitration hearing the essential claims and evidence on which the other relies. The best course of action for an arbitrator faced with an arbitrability objection to a new issue is to sustain the objection. The injured party may then be able to file a separate grievance over the new matter.

## C. PRINCIPLES OF INTERPRETATION

Apart from deciding questions of fact, the arbitrator's primary task is interpretation. The arbitrator must determine just what the parties meant when they adopted certain language, or how they would have intended their language to be applied in specific circumstances. Standardized contract language and a desire for predictability have caused arbitrators to follow a number of general principles of interpretation in fulfilling this task.

One should use these principles cautiously. The distinguished American Legal Realist Karl Llewellyn suggested a half century ago, perhaps with tongue in cheek, that every canon of interpretation had an equal and opposite canon. *Remarks on the Theory of Appellate Decision and the Rules or Canons About How Statutes Are to be Construed*, 3 Vanderbilt Law Review 395 (1950). More recently, Justice Antonin Scalia argued that Llewellyn was off base and that most of his "opposites" were merely limitations on the basic canon. A Matter of Interpretation: Federal Courts and the Law 25–29 (1997). In any event, principles are just that: guidelines, subject to variation in application. The reader looking for a detailed treatment of contract interpretation should read Jay E. Grenig, *Contract Interpretation and Respect for Prior Proceedings*, I Labor and Employment Arbitration Chapter 9 (Tim Bornstein, Ann Gosline, and Marc Greenbaum, eds., 2d ed. 1997).

## 1. If the Relevant Language is Clear and Unambiguous, the Arbitrator Should Apply It Without Recourse to Other Indications of Intent

This is of course simply a restatement of the "plain meaning" rule discussed in Chapter VIII. It belongs in this section as well because it functions as a rule of interpretation as well as one of admissibility. The cautions about the plain meaning rule expressed in the previous chapter apply here as well. Contract interpreters recognize that words are far more slippery than we once thought them to be. As a result, latent ambiguities—where the language itself seems clear but some extrinsic fact suggests another meaning—are easier to prove. An arbitrator must at least consider all the offered evidence on the preliminary question of whether the language at issue is truly "unambiguous." Before relying on the plain meaning rule, therefore, an advocate should reread Carlton Snow's definitive article, *Contract Interpretation: The Plain Meaning Rule in Labor Arbitration*, 55 Fordham Law Review 681 (1987).

Once the arbitrator has found that there is no patent or latent ambiguity, the next step follows as a matter of course: the arbitrator must apply the contract as the parties intended.

## 2. The Sounds of Silence: Interpretation Without Specific Language

Arbitrators frequently face difficult questions of interpretation arising from issues the contract does not address. Two principles help to resolve many of these questions:

***(a) Evidence of a Consistent Past Practice May Fill in Gaps and Supplement the Written Agreement***. An arbitrator may not change the parties' agreement, but the parties themselves are free to do so. Often they do so through their practices rather than through formal amendments. When, as discussed in Chapter VIII, there is proof that the parties have so amended their agreement—where a supplementary practice is clear, well-established, and mutually understood to be an accepted application—the arbitrator may use it as an interpretive aid. Some arbitrators have even used an accepted past practice to contradict apparently unambiguous language.

*(b) Management Retains all Rights Not Limited by the Agreement.* Usually termed the "reserved rights doctrine," this principle is embodies the argument that, because the employer possessed all rights to run the business before the union came on the scene, it must still possess those the union did not succeed in limiting. If this were not so, the argument goes, it would mean either that all former management rights passed silently to the union or that they simply disappeared; neither possibility is very reasonable. This principle is still the subject of some dispute in the arbitration community. One counter to the reserved rights doctrine is the "implied obligations" theory—that is, the assertion that unionization of an employer's workforce by itself imposes certain obligations on the employer.

Most arbitrators follow some form of the reserved rights doctrine, usually with a few qualifications. One such qualification is an implied "good faith" or "fair dealing" obligation, which simply recognizes that an employer may not use reserved rights to destroy others specified in the contract. An employer could not use a reserved right to subcontract in a manner that would abolish the bargaining unit, for example, or use its disciplinary power simply to avoid paying a negotiated pension.

A second important qualification is that the reserved rights principle applies only when there is no applicable contract provision. It does not limit the application of general language to specific cases. A general seniority clause may or may not require distribution of new equipment to the most senior employees first, but whether it does depends not on the reserved rights principle but on the interpretation of the seniority clause itself. A third qualification is that a binding past practice can limit reserved rights unless the contract provides otherwise.

## 3. Arbitrators Should Avoid Interpretations that Would Bring the Contract Into Conflict With Positive Law

We turn now to the interpretation of ambiguous language. The following principles do not appear in order of importance, but surely this is one of the first that ought to be applied. The earlier discussion of individual employment arbitration (Section IV. E.) considered some of the potential problems involved in arbitral decisions on statutory questions. There is no need to repeat that discussion here, for this rule of interpretation applies only in case of a recognized conflict with some legal requirement. Where one interpretation would force that conflict and another would avoid it, the prudent arbitrator should adopt the latter view, absent compelling evidence that the parties intended the former.

This principle rests on a presumption few people would question, that parties to contracts intend their agreements to be legal, if only to make them legally enforceable. Because no court will enforce an award ordering a party to violate the law, it would be unreasonable to assume that the parties would have wanted such an award.

## 4. Specific Language Controls General Language

"Specific language" refers to a provision covering a particular named category of persons or events. The principle simply holds that when such a provision potentially conflicts with general language that would apply to the disputed issue only by implication or extension, the parties presumably intended the specific provision to govern the case. Even specific language can be ambiguous, however, and therefore might require further interpretation.

## 5. Arbitrators Should Construe Ambiguous Language in Context

There would be no point in pulling a provision out of the contract and ignoring the rest of the document. An employment agreement is an interrelated, functioning entity; each clause should function as a part of that entity.

From this observation two more precise rules follow. First, the arbitrator should interpret each clause to make it compatible with the rest of the agreement. This means avoiding an interpretation that would nullify some other provision. If the parties wanted to nullify the other provision, they would hardly have included it in their contract. Put differently, the arbitrator should always interpret contracts to give effect to all their parts.

Second, the context may limit general language. For example, if a sentence providing that "seniority shall be applied in all cases where the most senior employee has the ability to do the work" appears in an article dealing with recalls to work after a layoff, the arbitrator should not apply the quoted phrase to promotions or other matters.

## 6. Arbitrators Should Give Words Their Normal Meaning Absent Proof that the Parties Intended Some Other Meaning

This principle is important but easily misunderstood. It simply states the assumption that people normally use words with their standard meaning in mind; if they have a special or technical meaning in mind, they will normally indicate that intention. Dictionaries and standard reference books are the best sources of common meanings. One implicit qualification of this rule is that the normal meaning should not produce unreasonable consequences. If it does, that fact itself may give good reason to believe that the parties intended the language in a special sense that would produce more reasonable results.

On the other hand, arbitrators should assume that parties use trade and technical terms with their trade or technical meanings in mind, at least unless there is clear evidence that they intended another meaning. A technical dictionary is just as appropriate for finding a technical definition as a general dictionary is for finding the ordinary meaning of a term.

## 7. Arbitrators Should Construe Ambiguous Language Against the Drafter

This principle of interpretation is to be used with great care, preferably only when no other rule of construction provides a satisfactory result. It rests on the belief that drafters can more easily prevent mistakes and should therefore bear the risks of their own ambiguity. Even leaving aside the occasional difficulty in determining whether one side can properly be termed the drafter of language both agreed to, there is another difficulty with the principle. Many interpretive problems arise in unforeseeable circumstances. Often it would be unfair to penalize a drafter for lacking superhuman perspicacity. That is why other principles of interpretation should be tried first. If all else fails, placing the burden on the drafter is probably a little fairer than tossing a coin.

## 8. Arbitrators Should Avoid Interpretations that Would Create a Forfeiture

Parties typically provide for a forfeiture (the loss of a right as a penalty for some fault) with some specificity. They often list the only conditions that would cause an employee to forfeit seniority, for example. Similarly, when they want a failure to comply with procedural steps in the grievance process to work a forfeiture of the right to arbitrate, their contract will usually say so in relatively clear terms.

It follows from this that arbitrators should not impose a forfeiture unless the parties' intent is clear or no other interpretation is reasonable. Several things could make the intent clear: explicit language, of course, or a consistent past practice ratified by readoption of general language. The context might also give such an indication. Prompt and efficient operation of the grievance and arbitration process is so important to most parties that a decision maker could reasonably assume they want filing deadlines followed strictly. Other steps of the process are not so crucial to efficient handling of grievances and are often held not to work forfeitures. If a union has taken a grievance through the four specified steps of the grievance procedure and timely demanded arbitration, for example, a day's delay in appointing its own member of the arbitration panel would probably not cause it to lose the right to arbitrate.

## 9. Arbitrators Should Avoid Interpretations that Would Produce Harsh, Absurd or Nonsensical Results, if Another Interpretation Would Lead to Just and Reasonable Results

The parties may occasionally provide for harsh penalties in a contract. A serious attendance problem in a plant might lead to a contract clause providing discharge for continued absences or to a clause prohibiting the arbitrator from modifying a penalty imposed by the employer. Arbitrators obviously must follow such clear intentions. Absent evidence of such clear intentions, it is more reasonable to assume that the parties did not expect their agreement to be unduly harsh. It is even less likely that they intended absurd or nonsensical results.

Thus when one possible interpretation would lead to harshness or absurdity, and another to justice and rationality, arbitrators naturally adopt the latter. This does not mean the arbitrator may amend any agreement to make it more just or reasonable; it simply provides guidance for exercising a choice when the agreement itself admits of several possibilities.

# CHAPTER X

# THE SUBJECT MATTER OF LABOR AND EMPLOYMENT ARBITRATION

Arbitration's subjects are as broad as the employment relationship itself. Collective and individual employment contracts can deal with the entire range of employment issues, from hiring to firing, including wages, fringe benefits, hours, work loads, job security, safety, and much more. The following pages provide only brief introductions to the most important subjects of arbitration.

## A. DISCIPLINE AND DISCHARGE

Discipline and discharge matters form the single largest group of arbitration cases, probably because the stakes are so high when a job is at risk. Protection against unjust discharge represents a marked departure from the employment-at-will doctrine that governs most employment relationships. These cases comprise nearly half of the typical arbitrator's work. In general, discipline cases are more fact-specific than many other arbitrations, because the controlling contract terms (like the requirement of "just cause") are too vague to provide much help.

## 1. The Just Cause Principle

Virtually all collective bargaining agreements, and many individual contracts of employment, provide that the employer may discipline the employee only for "just cause" (or some similar term). Although that phrase lacks detail, labor arbitrators have explicated it in tens of thousands of arbitration awards.

One important attempt to provide tangible guidelines was Arbitrator Carroll Daugherty's enumeration in *Grief Brothers Cooperage Corp.* (1964), and *Enterprise Wire Co.* (1966), of "seven tests" of just cause. He posed those tests as seven questions:

1. Did the company give to the employee forewarning or foreknowledge of the possible or probable disciplinary consequences of the employee's conduct?

2. Was the company's rule or managerial order reasonably related to (a) the orderly, efficient, and safe operation of the company's business and (b) the performance that the company might properly expect of the employee?

3. Did the company, before administering discipline to an employee, make an effort to discover whether the employee did in fact violate or disobey a rule or order of management?

4. Was the company's investigation conducted fairly and objectively?

5. At the investigation, did the "judge" obtain substantial evidence or proof that the employee was guilty as charged?

6. Has the company applied its rules, orders, and penalties evenhandedly and without discrimination to all employees?

7. Was the degree of discipline administered by the company in a particular case reasonably related to (a) the seriousness of the employee's proven offense and (b) the record of the employee in his service with the company?

Daugherty demanded an affirmative answer to each question before he would find an employer's disciplinary decision to be "just."

Although widely used by arbitrators, Daugherty's formulation has drawn withering criticism. In a paper delivered at the 1989 meeting of the National Academy of Arbitrators, for instance, Arbitrator Jack Dunsford recognized the usefulness of the seven tests "as an introduction to an academic discussion of just cause in the classroom, or a schematic for organizing a textbook or commentary," but asserted that

> as agenda for resolving disputes in arbitration, the tests are in my judgment misleading in substance and distracting in application. Worse yet, they assume controversial positions with regard to the role of the arbitrator without frankly addressing the value judgments they embody.

*Arbitral Discretion: The Tests of Just Cause*, 42 Proceedings of the National Academy of Arbitrators 23, 28 (1990). For example, Daugherty imposed out of nowhere a requirement that employers conduct pre-disciplinary investigations using only an official unconnected with the events at issue. In Daugherty's view, the arbitrator sat as a sort of "appellate court" over a managerial "trial court." That limited role contrasts with the normal expectation of parties and arbitrators alike that the arbitrator is to be a fact-finder. Moreover, Daugherty's tests are simplistically mechanical; they take no account of the flexibility needed in real world employment relations.

Dunsford attributes Daugherty's idiosyncratic view of arbitration to his work as a referee in Railway Labor Act cases. Unlike normal grievance arbitrators, RLA referees rely on documents and oral arguments without hearing witnesses or conducting other types of investigations. Whatever the merits of the seven tests in that environment, they are of limited use in other types of arbitration.

A more recent effort to construct a theory of just cause appears in a 1985 article by Roger Abrams and Dennis Nolan, *Toward a Theory of "Just Cause" in Employee Discipline Cases*, 1985 Duke Law Journal 594. The authors start with the concept of the "fundamental understanding" that marks every employment relationship:

> both parties realize that the employer must pay the agreed wages and benefits and that the em-

ployee must do "satisfactory" work. "Satisfactory" work, in this context, has four elements: (1) regular attendance, (2) obedience to reasonable work rules, (3) a reasonable quantity and quality of work, and (4) avoidance of any conduct that would interfere with the employer's ability to operate the business successfully.

The parties use the disciplinary process as one tool for the implementation of this bargain. Employers have at least three legitimate reasons for disciplining employees: rehabilitation, deterrence, and protection of profitability. Employees in turn have a legitimate desire for fairness in the procedure, including a proper allocation of the burden of proof (in labor arbitration cases, employers bear that burden, while in most individual statutory arbitrations, employees must prove the discipline improper) and other procedural rules; in assuring consistent treatment of similar cases; and in providing for consideration of mitigating factors. In short, disciplinary fairness requires "industrial due process," "industrial equal protection," and individualized treatment.

Theoretical formulations can help an advocate or arbitrator analyze a specific case, but they cannot eliminate the difficult task of judgment. As Dunsford puts it,

> That is, of course, always the rub: the recognition of that unvarnished element of discretionary judgment that the arbitrator must often bring to bear in a particular case, when the rules from

whatever source do not relieve the sharp and nagging uncertainty that surrounds a critical factor in a dispute. In order to perform the job honestly and effectively, the arbitrator is forced to go into uncharted terrain where rules do not reach.

## 2. Common Reasons for Discipline and Requirements for Just Cause

What reasons constitute just cause for discipline? Obviously there are some offenses universally recognized as serious enough to warrant discipline, even to the point of discharge for a first offense: physical assault, sabotage, theft, major dishonesty, flagrant insubordination, and so on. So basic are the reasons for prohibiting such conduct that most arbitrators do not even require employers to have a formal rule against it. In most other situations (for example attendance problems, inadequacies in quantity or quality of work, difficulty in working with supervisors, employees, or customers), just cause requires the employer to have and publicize an appropriate rule and to use "corrective discipline" before discharging an employee. "Corrective discipline" is a near-synonym for "progressive discipline," meaning that the employer should gradually increase penalties for subsequent offenses. The purposes of those requirements are to provide the employee with ample warning and full opportunity to correct problems.

A good example is *EG & G Mound Applied Technologies*. (Langdon Bell 1992). The employer, who operated a nuclear research facility for the Department of Energy, fired an employee for tampering with a safety system. The employee was annoyed by the "Muzak" played over the public address system and unplugged his unit at least once and turned down the volume on other occasions. The employer's disciplinary policy provided authorized discharge only for "continuing" poor performance or unacceptable behavior. The policy emphasized "corrective, rather than punitive action" except in the case of violation of serious work rules.

The arbitrator recognized the seriousness of the grievant's offense but found discharge improper because the employer failed to warn the employee that his conduct could lead to discharge and did not deal with similar tampering that occurred when the grievant was not present. "The penalty here imposed was either an over-reaction, or alternatively used as a stringent example so as to deter others from such conduct." The arbitrator reinstated the grievant but, because of the seriousness of the offense, he denied the employee back pay.

Just cause also requires an employer to consider aggravating and mitigating circumstances. In *Kaiser Permanente (Sunset Medical Office)* (Martin Henner 1992), the arbitrator reduced a discharge for serious absenteeism to a suspension without back pay because of the employee's long record of otherwise satisfactory service and because the absences stemmed from medical problems rather than from the employee's own fault.

### 3. Off–Duty Conduct

One of the knottiest issues in the just cause area involves conduct off the employer's premises on the employee's own time. However reprehensible an employee's off-duty conduct might be, employers are not society's chosen enforcers. As Yale Law Dean Harry Shulman held in an opinion while he was the designated umpire for Ford Motor Company and the United Auto Workers, "what the employee does outside the plant after working hours is normally no concern of the employer," *Ford Motor Co.* (1944). An employer has a legitimate interest in off-duty conduct only when that conduct in some way affects the enterprise. Arbitrators therefore insist that the employer prove some connection, or "nexus," between the conduct and the employer's business interests. For an extensive discussion of these issues, see Marvin F. Hill, Jr., and James A. Wright, Employee Lifestyle and Off–Duty Conduct Regulation (BNA 1993).

The required nexus can take any of several forms. Some conduct might have a direct impact on the employer, such as an after-work and off-premises attack on a supervisor resulting from a work-related dispute. Similarly, an employee's public criticism of the employer or its products may take place away from work but have very direct adverse effects on the business.

Other conduct may have a less obvious (perhaps only a potential) impact on the business. An employee who uses drugs immediately before work, for example, endangers lives while at work. An employee arrested for a serious crime may bring the employer into disrepute if the media mentions the place of employment. Some crimes, for example off-duty child abuse by a child care worker, may cast sufficient doubt on an employee's suitability for the job as to justify discharge even without proof of actual harm to the employer. Other employees or customers may refuse to deal with a particularly notorious employee.

In all these cases, the employee's off-duty conduct may justify discipline. In many other cases, it will not. In *Champion International* (Gordon Statham 1991), the arbitrator refused to sustain the grievance of an employee fired after a felony conviction for unlawful distribution of controlled substances. The negotiated Rules for Employee Conduct authorized discharge for a violation of civil or criminal law that "reflects unfavorably upon the Company, other employees, or upon the employee involved." The arbitrator found that the grievant's involvement with drugs was minimal and that the conviction had no effect on the business. Because the employer failed to establish the necessary nexus between the conduct and the employer's business interests, the arbitrator reinstated the employee. Strangely, though, the arbitrator denied back pay.

## B. MANAGEMENT RIGHTS

The theoretical framework of the management rights issue involves the two contradictory positions discussed in Chapter IX, the "reserved rights" and "implied obligations" doctrines. The practical framework involves the conflicting goals of management (organizational flexibility and efficiency) and of unions (chiefly job security, but also including predictability of managerial behavior). See generally, Marvin Hill, Jr., and Anthony Sinicropi, Management Rights: A Legal and Arbitral Analysis (BNA 1986).

A typical management rights clause in a collective bargaining agreement empowers the employer to hire, fire, and discipline employees, to decide the methods of production, to establish and change reasonable work rules, and so on. A strong management rights clause incorporates the reserved rights doctrine. It could do so by guaranteeing the specified managerial rights and all others not expressly limited by other provisions of the agreement. Many assertions of management rights in arbitration are merely glosses on other issues. For example, an employer defending a discharge decision may point to a portion of the management rights clause allowing it to discipline employees "for just cause." The critical dispute in such cases centers on the meaning of "just cause," not the meaning of "management rights."

The most common arbitration case presenting serious management rights issues involves an employer's change of working conditions or work rules. Under a contract allowing the employer to "establish necessary reasonable rules" and obliging it to "provide safe and clean working conditions," one employer banned smoking in the work place. Because the employer demonstrated business harms from employee smoking (higher absenteeism and lower productivity among smokers), the arbitrator found that the new rule was reasonable and was therefore permitted by the agreement. *Worthington Foods, Inc.* (Bruce McIntosh 1987).

Another employer, whose management rights clause merely authorized it to "manage its plant," unilaterally adopted a similar rule in even more pressing circumstances: the employer's products used asbestos, and smokers who work with asbestos are far more likely than non-smokers to develop lung cancer. Despite the medical justification for the no-smoking rule, the arbitrator found that the agreement did not allow the employer to adopt it unilaterally. *Nicolet Industries, Inc.* (Eli Rock 1978).

One important lesson from cases like these is that a vague statement of management rights carries no more weight than a platitude, while a specific and strong management rights clause can reserve a great deal of authority to management.

## C. SENIORITY

Seniority clauses are second only to just cause provisions in most unions' bargaining objectives. "Seniority" refers to an employee's length of service with an employer or industry, in a plant or department, or in a given job. Seniority in the abstract is meaningless. It becomes valuable only to the extent that some contractual provision or other authority requires its use for employment decisions. Seniority provisions in collective agreements define the term, establish its utility, and specify the ways employees lose seniority. Seniority clauses typically control (or at least influence) promotions, job bids, shift preferences, layoffs, and some types of fringe benefits such as vacation length and scheduling. See generally Roger I. Abrams and Dennis R. Nolan, *Seniority Rights Under the Collective Agreement*, 2 The Labor Lawyer 99 (1986).

The two primary categories of seniority are "competitive status seniority" (used to choose between employees for a scarce benefit such as a promotion) and "benefit seniority" (used to calculate eligibility for sick leave, vacation and holiday pay, and pensions). Because seniority is a neutral factor, unions also use it to limit management's discretion and thereby prevent favoritism and minimize competition between workers. The broader the seniority clause, the greater attention the employer must pay to seniority in making employment decisions.

Seniority grievances cover a wide area. Some deal with the acquisition, calculation, retention, or loss of seniority. Those issues are especially important to employees who fear layoffs. One common problem is in determining the appropriate seniority unit. Usually the collective agreement specifies whether an employee accumulates seniority in the job, department, plant, or other unit. An employee may even have several types of seniority depending on the matter in dispute: benefit seniority to determine the length of vacation, plant seniority to determine the order of layoffs, and job seniority to determine shift preferences, for example. Calculation issues most commonly involve breaks in service. Does an employee promoted out of the bargaining unit and later demoted back into it get credit for time spent as a supervisor? Does an employee on disability leave continue to accrue seniority?

Other grievances focus on the uses of seniority, seeking to determine who may use seniority for what employment decisions. Mergers and other corporate reorganizations frequently present these issues. If Company A acquires Company B, must it merge the seniority lists by total length of service ("dove-tailing"), or may it put the former Company B employees at the end of the list ("end-tailing")? The airline industry, which has seen many mergers and acquisitions, has produced a copious arbitration literature on the subject.

Still other grievances challenge the weight the employer assigns to seniority in making decisions such as promotions. There are several common terms used to describe the various options. A "straight seniority" clause makes the job decision turn solely on seniority. A "modified seniority" clause qualifies the seniority right in some way. For example, a "sufficient ability" clause requires the use of seniority so long as the senior employee is minimally qualified. A "relative ability" clause, in contrast, allows selection of a junior employee who is more qualified than the senior. "Hybrid clauses" require some consideration of both seniority and ability.

Because an employer's subjective ratings of competing employees could result in evasion of the seniority clause, many arbitrators expect the employer seeking to promote or retain the junior employee to prove that he or she is "head and shoulders" above the senior employee. In the usual case with a "hybrid clause," if the employer cannot show that the junior candidate for a promotion is distinctly more qualified than the senior, the employer must appoint the senior. *City of Fon du Lac* (Robert Moberly 1969).

## D. WAGES AND HOURS

### 1. Wage Disputes

Except in the relatively rare practice of interest arbitration, the determination of wages and hours is not a subject of arbitration. Nevertheless, other types of wage and hour issues frequently reach arbitration. Wage issues are particularly common because of the complexity of modern pay systems. In addition to (or instead of) a stated base rate, employees may have the possibility of piece rates or other productivity-based rates; profit-sharing or other bonuses; shift differentials; differentials for unpleasant or dangerous work; cost-of-living increments; and premium pay for overtime, holiday or vacation work, or for being "called in" or "reporting." For more detailed consideration of these issues, see Roger I. Abrams and Dennis R. Nolan, *Buying Employees' Time: Guaranteed Pay Under Collective Agreements*, 35 Syracuse law Review 867 (1984) and *Time at a Premium: The Arbitration of Overtime and Premium Pay Disputes*, 45 Ohio State Law Journal 837 (1984).

Overtime requirements produce the most arbitrations in the wage and hour category. These grievances can involve the employer's power to require overtime, selection of the proper employee to perform the overtime work, determination of the proper pay rate, and the remedy for improper assignment of overtime. Overtime disputes are complicated by the fact that employees differ in their attitudes toward overtime: some prefer leisure to extra income, while "overtime hounds" seek all the overtime they can find.

Many agreements oblige the employer to distribute overtime equally. These requirements balance employees' contradictory views by sharing both the burden and the benefit of overtime. Recognizing some employees' reluctance to work overtime, contracts often allow employees to decline overtime, thus leaving it to the overtime hounds. Typically, though, an employer may require a reluctant employee to work overtime if no qualified person volunteers. Once the agreement provides for equalization, an employer may not simply choose the most efficient or least expensive employees. *Colt Industries Operating Corp.* (William Belshaw 1979).

It is sometimes difficult to determine the proper remedy for an improper overtime bypass. If the employer should have offered A the work but instead gave it to B, to what remedy, if any, is A entitled? There are two main options, monetary relief and make-up relief. Monetary relief (giving the employee the overtime pay he or she would have earned) initially seems fair, but it usually produces a windfall: the grievant would receive pay without providing the overtime work the pay is supposed to compensate. The actual loss in such cases is the opportunity to *earn* overtime pay, not the pay itself. It is not unheard of for employees to encourage overtime bypasses so that they can later file a grievance for the overtime pay.

Often the fairer remedy is an extra opportunity to work overtime. That approach works only in certain circumstances, chiefly when the relevant work force at the time of the remedy is the same as it was at the date of the wrongful bypass. If the composition of the work unit has changed, an extra opportunity for A may deprive innocent new employee C of extra earnings. Similarly, if the agreement provides for equalization within a certain period, a make-up order may not be possible without distorting calculations for the next period. When a make-up opportunity is not feasible or would harm other employees, monetary relief is the lesser of the evils.

## 2. Hours Disputes

Disputes over hours are not as diverse as wage disputes. Hours disputes usually arise when an employer changes working hours or seeks to avoid premium pay for second and third shifts. The legitimacy of changes in working hours depends on the management rights clause and on the specificity of the premium pay provision.

One case raising both of these issues is *Goodyear Tire and Rubber Co.* (Gordon Knight 1980). The agreement called for a shift differential for employees working on the "Second shift, 3:00 pm to 11:00 pm." It also allowed the employer to adjust starting times "for any portion of employees." To meet certain production needs, the employer eliminated the second shift and then assigned three employees to a split shift from 11:00 am to 7:00 pm. It refused to pay premium pay for part of the split shift because no one worked the defined "second shift."

Rejecting the union's argument that the new shift was merely a subterfuge to deprive the union of the benefit of its bargain, Arbitrator Knight found that the parties carefully chose the contract's terms to make starting times (rather than working times) critical. Because the agreement allowed the employer to change starting times, there was no violation of the agreement. The arbitrator warned, however, that the employer could not avoid its premium pay obligation by making a trivial change. In the case before the arbitrator, though, the change in starting times was substantial.

Collective agreements often define a "normal" work day or work week. Unions occasionally interpret those provisions as absolute guarantees of work or as limits on the employer's authority to change working times. In *Anchor Hocking Corp.* (Roger Abrams 1983), the agreement defined a "normal" work day as eight hours. To cut costs, the employer adjusted assignments and reduced the number of hours many employees worked. The arbitrator held that the definition did not bar occasional variations in hours but did not permit a permanent reduction in hours. In *Ampco-Pittsburgh Corp.* (Steven Briggs 1982), on the other hand, the arbitrator held that a similar provision was not a guarantee of hours.

## E. FRINGE BENEFITS

Until well into the twentieth century, a worker's compensation consisted almost exclusively of a wage or salary. During the last sixty years or so, prodded by economic forces, marketplace changes, government regulations, and tax considerations, employers have paid employees in other ways—holidays and vacations, health benefits, sick leave, disability insurance, profit-sharing plans, pensions, and many others besides. Predictably, these "fringe benefits," as they are now known, have produced more than their share of arbitration cases.

Holiday pay, for instance presents problems of eligibility (has the employee met contractual prerequisites such as working the days before and after the holiday?), entitlement for holidays that fall during the employee's nonwork periods (layoffs, strikes, plant shutdowns, and the like), scheduling of holidays falling on nonwork days, and calculation of the amount of holiday pay (does the pay include shift differential?). See generally Roger I. Abrams and Dennis R. Nolan, *Resolving Holiday Pay Disputes in Labor Arbitration*, 33 Case Western Reserve Law Review 380 (1983).

In *Outboard Marine Corp.* (Louis Kesselman 1969), the agreement required employees to work "their full regularly scheduled work day" before and after the holiday "unless their absence on either of such days has been authorized by the Company." Employees on sick leave had to work just one of those days. The grievant was sick on December 26, but also left work a half-hour early on the 23rd to perform as a volunteer Santa Claus. His supervisor gave him permission to leave but reminded him to be sure to work the day after the holiday "if at all possible."

Although the employer argued that the supervisor lacked the authority to waive the contractual requirement, the arbitrator found that the supervisor was a representative of "the Company." The supervisor's implied condition of working the 26th was excused by the separate contractual exemption for sick leave. The arbitrator relied, as many arbitrators do, on the purpose of these "surrounding day" work requirements, to prevent employees from extending a holiday period. Because the grievant was not trying to extend his holiday, he was entitled to the holiday pay.

Vacation pay provisions are even more problematic than holiday pay rights. The arbitrated problems—eligibility, scheduling, calculation—are similar, but the details are far more complex. In addition to "surrounding day" eligibility requirements, vacation pay provisions usually include a minimum service threshold requirement (a year's service for two weeks of vacation, for example) and a minimum number of hours worked in some stated base period. There are often disputes over the permissible length of vacations (if the contract clause is not specific) and over the possible proration of vacation pay benefits if the employee has not fully satisfied the contractual eligibility requirements.

In addition to the holiday-pay scheduling problem presented by non-work periods, vacation pay provisions often use seniority or work needs to allow employees to take a vacation at a certain time. Employers sometimes schedule mandatory "vacations" during an indefinite layoff to minimize interruptions to production once work resumes. May an employer thus choose the date of an employee's vacation?

In addition to the calculation difficulties posed by a shift premium, vacation pay provisions open the door to differences over the rate of pay. Must the employer use the employee's current rate, even if that is not for some reason representative, or the average rate for the year? What is the appropriate rate when wages have risen after the qualifying year but before the employee takes the vacation? How is the employer to calculate vacation pay when the employee works on an incentive pay or piecerate basis? See generally, Roger I. Abrams and Dennis R. Nolan, *The Common Law of the Labor Agreement: Vacations*, 5 Industrial Relations Law Journal 603 (1983).

*Reichhold Chemicals, Inc.* (Paul Jackson 1976), illustrates one complexity. The union struck for three months during 1974. After the strike ended, the employer announced that it would reduce vacations by a quarter, effectively pro-rating the vacation benefit to account for the employees' reduced eligibility time. The agreement provided that time spent on a layoff would not count toward vacation pay but said nothing about time spent on strike. The union argued that the required "service" for vacation benefits meant the same as "seniority," which continued to accrue during the strike. Because the union's argument would mean that a year-long strike would entitle employees to a vacation, the arbitrator held instead that "service" meant time "worked."

Leaves of absence are another source of grievances. Sick leave is particularly difficult to administer because of the variety of medical reasons employees cite and because of employers' understandable fear that employees will abuse the contractual benefit. When may an employer demand medical proof of illness? Is a general statement from a doctor always sufficient? Funeral or bereavement leave clauses pose questions of which relatives an employee may leave work to bury, and whether the employee has to attend the funeral in order to qualify for the leave. Some contracts authorize employees to take leave for union business. How can the employer be sure the employee is actually doing union work during the absence?

## F. SUBCONTRACTING

Subcontracting—or "contracting out," as it is more accurately known—sometimes poses a conflict between efficiency and job security. The conflict may not be real, at least not in the long run, because only the efficient producers are likely to survive long enough to guarantee jobs, but it certainly seems real to the parties involved. Contract provisions dealing with subcontracting cover the gamut, from broad grants of contracting authority to employers to prohibitions on any subcontracting without mutual agreement. Some clauses require the employer merely to give the union advance notice of planned subcontracting. Others require negotiation. Some permit only "reasonable" contracting, while others prohibit subcontracting that would result in (or continue) layoffs of employees capable of performing the contracted work. The range of arbitrated disputes is equally wide. See generally, Roger I. Abrams and Dennis R. Nolan,

*Subcontracting Disputes in Labor Arbitration: Productive Efficiency versus Job Security*, 15 University of Toledo Law Review 7 (1983).

Contracting provisions at least give the arbitrator some guidance. The arbitrator's task is far more difficult when the contract is silent on the point. While the reserved rights doctrine would interpret contractual silence as a blank check for management, unrestricted subcontracting could eliminate the bargaining unit. Because the parties were unlikely to have left the employer the power to destroy the union, most arbitrators interpret even silent agreements to include some implied limitations. As Archibald Cox wrote forty years ago, the implied covenants of good faith and fair dealing bar an employer from seeking "a substitute labor supply at lower wages or inferior standards" but do not reach subcontracting "based on business considerations other than the cost of acquiring labor under the collective agreement." *The Legal Nature of Collective Bargaining Agreements*, 57 Michigan Law Review 1, 31–32 (1958).

A good example is the early case of *Allis-Chalmers Manufacturing Co.* (Russell Smith 1962). The employer subcontracted certain janitorial and manufacturing work while some employees who had done similar work were on layoff. The arbitrator rejected both the employer's claim of unrestricted freedom and the union's assertion that the contract impliedly banned all subcontracting. He held instead that the contract required only "good faith," which he defined as contracting out "on the basis of a rational consideration of factors related to the conduct of an efficient, economical operation, and with some regard for the interests and expectations of the employees affected." In both the janitorial and manufacturing subcontracting, the employer relied on rational considerations such as the need to guarantee timely performance, safety factors, and lower unit costs. The employer's decisions were thus in good faith and did not violate the agreement.

Subcontracting cases often pose difficult remedial decisions. If the employer breaches a promise to give the union a chance to discuss proposed contracting, what is the appropriate remedy? Because the agreement does not prevent the employer from ultimately going ahead with its plans, the union cannot prove any monetary loss, yet a mere finding of a breach with no remedy would allow the employer to avoid the agreement with impunity. If the employer breaches a flat prohibition on the challenged subcontracting, however, employees are entitled to compensation for the work they lost.

## G. UNION SECURITY

One of the newest subjects of arbitration has been union security. Federal law allows parties in the thirty states without right to work laws to negotiate compulsory union membership provisions. Unions defend these agreements as essential to deter "free riders," employees who would like to enjoy the negotiated benefits without paying their share of the costs. As the Supreme Court has interpreted the law, however, valid union security agreements may only force employees to pay dues and fees, not to become full members of the union. The compulsory payments can only cover union expenses related to its representation functions. Those limitations protect employees from becoming "forced riders." For a brief synopsis of the relevant law, see Laura J. Cooper and Dennis R. Nolan, Labor Arbitration: A Coursebook 226–33 (West Publishing Co. 1994).

Union security arbitrations come in two main forms. The most common is a grievance alleging that the employer failed to enforce a union security agreement against a dissenting employee. *Hartford Provision Co.* (Howard Sacks 1987), was just such a case. The employer defended its refusal to fire a reluctant employee on the basis that the employee was not eligible under federal law for inclusion within the bargaining unit. After first determining that he had both authority and reason to interpret the relevant statute, the arbitrator agreed with the employer and denied the grievance. *J.W. Wells Lumber Co.* (Robert Howlett 1964) turned on the meaning of a contract provision making payment of a service charge a "condition of employment." The employer refused to fire employees who declined to pay the fee, saying that dues collection was the union's responsibility. Arbitrator Howlett sustained the grievance, finding that the contract meant that defaulting employees "are not entitled to retain employee status."

The second common type of union security arbitration concerns the amount of fees a union may collect from represented employees who choose not to join the union. Unions naturally claim that almost all of their expenditures relate in some way to representation of employees covered by the collective agreement. Dissenting employees just as naturally disagree. Arbitration and court cases usually find that 85% or more of a union's expenditures meet the Supreme Court's standard of relevance. The disputed items, apart from obviously unchargeable expenditures like political contributions, usually involve minor payments for things like publications and parties.

*International Brotherhood of Firemen and Oilers, Local 100* (Nicholas Duda 1990), was somewhat unusual in that the local did not seek to charge represented employees for the 52% of its funds passed on to the international union and the local labor council. After finding that salaries, rent, meeting expenses, and the like obviously related to contract negotiation and administration, Arbitrator Duda was left with complaints about the local's purchase of a table for six at an AFL–CIO dinner and a lump sum given to a unit that split from the local. The former was not chargeable, he found, because the dinner was for union members only; the latter was chargeable, because it represented a disbursement of money contributed by the departing unit's members. That change increased the rebate dissenters were to receive from $5.68 a month (out of the monthly dues of $11) to $5.73.

Dissenting employees are at a marked disadvantage. Not only do the defendant union organizations control the critical information, the amount of money at stake is too small to make a challenge economically sensible. As a result, the few cases of this sort are usually subsidized by opponents of compulsory unionism such as the National Right to Work Legal Defense Fund.

## H. OCCUPATIONAL SAFETY AND HEALTH

Many collective bargaining agreements, particularly those covering hazardous occupations, contain provisions relating to occupational safety and health. Typically these provisions authorize or require the employer to take reasonable steps to protect bargaining unit employees. Many contracts establish a joint safety committee, and some provide for mutual determination of safety rules and practices.

Concern in recent years about safety and health on the job has led to a significant increase in arbitration awards dealing with this topic. The two major issues in these arbitrations are challenges to employer actions designed to promote safety or health, and discipline of employees for refusing to obey orders they believe would endanger themselves or others.

Even where the contract is silent on the point, arbitrators uniformly hold that an employer may impose and enforce reasonable safety rules. Safety, after all, is an obligation for all employers. Almost as uniformly, they hold that employers have the right and responsibility to take immediate action to eliminate a danger. For example, an employer may transfer or suspend an employee whose physical or mental problems present safety concerns. Similarly, even without express contractual authorization, an employer may require an employee on medical leave to provide a doctor's release before returning to work. An employer's safety rules and practices must of course meet the usual criteria of reasonableness: they must bear a clear relationship to their ostensible purpose, must be reasonable in content and fairly applied, and, in the case of work rules, must be adequately communicated to the affected employees.

Employees sometimes challenge rules the employer ostensibly adopts for their protection. From an employer's perspective, a ban on smoking contributes to employee health as well as to the employer's bottom line. From the employees' perspective, however, the ban may seem like an unwarranted interference with their liberty. So long as the employer's rule is sensitive—if, for example, it provides long notice of the proposed ban and offers smoking-cessation classes or medical support—an arbitrator is likely to find it a reasonable exercise of the employer's contractual right and duty to provide a safe work place.

There is more division on the second issue, discipline of employees who refuse assignments they believe to be dangerous. The usual "obey now, grieve later" rule applies in this context as well as others, but most arbitrators recognize a narrow implied exception to the rule for disobedience prompted by a reasonable belief that the order poses a serious imminent risk to health or safety. Certain risks are inherent in particular jobs, and these do not come within the exception. A roofer may not refuse a normal roofing assignment after developing a fear of heights, for example, nor may a utility lineman refuse to climb a normal pole because of fear of a shock. Moreover, the exception applies only to employees within the zone of danger; others who are not involved have no license to strike over the disputed assignment.

When such an issue arises, the arbitrator must find a formula that will distinguish between justified and unjustified fears. Their answers range from the purely subjective or "good faith" standard to the purely objective or "real and imminent danger" test. Most tend toward the objective approach, influenced, perhaps, by the Supreme Court's decision in *Gateway Coal v. United Mine Workers* (1974). The union in that case struck to enforce its demand that the employer suspend two foremen who allegedly falsified measurements of air flow in a mine, a matter of great concern to miners. The Court held that once the parties agreed to submit grievances to arbitration, the union could not strike in disregard of that agreement even over safety questions. Section 502 of the Labor–Management Relations Act, which provides that

> the quitting of labor by an employee or employees in good faith because of abnormally dangerous conditions for work at the place of employment of such employee or employees [shall not] be deemed a strike,

did not protect the union, said the Court. A union seeking to justify a contractually prohibited strike under Section 502 must present "ascertainable, objective evidence supporting its conclusion that an abnormally dangerous condition for work exists," not simply a generalized doubt about the competence of some supervisors. The *Gateway Coal* decision did not bind arbitrators, but many of them have taken a cue from it. Perhaps, too, arbitrators realize that a purely subjective approach would be open to serious abuse. Proving bad faith is almost impossible, so any employee who wanted to avoid a given assignment could escape discipline simply by claiming a safety concern.

\*

# APPENDICES

**App.**
- A. AAA Labor Arbitration Rules.
- B. AAA Expedited Labor Arbitration Procedures.
- C. AAA National Rules for the Resolution of Employment Disputes.
- D. AAA Excelleration Program.
- E. AAA Forms.
    1. Demand for Arbitration.
    2. Submission to Arbitration.
    3. List for Selection of Arbitrator.
    4. Notice of Appointment and Arbitrator's Oath.
    5. Notice of Hearing.
    6. Subpoena Duces Tecum.
    7. Stipulation.
    8. Award of Arbitrator.
    9. Arbitrator's Bill.
- F. FMCS Procedures for Arbitration Services.
- G. FMCS Expedited Arbitration Rules.
- H. FMCS Forms.
    1. Request for Arbitration Panel (FMCS Form R–19).
    2. Arbitrator's Report and Fee Statement (FMCS Form R–43).
- I. Code of Professional Responsibility for Arbitrators of Labor–Management Disputes.
- J. Federal Arbitration Act.
- K. Uniform Arbitration Act.
- L. A Due Process Protocol for Mediation and Arbitration of Statutory Disputes Arising Out of the Employment Relationship.

# APPENDIX A

# AAA LABOR ARBITRATION RULES

As amended and effective on January 1, 1996.

Copyright 1996 by the American Arbitration Association. All rights reserved.

*Analysis*

Introduction.

**Rule**
1. Agreement of Parties.
2. Name of Tribunal.
3. Administrator.
4. Delegation of Duties.
5. Panel of Labor Arbitrators.
6. Office of Tribunal.
7. Initiation Under an Arbitration Clause in a Collective Bargaining Agreement.
8. Answer.
9. Initiation Under a Submission.
10. Fixing of Locale.
11. Qualifications of Arbitrator.
12. Appointment From Panel
13. Direct Appointment by Parties.
14. Appointment of Neutral Arbitrator by Party–Appointed Arbitrators.
15. Number of Arbitrators.
16. Notice to Arbitrator of Appointment.
17. Disclosure and Challenge Procedure.
18. Vacancies.
19. Date, Time, and Place of Hearing.
20. Representation.

## AAA LABOR ARBITRATION RULES

21. Stenographic Record and Interpreters.
22. Attendance at Hearings.
23. Postponements.
24. Oaths.
25. Majority Decision.
26. Order of Proceedings.
27. Arbitration in the Absence of a Party or Representative.
28. Evidence.
29. Evidence by Affidavit and Filing of Documents.
30. Inspection.
31. Closing of Hearings.
32. Reopening of Hearings.
33. Waiver of Oral Hearings.
34. Waiver of Rules.
35. Extensions of Time.
36. Serving of Notice.
37. Time of Award.
38. Form of Award.
39. Award Upon Settlement.
40. Delivery of Award to Parties.
41. Release of Documents for Judicial Proceedings.
42. Judicial Proceedings and Exclusion of Liability.
43. Administrative Fees.
44. Expenses.
45. Communication with Arbitrator.
46. Interpretation and Application of Rules.

Administrative Fees.
  Initial Administrative Fee.
  Arbitrator Compensation.
  Additional Hearing Fees.
  Hearing Room Rental.
  Postponement Fees.

## Introduction

Every year, labor and management enter into thousands of collective bargaining agreements. Virtually all of these agreements provide for arbitration of unresolved grievances. For decades, the American Arbitration Association (AAA) has been a leading administrator of labor-management disputes.

The American Arbitration Association is a public-service, not-for-profit organization offering a broad range of dispute-resolution services to business executives, attorneys, individuals, trade associations, unions, management, consumers, families, communities, and all levels of government. Services are available through AAA headquarters in New York City and through offices located in major cities throughout the United States. Hearings may be held at locations convenient for the parties and are not limited to cities with AAA offices. In addition, the AAA serves as a center for education and training, issues specialized publications, and conducts research on all forms of out-of-court dispute settlement.

Arbitration is a tool of industrial relations. Like other tools, it has limitations as well as uses. In the hands of an expert, it produces useful results. When abused or made to do things for which it was never intended, the outcome can be disappointing. For these reasons, all participants in the process-union officials, employers, personnel executives, attorneys, and the arbitrators themselves-have an equal stake in orderly efficient, and constructive arbitration procedures. The AAA's Labor Arbitration Rules provide a time-tested method for efficient, fair, and economical resolution of labor-management disputes. By referring to them in a collective bargaining agreement, the parties can take advantage of these benefits.

The parties can provide for arbitration of future disputes by inserting the following clause into their contracts.

Any dispute, claim, or grievance arising from or relating to interpretation or application of this agreement shall be submitted to arbitration administered by the American Arbitration Association under its Labor Arbitration Rules. The parties further agree to accept the arbitrator's award as final and binding on them.

For relatively uncomplicated grievances, parties who use the labor arbitration services of the American Arbitration Association may agree to use expedited procedures that provide a prompt and inexpensive method for resolving disputes. This option responds to a concern about rising costs and delays in processing grievance-arbitration cases. The AAA's Expedited Labor Arbitration Procedures, by eliminating or streamlining certain steps, are intended to resolve cases within a month of the appointment of the arbitrator. The procedures may be found near the end of this document.

## Labor Arbitration Rules

### 1. Agreement of Parties

The parties shall be deemed to have made these rules a part of their arbitration agreement whenever, in a collective bargaining agreement or submission, they have provided for arbitration by the American Arbitration Association (hereinafter the AAA) or under its rules. These rules and any amendment thereof shall apply in the form obtaining when the arbitration is initiated. The parties, by written agreement, may vary the procedures set forth in these rules.

### 2. Name of Tribunal

Any tribunal constituted by the parties under these rules shall be called the Labor Arbitration Tribunal.

### 3. Administrator

When parties agree to arbitrate under these rules and an arbitration is instituted thereunder, they thereby authorize the AAA to administer the arbitration. The authority and obligations of the administrator are as provided in the agreement of the parties and in these rules.

### 4. Delegation of Duties

The duties of the AAA may be carried out through such representatives or committees as the AAA may direct.

### 5. Panel of Labor Arbitrators

The AAA shall establish and maintain a Panel of Labor Arbitrators and shall appoint arbitrators therefrom as hereinafter provided.

### 6. Office of Tribunal

The general office of the Labor Arbitration Tribunal is the headquarters of the AAA, which may, however, assign the administration of an arbitration to any of its regional offices.

### 7. Initiation Under an Arbitration Clause in a Collective Bargaining Agreement

Arbitration under an arbitration clause in a collective bargaining agreement under these rules may be initiated by either party in the following manner:

(a) by giving written notice to the other party of its intention to arbitrate (demand), which notice shall contain a statement setting forth the nature of the dispute and the remedy sought, and

(b) by filing at any regional office of the AAA three copies of the notice, together with a copy to the collective bargaining agreement or such parts thereof as relate to the dispute, including the arbitration provisions. After the arbitrator is appointed, no new or different claim may be submitted except with the consent of the arbitrator and all other parties.

## 8. Answer

The party upon whom the demand for arbitration is made may file an answering statement with the AAA ten days after notice from the AAA, simultaneously sending a copy to the other party, If no answer is filed, within the stated time, it will be treated as a denial of the claim. Failure to file an answer shall not operate to delay the arbitration.

## 9. Initiation Under a Submission

Parties to any, collective bargaining agreement may initiate an arbitration under these rules by filing at any regional office of the AAA two copies of a written agreement to arbitrate under these rules (submission), signed by the parties and setting forth the nature of the dispute and the remedy sought.

## 10. Fixing of Locale

The parties may mutually agree on the locale where the arbitration is to be held. If the locale is not designated in the collective bargaining agreement or submission, and if there is a dispute as to the appropriate locale, the AAA shall have the power to determine the locale and its decision shall be binding.

## 11. Qualifications of Arbitrator

Any neutral arbitrator appointed pursuant to Section 12, 13, or 14 or selected by mutual choice of the parties or their appointees, shall be subject to disqualification for the reasons specified in Section 17. If the parties specifically so agree in writing, the arbitrator shall not be subject to disqualification for those reasons.

Unless the parties agree otherwise, an arbitrator selected unilaterally by one party is a party-appointed arbitrator and ь not subject to disqualification pursuant to Section 17.

The term "arbitrator" in these rules refers to the arbitration panel, whether composed of one or more arbitrators and whether the arbitrators are neutral or party appointed.

## 12. Appointment From Panel

If the parties have not appointed an arbitrator and have not provided any other method of appointment, the arbitrator shall be appointed in the following manner: immediately after the filing of the demand or submission, the AAA shall submit simultaneously to each party an identical list of names of persons chosen from the Panel of Labor Arbitrators. Each party shall have ten days from the mailing date in which to strike any name to which it objects, number the remaining names to indicate the order of preference, and return the list to the AAA.

If a party does not return the list within the time specified, all persons named therein shall be deemed acceptable.

From among the persons who have been approved on both lists, and in accordance with the designated order of mutual preference, the AAA shall invite the acceptance of an arbitrator to serve. If the parties fail to agree upon any of the persons named, if those named decline or are unable to act, or if for any other reason the appointment cannot be made from the submitted lists, the administrator shall have the power to make the appointment from among other members of the panel without the submission of any additional list.

## 13. Direct Appointment by Parties

If the agreement of the parties names an arbitrator or specifies a method of appointing an arbitrator, that designation or method shall be followed. The notice of appointment, with the name and address of the arbitrator, shall be filed with the AAA by the appointing party. Upon the request of any appointing party, the AAA shall submit a list of members of the panel from which the party may, if it so desires, make the appointment.

If the agreement specifies a period of time within which an arbitrator shall be appointed and any party fails to make an appointment within that period, the AAA may make the appointment.

If no period of time is specified in the agreement, the AAA shall notify the parties to make the appointment and if within ten days thereafter such arbitrator has not been so appointed, the AAA shall make the appointment.

## 14. Appointment of Neutral Arbitrator by Party–Appointed Arbitrators

If the parties have appointed their arbitrators or if either or both of them have been appointed as provided in Section 13, and have authorized those arbitrators to appoint a neutral arbitrator within a specified time and no appointment is made within that time or any agreed extension thereof, the AAA may appoint a neutral arbitrator who shall act as chairperson.

If no period of time is specified for appointment of the neutral arbitrator and the parties do not make the appointment within ten days from the date of the appointment of the last party-appointed arbitrator, the AAA shall appoint a neutral arbitrator who shall act as chairperson.

If the parties have agreed that the arbitrators shall appoint the neutral arbitrator from the panel, the AAA shall furnish to the party-appointed arbitrators, in the manner prescribed in Section 12, a list selected from the panel, and the appointment of the neutral arbitrator shall be made as prescribed in that section.

## 15. Number of Arbitrators

If the arbitration agreement does not specify the number of arbitrators, the dispute shall be heard and determined by one arbitrator, unless the parties otherwise agree.

### 16. Notice to Arbitrator of Appointment

Notice of the appointment of the neutral arbitrator shall be mailed to the arbitrator by the AAA and the signed acceptance of the arbitrator shall be filed with the AAA prior to the opening of the first hearing.

### 17. Disclosure and Challenge Procedure

No person shall serve as a neutral arbitrator in any arbitration under these rules in which that person has any financial or personal interest in the result of the arbitration. Any prospective or designated neutral arbitrator shall immediately disclose any circumstance likely to affect impartiality, including any, bias or financial or personal interest in the result of the arbitration. Upon receipt of this information from the arbitrator or another source, the AAA shall communicate the information to the parties and, if it deems it appropriate to do so, to the arbitrator.

Upon objection of a party to the continued service of a neutral arbitrator, the AAA, after consultation with the parties and the arbitrator, shall determine whether the arbitrator should be disqualified and shall inform the parties of its decision, which shall be conclusive.

### 18. Vacancies

If any arbitrator should resign, die, or otherwise be unable to perform the duties of the office, the AAA shall, on proof satisfactory to it, declare the office vacant. Vacancies shall be filled in the same manner as that governing, the making of the original appointment, and the matter shall be reheard by the new arbitrator.

### 19. Date, Time, and Place of Hearing

The arbitrator shall fix the date, time, and place for each hearing. At least five days prior thereto, the AAA shall mail notice of the date, time, and place of hearing to each party, unless the parties otherwise agree.

## 20. Representation

Any party may be represented by counsel or other authorized representative.

## 21. Stenographic Record and Interpreters

Any party wishing a stenographic record shall make arrangements directly with a stenographer and shall notify the other parties of such arrangements in advance of the hearing. The requesting party or parties shall pay the cost of the record. If the transcript is agreed by the parties to be or, in appropriate cases, determined by the arbitrator to be the official record of the proceeding, it must be made available to the arbitrator and to the other party for inspection, at a time and place determined by the arbitrator.

Any party wishing an interpreter shall make all arrangements directly with the interpreter and shall assume the costs of the service.

## 22. Attendance at Hearings

Persons having a direct interest in the arbitration are entitled to attend hearings. The arbitrator shall have the power to require the retirement of any witness or witnesses during the testimony of other witnesses. It shall be discretionary with the arbitrator to determine the propriety of the attendance of any other person.

## 23. Postponements

The arbitrator for good cause shown may postpone the hearing upon the request of a party or upon his or her own initiative and shall postpone when all of the parties agree thereto.

### 24. Oaths

Before proceeding with the first hearing, each arbitrator may take an oath of office and, if required by law, shall do so. The arbitrator may require witnesses to testify under oath administered by any duly qualified person and, if required by law or requested by either party, shall do so.

### 25. Majority Decision

Whenever there is more than one arbitrator, all decisions of the arbitrators shall be by majority vote. The award shall also be made by majority vote unless the concurrence of all is expressly required.

### 26. Order of Proceedings

A hearing shall be opened by the filing of the oath of the arbitrator, where required; by the recording of the date, time, and place of the hearing and the presence of the arbitrator, the parties, and counsel, if any; and by the receipt by the arbitrator of the demand and answer, if any, or the submission.

Exhibits may, when offered by either party, be received in evidence by the arbitrator. The names and addresses of all witnesses and exhibits in order received shall be made a part of the record.

The arbitrator may vary the normal procedure under which the initiating party first presents its claim, but in any case shall afford full and equal opportunity to all parties for the presentation of relevant proofs.

### 27. Arbitration in the Absence of a Party or Representative

Unless the law provides to the contrary, the arbitration may proceed in the absence of any party or representative who, after due notice, fails to be present or fails to obtain a postponement. An award shall not be made solely on the default of a party. The arbitrator shall require the other party to submit such evidence as may be required for the making of an award.

## 28. Evidence

The parties may offer such evidence as is relevant and material to the dispute, and shall produce such additional evidence as the arbitrator may deem necessary to an understanding and determination of the dispute. An arbitrator authorized by law to subpoena witnesses and documents may do so independently or upon the request of any party. The arbitrator shall be the judge of the relevance and materiality of the evidence offered and conformity to legal rules of evidence shall not be necessary. All evidence shall be taken in the presence of all of the arbitrators and all of the parties except where any of the parties is absent in default or has waived the right to be present.

## 29. Evidence by Affidavit and Filing of Documents

The arbitrator may receive and consider the evidence of witnesses by affidavit, giving it only such weight as seems proper after consideration of any objection made to its admission.

All documents that are not filed with the arbitrator at the hearing, but arranged at the hearing or subsequently by agreement of the parties to be submitted, shall be filed with the AAA for transmission to the arbitrator. All parties shall be afforded opportunity to examine such documents.

## 30. Inspection

Whenever the arbitrator deems it necessary, he or she may make an inspection in connection with the subject matter of the dispute after written notice to the parties, who may, if they so desire, be present at the inspection.

### 31. Closing of Hearings

The arbitrator shall inquire of all parties whether they have any further proof to offer or witness to be heard. Upon receiving negative replies or if satisfied that the record is complete, the arbitrator shall declare the hearings closed and a minute thereof shall be recorded. If briefs or other documents are to be filed, the hearings shall be declared closed as of the final date set by the arbitrator for filing with the AAA. If documents are to be filed as provided in Section 29 and the date for their receipt is later than the date set for the receipt of briefs, the later date shall be the date of closing the hearing. The time limit within which the arbitrator is required to make an award shall commence to run, in the absence of another agreement by the parties, upon the closing of the hearings.

### 32. Reopening of Hearings

The hearings may for good cause shown be reopened by the arbitrator at will or on the motion of either party at any time before the award is made but, if the reopening of the hearings would prevent the making of the award within the specific time agreed upon by the parties in the contract out of which the controversy has arisen, the matter may not be reopened unless both parties agree to extend the time. When no specific date is fixed in the contract, the arbitrator may reopen the hearings and shall have thirty days from the closing of the reopened hearings within which to make an award.

### 33. Waiver of Oral Hearings

The parties may provide, by written agreement, for the waiver of oral hearings. If the parties are unable to agree as to the procedure, the AAA shall specify a fair and equitable procedure.

## 34. Waiver of Rules

Any party who proceeds with the arbitration after knowledge that any provision or requirement of these rules has not been complied with and who fails to state an objection thereto in writing shall be deemed to have waived the right to object.

## 35. Extensions of Time

The parties may modify any period of time by mutual agreement. The AAA or the arbitrator may for good cause extend any period of time established by these rules, except the time for making the award. The AAA shall notify the parties of any such extension of time and its reason therefor.

## 36. Serving of Notice

Each party to a submission or other agreement that provides for arbitration under these rules shall be deemed to have consented and shall consent that any papers, notices, or process necessary or proper for the initiation or continuation of an arbitration under these rules; for any court action in connection therewith, or for the entry of judgment on an award made thereunder may be served upon the party by mail addressed to the party, or its representative at the last known address or by personal service, in or outside the state where the arbitration is to be held.

The AAA and the parties may also use facsimile transmission, telex, telegram, or other written forms of electronic communication to give the notices required by these rules.

## 37. Time of Award

The award shall be rendered promptly by the arbitrator and, unless otherwise agreed by the parties or specified by law, no later than thirty days from the date of closing the hearings, with five additional days for mailing if briefs are to be filed.

If oral hearings have been waived, the award shall be rendered no later than thirty days from the date of transmitting the final statements and proofs to the arbitrator.

## 38. Form of Award

The award shall be in writing and shall be signed either by the neutral arbitrator or by a concurring majority if there is more than one arbitrator. The parties shall advise the AAA whenever they do not require the arbitrator to accompany the award with an opinion.

## 39. Award Upon Settlement

If the parties settle their dispute during the course of the arbitration, the arbitrator may, upon their request, set forth the terms of the agreed settlement in an award.

## 40. Delivery of Award to Parties

Parties shall accept as legal delivery of the award the placing of the award or a true copy thereof in the mail by the AAA, addressed to the party at its last known address or to its representative; personal service of the award; or the filing of the award in any other manner that is permitted by law.

## 41. Release of Documents for Judicial Proceedings

The AAA shall, upon the written request of a party, furnish to such party, at its expense, certified facsimiles of any papers in the AAA's possession that may be required in Judicial proceedings relating to the arbitration.

## 42. Judicial Proceedings and Exclusion of Liability

(a) Neither the AAA nor any arbitrator in a proceeding under these rules is a necessary party in judicial proceedings relating to the arbitration.

(b) Neither the AAA nor any arbitrator shall be liable to any party for any act or omission in connection with any arbitration conducted under these rules.

## 43. Administrative Fees

As a not-for-profit organization, the AAA shall prescribe an administrative fee schedule to compensate it for the cost of providing administrative services. The schedule in effect at the time of filing shall be applicable.

## 44. Expenses

The expenses of witnesses for either side shall be paid by the party producing such witnesses.

Expenses of the arbitration, other than the cost of the stenographic record, including required traveling and other expenses of the arbitrator and of AAA representatives and the expenses of any witness or the cost of any proof produced at the direct request of the arbitrator, shall be borne equally by the parties, unless they agree otherwise, or unless the arbitrator, in the award, assesses such expenses or any part hereof against any specified party or parties.

## 45. Communication with Arbitrator

There shall be no communication between the parties and a neutral arbitrator other than at oral hearings, unless the parties and the arbitrator agree otherwise. Any other oral or written communication from the parties to the arbitrator shall be directed to the AAA for transmittal to the arbitrator.

## 46. Interpretation and Application of Rules

The arbitrator shall interpret and apply these rules insofar as they relate to the arbitrator's powers and duties. When there is more than one arbitrator and a difference arises among them concerning the meaning or application of any such rule, it shall be decided by a majority vote. If that is unobtainable, the arbitrator or either party may refer the question to the AAA for final decision. All other rules shall be interpreted and applied by the AAA.

## Administrative Fees

### Initial Administrative Fee

The initial administrative fee is $150 for each party, due and payable at the time of filing. No refund of the initial fee is made when a matter is withdrawn or settled after the filing of the demand for arbitration or submissions

### Arbitrator Compensation

Unless mutually agreed otherwise, the arbitrator's compensation shall be borne equally by the parties, in accordance with the fee structure disclosed in the arbitrator's biographical profile submitted to the parties.

### Additional Hearing Fees

A fee of $50 is payable by each party for each hearing held after the first hearing.

### Hearing Room Rental

Hearing rooms for second and subsequent hearings are available on a rental basis at AAA offices. Check with your local office for specific availability and rates.

### Postponement Fees

A fee of $150 is payable by a party causing a postponement of any scheduled hearing.

# APPENDIX B
# AAA EXPEDITED LABOR ARBITRATION PROCEDURES

- E1. Agreement of Parties.
- E2. Appointment of Neutral Arbitrator.
- E3. Qualifications of Neutral Arbitrator.
- E4. Vacancies.
- E5. Date, Time, and Place of Hearing.
- E6. No Stenographic Record.
- E7. Proceedings.
- E8. Posthearing Briefs.
- E9. Time of Award.
- E10. Form of Award.

   Administrative Fees.
   Initial Administrative Fee.
   Arbitrator Compensation.
   Additional Hearing Fees.
   Hearing Room Rental.
   Postponement Fees.

In response to the concern of parties over rising costs and delays in grievance arbitration, the American Arbitration Association has established expedited procedures under which cases are scheduled promptly and awards rendered no later than seven days after the hearings. In return for giving up certain features of traditional labor arbitration, such as transcripts, briefs, and extensive opinions, the parties using these simplified procedures can get quick decisions and realize certain cost savings.

Leading labor arbitrators have indicated a willingness to offer their services under these procedures, and the Association makes every effort to assign the best possible arbitrators with early available hearing dates. Since the establishment of these procedures, an ever increasing number of parties has taken advantage of them.

## E1. Agreement of Parties

These procedures shall apply whenever the parties have agreed to arbitrate under them, the Streamlined Labor Arbitration Rules, or the Expedited Labor Arbitration Rules of the American Arbitration Association, in the form obtaining when the arbitration is initiated.

These procedures shall be applied as set forth below, in addition to any other portion of the Labor Arbitration Rules that is not in conflict with these expedited procedures.

## E2. Appointment of Neutral Arbitrator

The AAA shall appoint a single neutral arbitrator from its Panel of Labor Arbitrators, who shall hear and determine the case promptly.

## E3. Qualifications of Neutral Arbitrator

No person shall serve as a neutral arbitrator in any arbitration in which that person has any financial or personal interest in the result of the arbitration. Prior to accepting an appointment, the prospective arbitrator shall disclose any circumstance likely to prevent a prompt hearing or to create a presumption of bias. Upon receipt of such information, the AAA shall immediately replace that arbitrator or communicate the information to the parties.

### E4. Vacancies

The AAA is authorized to substitute another arbitrator if a vacancy occurs or if an appointed arbitrator is unable to serve promptly.

### E5. Date, Time, and Place of Hearing

The arbitrator shall fix the date, time, and place of the hearing, notice of which must be given at least 24 hours in advance. Such notice may be given orally or by facsimile.

### E6. No Stenographic Record

There shall be no stenographic record of the proceedings.

### E7. Proceedings

The hearing shall be conducted by the arbitrator in whatever manner will most expeditiously permit full presentation of the evidence and arguments of the parties. The arbitrator shall make an appropriate minute of the proceedings. Normally, the hearing, shall be completed within one day. In unusual circumstances and for good cause shown, the arbitrator may schedule an additional hearing to be held within seven days.

### E8. Posthearing Briefs

There shall be no post-hearing briefs.

### E9. Time of Award

The award shall be rendered promptly by the arbitrator and, unless otherwise agreed by the parties, no later than seven days from the date of the closing, of the hearing.

### E10. Form of Award

The award shall be in writing and shall be signed by the arbitrator. If the arbitrator determines that an opinion is necessary, it shall be in summary form.

## Administrative Fees

### Initial Administrative Fee

The initial administrative fee is $75 for each party, due and payable at the time of filing. No refund of the initial fee is made when a matter is withdrawn or settled after the filing of the demand for arbitration or submission.

### Arbitrator Compensation

Unless mutually agreed otherwise, the arbitrator's compensation shall be borne equally by the parties, in accordance with the fee structure disclosed in the arbitrator's biographical profile submitted to the parties.

### Additional Hearing Fees

A fee of $50 is payable by each party for each hearing held after the first hearing.

### Hearing Room Rental

Hearing rooms for second and subsequent hearings are available on a rental basis at AAA offices. Check with your local office for specific availability and rates.

### Postponement Fees

A fee of $150 is payable by a party causing a postponement of any scheduled hearing.

# APPENDIX C

# AAA NATIONAL RULES FOR THE RESOLUTION OF EMPLOYMENT DISPUTES

Effective June 1, 1997.

Copyright 1997 by the American Arbitration Association. All rights reserved.

## NATIONAL RULES FOR THE RESOLUTION OF EMPLOYMENT DISPUTES

*Analysis*

**Rule**
1. Applicable Rules of Arbitration.
2. Notification.
3. AAA as Administrator of the Arbitration.
4. Initiation of Arbitration.
5. Changes of Claim.
6. Administrative and Mediation Conferences.
7. Discovery.
8. Arbitration Management Conference.
9. Location of the Arbitration.
10. Date and Time of Hearing.
11. Qualifications to Serve as Arbitrator and Rights of Parties to Disqualify Arbitrator.
12. Number and Appointment of Neutral Arbitrators.
13. Vacancies.
14. Representation.
15. Attendance at Hearings.
16. Confidentiality of Hearings.
17. Postponements.

18. Oaths.
19. Majority Decision.
20. Order of Proceedings and Communication With Arbitrators.
21. Arbitration in the Absence of a Party or Representative.
22. Evidence.
23. Evidence by Affidavit or Declaration and Post–Hearing Filing of Documents or Other Evidence.
24. Inspection or Investigation.
25. Interim Measures.
26. Closing of Hearing.
27. Reopening of Hearing.
28. Waiver of Oral Hearing.
29. Waiver of Objection/Lack of Compliance with These Rules.
30. Extensions of Time.
31. Serving of Notice.
32. The Award.
33. Release of Documents for Judicial Proceedings.
34. Judicial Proceedings and Exclusion of Liability.
35. Administrative Fees.
36. Expenses.
37. Neutral Arbitrator's Compensation.
38. Deposits.
39. Interpretation and Application of Rules.

Administrative Fee Schedule.
    Administrative Fee.
    Filing Fees.
    Hearing Fees.
    Postponement/Cancellation Fees.
    Hearing Room Rental.
    Suspension for Nonpayment.

## NATIONAL RULES FOR THE RESOLUTION OF EMPLOYMENT DISPUTES

### 1. Applicable Rules of Arbitration

The parties shall be deemed to have made these rules a part of their arbitration agreement whenever they have provided for arbitration by the American Arbitration Association (hereinafter "AAA") or under its National Rules for the Resolution of Employment Disputes. If a party establishes that an adverse material inconsistency exists between the arbitration agreement and these rules, the arbitrator shall apply these rules.

If, within thirty (30) days after the Association's commencement of administration, a party seeks judicial intervention with respect to a pending arbitration, the Association will suspend administration for sixty (60) days to permit the party to obtain a stay of arbitration from the court.

These rules, and any amendment of them, shall apply in the form obtaining at the time the demand for arbitration or submission is received by the AAA.

### 2. Notification

An employer intending to incorporate these rules or to refer to the dispute resolution services of the AAA in an employment ADR plan, shall, at least thirty (30) days prior to the planned effective date of the program:

i) notify the Association of its intention to do so; and,

ii) provide the Association with a copy of the employment dispute resolution plan.

Compliance with this requirement shall not preclude an arbitrator from entertaining challenges as provided in Section 1. If an employer does not comply with this requirement, the Association reserves the right to decline its administrative services.

## 3. AAA as Administrator of the Arbitration

When parties agree to arbitrate under these rules, or when they provide for arbitration by the AAA and an arbitration is initiated under these rules, they thereby authorize the AAA to administer the arbitration. The authority and duties of the AAA are prescribed in these rules, and may be carried out through such of the AAA's representatives as it may direct.

## 4. Initiation of Arbitration

Arbitration shall be initiated in the following manner:

a. The parties may submit a joint request for arbitration.

b. In the absence of a joint request for arbitration:

(i) The initiating party (hereinafter "Claimant[s]") shall:

(1) File a written notice (hereinafter "Demand") of its intention to arbitrate at any regional office of the AAA, within the time limit established by the applicable statute of limitations if the dispute involves statutory rights. If no statutory rights are involved, the time limit established by the applicable arbitration agreement shall be followed. Any dispute over such issues shall be referred to the arbitrator. The filing shall be made in duplicate, and each copy shall include the applicable arbitration agreement. The Demand shall set forth the names, addresses, and telephone numbers of the parties; a brief statement of the nature of the dispute; the amount in controversy, if any; the remedy sought; and requested hearing location.

(2) Simultaneously mail a copy of the Demand to the other party (hereinafter "Respondent[s]").

(3) Include with its Demand the applicable filing fee, unless the parties agree to some other method of fee advancement.

(ii) The Respondent(s) shall file an Answer with the AAA within ten (10) days after the date of the letter from the AAA acknowledging receipt of the Demand. The Answer shall provide the Respondent's brief response to the claim and the issues presented. The Respondent(s) shall make its filing in duplicate with the AAA, and simultaneously shall mail a copy of the Answer to the Claimant.

(iii) The Respondent(s):

(1) May file a counterclaim with the AAA within ten (10) days after the letter from the AAA acknowledging receipt of the Demand. The filing shall be made in duplicate. The counterclaim shall set forth the nature of the claim, the amount in controversy, if any, and the remedy sought.

(2) Simultaneously shall mail a copy of any counterclaim to the Claimant.

(3) Shall include with its filing the applicable filing fee provided for by these rules.

(iv) The Claimant shall file an Answer to the counterclaim with the AAA within ten (10) days after the date of the letter from the AAA acknowledging receipt of the counterclaim. The Answer shall provide Claimant's brief response to the counterclaim and the issues presented. The Claimant shall make its filing in duplicate with the AAA, and simultaneously shall mail a copy of the Answer to the Respondent(s).

c. The form of any filing in these rules shall not be subject to technical pleading requirements.

## 5. Changes of Claim

Before the appointment of the Arbitrator, if either party desires to offer a new or different claim or counterclaim, such party must do so in writing by filing a written statement with the AAA and simultaneously mailing a copy to the other party(s), who shall have ten (10) days from the date of such mailing within which to file an Answer with the AAA. After the appointment of the arbitrator, a party may offer a new or different claim or counterclaim only in the discretion of the arbitrator.

## 6. Administrative and Mediation Conferences

Before the appointment of the arbitrator, any party may request, or the AAA, in its discretion, may schedule an administrative conference with a representative of the AAA and the parties and/or their representatives. The purpose of the administrative conference is to organize and expedite the arbitration, explore its administrative aspects, establish the most efficient means of selecting an arbitrator, and to consider mediation as a dispute resolution option. There is no administrative fee for this service.

At any time after the filing of the Demand, with the consent of the parties, the AAA will arrange a mediation conference under its Mediation Rules to facilitate settlement. The mediator shall not be any arbitrator appointed to the case, except by mutual agreement of the parties. There is no administrative fee for initiating a mediation under AAA Mediation Rules for parties to a pending arbitration.

## 7. Discovery

The arbitrator shall have the authority to order such discovery, by way of deposition, interrogatory, document production, or otherwise, as the arbitrator considers necessary to a full and fair exploration of the issues in dispute, consistent with the expedited nature of arbitration.

## 8. Arbitration Management Conference

As soon as possible after the appointment of the arbitrator, but not later than sixty (60) days thereafter, the arbitrator shall conduct an Arbitration Management Conference with the parties and/or their representatives, in person or by telephone, to explore and resolve matters that will expedite the arbitration proceedings. The specific matters to be addressed include:

   (i) the issues to be arbitrated;
  (ii) the date, time, place and estimated duration of the hearing;
 (iii) the resolution of outstanding discovery issues and establishment of discovery parameters;
 (iv) the law, standards, rules of evidence and burdens of proof that are to apply to the proceeding;
  (v) the exchange of stipulations and declarations regarding facts, exhibits, witnesses and other issues;
 (vi) the names of witnesses (including expert witnesses), the scope of witness testimony, and witness exclusion;
(vii) the value of bifurcating the arbitration into a liability phase and damages phase;
(viii) the need for a stenographic record;
 (ix) whether the parties will summarize their arguments orally or in writing;
  (x) the form of the award;
 (xi) any other issues relating to the subject or conduct of the arbitration;
(xii) the allocation of attorney's fees and costs.

The arbitrator shall issue oral or written orders reflecting his or her decisions on the above matters and may conduct additional conferences when the need arises.

There is no AAA administrative fee for an Arbitration Management Conference.

## 9. Location of the Arbitration

The parties may designate the location of the arbitration by mutual agreement. In the absence of such agreement before the appointment of the arbitrator, any party may request a specific hearing location by notifying the AAA in writing and simultaneously mailing a copy of the request to the other party(s). If the AAA receives no objection within ten (10) days of the date of the request, the hearing shall be held at the requested location. If a timely objection is filed with the AAA, the AAA shall have the power to determine the location and its decision shall be final and binding. After the appointment of the arbitrator, the arbitrator shall resolve all disputes regarding the location of the hearing.

## 10. Date and Time of Hearing

The arbitrator shall have the authority to set the date and time of the hearing in consultation with the parties.

## 11. Qualifications to Serve as Arbitrator and Rights of Parties to Disqualify Arbitrator

a. Standards of Experience and Neutrality.

(i) Arbitrators serving under these rules shall be experienced in the field of employment law.

(ii) Arbitrators serving under these rules shall have no personal or financial interest in the results of the proceedings in which they are appointed and shall have no relation to the underlying dispute or to the parties or their counsel that may create an appearance of bias.

(iii) The roster of available arbitrators will be established on a non-discriminatory basis, diverse by gender, ethnicity, background and qualifications.

(iv) The Association may, upon request of a party or upon its own initiative, supplement the list of proposed arbitrators in disputes arising out of individually negotiated employment contracts with persons from the regular Commercial Roster, to allow the Association to respond to the particular needs of the dispute. In multi-arbitrator disputes, at least one of the arbitrators shall be experienced in the field of employment law.

b. Standards of Disclosure by Arbitrator

Prior to accepting appointment, the prospective arbitrator shall disclose all information that might be relevant to the standards of neutrality set forth in this Section, including but not limited to service as a neutral in any past or pending case involving any of the parties, or that may prevent a prompt hearing.

c. Disqualification for Failure to Meet Standards of Experience and Neutrality.

An arbitrator may be disqualified in two ways:

(i) No later than ten (10) days after the appointment of the arbitrator, all parties jointly may challenge the qualifications of an Arbitrator by communicating their objection to the AAA in writing. Upon receipt of a joint objection, the arbitrator shall be replaced.

(ii) Any party may challenge the qualifications of an arbitrator by communicating its objection to the AAA in writing. Upon receipt of the objection, the AAA either shall replace the arbitrator or communicate the objection to the other parties. If any party believes that the objection does not merit disqualification of the arbitrator, the party shall so communicate to the AAA and to the other parties within ten (10) days of the receipt of the objection from the AAA. Upon objection of a party to the service of an arbitrator, the AAA shall determine whether the arbitrator should be disqualified and shall inform the parties of its decision, which shall be conclusive.

## 12. Number and Appointment of Neutral Arbitrators

a. If the parties do not specify the number of arbitrators, the dispute shall be heard and determined by one arbitrator. If the parties cannot agree upon the number of arbitrators, the AAA shall have the authority to determine the number of arbitrators.

b. If the parties have not appointed an arbitrator and have not provided any method of appointment, the arbitrator shall be appointed in the following manner:

(i) Immediately after it receives the Demand, the AAA shall mail simultaneously to each party a letter containing an identical list of the names of all arbitrators who are members of the regional Employment Dispute Resolution Roster. To the extent possible, the AAA will provide the names of the parties or their representatives in recent cases decided by the listed arbitrators.

(ii) Each party shall have ten (10) days from the date of the letter in which to select the name of a mutually acceptable arbitrator to hear and determine their dispute. If the parties cannot agree upon a mutually acceptable arbitrator, they shall so notify the AAA. Within ten (10) days of the receipt of that notice, the AAA shall send the parties a shorter list of arbitrators who are members of the regional Employment Dispute Resolution Roster. Each party shall have ten (10) days from the date of the letter containing the revised list to strike any names objected to, number the remaining names in order of preference, and return the list to the AAA. If a party does not return the list within the time specified, all of the listed persons shall be deemed acceptable to that party.

(iii) The AAA shall invite the acceptance of the arbitrator, whom both parties have selected as mutually acceptable or, in the case of resort to the ranking procedure, the arbitrator who has received the highest rating in the order of preference that the parties have specified.

(iv) If the parties fail to agree on any of the persons whom the AAA submits for consideration, or if mutually acceptable arbitrators are unable to act, or if for any other reason the appointment cannot be made from the list of persons whom the AAA submits for consideration, the AAA shall have the power to make the appointment from among other members of the Roster without the submission of additional lists.

## 13. Vacancies

If for any reason an arbitrator is unable to perform the duties of the office, the AAA may, on proof satisfactory to it, declare the office vacant. The vacancy shall be filled in accordance with applicable provisions of these rules.

In the event of a vacancy in a panel of neutral arbitrators after the hearings have commenced, the remaining arbitrator or arbitrators may continue with the hearing and determination of the controversy, unless the parties agree otherwise.

## 14. Representation

Any party may be represented by counsel or by any other person whom the party designates. For parties without representation, the AAA will, upon request, provide reference to institutions which might offer assistance. A party who intends to be represented shall notify the other party and the AAA of the name and address of the representative at least ten (10) days prior to the date set for the hearing or conference at which that person is first to appear. If a representative files a Demand or an Answer, the obligation to give notice of representative status is deemed satisfied.

## 15. Attendance at Hearings

The arbitrator shall have the authority to exclude witnesses, other than a party, from the hearing during the testimony of any other witness. The arbitrator also shall have the authority to decide whether any person who is not a witness may attend the hearing.

### 16. Confidentiality of Hearings

The arbitrator shall maintain the confidentiality of the hearings and shall have the authority to make appropriate rulings to safeguard that confidentiality, unless the parties agree otherwise or the law provides to the contrary.

### 17. Postponements

The arbitrator: (1) may postpone any hearing upon the request of a party for good cause shown; (2) must postpone any hearing upon the mutual agreement of the parties; and (3) may postpone any hearing on his or her own initiative.

### 18. Oaths

Before proceeding with the first hearing, each arbitrator may take an oath of office and, if required by law, shall do so. The arbitrator may require witnesses to testify under oath administered by any duly qualified person and, if it is required by law or requested by any party, shall do so.

### 19. Majority Decision

All decisions and awards of the arbitrators must be by a majority, unless the unanimous decision of all arbitrators is expressly required by the arbitration agreement or by law.

### 20. Order of Proceedings and Communication With Arbitrators

A hearing shall be opened by: (1) filing the oath of the arbitrator, where required; (2) recording the date, time, and place of the hearing; (3) recording the presence of the arbitrator, the parties, and their representatives, if any; and (4) receiving into the record the Demand and the Answer, if any. The arbitrator may, at the beginning of the hearing, ask for statements clarifying the issues involved.

The parties shall bear the same burdens of proof and burdens of producing evidence as would apply if their claims and counterclaims had been brought in court.

Witnesses for each party shall submit to direct and cross examination as approved by the arbitrator.

With the exception of the rules regarding the allocation of the burdens of proof and going forward with the evidence, the arbitrator has the authority to set the rules for the conduct of the proceedings and shall exercise that authority to afford a full and equal opportunity to all parties to present any evidence that the arbitrator deems material and relevant to the resolution of the dispute.

Documentary and other forms of physical evidence, when offered by either party, may be received in evidence by the arbitrator.

The names and addresses of all witnesses and a description of the exhibits in the order received shall be made a part of the record.

There shall be no ex parte communication with the arbitrator, unless the parties and the arbitrator agree to the contrary in advance of the communication.

## 21. Arbitration in the Absence of a Party or Representative

Unless the law provides to the contrary, the arbitration may proceed in the absence of any party or representative who, after due notice, fails to be present or fails to obtain a postponement. An award shall not be based solely on the default of a party. The arbitrator shall require the party who is present to present such evidence as the arbitrator may require for the making of the award.

## 22. Evidence

The parties may offer such evidence as is relevant and material to the dispute and shall produce such evidence as the arbitrator deems necessary to an understanding and determination of the dispute. An arbitrator or other person authorized by law to subpoena witnesses or documents may do so upon the request of any party or independently.

The arbitrator shall be the judge of the relevance and materiality of the evidence offered, and conformity to legal rules of evidence shall not be necessary. The arbitrator may in his or her discretion direct the order of proof, bifurcate proceedings, exclude cumulative or irrelevant testimony or other evidence, and direct the parties to focus their presentations on issues the decision of which could dispose of all or part of the case. All evidence shall be taken in the presence of all of the arbitrators and all of the parties, except where any of the parties is absent, in default, or has waived the right to be present.

## 23. Evidence by Affidavit or Declaration and Post–Hearing Filing of Documents or Other Evidence

The arbitrator may receive and consider the evidence of witnesses by affidavit, but shall give it only such weight as the arbitrator deems it entitled to after consideration of any objection made to its admission.

If the parties agree or the arbitrator directs that documents or other evidence may be submitted to the arbitrator after the hearing, the documents or other evidence shall be filed with the AAA for transmission to the arbitrator, unless the parties agree to a different method of distribution. All parties shall be afforded an opportunity to examine such documents or other evidence and to lodge appropriate objections, if any.

## 24. Inspection or Investigation

An arbitrator finding it necessary to make an inspection or investigation in connection with the arbitration shall direct the AAA to so advise the parties. The arbitrator shall set the date and time, and the AAA shall notify the parties. Any party who so desires may be present during the inspection or investigation. In the event that one or all parties are not present during the inspection or investigation, the arbitrator shall make an oral or written report to the parties and afford them an opportunity to comment.

## 25. Interim Measures

At the request of any party, the arbitrator may take whatever interim measures he or she deems necessary with respect to the dispute, including measures for the conservation of property.

Such interim measures may be taken in the form of an interim award and the arbitrator may require security for the costs of such measures.

## 26. Closing of Hearing

The arbitrator shall specifically inquire of all parties whether they have any further proofs to offer or witnesses to be heard. Upon receiving negative replies or if satisfied that the record is complete, the arbitrator shall declare the hearing closed.

If briefs are to be filed, the hearing shall be declared closed as of the final date set by the arbitrator for the receipt of briefs. If documents are to be filed as provided in Section 23 and the date set for their receipt is later than that set for the receipt of briefs, the later date shall be the date of closing the hearing. The time limit within which the arbitrator is required to make the award shall commence to run, in the absence of other agreements by the parties, upon closing of the hearing.

### 27. Reopening of Hearing

The hearing may be reopened by the arbitrator upon the arbitrator's initiative, or upon application of a party for cause shown, at any time before the award is made. If reopening the hearing would prevent the making of the award within the specific time agreed on by the parties in the contract(s), out of which the controversy has arisen, the matter may not be reopened unless the parties agree on an extension of time. When no specific date is fixed in the contract, the arbitrator may reopen the hearing and shall have thirty (30) days from the closing of the reopened hearing within which to make an award.

### 28. Waiver of Oral Hearing

The parties may provide, by written agreement, for the waiver of oral hearings in any case. If the parties are unable to agree as to the procedure, the AAA shall specify a fair and equitable procedure.

### 29. Waiver of Objection/Lack of Compliance with These Rules

Any party who proceeds with the arbitration after knowledge that any provision or requirement of these rules has not been complied with, and who fails to state objections thereto in writing, shall be deemed to have waived the right to object.

### 30. Extensions of Time

The parties may modify any period of time by mutual agreement. The AAA or the arbitrator may for good cause extend any period of time established by these rules, except the time for making the award. The AAA shall notify the parties of any extension.

## 31. Serving of Notice

Each party shall be deemed to have consented that any papers, notices, or process necessary or proper for the initiation or continuation of an arbitration under these rules; for any court actions in connection therewith; or for the entry of judgment on an award made under these procedures, may be served on a party by mail addressed to the party or its representative at the last known address or by personal service, in or outside the state where the arbitration is to be held.

The AAA and the parties may also use facsimile transmission, telex, telegram, or other written forms of electronic communication to give the notices required by these rules.

## 32. The Award

a. The award shall be made promptly by the arbitrator and, unless otherwise agreed by the parties or specified by law, no later than thirty (30) days from the date of closing of the hearing or, if oral hearings have been waived, from the date of the AAA's transmittal of the final statements and proofs to the arbitrator.

b. The award shall be in writing and shall be signed by a majority of the arbitrators and shall provide the written reasons for the award unless the parties agree otherwise. It shall be executed in the manner required by law.

c. The arbitrator may grant any remedy or relief that the arbitrator deems just and equitable, including any remedy or relief that would have been available to the parties had the matter been heard in court. The arbitrator shall, in the award, assess arbitration fees, expenses, and compensation as provided in Sections 35, 36, and 37 in favor of any party and, in the event any administrative fees or expenses are due the AAA, in favor of the AAA.

d. The arbitrator shall have the authority to provide for the reimbursement of representative's fees, in whole or in part, as part of the remedy, in accordance with applicable law.

e. If the parties settle their dispute during the course of the arbitration, the arbitrator may set forth the terms of the settlement in a consent award.

f. The parties shall accept as legal delivery of the award the placing of the award or a true copy thereof in the mail, addressed to a party or its representative at the last known address, personal service of the award, or the filing of the award in any manner that may be required by law.

g. The arbitrator's award shall be final and binding. Judicial review shall be limited, as provided by law.

### 33. Modification of Award

Within twenty (20) days after the transmittal of an award, any party, upon notice to the other parties, may request the arbitrator to correct any clerical, typographical, technical or computational error in the award. The arbitrator is not empowered to redetermine the merits of any claim already decided.

The other parties shall be given ten (10) days to respond to the request. The arbitrator shall dispose of the request within twenty (20) days after transmittal by the AAA to the arbitrator of the request and any response thereto.

If applicable law requires a different procedural time frame, that procedure shall be followed.

### 34. Release of Documents for Judicial Proceedings

The AAA shall, upon the written request of a party, furnish to the party, at that party's expense, certified copies of any papers in the AAA's case file that may be required in judicial proceedings relating to the arbitration.

## 35. Judicial Proceedings and Exclusion of Liability

a. No judicial proceeding by a party relating to the subject matter of the arbitration shall be deemed a waiver of the party's right to arbitrate.

b. Neither the AAA nor any arbitrator in a proceeding under these rules is or shall be considered a necessary or proper party in judicial proceedings relating to the arbitration.

c. Parties to these procedures shall be deemed to have consented that judgment upon the arbitration award may be entered in any federal or state court having jurisdiction.

d. Neither the AAA nor any arbitrator shall be liable to any party for any act or omission in connection with any arbitration conducted under these procedures.

## 36. Administrative Fees

As a not-for-profit organization, the AAA shall prescribe filing and other administrative fees to compensate it for the cost of providing administrative services. The AAA administrative fee schedule, in effect at the time the demand for arbitration or submission agreement is received, shall be applicable.

The filing fee shall be advanced by the initiating party or parties, subject to final apportionment by the arbitrator in the award.

The AAA may, in the event of extreme hardship on any party, defer or reduce the administrative fees.

### 37. Expenses

Unless otherwise agreed by the parties, the expenses of witnesses for either side shall be borne by the party producing such witnesses. All expenses of the arbitration, including required travel and other expenses of the arbitrator, AAA representatives, and any witness and the costs relating to any proof produced at the direction of the arbitrator, shall be borne equally by the parties, unless they agree otherwise or unless the arbitrator directs otherwise in the award.

### 38. Neutral Arbitrator's Compensation

Arbitrators shall charge a rate consistent with the arbitrator's stated rate of compensation. If there is disagreement concerning the terms of compensation, an appropriate rate shall be established with the arbitrator by the AAA and confirmed to the parties.

Any arrangement for the compensation of a neutral arbitrator shall be made through the AAA and not directly between the parties and the arbitrator. Payment of the arbitrator's fees and expenses shall be made by the AAA from the fees and moneys collected by the AAA from the parties for this purpose.

### 39. Deposits

The AAA may require the parties to deposit in advance of any hearings such sums of money as it deems necessary to cover the expenses of the arbitration, including the arbitrator's fee, if any, and shall render an accounting to the parties and return any unexpended balance at the conclusion of the case.

### 40. Interpretation and Application of Rules

The arbitrator shall interpret and apply these rules as they relate to the arbitrator's powers and duties. When there is more than one arbitrator and a difference arises among them concerning the meaning or application of these rules, it shall be resolved by a majority vote. If that is not possible, either an arbitrator or a party may refer the question to the AAA for final decision. All other procedures shall be interpreted and applied by the AAA.

## ADMINISTRATIVE FEE SCHEDULE

### Administrative Fee

The AAA's administrative fees are based on filing and service charges. Arbitrator compensation is not included in this schedule. Unless the parties agree otherwise, arbitrator compensation and administrative fees are subject to allocation by the arbitrator in the award.

### Filing Fees

For disputes which arise out of employer-promulgated plans:

In cases before a single arbitrator, a nonrefundable filing fee in the amount of $500 is payable in full by a filing party when a claim is filed, unless the plan provides otherwise.

In cases before three or more arbitrators, a nonrefundable filing fee in the amount of $1,500 is payable in full by a filing party when a claim is filed, unless the plan provides otherwise.

### Hearing Fees

For each day of hearing held before a single arbitrator, an administrative fee of $150 is payable by each party.

For each day of hearing held before a multi-arbitrator panel, an administrative fee of $250 is payable by each party.

There is no AAA hearing fee for the initial Arbitration Management Conference.

## Postponement/Cancellation Fees

A fee of $150 is payable by a party causing a postponement of any hearing scheduled before a single arbitrator.

A fee of $250 is payable by a party causing a postponement of any hearing scheduled before a multi-arbitrator panel.

## Hearing Room Rental

The hearing fees described above do not cover the rental of hearing rooms, which are available on a rental basis. Check with the administrator for availability and rates.

## Suspension for Nonpayment

If arbitrator compensation or administrative charges have not been paid in full, the administrator may so inform the parties in order that one of them may advance the required payment. If such payments are not made, the tribunal may order the suspension or termination of the proceedings. If no arbitrator has yet been appointed, the administrator may suspend the proceedings.

For disputes which arise out of all other employment contracts, please refer to the Administrative Fee Schedule in the Commercial Arbitration Rules.

[Employment Mediation Rules Omitted]

# APPENDIX D

# AAA EXCELLERATION PROGRAM

Copyright 1996 by the American Arbitration Association. All rights reserved.

1. Agreement of Parties.
2. Appointment of Neutral Arbitrator.
3. Qualifications of Neutral Arbitrator.
4. Vacancies.
5. Date, Time, and Place of Hearing.
6. No Stenographic Record.
7. Proceedings.
8. Desk Arbitration.
9. Posthearing Briefs.
10. Time of Award.
11. Form of Award.

Administrative Fees.

### The EXCELLERATION Program

Responding to concerns over rising costs and delays in grievance arbitration, a joint committee of labor and management leaders cooperated with the American Arbitration Association in establishing The EXCELLERATION Program. Features of the Program include scheduling of hearings within 15 days of filing with the AAA and awards rendered no later than 24 hours after the hearing. In return for giving up certain features of traditional labor arbitration, such as transcripts, briefs, and extensive opinions, the parties using these simplified procedures can get prompt decisions and cost savings.

A national roster of arbitrators selected from among the most active members of the National Academy of Arbitrators has been established by a joint labor/management committee. The AAA will appoint arbitrators to hear cases submitted under this Program from the aforementioned roster.

A special feature of the Program is the opportunity, if the parties agree, to have the matter decided by the arbitrator based on written submissions only, without the necessity of conducting an oral hearing.

Leading labor arbitrators have indicated a willingness to offer their services under these procedures, and the Association will only assign experienced, qualified arbitrators available to hear cases within 15 days of filing.

## 1. Agreement of Parties

These procedures shall apply whenever the parties have agreed to arbitrate under them.

## 2. Appointment of Neutral Arbitrator

The AAA shall appoint a single neutral arbitrator from its Panel of Labor Arbitrators qualified under this Program. The arbitrator shall hear and determine the case within 15 days of submission of the matter to the AAA.

## 3. Qualifications of Neutral Arbitrator

No person shall serve as a neutral arbitrator in any arbitration in which that person has any financial or personal interest in the result of the arbitration. Prior to accepting an appointment, the prospective arbitrator shall disclose any circumstance likely to prevent a prompt hearing or to create a presumption of bias. Upon receipt of such information, the AAA shall immediately replace that arbitrator or communicate the information to the parties.

### 4. Vacancies

The AAA is authorized to substitute another arbitrator if a vacancy occurs or if an appointed arbitrator is unable to serve promptly.

### 5. Date, Time, and Place of Hearing

The arbitrator shall fix the date, time, and place of the hearing, notice of which must be given at least 24 hours in advance. Such notice may be given orally or by facsimile.

### 6. No Stenographic Record

There shall be no stenographic record of the proceedings.

### 7. Proceedings

The hearing shall be conducted by the arbitrator in whatever manner will most expeditiously permit full presentation of the evidence and arguments of the parties. The arbitrator shall make appropriate minutes of the proceedings. Normally, the hearing shall be completed within 3 hours. In unusual circumstances and for good cause shown, the arbitrator may schedule an additional hearing to be held promptly.

### 8. Desk Arbitration

When the parties agree that the matter will be decided on the basis of document submission, each shall send two copies of their respective documentation to the AAA and to each other within seven days of the filing. The parties will have an additional seven days to file any answering statements with the AAA and each other. Thereafter, the

AAA shall forward the documents to the arbitrator, which shall be done within seven days.

## 9. Posthearing Briefs

There shall be no posthearing briefs.

## 10. Time of Award

The award shall be rendered promptly by the arbitrator no later than 24 hours from the date of the closing of the hearing unless otherwise agreed by the parties.

## 11. Form of Award

The award shall be in writing and shall be signed by the arbitrator. The award will specify the remedy, if any, and there will be no opinion unless all parties agree or one is otherwise required. If an opinion is required, the parties will share the additional arbitrator compensation.

## Administrative Fees

### Program Fee

A fee of $275 per party is due to the AAA within 45 days of submission of the case to the Program. This fee includes the administrative fee of the AAA ($200) as well as 3 hours' compensation for the arbitrator ($350).

If the case goes beyond 3 hours, the parties will be billed for additional arbitrators' compensation on a pro rata basis.

A surcharge of $35 will be due from any party that does not pay the Program fee within 45 days.

### Additional Hearing Fees

A fee of $50 is payable by each party for each hearing held after the first hearing.

## Hearing Room Rental

There may be a rental fee for the use of an AAA hearing room. Please check with the local AAA regional office for availability and rates.

## Postponement Fees

A fee of $50 is payable by a party causing a postponement of any scheduled hearing.

# APPENDIX E
# AAA FORMS

1. Demand for Arbitration.
2. Submission to Arbitration.
3. List for Selection of Arbitrator.
4. Notice of Appointment and Arbitrator's Oath.
5. Notice of Hearing.
6. Subpoena Duces Tecum.
7. Stipulation.
8. Award of Arbitrator.
9. Arbitrator's Bill.

# Form 1. Demand for Arbitration

## American Arbitration Association

*MEDIATION  Please consult the AAA regarding mediation procedures. If you want the AAA to contact the other party and attempt to arrange a mediation, please check this box.* ☐

### VOLUNTARY LABOR ARBITRATION RULES
### DEMAND FOR ARBITRATION

DATE: _____

TO: Name _____
(of the party upon whom the demand is made)

Address _____

City and State _____ ZIP Code _____

Telephone ( ) _____ Fax _____

Name of Representative _____
(if known)

Representative's Address _____

City and State _____ ZIP Code _____

Telephone ( ) _____ Fax _____

The named claimant, a party to an arbitration agreement contained in a written contract, dated _____ _____, providing for arbitration under the Voluntary Labor Arbitration Rules, hereby demands arbitration thereunder.

(Attach the arbitration clause or quote it hereunder.)

NATURE OF DISPUTE:

CLAIM OR RELIEF SOUGHT: (amount, if any)

HEARING LOCALE REQUESTED: _____
(City and State)

You are hereby notified that copies of our arbitration agreement and of this demand are being filed with the American Arbitration Association at its _____ office, with the request that it commence the administration of the arbitration. Under the rules, you may file an answering statement after notice from the administrator.

Signed _____ Title _____
(may be signed by a representative)

Name of Claimant _____

Address (to be used in connection with this case) _____

City and State _____ ZIP Code _____

Telephone ( ) _____ Fax _____

Name of Representative _____

Representative's Address _____

City and State _____ ZIP Code _____

Telephone ( ) _____ Fax _____

To institute proceedings, please send three copies of this demand with the administrative fee, as provided for in the rules, to the AAA. Send the original demand to the respondent.

Form L2-2/90

## APPENDIX E

## Form 2. Submission to Arbitration

# American Arbitration Association

### SUBMISSION TO ARBITRATION

Date:

The named Parties hereby submit the following dispute to arbitration under the VOLUNTARY LABOR ARBITRATION RULES of the American Arbitration Association:

We agree that we will abide by and perform any Award rendered hereunder and that a judgment may be entered upon the Award.

Employer

Signed by                        Title

Address

Union                            Local

Signed by                        Title

Address

PLEASE FILE TWO COPIES

## Form 3. List for Selection of Arbitrator

# American Arbitration Association

**Do not send this form to the other party.**

CASE NUMBER: _____ DATE LIST SUBMITTED: _____

PARTIES: _____ AND _____

### LIST FOR SELECTION OF ARBITRATOR(S)

After striking the name of any unacceptable arbitrator(s), please indicate your order of preference by number. We will try to appoint arbitrator(s) mutually acceptable who can hear your case promptly. Leave as many names as possible.

NOTE: Biographical information is attached. Unless your response is received by the Association by _____, all names submitted may be deemed acceptable.

### REQUEST FOR DATES

To enable the arbitrator(s) to avoid fixing an inconvenient hearing date, please cross off the dates that are not acceptable for a hearing, but leave as many days as possible so that the first mutually agreeable date for hearing may be set. If a mutually agreeable date is not available for these two months, the arbitrator(s) is/are empowered under the rules to fix the time and place for each hearing. If this form is not returned by _____, it will be assumed that any open date is satisfactory to you. The hearing will then be scheduled for a date preferred by the other party.

**NOTE: Saturdays, Sundays, and other unavailable days have been marked off.**

Month of _____

| 1 | 2 | 3 | 4 | 5 | 6 | 7 |
|---|---|---|---|---|---|---|
| 8 | 9 | 10 | 11 | 12 | 13 | 14 |
| 15 | 16 | 17 | 18 | 19 | 20 | 21 |
| 22 | 23 | 24 | 25 | 26 | 27 | 28 |
| 29 | 30 | 31 | | | | |

Month of _____

| 1 | 2 | 3 | 4 | 5 | 6 | 7 |
|---|---|---|---|---|---|---|
| 8 | 9 | 10 | 11 | 12 | 13 | 14 |
| 15 | 16 | 17 | 18 | 19 | 20 | 21 |
| 22 | 23 | 24 | 25 | 26 | 27 | 28 |
| 29 | 30 | 31 | | | | |

Please note that hearings generally commence at _____ a.m./p.m.

I anticipate that my case will require _____ hours/days of hearing.

PARTY: _____

BY: _____ TITLE: _____

Your telephone or fax response to this inquiry will be appreciated and will expedite administration. Please refer to the telephone and fax numbers on the enclosed letterhead.

Form G4—4/89

## Form 4. Notice of Appointment and Arbitrator's Oath

**AMERICAN ARBITRATION ASSOCIATION**

In the Matter of the Arbitration between

Re:

### NOTICE OF APPOINTMENT

TO:
\*\*\*\*\*\*\*\*\*\*\*\*\*\*\*\*\*\*\*\*\*\*\*\*\*\*\*\*\*\*\*\*\*\*\*\*\*\*\*\*\*\*\*\*\*\*\*\*\*\*\*\*\*\*\*\*\*\*\*\*\*\*

You have been selected as arbitrator in the above case. If you are able to accept this responsibility, please sign below and return.

The Code of Professional Responsibility for Arbitrators of Labor-Management Disputes requires certain disclosures so that the parties can have complete confidence in the arbitrator's impartiality. Therefore, please disclose any current or past managerial, representational, or consultative relationship with the employer or labor organization involved in this proceeding, as well as any close personal relationship or other circumstances that might reasonably raise a question as to your impartiality. If you are serving concurrently as an advocate for or representative of parties in labor relations matters, or have done so in recent years, you should also disclose such activities before accepting appointment. Disclosure must also be made of any pertinent pecuniary interest. If you are aware of any such relationship, please describe it below. And, if any such relationship arises during the course of the arbitration, it must also be disclosed. The AAA will bring the facts to the attention of the parties.

\_\_\_\_\_ I HAVE NOTHING TO DISCLOSE.
\_\_\_\_\_ I HEREBY DISCLOSE THE FOLLOWING:

### ARBITRATOR'S OATH

, being duly sworn, hereby accept this appointment and will faithfully and fairly hear and decide the matters in controversy between the above-named parties, in accordance with their Arbitration Agreement, and will make an Award according to the best of the my understanding.

Dated _____    Signed _____

**NOTICE TO THE ARBITRATOR:** Please execute and return one copy to this office.

**ARBITRATOR'S PER DIEM:**

## Form 5. Notice of Hearing

# American Arbitration Association

### NOTICE OF HEARING

DATE:

TO: IN THE MATTER OF THE ARBITRATION BETWEEN:

PLEASE TAKE NOTICE that a hearing in the above-entitled arbitration will be held as follows.

Place

Date

Hour

Arbitrator(s)

NOTE:

Please attend promptly with your witnesses
and be prepared to present your proofs.

_____
Case Administrator

NOTICE: The arbitrator(s) have arranged their schedule and reserved the above date(s) based on the advice of the parties. Therefore, every effort should be made to appear on the date(s) scheduled. In the event that unforeseen circumstances make it impossible to attend the hearing as scheduled, a party requesting a postponement should obtain the agreement of the other party. If there is no mutual agreement, the arbitrator(s) will make a determination. *All requests for postponements must be communicated to the case administrator (not the arbitrator).* There should be no communication between the parties and the neutral arbitrator(s) other than at oral hearings. Postponements are subject to an AAA fee assessment, as set forth in the rules. In some instances, postponements are subject to cancellation fees by the arbitrator(s).

Any party wishing a stenographic record must make the arrangements directly with a stenographer and notify the other parties of such arrangements in advance of the hearing.

CC: The Arbitrator(s) Form 8-3/92

## Form 6. Subpoena Duces Tecum

**The Arbitration Tribunals of the American Arbitration Association**

In the Matter of the Arbitration between

Subpoena Duces Tecum
(Documents)

FROM THE PEOPLE OF THE STATE OF

to

GREETING:

WE COMMAND YOU that, all business and excuses being laid aside, you and each of you appear and attend before

, arbitrators(s)

acting under the arbitration law of this state, at

_____
(address)

on the      day of            , 19   , at       o'clock, to testify and give evidence in a certain arbitration, then and there to be held between the above entitled parties, and that you bring with you and produce certain

now in your custody.

Request by: _____   Signed: _____

_____              Signed: _____
Name of Representative                          Arbitrator(s)

_____
Address            ZIP Code

_____
Telephone

Dated: _____

Form G10–11/89

# Form 7. Stipulation

# American Arbitration Association

**Stipulation**

In the Matter of the Arbitration between

Case Number:

IT IS HEREBY STIPULATED AND AGREED between the Parties to the above entitled Arbitration that

---

(Name of Party)          (Name of Party)

(Signed by)          (Signed by)

(Title and Date)          (Title and Date)

Case No.

FORM STIP-1-AAA

## Form 8. Award of Arbitrator

# American Arbitration Association

_____ ARBITRATION TRIBUNAL

In the Matter of the Arbitration between

CASE NUMBER:

### AWARD OF ARBITRATOR(S)

I (WE), THE UNDERSIGNED ARBITRATOR(S), having been designated in accordance with the arbitration agreement entered into by the above-named parties and dated             and having been duly sworn and having duly heard the proofs and allegations of the parties, AWARD as follows:

| (Date) | (Signature of Arbitrator) |

STATE OF

COUNTY OF  } SS:

On this       day of              , 19    , before me personally came and appeared                              , to me known and known to me to be the individual(s) described in and who executed the foregoing instrument, and  he  acknowledged to me that  he  executed the same.

Form G3–9/92

## Form 9. Arbitrator's Bill

**ARBITRATOR'S BILL**

This bill is submitted on behalf of the arbitrator.

Arbitrator _____  Case Number _____

Address _____  Number of Grievances _____

_____  Arbitrator Control No. _____

**Make your check payable to, and mail it directly to, the arbitrator.**

UNION

EMPLOYER

**This area is to be completed by the arbitrator.**

ARBITRATOR COMPENSATION

Number of Hearing Days _____ @ $ _____ = $ _____
Hearing Dates _____
Study/Preparation Days (if available) _____ @ $ _____ = $ _____
Study and Preparation Dates _____
Other (Specify.) _____ _____ @ $ _____ = $ _____
                                                   FEE $ _____

ARBITRATOR EXPENSES

Transportation     $ _____
Hotel              $ _____
Meals              $ _____
Other (Specify.) _____ $ _____
                              EXPENSES $ _____
                              TOTAL $ _____

PAYABLE BY _____ $ _____
PAYABLE BY _____ $ _____

Arbitrator Signature _____ Date _____
Social-Security Number _____

Form 116-10/95

# APPENDIX F

# FMCS PROCEDURES FOR ARBITRATION SERVICES

## PART 1404—ARBITRATION SERVICES

### Subpart A—Arbitration Policy; Administration of Roster.

Sec.
1404.1 Scope and authority.
1404.2 Policy.
1404.3 Administrative responsibilities.

### Subpart B—Roster of Arbitrators; Admission and Retention.

1404.4 Roster and status of members.
1404.5 Listing on the roster; criteria for listing and retention.
1404.6 Inactive status.
1404.7 Listing fee.

### Subpart C—Procedures for Arbitration Services.

1404.8 Freedom of choice.
1404.9 Procedures for requesting arbitration lists and panels.
1404.10 Arbitrability.
1404.11 Nominations of arbitrators—Standard and nonstandard panels.
1404.12 Selection by parties and appointments of arbitrators.
1404.13 Conduct of hearings.

1404.14 Decision and award.
1404.15 Fees and charges of arbitrators.
1404.16 Reports and biographical sketches.

Appendix to Part 1404—Arbitration Policy;
Schedule of Fees.

**AUTHORITY:** 29 U.S.C. 172 and 29 U.S.C. 173 et seq.

## Subpart A—Arbitration Policy; Administration of Roster

### 1404.1 Scope and Authority

This chapter is issued by the Federal Mediation and Conciliation Service (FMCS) under Title II of the Labor Management Relations Act of 1947 (Pub L. 80–101) as amended. It applies to all arbitrators listed on the FMCS Roster of Arbitrators, to all applicants for listing on the Roster, and to all persons or parties seeking to obtain from FMCS either names or panels of names of arbitrators listed on the Roster in connection with disputes which are to be submitted to arbitration or factfinding.

### 1404.2 Policy

The labor policy of the United States promotes and encourages the use of voluntary arbitration to resolve disputes over the interpretation or application of collective bargaining agreements. Voluntary arbitration and factfinding are important features of constructive employment relations as alternatives to economic strife.

### 1404.3 Administrative Responsibilities

(a) *Director.* The Director of FMCS has responsibility for all aspects of FMCS arbitration activities and is the final agency authority on all questions concerning the Roster and FMCS arbitration procedures.

(b) *Office of Arbitration Services.* The Office of Arbitration Services (OAS) maintains a Roster of Arbitrators (the Roster); administers Subpart C of this part (Procedures for Arbitration Services); assists, promotes, and cooperates in the establishment of programs for training and developing new arbitrators; and provides names or panels of names of listed arbitrators to parties requesting them.

(c) *Arbitrator Review Board.* The Arbitrator Review Board shall consist of a chairman and members appointed by the Director who shall serve at the Director's pleasure. The Board shall be composed entirely of full-time officers or employees of the Federal Government and shall establish procedures for carrying out its duties.

(1) *Duties of the Board.* The Board shall:

(i) Review the qualifications of all applicants for listing on the Roster, interpreting and applying the criteria set forth in Section 1404.5;

(ii) Review the status of all persons whose continued eligibility for listing on the Roster has been questioned under subsection 1404.5;

(iii) Recommend to the Director the acceptance or rejection of applicants for listing on the Roster, or the withdrawal of listing on the Roster for any of the reasons set forth in this part;

(iv) At the request of the Director of FMCS, review arbitration policies and procedures, including all regulations and written guidance regarding the use of the FMCS arbitrators, and make recommendations regarding such policies and procedures to the Director.

(2) [Reserved]

## Subpart B—Roster of Arbitrators; Admission and Retention

### 1404.4 Roster and Status of Members

(a) *The Roster.* FMCS shall maintain a Roster of labor arbitrators consisting of persons who meet the criteria for listing contained in 1404.5 and who remain in good standing.

(b) *Adherence of Standards and Requirements.* Persons listed on the Roster shall comply with FMCS rules and regulations pertaining to arbitration and with such guidelines and procedures as may be issued by the OAS pursuant to Subpart C of this part. Arbitrators shall conform to the ethical standards and procedures set forth in the Code of Professional Responsibility for Arbitrators of Labor Management Disputes, as approved by the National Academy of Arbitrators, Federal Mediation and Conciliation Service, and the American Arbitration Association.

(c) *Status of Arbitrators.* Persons who are listed on the Roster and are selected or appointed to hear arbitration matters or to serve as factfinders do not become employees of the Federal Government by virtue of their selection or appointment. Following selection or appointment, the arbitrator's relationship is solely with the parties to the dispute, except that arbitrators are subject to certain reporting requirements and to standards of conduct as set forth in this Part.

(d) *Role of FMCS.* FMCS has no power to:

(1) Compel parties to appear before an arbitrator;

(2) Enforce an agreement to arbitrate;

(3) Compel parties to arbitrate any issue;

(4) Influence, alter, or set aside decisions of arbitrators on the Roster;

(5) Compel, deny, or modify payment of compensation to an arbitrator.

(e) *Nominations and Panels.* On request of the parties to an agreement to arbitrate or engage in factfinding, or where arbitration or factfinding may be provided for by statute, OAS will provide names or panels of names for a nominal fee. Procedures for obtaining these services are outlined in Subpart C of this part. Neither the submission of a nomination or panel nor the appointment of an arbitrator constitutes a determination by FMCS that an agreement to arbitrate or enter factfinding proceedings exists; nor does such action constitute a ruling that the matter in controversy is arbitrable under any agreement.

(f) *Rights of Persons Listed on the Roster.* No person shall have any right to be listed or to remain listed on the Roster. FMCS retains its authority and responsibility to assure that the needs of the parties using its services are served. To accomplish this purpose, FMCS may establish procedures for the preparation of panels or the appointment of arbitrators or factfinders which include consideration of such factors as background and experience, availability, acceptability, geographical location, and the expressed preferences of the parties. FMCS may also establish procedures for the removal from the Roster of those arbitrators who fail to adhere to provisions contained in this part.

## 1404.5 Listing on the Roster; Criteria for Listing and Retention

Persons seeking to be listed on the Roster must complete and submit an application form which may be obtained from OAS. Upon receipt of an executed application, OAS will review the application, assure that it is complete, make such inquiries as are necessary, and submit the application to the Arbitrator Review Board. The Board will review the completed application under the criteria in paragraphs (a), (b), and 8 of this section, and will forward to the FMCS Director its recommendation as to whether or not the applicant meets the criteria for listing on the Roster. The Director shall make all final decisions as to whether an applicant may be listed on the Roster. Each applicant shall be notified in writing of the Director's decision and the reasons therefor.

(a) *General Criteria.* Applicants for the Roster will be listed on the Roster upon a determination that they are experienced, competent, and acceptable in decision-making roles in the resolution of labor relations disputes.

(b) *Proof of Qualification.* Qualifications for listing on the Roster may be demonstrated by submission of five (5) arbitration awards prepared by the applicant while serving as an impartial arbitrator of record chosen by the parties to labor disputes arising under collective bargaining agreements. The Board will consider experience in relevant positions in collective bargaining or as a judge or hearing examiner in labor relations controversies as a substitute for such awards.

(c) *Advocacy.* Any person who at the time of application is an advocate as defined in paragraph (c)(1) of this section, must agree to cease such activity before being recommended for listing on the Roster by the Board. Except in the case of persons listed on the Roster as advocates before November 17, 1976, any person who did not divulge his or her advocacy at the time of listing or who becomes an advocate while listed on the Roster, shall be recommended for removal by the Board after the fact of advocacy is revealed.

   (1) *Definition of Advocacy.* An advocate is a person who represents employers, labor organizations, or individuals as an employee, attorney, or consultant, in matters of labor relations, including but not limited to the subjects of union representation and recogni-

tion matters, collective bargaining, arbitration, unfair labor practices, equal employment opportunity, and other areas generally recognized as constituting labor relations. The definition includes representatives of employers or employees in individual cases or controversies involving worker's compensation, occupational health or safety, minimum wage, or other labor standards matters. This definition of advocate also includes a person who is directly associated with an advocate in a business or professional relationship as, for example, partners or employees of a law firm. Consultants engaged only in joint education or training or other non-adversarial activities will not be deemed as advocates.

(d) *Duration of Listing, Retention.* Listing on the Roster shall be by decision of the Director of FMCS based upon the recommendations of the Arbitrator Review Board. The Board may recommend, and the Director may remove, any person listed on the Roster, for violation of this part and/or the Code of Professional Responsibility. Notice of cancellation or suspension shall be given to a person listed on the Roster whenever a Roster member:

(1) No longer meets the criteria for admission;

(2) Has become an advocate as defined in paragraph 8 of this section;

(3) Has been repeatedly or flagrantly delinquent in submitting awards;

(4) Has refused to make reasonable and periodic reports in a timely manner to FMCS, as required in Subpart C of this part, concerning activities pertaining to arbitration;

(5) Has been the subject of complaints by parties who use FMCS services, and the Board after appropriate inquiry, concludes that just cause for cancellation has been shown;

(6) Is determined by the Director to be unacceptable to the parties who use FMCS arbitration services; the Director may base a determination of unacceptability on FMCS records which show the number of times the arbitrator's name has been proposed to the parties and the number of times it has been selected. Such cases will be reviewed for extenuating circumstances, such as length of time on the Roster or prior history.

(e) The Board may, at its discretion, conduct an inquiry into the facts of any proposed removal from the Roster. An arbitrator listed on the Roster may only be removed after 60–day notice and an opportunity to submit a response or information showing why the listing should not be canceled. The Board may recommend to the Director whether to remove an arbitrator from the Roster. All determinations to remove an arbitrator from the Roster shall be made by the Director. Removals may be for a period of up to two (2) years, after which the arbitrator may seek reinstatement.

(f) The Director of OAS may suspend for a period not to exceed 180 days any person listed on the Roster who has violated any of the criteria in paragraph (d) of this section. Arbitrators shall be promptly notified of a suspension. They may appeal a suspension to the Arbitrator Review Board, which shall make a recommendation to the Director of FMCS. The decision of the Director of FMCS shall constitute the final action of the agency.

## 1404.6 Inactive Status

A member of the Roster who continues to meet the criteria for listing on the Roster may request that he or she be put in an inactive status on a temporary basis because of ill health, vacation, schedule, or other reasons.

### 1404.7 Listing Fee

All arbitrators will be required to pay an annual fee for listing on the Roster as set forth in the Appendix to this part.

### Subpart C—Procedures for Arbitration Services

### 1404.8 Freedom of Choice

Nothing contained in this part should be construed to limit the rights of parties who use FMCS arbitration services to jointly select any arbitrator or arbitration procedure acceptable to them. Once a request is made to OAS, all parties are subject to the procedures contained in this part.

### 1404.9 Procedures for Requesting Arbitration Lists and Panels

(a) The Office of Arbitration Services (OAS) has been delegated the responsibility for administering all requests for arbitration services. Requests should be addressed to the Federal Mediation and Conciliation Service, Office of Arbitration Services, Washington, DC 20427.

(b) The OAS will refer a panel of arbitrators to the parties upon request. The parties are encouraged to make joint requests. In the event, however, that the request is made by only one party, the OAS will submit a panel of arbitrators. However, the issuance of a panel—pursuant to either joint or unilateral request—is nothing more than a response to a request. It does not signify the adoption of any position by the FMCS regarding the arbitrability of any dispute or the terms of the parties' contract.

(c) As an alternative to a request for a panel of names, OAS will, upon written request, submit a list of all arbitrators and their biographical sketches from a designated geographical area. The parties may then select and deal directly with an arbitrator of their choice, with no further involvement of FMCS with the parties or the arbitrator. The parties may also request FMCS to make a direct appointment of their selection. In such a situation, a case number will be assigned.

(d) The OAS reserves the right to decline to submit a panel or make appointments of arbitrators, if the request submitted is overly burdensome or otherwise impracticable. The OAS, in such circumstances, may refer the parties to an FMCS mediator to help in the design of an alternative solution. The OAS may also decline to service any requests from parties with a demonstrated history of non-payment of arbitrator fees or other behavior which constrains the spirit or operation of the arbitration process.

(e) The parties are required to use the Request for Arbitration Panel (Form R–43), which has been prepared by the OAS and is available in quantity upon request to the Federal Mediation and Conciliation Service, Office of Arbitration Services, Washington, DC 20427, or by calling (202) 606–5111 or at www.fmcs.gov. Requests that do not contain all required information requested on the R–43 in typewritten form may be rejected.

(f) Requests made by only one party, for a service other than the furnishing of a standard list or panel of seven (7) arbitrators, will not be honored unless authorized by the applicable collective bargaining agreement. This includes unilateral requests for a second or third panel or for a direct appointment of an arbitrator.

(g) The OAS will charge a nominal fee for all requests for lists, panels, and other major services. Payments for these services must be received with the request for services before the service is delivered and may be paid by either labor or management or both. A schedule of fees is listed in the Appendix to this part.

## 1404.10 Arbitrability

The OAS will not decide the merits of a claim by either party that a dispute is not subject to arbitration.

## 1404.11 Nominations of Arbitrators

(a) The parties may also request a randomly selected panel containing the names of seven (7) arbitrators accompanied by a biographical sketch for each member of the panel. This sketch states the background, qualifications, experience, and all fees as furnished to the OAS by the arbitrator. Requests for a panel of seven (7) arbitrators, whether joint or unilateral, will be honored. Requests for a panel of other than seven (7) names, for a direct appointment of an arbitrator, for special qualifications or other service will not be honored unless jointly submitted or authorized by the applicable collective bargaining agreement. Alternatively, the parties may request a list and biographical sketches of some or all arbitrators in one or more designated geographical areas. If the parties can agree on the selection of an arbitrator, they may appoint their own arbitrator directly without any further case tracking by FMCS. No case number will be assigned.

(b) All panels submitted to the parties by the OAS, and all letters issued by the OAS making a direct appointment, will have an assigned FMCS case number. All future communications between the parties and the OAS should refer to this case number.

(c) The OAS will provide a randomly selected panel of arbitrators located in state(s) in proximity of the hearing site. The parties may request special qualifications of arbitrators experienced in certain issues or industries or that possess certain backgrounds. The OAS has no obligation to put an individual on any given panel, or on a minimum number of panels in any fixed period. In general:

(1) The geographic location of arbitrators placed on panels is governed by the site of the dispute as stated on the request received by the OAS.

(2) If at any time both parties request that a name or names be included, or omitted, from a panel, such name or names will be included, or omitted, unless the number of names is excessive. These inclusions/exclusions may not discriminate against anyone because of age, race, gender, ethnicity or religious beliefs.

(d) If the parties do not agree on an arbitrator from the first panel, the OAS will furnish a second and third panel to the parties upon joint request and payment of an additional fee. Requests for a second or third panel should be accompanied by a brief explanation as to why the previous panel(s) was inadequate. If parties are unable to agree on a selection after having received three panels, the OAS will make a direct appointment upon joint request.

## 1404.12 Selection by Parties and Appointments of Arbitrators

(a) After receiving a panel of names, the parties must notify the OAS of their selection of an arbitrator or of the decision not to proceed with arbitration. Upon notification of the selection of an arbitrator, the OAS will make a formal appointment of the arbitrator. The arbitrator, upon notification of appointment, is expected to communicate with the parties within 14 days to arrange for preliminary matters, such as the date and place of hearing. Should an arbitrator be notified directly by the parties that he or she has been selected, the Arbitrator must promptly notify the OAS of the selection and his or her willingness to serve. If the parties settle a case prior to the hearing, the parties must inform the arbitrator as well as the OAS.

Consistent failure to follow these procedures may lead to a denial of future OAS service.

(b) If the parties request a list of names and biographical sketches rather than a panel, they may choose to appoint and contact an arbitrator directly. In this situation, neither the parties nor the arbitrator is required to furnish any additional information to FMCS and no case number will be assigned.

(c) Where the parties' collective bargaining agreement is silent on the manner of selecting arbitrators, the parties may wish to consider any jointly determined method or one of the following methods for selection of an arbitrator from a panel:

(1) Each party alternately strikes a name from the submitted panel until one remains, **or**

(2) Each party advises the OAS of its order of preference by numbering each name on the panel and submitting the numbered lists in writing to the OAS. The name that has the lowest combined number will be appointed.

(3) In those situations where the parties separately notify the OAS of their preferred selections, once the OAS receives the preferred selection from one party, it will notify the other party that it has fourteen (14) days in which to submit its selections. If that party fails to respond within the deadline, the first party's choice will be honored. If, within 14 days, a second panel is requested and is allowed by the collective bargaining agreement, the requesting party must pay a fee for the second panel.

(d) The OAS will make a direct appointment of an arbitrator only upon joint request unless authorized by the applicable collective bargaining agreement.

(e) The issuance of a panel of names or a direct appointment in no way signifies a determination on arbitrability or an interpretation of the terms and conditions of the collective bargaining agreement. The resolution of such disputes rests solely with the parties.

### 1404.13  Conduct of Hearings

All proceedings conducted by the arbitrators shall be in conformity with the contractual obligations of the parties. The arbitrator shall comply with 1404.4(b). The conduct of the arbitration proceeding is under the arbitrator's jurisdiction and control, and the arbitrator's decision shall be based upon the evidence and testimony presented at the hearing or otherwise incorporated in the record of the proceeding. The arbitrator may, unless prohibited by law, proceed in the absence of any party who, after due notice, fails to be present or to obtain a postponement. An award rendered in an *ex parte* proceeding of this nature must be based upon evidence presented to the arbitrator.

### 1404.14  Decision and Award

(a) Arbitrators shall make awards no later than 60 days from the date of the closing of the record as determined by the arbitrator, unless otherwise agreed upon by the parties or specified by the collective bargaining agreement or law. However, failure to meet the 60 day deadline will not invalidate the process or award. A failure to render timely awards reflects upon the performance of an arbitrator and may lead to removal from the FMCS Roster.

(b) The parties should inform the OAS whenever a decision is unduly delayed. The arbitrator shall notify the OAS if and when the arbitrator (1) cannot schedule, hear, and render decisions promptly, or (2) learns a dispute has been settled by the parties prior to the decision.

(c) Within 15 days after an award has been submitted to the parties, the arbitrator shall submit an Arbitrator's Report and Fee Statement (Form R–19) to OAS showing a breakdown of the fee and expense charges so that the OAS may review conformance with stated charges under Section 1404.11(a). The Form R–19 is not to be used to invoice the parties.

(d) While FMCS encourages the publication of arbitration awards, arbitrators should not publicize awards if objected to by one of the parties.

### 1404.15 Fees and Charges of Arbitrators

(a) FMCS will charge all arbitrators an annual fee to be listed on the Roster. All arbitrators listed on the Roster may charge a per diem and other predetermined fees for services, if the amount of such fees have been provided in advance to FMCS. Each arbitrator's maximum per diem and other fees are set forth on a biographical sketch which is sent to the parties when panels are submitted. The arbitrator shall not change any fee or add charges without giving at least 30 days advance written notice to FMCS. Arbitrators with dual business addresses must bill the parties for expenses from the least expensive business address to the hearing site.

(b) In cases involving unusual amounts of time and expenses relative to the pre-hearing and post-hearing administration of a particular case, an administrative charge may be made by the arbitrator.

(c) Arbitrators shall divulge all charges to the parties and obtain agreement thereto immediately after appointment.

(d) The OAS requests that it be notified of any arbitrator's deviation from the policies expressed in this part. While the OAS does not resolve individual fee disputes, repeated complaints concerning the fees charged by an arbitrator will be brought to the attention of the Arbitrator Review Board for consideration. Similarly, repeated complaints by arbitrators concerning non-payment of fees by the parties may lead to the denial of services or other actions by the OAS.

### 1404.16 Reports and Biographical Sketches

(a) Arbitrators listed on the Roster shall execute and return all documents, forms and reports required by the OAS. They shall also keep the OAS informed of changes of address, telephone number, availability, and of any business or other connection or relationship which involves labor-management relations or which creates or gives the appearance of advocacy as defined in Section 1404.5 (c ) (1).

(b) The OAS will provide biographical sketches on each person admitted to the Roster from information supplied by applicants. Arbitrators may request revision of biographical information at later dates to reflect changes in fees, the existence of additional charges, or other relevant data. The OAS reserves the right to decide and approve the format and content of biographical sketches.

# APPENDIX G

# FMCS EXPEDITED ARBITRATION RULES

## Subpart D—Expedited Arbitration

In an effort to reduce the time and expense of some grievance arbitrations, FMCS is offering expedited procedures that may be appropriate in certain non-precedential cases or those that do not involve complex or unique issues. Expedited Arbitration is intended to be a mutually agreed upon process whereby arbitrator appointments, hearings and awards are acted upon quickly by the parties, FMCS, and the arbitrators. The process is streamlined by mandating short deadlines and eliminating requirements for transcripts, briefs and lengthy opinions.

## 1404.18 Procedures for Requesting Expedited Panels

(a) With the exception of the specific changes noted in this Subpart, all FMCS rules and regulations governing its arbitration services shall apply to Expedited Arbitration.

(b) Upon receipt of a joint Request for Arbitration Panel (Form R–43) indicating that expedited services are desired by both parties, the OAS will refer a panel of arbitrators.

(c) A panel of arbitrators submitted by the OAS in expedited cases shall be valid for up to 30 days. Only one panel will be submitted per case. If the parties are unable to mutually agree upon an arbitrator or if prioritized selections are not received from both parties within 30 days, the OAS will make a direct appointment of an arbitrator not on the original panel.

(d) If the parties mutually select an arbitrator, but the arbitrator is not available, the parties may select a second name from the same panel or the OAS will make a direct appointment of another arbitrator not listed on the original panel.

### 1404.19 Arbitration Process

(a) Once notified of the expedited case appointment by the OAS, the arbitrator must contact the parties within seven (7) calendar days.

(b) The parties and the arbitrator must attempt to schedule a hearing within 30 days of the appointment date.

(c) Absent mutual agreement, all hearings will be concluded within one day. No transcripts of the proceedings will be made and the filing of post-hearing briefs will not be allowed.

(d) All awards must be completed within seven (7) working days after the hearing. These awards are expected to be brief, concise, and not require extensive written opinion or research time.

### 1404.20 Arbitrator Eligibility

In an effort to increase exposure for new arbitrators, those arbitrators who have been listed on the Roster of Arbitrators for a period of five (5) years or less will be automatically placed on expedited panels submitted to the parties. However, all panels will also contain the names of at least two more senior arbitrators. In addition, the parties may jointly request a larger pool of arbitrators or a direct appointment of any arbitrator of their choice who is listed on the Roster.

## 1404.21 Proper Use of Expedited Arbitration

(a) FMCS reserves the right to cease honoring requests for Expedited Arbitration if a pattern of misuse of this process becomes apparent. Misuse may be indicated by the parties' frequent delaying of the process or referral of inappropriate cases.

(b) Arbitrators who exhibit a pattern of unavailability for appointments or who are repeatedly unable to schedule hearings or render awards within established deadlines will, after written warning, be considered ineligible for appointment for this service.

## Appendix Schedule of Fees

Annual listing fee for all arbitrators: $100 for the first address; $50 for second address.

Request for panel of arbitrators: $30 for each panel request (includes subsequent appointment).

Direct appointment of arbitrator $20 per appointment when a panel is not used.

List and biographical sketches of $10 per request plus $.10 per page arbitrators in a specific area.

# APPENDIX H
# FMCS FORMS

1. Request for Arbitration Panel (FMCS Form R–43).
2. Arbitrator's Report and Fee Statement.

# Form 1. Request for Arbitration Panel (FMCS Form R–43)

FMCS Form R-43
Revised June 1997

FEDERAL MEDIATION AND CONCILIATION SERVICE
WASHINGTON, D.C. 20427

Form Approved
OMB NO. 3076-0002
Expires 8-31-98

REQUEST FOR ARBITRATION PANEL

To: Office of Arbitration Services
Federal Mediation and Conciliation Service
Washington, D.C. 20427
or FAX (202) 606-3749

Date _____

☐ Please check if this panel is under FMCS Expedited Arbitration procedures. A joint request is required.

1. Name of Employer _____

   Name and Address of Representative to Receive Panel
   _____ *(Name)*
   _____ *(Street)*
   _____ *(City, State, Zip)*

   Telephone (include area code) _____ Fax (include area code) _____

2. Name of Union and Local No. _____

   Name and Address of Representative to Receive Panel
   _____ *(Name)*
   _____ *(Street)*
   _____ *(City, State, Zip)*

   Telephone (include area code) _____ Fax (include area code) _____

3. Site of Dispute _____ *(City, State, Zip)*

4. Type of Issue _____ *(Discharge, Holiday, Pay, Sick Leave, etc.)*

5. A panel of seven (7) names is usually provided; *If you desire a different number, please indicate:* _____

6. Type of Industry   ☐ Private Sector   ☐ Public Sector   ☐ Federal Sector

7. Special Requirements _____
   *(SPECIAL ARBITRATOR QUALIFICATIONS, TIME LIMITATIONS ON HEARING OR DECISION, GEOGRAPHICAL RESTRICTIONS, ETC.)*

8. Fee Enclosed *(Check One)*   ☐ Check   ☐ Money Order   Credit Card:   ☐ Visa   ☐ Master Card

   Name as it appears on Credit Card _____

   Card Number _____ Exp. ___ / ___

   For Federal Agencies: ALC _____

9. Signatures (Joint) _____ _____
   *(Union)* *(Employer)*

A submission will be made based on the request of a single party. However, a submission of a panel should not be construed as anything more than compliance with a request and does not reflect on the substance or arbitrability of the issue in dispute.

PAPERWORK REDUCTION ACT NOTICE: The estimated burden associated with this collection of information is 10 minutes per respondent. Comments concerning the accuracy of this burden estimate and suggestions for reducing this burden should be sent to Office of General Counsel, Federal Mediation and Conciliation Service, 2100 K Street, N.W., Washington DC 20427. Persons are not required to respond to this collection of information unless it displays the current valid OMB control number.

# Form 2. Arbitrator's Report and Fee Statement (FMCS Form R–19)

FMCS Form R-19
Revised AUGUST 1996

FEDERAL MEDIATION AND CONCILIATION SERVICE
WASHINGTON, D.C. 20427
**ARBITRATOR'S REPORT AND FEE STATEMENT**

Form Approved
OMB No. 3076-0003
Expires 8/31/98

FILE NO. _____ ARBITRATOR _____ DATE OF AWARD _____

I. COMPANY _____
                  (Name)            (City)         (State)       (Zip Code)

II. UNION _____
              (Name)          (Local No.)          (Affiliation)

III. ISSUES: *(Please check either a or b, and complete c and d)*

a. ☐ New or reopened contract terms
b. ☐ Contract interpretation or application
c.   Issue or Issues *(Please check only one issue per grievance)*
  1. ☐ Discharge and disciplinary actions
  2. ☐ Incentive rates or standards
  3. ☐ Job evaluation
  4. ☐ Work assignment
  5. ☐ Job classification
6. Seniority:
  ☐ a. Promotion and upgrading
  ☐ b. Layoff, bumping and recall
  ☐ c. Transfer
  ☐ d. Other
7. Overtime:
  a. ☐ Overtime pay
  b. ☐ Overtime distribution
  c. ☐ Compulsory overtime
  d. ☐ Other
8. ☐ Union officers - superseniority and union business
9. ☐ Strike or lockout issues *(excluding disciplinary actions)*

10. ☐ Vacations and vacation pay
11. ☐ Holidays and holiday pay
12. ☐ Scheduling of work
13. ☐ Reporting, call-in and call-back pay
14. ☐ Health and welfare
15. ☐ Pensions
16. ☐ Other fringe benefits
17. Scope of agreement:
  ☐ a. Subcontracting
  ☐ b. Jurisdictional disputes
  ☐ c. Foreman, supervision, etc.
  ☐ d. Mergers, consolidations, accretion, other plants
18. ☐ Working conditions, including safety
19. ☐ Severance pay
20. ☐ Rate of pay
21. ☐ Discrimination
22. ☐ Management rights
23. ☐ Job posting & bidding
24. ☐ Wage issues
25. ☐ Miscellaneous

d. Was arbitrability of grievance involved? ☐ Yes ☐ No If yes, check one or both ☐ Procedural ☐ Substantive

4. Hearing:
  a. Were briefs filed? ☐ Yes ☐ No If yes, give date _____
  b. Was transcript taken? ☐ Yes ☐ No      d. Dates of Hearing: _____
  c. Number of grievances: _____    e. Date of grievance _____
                                                             f. Was there any waiver by parties on date the award was due?
                                                                                                       Yes ☐ No ☐

5. FEES AND DAYS: For services as Arbitrator
  No. of Days: _____ + _____ + _____ = _____ x $ _____ = $ _____
               Hearings     Travel     Study     Total    Per Diem Rate    Total Fee
  Expenses:   Transportation $ _____ + Other $ _____ = $ _____
                                                                                           Total Expenses

Amount payable by Company $ _____

Amount payable by Union $ _____                                TOTAL $ _____

6. PANEL: If tripartite panel or more than one arbitrator made the award, check here _____

7. Date of this Report _____ Signature _____

*Please do not write below this line*

DATE CLOSED: _____ REVIEWED BY: _____

PAPERWORK REDUCTION ACT NOTICE: The estimated burden associated with this collection of information is one and one-hour per respondent, comments concerning the accuracy of this burden estimate and suggestions for reducing this burden should be sent to the Director of Arbitration Services, Federal Mediation and Conciliation Service (FMCS), 2100 K Street, N.W., Washington, D.C. 20427. Persons are not required to respond to this collection of information unless it displays the currently valid OMB control number.

# APPENDIX I

# CODE OF PROFESSIONAL RESPONSIBILITY FOR ARBITRATORS OF LABOR–MANAGEMENT DISPUTES

**CODE OF PROFESSIONAL RESPONSIBILITY FOR ARBITRATORS OF LABOR–MANAGEMENT DISPUTES OF THE NATIONAL ACADEMY OF ARBITRATORS, AMERICAN ARBITRATION ASSOCIATION, AND FEDERAL MEDIATION AND CONCILIATION SERVICE, As amended and in effect May 30, 1996.**

## FOREWORD

This "Code of Professional Responsibility for Arbitrators of Labor–Management Disputes" supersedes the "Code of Ethics and Procedural Standards for Labor–Management Arbitration," approved in 1951 by a Committee of the American Arbitration Association, by the National Academy of Arbitrators, and by representatives of the Federal Mediation and Conciliation Service.

Revision of the 1951 Code was initiated officially by the same three groups in October, 1972. The following members of a Joint Steering Committee were designated to draft a proposal:

Chair

William E. Simkin

Representing American Arbitration Association

Frederick H. Bullen

Donald B. Straus

Representing Federal Mediation and Conciliation Service

Lawrence B. Babcock, Jr.

L. Lawrence Schultz

Representing National Academy of Arbitrators

Sylvester Garrett

Ralph T. Seward

The proposal of the Joint Steering Committee was issued on November 30, 1974, and thereafter adopted by all three sponsoring organizations. Reasons for Code revision should be noted briefly. Ethical considerations and procedural standards were deemed to be sufficiently intertwined to warrant combining the subject matter of Parts I and II of the 1951 Code under the caption of "Professional Responsibility." It also seemed advisable to eliminate admonitions to the parties (Part III of the 1951 Code) except as they appear incidentally in connection with matters primarily involving responsibilities of arbitrators. The substantial growth of third-party participation in dispute resolution in the public sector required consideration, as did the fact that the arbitration of new contract terms had become more significant. Finally, during the interval of more than two decades, new problems had emerged as private-sector grievance arbitration matured and became more diversified.

In 1985, the provisions of 2 C. 1. c. were amended to specify certain procedures, deemed proper, which could be followed by an arbitrator seeking to determine if the parties are willing to consent to publication of an award.

In 1996, the wording of the Preamble was amended to reflect the intent that the provisions of the Code apply to covered arbitrators who agree to serve as impartial third parties in certain arbitration and related procedures, dealing with the rights and interests of employees in connection with their employment and/or representation by a union. Simultaneously, the provisions of 2 A. 3. were amended to make clear that an arbitrator has no obligation to accept an appointment to arbitrate under dispute procedures adopted unilaterally by an employer or union and to identify additional disclosure responsibilities for arbitrators who agree to serve under such procedures.

## TABLE OF CONTENTS

FOREWORD
TABLE OF CONTENTS
PREAMBLE
1. ARBITRATOR'S QUALIFICATIONS AND RESPONSIBILITIES TO THE PROFESSION
   A. General Qualifications.
   B. Qualification for Special Cases.
   C. Responsibilities to the Profession.
2. RESPONSIBILITIES TO THE PARTIES
   A. Recognition of Diversity in Arbitration Arrangements.
   B. Required Disclosures.
   C. Privacy of Arbitration.
   D. Personal Relationships With the Parties.
   E. Jurisdiction.
   F. Mediation by an Arbitrator.
   G. Reliance by an Arbitrator on Other Awards.
   H. Use of Assistants.
   I. Consent Awards.
   J. Avoidance of Delay.
   K. Fees and Expenses.
3. RESPONSIBILITIES TO ADMINISTRATIVE AGENCIES
   A. General Responsibilities.
4. PREHEARING CONDUCT
5. HEARING CONDUCT
   A. General Principles.
   B. Transcripts or Recordings.

C. Ex Parte Hearings.
D. Plant Visits.
E. Bench Decisions or Expedited Awards.
6. POST HEARING CONDUCT
   A. Post Hearing Briefs and Submissions.
   B. Disclosure of Terms of Award.
   C. Awards and Opinions.
   D. Clarification of Interpretation of Awards.
   E. Enforcement of Award.

## PREAMBLE

### Background

The provisions of this Code deal with the voluntary arbitration of labor-management disputes and certain other arbitration and related procedures which have developed or become more common since it was first adopted.

Voluntary arbitration rests upon the mutual desire of management and labor in each collective bargaining relationship to develop procedures for dispute settlement which meet their own particular needs and obligations. No two voluntary systems, therefore, are likely to be identical in practice. Words used to describe arbitrators (Arbitrator, Umpire, Impartial Chair, Chair of Arbitration Board, etc.) may suggest typical approaches, but actual differences within any general type of arrangement may be as great as distinctions often made among the several types.

Arbitrators of labor-management disputes are sometimes asked to serve as impartial third parties under a variety of arbitration and related procedures dealing with the rights and interests of employees in connection with their employment and/or representation by a union. In some cases these procedures may not be the product of voluntary agreement between management and labor. They may be established by statute or ordinance, *ad hoc* agreement, individual employment contract, or through procedures unilaterally adopted by employers and unions. Some of the procedures may be designed to resolve disputes over new or revised contract terms, where the arbitrator may be referred to as a Fact Finder or a member of an Impasse Panel or Board of Inquiry, or the like. Others may be designed to resolve disputes over wrongful termination or other employment issues arising under the law, an implied or explicit individual employment contract, or an agreement to resolve a lawsuit. In some such cases the arbitrator may be referred to as an Appeal Examiner, Hearing Officer, Referee, or other like titles. Finally, some procedures may be established by employers to resolve employment disputes under personnel policies and handbooks or established by unions to resolve disputes with represented employees in agency shop or fair share cases.

The standards of professional responsibility set forth in this Code are intended to guide the impartial third party serving in all of these diverse procedures.

## Scope of Code

This Code is a privately developed set of standards of professional behavior for arbitrators who are subject to its provisions. It applies to voluntary arbitration of labor-management disputes and the other arbitration and related procedures described in the Preamble, hereinafter referred to as "covered arbitration dispute procedures."

The word "arbitrator," as used hereinafter in the Code, is intended to apply to any impartial person, irrespective of specific title, who serves in a covered arbitration dispute procedure in which there is conferred authority to decide issues or to make formal recommendations.

The Code is not designed to apply to mediation or conciliation, as distinguished from arbitration, nor to other procedures in which the third party is not authorized in advance to make decisions or recommendations. It does not apply to partisan representatives on tripartite boards. It does not apply to commercial arbitration or to uses of arbitration other than a covered arbitration dispute procedure as defined above.

## Format of Code

**Bold Face** type, sometimes including explanatory material, is used to set forth general principles. *Italics* are used for amplification of general principles. Ordinary type is used primarily for illustrative or explanatory comment.

## Application of Code

Faithful adherence by an arbitrator to this Code is basic to professional responsibility.

The National Academy of Arbitrators will expect its members to be governed in their professional conduct by this Code and stands ready, through its Committee on Professional Responsibility and Grievances, to advise its members as to the Code's interpretation. The American Arbitration Association and the Federal Mediation and Conciliation Service will apply the Code to the arbitrators on their rosters in cases handled under their respective appointment or referral procedures. Other arbitrators and administrative agencies may, of course, voluntarily adopt the Code and be governed by it.

In interpreting the Code and applying it to charges of professional misconduct, under existing or revised procedures of the National Academy of Arbitrators and of the administrative agencies, it should be recognized that while some of its standards express ethical principles basic to the arbitration profession, others rest less on ethics than on considerations of good practice. Experience has shown the difficulty of drawing rigid lines of distinction between ethics and good practice, and this Code does not attempt to do so. Rather, it leaves the gravity of alleged misconduct and the extent to which ethical standards have been violated to be assessed in the light of the facts and circumstances of each particular case.

1

## ARBITRATOR'S QUALIFICATIONS AND RESPONSIBILITIES TO THE PROFESSION

### A. General Qualifications

**1. Essential personal qualifications of an arbitrator include honesty, integrity, impartiality and general competence in labor relations matters.**

**An arbitrator must demonstrate ability to exercise these personal qualities faithfully and with good judgment, both in procedural matters and in substantive decisions.**

  a. Selection by mutual agreement of the parties or direct designation by an administrative agency are the effective methods of appraisal of this combination of an individual's potential and performance, rather than the fact of placement on a roster of an administrative agency or membership in a professional association of arbitrators.

**2. An arbitrator must be as ready to rule for one party as for the other on each issue, either in a single case or in a group of cases. Compromise by an arbitrator for the sake of attempting to achieve personal acceptability is unprofessional.**

### B. Qualifications for Special Cases

**1. When an arbitrator decides that a case requires specialized knowledge beyond the arbitrator's competence, the arbitrator must decline**

## appointment, withdraw, or request technical assistance.

a. An arbitrator may be qualified generally but not for specialized assignments. Some types of incentive, work standard, job evaluation, welfare program, pension, or insurance cases may require specialized knowledge, experience or competence. Arbitration of contract terms also may require distinctive background and experience.

b. Effective appraisal by an administrative agency or by an arbitrator of the need for special qualifications requires that both parties make known the special nature of the case prior to appointment of the arbitrator.

### C. Responsibilities to the Profession

**1. An arbitrator must uphold the dignity and integrity of the office and endeavor to provide effective service to the parties.**

a. To this end, an arbitrator should keep current with principles, practices and developments that are relevant to the arbitrator's field of practice.

**2. An experienced arbitrator should cooperate in the training of new arbitrators.**

**3. An arbitrator must not advertise or solicit arbitration assignments.**

a. For purposes of this standard, advertising shall not include:

(1) providing accurate, objectively verifiable biographical information (including fees and expenses) for inclusion in administrative agency arbitration rosters, dispute resolution directories, and

(2) providing name, address, phone numbers and identification as an arbitrator in telephone directo-

ries, change of address and/or change of services offered announcements.

b. Information provided under paragraph (a) may not include editorial or adjectival comments concerning the arbitrator's qualifications.

c. It is a matter of personal preference whether an arbitrator includes "Labor Arbitrator" or similar titles on professional letterheads, cards and announcements.

d. Solicitation, as prohibited by this section, includes the making of requests for arbitration work through personal contacts with individual parties, orally or in writing.

2

## RESPONSIBILITIES TO THE PARTIES

### A. Recognition of Diversity in Arbitration Arrangements

**1. An arbitrator should conscientiously endeavor to understand and observe, to the extent consistent with professional responsibility, the significant principles governing each arbitration system in which the arbitrator serves.**

a. Recognition of special features of a particular arbitration arrangement can be essential with respect to procedural matters and may influence other aspects of the arbitration process.

**2. Such understanding does not relieve an arbitrator from a corollary responsibility to seek to discern and refuse to lend approval or consent to any collusive attempt by the parties to use arbitration for an improper purpose.**

**3. An arbitrator who is asked to arbitrate a dispute under a procedure established unilaterally**

**by an employer or union, to resolve an employment dispute or agency shop or fair share dispute, has no obligation to accept such appointment. Before accepting such an appointment, an arbitrator should consider the possible need to disclose the existence of any ongoing relationships with the employer or union.**

    a. If the arbitrator is already serving as an umpire, permanent arbitrator or panel member under a procedure where the employer or union has the right unilaterally to remove the arbitrator from such a position, those facts should be disclosed.

### B. Required Disclosures

**1. Before accepting an appointment, an arbitrator must disclose directly or through the administrative agency involved, any current or past managerial, representational, or consultative relationship with any company or union involved in a proceeding in which the arbitrator is being considered for appointment or has been tentatively designated to serve. Disclosure must also be made of any pertinent pecuniary interest.**

    a. The duty to disclose includes membership on a Board of Directors, full-time or part-time service as a representative or advocate, consultation work for a fee, current stock or bond ownership (other than mutual fund shares or appropriate trust arrangements) or any other pertinent form of managerial, financial or immediate family interest in the company or union involved.

**2. When an arbitrator is serving concurrently as an advocate for or representative of other companies or unions in labor relations matters, or has done so in recent years, such activities must be disclosed before accepting appointment as an arbitrator.**

**An arbitrator must disclose such activities to an administrative agency if on that agency's active roster or seeking placement on a roster. Such disclosure then satisfies this requirement for cases handled under that agency's referral.**

   a. It is not necessary to disclose names of clients or other specific details. It is necessary to indicate the general nature of the labor relations advocacy or representational work involved, whether for companies or unions or both, and a reasonable approximation of the extent of such activity.

   b. *An arbitrator on an administrative agency's roster has a continuing obligation to notify the agency of any significant changes pertinent to this requirement.*

   c. When an administrative agency is not involved, an arbitrator must make such disclosure directly unless the arbitrator is certain that both parties to the case are fully aware of such activities.

**3. An arbitrator must not permit personal relationships to affect decision-making.**

**Prior to acceptance of an appointment, an arbitrator must disclose to the parties or to the administrative agency involved any close personal relationship or other circumstance, in addition to those specifically mentioned earlier in this section, which might reasonably raise a question as to the arbitrator's impartiality.**

   a. Arbitrators establish personal relationships with many company and union representatives, with fellow arbitrators, and with fellow members of various professional associations. There should be no attempt to be secretive about such friendships or acquaintances but disclosure is not necessary unless some feature of a particular relationship might reasonably appear to impair impartiality.

**4. If the circumstances requiring disclosure are not known to the arbitrator prior to acceptance of appointment, disclosure must be made when such circumstances become known to the arbitrator.**

**5. The burden of disclosure rests on the arbitrator. After appropriate disclosure, the arbitrator may serve if both parties so desire. If the arbitrator believes or perceives that there is a clear conflict of interest, the arbitrator should withdraw, irrespective of the expressed desires of the parties.**

### C. Privacy of Arbitration

**1. All significant aspects of an arbitration proceeding must be treated by the arbitrator as confidential unless this requirement is waived by both parties or disclosure is required or permitted by law.**

a. Attendance at hearings by persons not representing the parties or invited by either or both of them should be permitted only when the parties agree or when an applicable law requires or permits. Occasionally, special circumstances may require that an arbitrator rule on such matters as attendance and degree of participation of counsel selected by a grievant.

b. *Discussion of a case at any time by an arbitrator with persons not involved directly should be limited to situations where advance approval or consent of both parties is obtained or where the identity of the parties and details of the case are sufficiently obscured to eliminate any realistic probability of identification.*

A commonly recognized exception is discussion of a problem in a case with a fellow arbitrator. *Any such discussion does not relieve the arbitrator who is acting in the case from sole responsibility for the decision and the discussion must be considered as confidential.*

Discussion of aspects of a case in a classroom without prior specific approval of the parties is not a violation provided the arbitrator is satisfied that there is no breach of essential confidentiality.

c. *It is a violation of professional responsibility for an arbitrator to make public an award without the consent of the parties.*

*An arbitrator may ask the parties whether they consent to the publication of the award either at the hearing or at the time the award is issued.*

*(1) If such question is asked at the hearing it should be asked in writing as follows:*

"*Do you consent to the submission of the award in this matter for publication?*

*( )      ( )*
*YES     NO*

*If you consent you have the right to notify the arbitrator within 30 days after the date of the award that you revoke your consent.*"

*It is desirable but not required that the arbitrator remind the parties at the time of the issuance of the award of their right to withdraw their consent to publication.*

(2) If the question of consent to the publication of the award is raised at the time the award is issued, the arbitrator may state in writing to each party that failure to answer the inquiry within 30 days will be considered an implied consent to publish.

d. It is not improper for an arbitrator to donate arbitration files to a library of a college, university or similar institution without prior consent of all parties involved. When the circumstances permit, there should be deleted from such donations any cases concerning which one or both of the parties have expressed a desire for privacy. As an additional safeguard, an arbitrator may also decide to withhold recent cases or indicate to the donee a time interval before such cases can be made generally available.

e. *Applicable laws, regulations, or practices of the parties may permit or even require exceptions to the above noted principles of privacy.*

### D. Personal Relationships with the Parties

**1. An arbitrator must make every reasonable effort to conform to arrangements required by an administrative agency or mutually desired by the parties regarding communications and personal relationships with the parties.**

a. *Only an "arm's-length" relationship may be acceptable to the parties in some arbitration arrangements or may be required by the rules of an administrative agency. The arbitrator should then have no contact of consequence with representatives of either party while handling a case without the other party's presence or consent.*

b. *In other situations, both parties may want communications and personal relationships to be less formal. It is then appropriate for the arbitrator to respond accordingly.*

### E. Jurisdiction

**1. An arbitrator must observe faithfully both the limitations and inclusions of the jurisdiction conferred by an agreement or other submission under which the arbitrator serves.**

**2. A direct settlement by the parties of some or all issues in a case, at any stage of the proceedings,**

**must be accepted by the arbitrator as removing further jurisdiction over such issues.**

### F. Mediation by an Arbitrator

**1. When the parties wish at the outset to give an arbitrator authority both to mediate and to decide or submit recommendations regarding residual issues, if any, they should so advise the arbitrator prior to appointment. If the appointment is accepted, the arbitrator must perform a mediation role consistent with the circumstances of the case.**

a. Direct appointments, also, may require a dual role as mediator and arbitrator of residual issues. This is most likely to occur in some public sector cases.

**2. When a request to mediate is first made after appointment, the arbitrator may either accept or decline a mediation role.**

a. *Once arbitration has been invoked, either party normally has a right to insist that the process be continued to decision.*

b. *If one party requests that the arbitrator mediate and the other party objects, the arbitrator should decline the request.*

c. *An arbitrator is not precluded from suggesting mediation. To avoid the possibility of improper pressure, the arbitrator should not so suggest unless it can be discerned that both parties are likely to be receptive. In any event, the arbitrator's suggestion should not be pursued unless both parties readily agree.*

### G. Reliance by an Arbitrator on Other Arbitration Awards or on Independent Research

**1. An arbitrator must assume full personal responsibility for the decision in each case decided.**

## CODE OF PROFESSIONAL RESPONSIBILITY   441

a. *The extent, if any, to which an arbitrator properly may rely on precedent, on guidance of other awards, or on independent research is dependent primarily on the policies of the parties on these matters, as expressed in the contract, or other agreement, or at the hearing.*

b. When the mutual desires of the parties are not known or when the parties express differing opinions or policies, the arbitrator may exercise discretion as to these matters, consistent with the acceptance of full personal responsibility for the award.

### H. Use of Assistants

**1. An arbitrator must not delegate any decision-making function to another person without consent of the parties.**

a. *Without prior consent of the parties, an arbitrator may use the services of an assistant for research, clerical duties, or preliminary drafting under the direction of the arbitrator, which does not involve the delegation of any decision-making function.*

b. *If an arbitrator is unable, because of time limitations or other reasons, to handle all decision-making aspects of a case, it is not a violation of professional responsibility to suggest to the parties an allocation of responsibility between the arbitrator and an assistant or associate. The arbitrator must not exert pressure on the parties to accept such a suggestion.*

### I. Consent Awards

**1. Prior to issuance of an award, the parties may jointly request the arbitrator to include in the award certain agreements between them, concerning some or all of the issues. If the arbitrator believes that a suggested award is proper, fair, sound, and lawful, it is consistent with professional responsibility to adopt it.**

a. *Before complying with such a request, an arbitrator must be certain of understanding the suggested settlement adequately in order to be able to appraise its terms. If it appears that pertinent facts or circumstances may not have been disclosed, the arbitrator should take the initiative to assure that all significant aspects of the case are fully understood. To this end, the arbitrator may request additional specific information and may question witnesses at a hearing.*

## J. Avoidance of Delay

**1. It is a basic professional responsibility of an arbitrator to plan a work schedule so that present and future commitments will be fulfilled in a timely manner.**

a. *When planning is upset for reasons beyond the control of the arbitrator, every reasonable effort should nevertheless be exerted to fulfill all commitments. If this is not possible, prompt notice at the arbitrator's initiative should be given to all parties affected. Such notices should include reasonably accurate estimates of any additional time required. To the extent possible, priority should be given to cases in process so that other parties may make alternative arbitration arrangements.*

**2. An arbitrator must cooperate with the parties and with any administrative agency involved in avoiding delays.**

a. *An arbitrator on the active roster of an administrative agency must take the initiative in advising the agency of any scheduling difficulties that can be foreseen.*

b. *Requests for services, whether received directly or through an administrative agency, should be declined if the arbitrator is unable to schedule a hearing as soon as the parties wish. If the parties, nevertheless, jointly desire to obtain the services of the arbitrator and the arbitrator agrees, arrangements should be made by agreement that the arbitrator confidently expects to fulfill.*

c. *An arbitrator may properly seek to persuade the parties to alter or eliminate arbitration procedures or tactics that cause unnecessary delay.*

**3. Once the case record has been closed, an arbitrator must adhere to the time limits for an award, as stipulated in the labor agreement or as provided by regulation of an administrative agency or as otherwise agreed.**

a. *If an appropriate award cannot be rendered within the required time, it is incumbent on the arbitrator to seek an extension of time from the parties.*

b. If the parties have agreed upon abnormally short time limits for an award after a case is closed, the arbitrator should be so advised by the parties or by the administrative agency involved, prior to acceptance of appointment.

## K. Fees and Expenses

**1. An arbitrator occupies a position of trust in respect to the parties and the administrative agencies. In charging for services and expenses, the arbitrator must be governed by the same high standards of honor and integrity that apply to all other phases of arbitration work.**

**An arbitrator must endeavor to keep total charges for services and expenses reasonable and consistent with the nature of the case or cases decided.**

**Prior to appointment, the parties should be aware of or be able readily to determine all significant aspects of an arbitrator's bases for charges for fees and expenses.**

a. *Services Not Primarily Chargeable on a per Diem Basis*

By agreement with the parties, the financial aspects of many "permanent" arbitration assignments, of some interest disputes, and of some "ad hoc" grievance assignments do not include a per diem fee for services as a primary part of the total understanding. *In such situations, the arbitrator must adhere faithfully to all agreed-upon arrangements governing fees and expenses.*

b. *Per Diem Basis for Charges for Services*

(1) *When an arbitrator's charges for services are determined primarily by a stipulated per diem fee, the arbitrator should establish in advance the bases for application of such per diem fee and for determination of reimbursable expenses.*

Practices established by an arbitrator should include the basis for charges, if any, for:

(a) hearing time, including the application of the stipulated basic per diem hearing fee to hearing days of varying lengths;

(b) study time;

(c) necessary travel time when not included in charges for hearing time;

(d) postponement or cancellation of hearings by the parties and the circumstances in which such charges will normally be assessed or waived;

(e) office overhead expenses (secretarial, telephone, postage, etc.);

(f) the work of paid assistants or associates.

(2) *Each arbitrator should be guided by the following general principles:*

(a) *Per diem charges for a hearing should not be in excess of actual time spent or allocated for the hearing.*

(b) *Per diem charges for study time should not be in excess of actual time spent.*

(c) *Any fixed ratio of study days to hearing days, not agreed to specifically by the parties, is inconsistent with the per diem method of charges for services.*

(d) *Charges for expenses must not be in excess of actual expenses normally reimbursable and incurred in connection with the case or cases involved.*

(e) *When time or expense are involved for two or more sets of parties on the same day or trip, such time or expense charges should be appropriately prorated.*

(f) *An arbitrator may stipulate in advance a minimum charge for a hearing without violation of (a) or (e) above.*

(3) *An arbitrator on the active roster of an administrative agency must file with the agency the individual bases for determination of fees and expenses if the agency so requires. Thereafter, it is the responsibility of each such arbitrator to advise the agency promptly of any change in any basis for charges.*

Such filing may be in the form of answers to a questionnaire devised by an agency or by any other method adopted by or approved by an agency.

*Having supplied an administrative agency with the information noted above, an arbitrator's professional responsibility of disclosure under this Code with respect to fees and expenses has been satisfied for cases referred by that agency.*

*(4) If an administrative agency promulgates specific standards with respect to any of these matters which are in addition to or more restrictive than an individual arbitrator's standards, an arbitrator on its active roster must observe the agency standards for cases handled under the auspices of that agency, or decline to serve.*

*(5) When an arbitrator is contacted directly by the parties for a case or cases, the arbitrator has a professional responsibility to respond to questions by submitting the bases for charges for fees and expenses.*

*(6) When it is known to the arbitrator that one or both of the parties cannot afford normal charges, it is consistent with professional responsibility to charge lesser amounts to both parties or to one of the parties if the other party is made aware of the difference and agrees.*

*(7) If an arbitrator concludes that the total of charges derived from the normal basis of calculation is not compatible with the case decided, it is consistent with professional responsibility to charge lesser amounts to both parties.*

**2. An arbitrator must maintain adequate records to support charges for services and expenses and must make an accounting to the parties or to an involved administrative agency on request.**

## 3

## RESPONSIBILITIES TO ADMINISTRATIVE AGENCIES

### A. General Responsibilities

**1. An arbitrator must be candid, accurate, and fully responsive to an administrative agency concerning qualifications, availability, and all other pertinent matters.**

## CODE OF PROFESSIONAL RESPONSIBILITY

**2. An arbitrator must observe policies and rules of an administrative agency in cases referred by that agency.**

**3. An arbitrator must not seek to influence an administrative agency by any improper means, including gifts or other inducements to agency personnel.**

    a. It is not improper for a person seeking placement on a roster to request references from individuals having knowledge of the applicant's experience and qualifications.

    b. Arbitrators should recognize that the primary responsibility of an administrative agency is to serve the parties.

### 4
### PREHEARING CONDUCT

**1. All prehearing matters must be handled in a manner that fosters complete impartiality by the arbitrator.**

    a. The primary purpose of prehearing discussions involving the arbitrator is to obtain agreement on procedural matters so that the hearing can proceed without unnecessary obstacles. If differences of opinion should arise during such discussions and, particularly, if such differences appear to impinge on substantive matters, the circumstances will suggest whether the matter can be resolved informally or may require a prehearing conference or, more rarely, a formal preliminary hearing. When an administrative agency handles some or all aspects of the arrangements prior to a hearing, the arbitrator will become involved only if differences of some substance arise.

    b. *Copies of any prehearing correspondence between the arbitrator and either party must be made available to both parties.*

# 5
# HEARING CONDUCT

## A. General Principles

**1. An arbitrator must provide a fair and adequate hearing which assures that both parties have sufficient opportunity to present their respective evidence and argument.**

a. *Within the limits of this responsibility, an arbitrator should conform to the various types of hearing procedures desired by the parties.*

b. An arbitrator may: encourage stipulations of fact; restate the substance of issues or arguments to promote or verify understanding; question the parties' representatives or witnesses, when necessary or advisable, to obtain additional pertinent information; and request that the parties submit additional evidence, either at the hearing or by subsequent filing.

c. *An arbitrator should not intrude into a party's presentation so as to prevent that party from putting forward its case fairly and adequately.*

## B. Transcripts or Recordings

**1. Mutual agreement of the parties as to use or non-use of a transcript must be respected by the arbitrator.**

a. *A transcript is the official record of a hearing only when both parties agree to a transcript or an applicable law or regulation so provides.*

b. An arbitrator may seek to persuade the parties to avoid use of a transcript, or to use a transcript if the nature of the case appears to require one. *However, if an arbitrator intends to make appointment to a case contingent on mutual agreement to a transcript, that requirement must be made known to both parties prior to appointment.*

c. If the parties do not agree to a transcript, an arbitrator may permit one party to take a transcript at its own cost. The arbitrator may also make appropriate arrangements under which the other party may have access to a copy, if a copy is provided to the arbitrator.

d. Without prior approval, an arbitrator may seek to use a personal tape recorder to supplement note taking. The arbitrator should not insist on such a tape recording if either or both parties object.

### C. Ex Parte Hearings

**1. In determining whether to conduct an ex parte hearing, an arbitrator must consider relevant legal, contractual, and other pertinent circumstances.**

**2. An arbitrator must be certain, before proceeding ex parte, that the party refusing or failing to attend the hearings has been given adequate notice of the time, place, and purposes of the hearing.**

### D. Plant Visits

**1. An arbitrator should comply with a request of any party that the arbitrator visit a work area pertinent to the dispute prior to, during, or after a hearing. An arbitrator may also initiate such a request.**

a. *Procedures for such visits should be agreed to by the parties in consultation with the arbitrator.*

### E. Bench Decisions or Expedited Awards

**1. When an arbitrator understands, prior to acceptance of appointment, that a bench decision is expected at the conclusion of the hearing, the arbi-**

**trator must comply with the understanding unless both parties agree otherwise.**

a. *If notice of the parties' desire for a bench decision is not given prior to the arbitrator's acceptance of the case, issuance of such a bench decision is discretionary.*

b. *When only one party makes the request and the other objects, the arbitrator should not render a bench decision except under most unusual circumstances.*

**2. When an arbitrator understands, prior to acceptance of appointment, that a concise written award is expected within a stated time period after the hearing, the arbitrator must comply with the understanding unless both parties agree otherwise.**

## 6
## POST HEARING CONDUCT

### A. Post Hearing Briefs and Submissions

**1. An arbitrator must comply with mutual agreements in respect to the filing or nonfiling of post hearing briefs or submissions.**

a. An arbitrator may either suggest the filing of post hearing briefs or other submissions or suggest that none be filed.

b. When the parties disagree as to the need for briefs, an arbitrator may permit filing but may determine a reasonable time limitation.

**2. An arbitrator must not consider a post hearing brief or submission that has not been provided to the other party.**

### B. Disclosure of Terms of Award

**1. An arbitrator must not disclose a prospective award to either party prior to its simultaneous issuance to both parties or explore possible alternative awards unilaterally with one party, unless both parties so agree.**

a. Partisan members of tripartite boards may know prospective terms of an award in advance of its issuance. Similar situations may exist in other less formal arrangements mutually agreed to by the parties. In any such situation, the arbitrator should determine and observe the mutually desired degree of confidentiality.

## C. Awards and Opinions

**1. The award should be definite, certain, and as concise as possible.**

a. When an opinion is required, factors to be considered by an arbitrator include: desirability of brevity, consistent with the nature of the case and any expressed desires of the parties; need to use a style and form that is understandable to responsible representatives of the parties, to the grievant and supervisors, and to others in the collective bargaining relationship; necessity of meeting the significant issues; forthrightness to an extent not harmful to the relationship of the parties; and avoidance of gratuitous advice or discourse not essential to disposition of the issues.

## D. Clarification of Interpretation of Awards

**1. No clarification or interpretation of an award is permissible without the consent of both parties.**

**2. Under agreements which permit or require clarification or interpretation of an award, an arbitrator must afford both parties an opportunity to be heard.**

## E. Enforcement of Award

**1. The arbitrator's responsibility does not extend to the enforcement of an award.**

**2. In view of the professional and confidential nature of the arbitration relationship, an arbitrator should not voluntarily participate in legal enforcement proceedings.**

# APPENDIX J

# THE FEDERAL ARBITRATION ACT

## UNITED STATES CODE
## TITLE 9. ARBITRATION
## CHAPTER 1—GENERAL PROVISIONS

### § 1. "Maritime transactions" and "commerce" defined; exceptions to operation of title

"Maritime transactions", as herein defined, means charter parties, bills of lading of water carriers, agreements relating to wharfage, supplies furnished vessels or repairs to vessels, collisions, or any other matters in foreign commerce which, if the subject of controversy, would be embraced within admiralty jurisdiction; "commerce", as herein defined, means commerce among the several States or with foreign nations, or in any Territory of the United States or in the District of Columbia, or between any such Territory and another, or between any such Territory and any State or foreign nation, or between the District of Columbia and any State or Territory or foreign nation, but nothing herein contained shall apply to contracts of employment of seamen, railroad employees, or any other class of workers engaged in foreign or interstate commerce.

### § 2. Validity, irrevocability and enforcement of agreements to arbitrate

A written provision in any maritime transaction or a contract evidencing a transaction involving commerce to settle by arbitration a controversy thereafter arising out of such contract or transaction, or the refusal to perform the whole or any part thereof, or an agreement in writing to submit to arbitration an existing controversy arising out of such a contract, transaction, or refusal, shall be valid, irrevocable, and enforceable, save upon such grounds as exist at law or in equity for the revocation of any contract.

## § 3. Stay of proceedings where issue therein referable to arbitration

If any suit or proceeding be brought in any of the courts of the United States upon any issue referable to arbitration under an agreement in writing for such arbitration, the court in which such suit is pending, upon being satisfied that the issue involved in such suit or proceeding is referable to arbitration under such an agreement, shall on application of one of the parties stay the trial of the action until such arbitration has been had in accordance with the terms of the agreement, providing the applicant for the stay is not in default in proceeding with such arbitration.

## § 4. Failure to arbitrate under agreement; petition to United States court having jurisdiction for order to compel arbitration; notice and service thereof; hearing and determination

A party aggrieved by the alleged failure, neglect, or refusal of another to arbitrate under a written agreement for arbitration may petition any United States district court which, save for such agreement, would have jurisdiction under Title 28, in a civil action or in admiralty of the subject matter of a suit arising out of the controversy between the parties, for an order directing that such arbitration proceed in the manner provided for in such agreement. Five days' notice in writing of such application shall be served upon the party in default. Service thereof shall be made in the manner provided by the Federal Rules of Civil Procedure. The court shall hear the parties, and upon being satisfied that the making of the agreement for arbitration or the failure to comply therewith is not in issue, the court shall make an order directing the parties to proceed to arbitration in accordance with the terms of the agreement. The hearing and proceedings, under such agreement, shall be within the district in which the petition for an order directing such arbitration is filed. If the making of the arbitration agreement or the failure, neglect, or refusal to perform the same be in issue, the court shall proceed summarily to the trial thereof. If no jury trial be demanded by the party alleged to be in default, or if the matter in dispute is within admiralty jurisdiction, the court shall hear and determine such issue. Where such an issue is raised, the party alleged to be in default may, except in cases of admiralty, on or before the return day of the notice of application, demand a jury trial of such issue, and upon such demand the court shall make an order referring the issue or issues to a jury in the manner provided by the Federal Rules of Civil Procedure, or may specially call a jury for that purpose. If the jury find that no agreement in writing for arbitration was made or that there is no default in proceeding thereunder, the proceeding shall be dismissed. If the jury find that an agreement for arbitration was made in writing and that there is a default in proceeding thereunder, the court shall make an order summarily directing the parties to proceed with the arbitration in accordance with the terms thereof.

## § 5. Appointment of arbitrators or umpire

If in the agreement provision be made for a method of naming or appointing an arbitrator or arbitrators or an umpire, such method shall be followed; but if no method be provided therein, or if a method be provided and any party thereto shall fail to avail himself of such method, or if for any other reason there shall be a lapse in the naming of an arbitrator or arbitrators or umpire, or in filling a vacancy, then upon the application of either party to the controversy the court shall designate and appoint an arbitrator or arbitrators or umpire, as the case may require, who shall act under the said agreement with the same force and effect as if he or they had been specifically named therein; and unless otherwise provided in the agreement the arbitration shall be by a single arbitrator.

## § 6. Application heard as motion

Any application to the court hereunder shall be made and heard in the manner provided by law for the making and hearing of motions, except as otherwise herein expressly provided.

## § 7. Witnesses before arbitrators; fees; compelling attendance

The arbitrators selected either as prescribed in this title or otherwise, or a majority of them, may summon in writing any person to attend before them or any of them as a witness and in a proper case to bring with him or them any book, record, document, or paper which may be deemed material as evidence in the case. The fees for such attendance shall be the same as the fees of witnesses before masters of the United States courts. Said summons shall issue in the name of the arbitrator or arbitrators, or a majority of them, and shall be signed by the arbitrators, or a majority of them, and shall be directed to the said person and shall be served in the same manner as subpoenas to appear and testify before the court; if any person or persons so summoned to testify shall refuse or neglect to obey said summons, upon petition the United States district court for the district in which such arbitrators, or a majority of them, are sitting may compel the attendance of such person or persons before said arbitrator or arbitrators, or punish said person or persons for contempt in the same manner provided by law for securing the attendance of witnesses or their punishment for neglect or refusal to attend in the courts of the United States.

## § 8. Proceedings begun by libel in admiralty and seizure of vessel or property

If the basis of jurisdiction be a cause of action otherwise justiciable in admiralty, then, notwithstanding anything herein to the contrary, the party claiming to be aggrieved may begin his proceeding hereunder by libel and seizure of the vessel or other property of the other party according to the usual course of admiralty proceedings, and the court shall then have jurisdiction to direct the parties to proceed with the arbitration and shall retain jurisdiction to enter its decree upon the award.

## § 9. Award of arbitrators; confirmation; jurisdiction; procedure

If the parties in their agreement have agreed that a judgment of the court shall be entered upon the award made pursuant to the arbitration, and shall specify the court, then at any time within one year after the award is made any party to the arbitration may apply to the court so specified for an order confirming the award, and thereupon the court must grant such an order unless the award is vacated, modified, or corrected as prescribed in sections 10 and 11 of this title. If no court is specified in the agreement of the parties, then such application may be made to the United States court in and for the district within which such award was made. Notice of the application shall be served upon the adverse party, and thereupon the court shall have jurisdiction of such party as though he had appeared generally in the proceeding. If the adverse party is a resident of the district within which the award was made, such service shall be made upon the adverse party or his attorney as prescribed by law for service of notice of motion in an action in the same court. If the adverse party shall be a nonresident, then the notice of the application shall be served by the marshal of any district within which the adverse party may be found in like manner as other process of the court.

## § 10. Same; vacation; grounds; rehearing

(a) In any of the following cases the United States court in and for the district wherein the award was made may make an order vacating the award upon the application of any party to the arbitration—(1) Where the award was procured by corruption, fraud, or undue means.

(2) Where there was evident partiality or corruption in the arbitrators, or either of them.

(3) Where the arbitrators were guilty of misconduct in refusing to postpone the hearing, upon sufficient cause shown, or in refusing to hear evidence pertinent and material to the controversy; or of any other misbehavior by which the rights of any party have been prejudiced.

(4) Where the arbitrators exceeded their powers, or so imperfectly executed them that a mutual, final, and definite award upon the subject matter submitted was not made.

(5) Where an award is vacated and the time within which the agreement required the award to be made has not expired the court may, in its discretion, direct a rehearing by the arbitrators.

(b) The United States district court for the district wherein an award was made that was issued pursuant to section 580 of title 5 may make an order vacating the award upon the application of a person, other than a party to the arbitration, who is adversely affected or aggrieved by the award, if the use of arbitration or the award is clearly inconsistent with the factors set forth in section 572 of title 5.

## § 11. Same; modification or correction; grounds; order

In either of the following cases the United States court in and for the district wherein the award was made may make an order modifying or correcting the award upon the application of any party to the arbitration—

(a) Where there was an evident material miscalculation of figures or an evident material mistake in the description of any person, thing, or property referred to in the award.

(b) Where the arbitrators have awarded upon a matter not submitted to them, unless it is a matter not affecting the merits of the decision upon the matter submitted.

(c) Where the award is imperfect in matter of form not affecting the merits of the controversy.

The order may modify and correct the award, so as to effect the intent thereof and promote justice between the parties.

## § 12. Notice of motions to vacate or modify; service; stay of proceedings

Notice of a motion to vacate, modify, or correct an award must be served upon the adverse party or his attorney within three months after the award is filed or delivered. If the adverse party is a resident of the district within which the award was made, such service shall be made upon the adverse party or his attorney as prescribed by law for service of notice of motion in an action in the same court. If the adverse party shall be a nonresident then the notice of the application shall be served by the marshal of any district within which the adverse party may be found in like manner as other process of the court. For the purposes of the motion any judge who might make an order to stay the proceedings in an action brought in the same court may make an order, to be served with the notice of motion, staying the proceedings of the adverse party to enforce the award.

## § 13. Papers filed with order on motions; judgment; docketing; force and effect; enforcement

The party moving for an order confirming, modifying, or correcting an award shall, at the time such order is filed with the clerk for the entry of judgment thereon, also file the following papers with the clerk:

(a) The agreement; the selection or appointment, if any, of an additional arbitrator or umpire; and each written extension of the time, if any, within which to make the award.

(b) The award.

(c) Each notice, affidavit, or other paper used upon an application to confirm, modify, or correct the award, and a copy of each order of the court upon such an application.

The judgment shall be docketed as if it was rendered in an action.

The judgment so entered shall have the same force and effect, in all respects, as, and be subject to all the provisions of law relating to, a judgment in an action; and it may be enforced as if it had been rendered in an action in the court in which it is entered.

## § 14. Contracts not affected

This title shall not apply to contracts made prior to January 1, 1926.

## § 15. Inapplicability of the Act of State doctrine

Enforcement of arbitral agreements, confirmation of arbitral awards, and execution upon judgments based on orders confirming such awards shall not be refused on the basis of the Act of State doctrine.

## § 16. Appeals

(a) An appeal may be taken from—

(1) an order—

(A) refusing a stay of any action under section 3 of this title,

(B) denying a petition under section 4 of this title to order arbitration to proceed,

(C) denying an application under section 206 of this title to compel arbitration,

(D) confirming or denying confirmation of an award or partial award, or

(E) modifying, correcting, or vacating an award;

(2) an interlocutory order granting, continuing, or modifying an injunction against an arbitration that is subject to this title; or

(3) a final decision with respect to an arbitration that is subject to this title.

(b) Except as otherwise provided in section 1292(b) of title 28, an appeal may not be taken from an interlocutory order—

(1) granting a stay of any action under section 3 of this title;

(2) directing arbitration to proceed under section 4 of this title;

(3) compelling arbitration under section 206 of this title; or

(4) refusing to enjoin an arbitration that is subject to this title.

# APPENDIX K

# UNIFORM ARBITRATION ACT

## § 1. Validity of Arbitration Agreement

A written agreement to submit any existing controversy to arbitration or a provision in a written contract to submit to arbitration any controversy thereafter arising between the parties is valid, enforceable and irrevocable, save upon such grounds as exist at law or in equity for the revocation of any contract. This act also applies to arbitration agreements between employers and employees or between their respective representatives [unless otherwise provided in the agreement].

## § 2. Proceedings to Compel or Stay Arbitration

(a) On application of a party showing an agreement described in Section 1, and the opposing party's refusal to arbitrate, the Court shall order the parties to proceed with arbitration, but if the opposing party denies the existence of the agreement to arbitrate, the Court shall proceed summarily to the determination of the issue so raised and shall order arbitration if found for the moving party, otherwise, the application shall be denied.

(b) On application, the court may stay an arbitration proceeding commenced or threatened on a showing that there is no agreement to arbitrate. Such an issue, when in substantial and bona fide dispute, shall be forthwith and summarily tried and the stay ordered if found for the moving party. If found for the opposing party, the court shall order the parties to proceed to arbitration.

(c) If an issue referable to arbitration under the alleged agreement is involved in an action or proceeding pending in a court having jurisdiction to hear applications under subdivision (a) of this Section, the application shall be made therein. Otherwise and subject to Section 18, the application may be made in any court of competent jurisdiction.

(d) Any action or proceeding involving an issue subject to arbitration shall be stayed if an order for arbitration or an application therefor has been made under this section or, if the issue is severable, the stay may be with respect thereto only. When the application is made in such action or proceeding, the order for arbitration shall include such stay.

(e) An order for arbitration shall not be refused on the ground that the claim in issue lacks merit or bona fides or because any fault or grounds for the claim sought to be arbitrated have not been shown.

## § 3. Appointment of Arbitrators by Court

If the arbitration agreement provides a method of appointment of arbitrators, this method shall be followed. In the absence thereof, or if the agreed method fails or for any reason cannot be followed, or when an arbitrator appointed fails or is unable to act and his successor has not been duly appointed, the court on application of a party shall appoint one or more arbitrators. An arbitrator so appointed has all the powers of one specifically named in the agreement.

## § 4. Majority Action by Arbitrators

The powers of the arbitrators may be exercised by a majority unless otherwise provided by the agreement or by this act.

## § 5. Hearing

Unless otherwise provided by the agreement:

(a) The arbitrators shall appoint a time and place for the hearing and cause notification to the parties to be served personally or by registered mail not less than five days before the hearing. Appearance at the hearing waives such notice. The arbitrators may adjourn the hearing from time to time as necessary and, on request of a party and for good cause, or upon their own motion may postpone the hearing to a time not later than the date fixed by the agreement for making the award unless the parties consent to a later date. The arbitrators may hear and determine the controversy upon the evidence produced notwithstanding the failure of a party duly notified to appear. The court on application may direct the arbitrators to proceed promptly with the hearing and determination of the controversy.

(b) The parties are entitled to be heard, to present evidence material to the controversy and to cross-examine witnesses appearing at the hearing.

(c) The hearing shall be conducted by all the arbitrators but a majority may determine any question and render a final award. If, during the course of the hearing, an arbitrator for any reason ceases to act, the remaining arbitrator or arbitrators appointed to act as neutrals may continue with the hearing and determination of the controversy.

## § 6. Representation by Attorney

A party has the right to be represented by an attorney at any proceeding or hearing under this act. A waiver thereof prior to the proceeding or hearing is ineffective.

## § 7. Witnesses, Subpoenas, Depositions

(a) The arbitrators may issue (cause to be issued) subpoenas for the attendance of witnesses and for the production of books, records, documents and other evidence, and shall have the power to administer oaths. Subpoenas so issued shall be served, and upon application to the

Court by a party or the arbitrators, enforced, in the manner provided by law for the service and enforcement of subpoenas in a civil action.

(b) On application of a party and for use as evidence, the arbitrators may permit a deposition to be taken, in the manner and upon the terms designated by the arbitrators, of a witness who cannot be subpoenaed or is unable to attend the hearing.

(c) All provisions of law compelling a person under subpoena to testify are applicable.

(d) Fees for attendance as a witness shall be the same as for a witness in the .......... Court.

## § 8. Award

(a) The award shall be in writing and signed by the arbitrators joining in the award. The arbitrators shall deliver a copy to each party personally or by registered mail, or as provided in the agreement.

(b) An award shall be made within the time fixed therefor by the agreement or, if not so fixed, within such time as the court orders on application of a party. The parties may extend the time in writing either before or after the expiration thereof. A party waives the objection that an award was not made within the time required unless he notifies the arbitrators of his objection prior to the delivery of the award to him.

## § 9. Change of Award by Arbitrators

On application of a party or, if an application to the court is pending under Sections 11, 12 or 13, on submission to the arbitrators by the court under such conditions as the court may order, the arbitrators may modify or correct the award upon the grounds stated in paragraphs (1) and (3) of subdivision (a) of Section 13, or for the purpose of clarifying the award. The application shall be made within twenty days after delivery of the award to the applicant. Written notice thereof shall be given forthwith to the opposing party, stating he must serve his objections thereto, if any, within ten days from the notice. The award so modified or corrected is subject to the provisions of Sections 11, 12 and 13.

## § 10. Fees and Expenses of Arbitration

Unless otherwise provided in the agreement to arbitrate, the arbitrators' expenses and fees, together with other expenses, not including counsel fees, incurred in the conduct of the arbitration, shall be paid as provided in the award.

## § 11. Confirmation of an Award

Upon application of a party, the Court shall confirm an award, unless within the time limits hereinafter imposed grounds are urged for vacating or modifying or correcting the award, in which case the court shall proceed as provided in Sections 12 and 13.

## § 12. Vacating an Award

(a) Upon application of a party, the court shall vacate an award where:

(1) The award was procured by corruption, fraud or other undue means;

(2) There was evident partiality by an arbitrator appointed as a neutral or corruption in any of the arbitrators or misconduct prejudicing the rights of any party;

(3) The arbitrators exceeded their powers;

(4) The arbitrators refused to postpone the hearing upon sufficient cause being shown therefor or refused to hear evidence material to the controversy or otherwise so conducted the hearing, contrary to the provisions of Section 5, as to prejudice substantially the rights of a party; or

(5) There was no arbitration agreement and the issue was not adversely determined in proceedings under Section 2 and the party did not participate in the arbitration hearing without raising the objection; but the fact that the relief was such that it could not or would not be granted by a court of law or equity is not ground for vacating or refusing to confirm the award.

(b) An application under this Section shall be made within ninety days after delivery of a copy of the award to the applicant, except that, if predicated upon corruption, fraud or other undue means, it shall be made within ninety days after such grounds are known or should have been known.

(c) In vacating the award on grounds other than stated in clause (5) of Subsection (a) the court may order a rehearing before new arbitrators chosen as provided in the agreement, or in the absence thereof, by the court in accordance with Section 3, or if the award is vacated on grounds set forth in clauses (3) and (4) of Subsection (a) the court may order a rehearing before the arbitrators who made the award or their successors appointed in accordance with Section 3. The time within which the agreement requires the award to be made is applicable to the rehearing and commences from the date of the order.

(d) If the application to vacate is denied and no motion to modify or correct the award is pending, the court shall confirm the award. As amended Aug. 1956.

## § 13. Modification or Correction of Award

(a) Upon application made within ninety days after delivery of a copy of the award to the applicant, the court shall modify or correct the award where:

(1) There was an evident miscalculation of figures or an evident mistake in the description of any person, thing or property referred to in the award;

(2) The arbitrators have awarded upon a matter not submitted to them and the award may be corrected without affecting the merits of the decision upon the issues submitted; or

(3) The award is imperfect in a matter of form, not affecting the merits of the controversy.

(b) If the application is granted, the court shall modify and correct the award so as to effect its intent and shall confirm the award as so modified and corrected. Otherwise, the court shall confirm the award as made.

(c) An application to modify or correct an award may be joined in the alternative with an application to vacate the award.

## § 14. Judgment or Decree on Award

Upon the granting of an order confirming, modifying or correcting an award, judgment or decree shall be entered in conformity therewith and be enforced as any other judgment or decree. Costs of the application and of the proceedings subsequent thereto, and disbursements may be awarded by the court.

## § 15. Judgment Roll, Docketing

(a) On entry of judgment or decree, the clerk shall prepare the judgment roll consisting, to the extent filed, of the following:

(1) The agreement and each written extension of the time within which to make the award;

(2) The award;

(3) A copy of the order confirming, modifying or correcting the award; and

(4) A copy of the judgment or decree.

(b) The judgment or decree may be docketed as if rendered in an action.

## § 16. Applications to Court

Except as otherwise provided, an application to the court under this act shall be by motion and shall be heard in the manner and upon the notice provided by law or rule of court for the making and hearing of motions. Unless the parties have agreed otherwise, notice of an initial application for an order shall be served in the manner provided by law for the service of a summons in an action.

## § 17. Court, Jurisdiction

The term "court" means any court of competent jurisdiction of this State. The making of an agreement described in Section 1 providing for arbitration in this State confers jurisdiction on the court to enforce the agreement under this Act and to enter judgment on an award thereunder.

## § 18. Venue

An initial application shall be made to the court of the [county] in which the agreement provides the arbitration hearing shall be held or, if the hearing has been held, in the county in which it was held. Otherwise the application shall be made in the [county] where the adverse party resides or has a place of business or, if he has no residence or place of business in this State, to the court of any [county]. All subsequent applications shall be made to the court hearing the initial application unless the court otherwise directs.

## § 19. Appeals

(a) An appeal may be taken from:

(1) An order denying an application to compel arbitration made under Section 2;

(2) An order granting an application to stay arbitration made under Section 2(b);

(3) An order confirming or denying confirmation of an award;

(4) An order modifying or correcting an award;

(5) An order vacating an award without directing a rehearing; or

(6) A judgment or decree entered pursuant to the provisions of this act.

(b) The appeal shall be taken in the manner and to the same extent as from orders or judgments in a civil action.

## § 20. Act Not Retroactive

This act applies only to agreements made subsequent to the taking effect of this act.

## § 21. Uniformity of Interpretation

This act shall be so construed as to effectuate its general purpose to make uniform the law of those states which enact it.

## § 22. Constitutionality

If any provision of this act or the application thereof to any person or circumstance is held invalid, the invalidity shall not affect other provisions or applications of the act which can be given effect without the invalid provision or application, and to this end the provisions of this act are severable.

## § 23. Short Title

This act may be cited as the Uniform Arbitration Act.

## § 24. Repeal

All acts or parts of acts which are inconsistent with the provisions of this act are hereby repealed.

## § 25. Time of Taking Effect

This act shall take effect . . . .

# APPENDIX L

# A DUE PROCESS PROTOCOL FOR MEDIATION AND ARBITRATION OF STATUTORY DISPUTES ARISING OUT OF THE EMPLOYMENT RELATIONSHIP

The following protocol is offered by the undersigned individuals, members of the Task Force on Alternative Dispute Resolution in Employment, as a means of providing due process in the resolution by mediation and binding arbitration of employment disputes involving statutory rights. The signatories were designated by their respective organizations, but the protocol reflects their personal views and should not be construed as representing the policy of the designating organizations.

## GENESIS

This Task Force was created by individuals from diverse organizations involved in labor and employment law to examine questions of due process arising out of the use of mediation and arbitration for resolving employment disputes. In this protocol we confine ourselves to statutory disputes.

The members of the Task Force felt that mediation and arbitration of statutory disputes conducted under proper due process safeguards should be encouraged in order to provide expeditious, accessible, inexpensive and fair private enforcement of statutory employment disputes for the 100,000,000 members of the workforce who might not otherwise have ready, effective access to administrative or judicial relief. They also hope that such a system will serve to reduce the delays which now arise out of the huge backlog of cases pending before administrative agencies and courts and that it will help forestall an even greater number of such cases.

## A. Pre or Post Dispute Arbitration

The Task Force recognizes the dilemma inherent in the timing of an agreement to mediate and/or arbitrate statutory disputes. It did not achieve consensus on this difficult issue. The views in this spectrum are set forth randomly, as follows:

Employers should be able to create mediation and/or arbitration systems to resolve statutory claims, but any agreement to mediate and/or arbitrate disputes should be informed, voluntary, and not a condition of initial or continued employment.

Employers should have the right to insist on an agreement to mediate and/or arbitrate statutory disputes as a condition of initial or continued employment. Postponing such an agreement until a dispute actually arises, when there will likely exist a stronger re-disposition to litigate, will result in very few agreements to mediate and/or arbitrate, thus negating the likelihood of effectively utilizing alternative dispute resolution and overcoming the problems of administrative and judicial delays which now plague the system.

Employees should not be permitted to waive their right to judicial relief of statutory claims arising out of the employment relationship for any reason.

Employers should be able to create mediation and/or arbitration systems to resolve statutory claims, but the decision to mediate and/or arbitrate individual cases should not be made until after the dispute arises.

The Task Force takes no position on the timing of agreements to mediate and/or arbitrate statutory employment disputes, though it agrees that such agreements be knowingly made. The focus of this protocol is on standards of exemplary due process.

## B. Right of Representation

### 1. Choice of Representative

Employees considering the use of or, in fact, utilizing mediation and/or arbitration procedures should have the right to be represented by a spokesperson of their own choosing. The mediation and arbitration procedure should so specify and should include reference to institutions which might offer assistance, such as bar associations, legal service associations, civil rights organizations, trade unions, etc.

### 2. Fees for Representation

The amount and method of payment for representation should be determined between the claimant and the representative. We recommend, however, a number of existing systems which provide employer reimbursement of at least a portion of the employee's attorney fees, especially for lower paid employees. The arbitrator should have the authority to provide for fee reimbursement, in whole or in part, as part of the remedy in accordance with applicable law or in the interests of justice.

### 3. Access to Information

One of the advantages of arbitration is that there is usually less time and money spent in pre-trial discovery. Adequate but limited pre-trial discovery is to be encouraged and employees should have access to all information reasonably relevant to mediation and/or arbitration of their claims. The employees' representative should also have reasonable pre-hearing and hearing access to all such information and documentation.

Necessary pre-hearing depositions consistent with the expedited nature of arbitration should be available. We also recommend that prior to selection of an arbitrator, each side should be provided with the names, addresses and phone numbers of the representatives of the parties in that arbitrator's six most recent cases to aid them in selection.

## C. Mediator and Arbitrator Qualification

1. Roster Membership

Mediators and arbitrators selected for such cases should have skill in the conduct of hearings, knowledge of the statutory issues at stake in the dispute, and familiarity with the workplace and employment environment. The roster of available mediators and arbitrators should be established on a non-discriminatory basis, diverse by gender, ethnicity, background, experience, etc. to satisfy the parties that their interest and objectives will be respected and fully considered.

Our recommendation is for selection of impartial arbitrators and mediators. We recognize the right of employers and employees to jointly select as mediator and/or arbitrator one in whom both parties have requisite trust, even though not possessing the qualifications here recommended, as most promising to bring finality and to withstand judicial scrutiny. The existing cadre of labor and employment mediators and arbitrators, some lawyers, some not, although skilled in conducting hearings and familiar with the employment milieu is unlikely, without special training, to consistently possess knowledge of the statutory environment in which these disputes arise and of the characteristics of the non-union workplace.

There is a manifest need for mediators and arbitrators with expertise in statutory requirements in the employment field who may, without special training, lack experience in the employment area and in the conduct of arbitration hearings and mediation sessions. Reexamination of rostering eligibility by designating agencies, such as the American Arbitration Association, may permit the expedited inclusion in the pool of this most valuable source of expertise.

The roster of arbitrators and mediators should contain representatives with all such skills in order to meet the diverse needs of this caseload.

Regardless of their prior experience, mediators and arbitrators on the roster must be independent of bias toward either party. They should reject cases if they believe the procedure lacks requisite due process.

2. Training

The creation of a roster containing the foregoing qualifications dictates the development of a training program to educate existing and potential labor and employment mediators and arbitrators as to the statutes, including substantive, procedural and remedial issues to be confronted and to train experts in the statutes as to employer procedures governing the employment relationship as well as due process and fairness in the conduct and control of arbitration hearings and mediation sessions.

Training in the statutory issues should be provided by the government agencies, bar associations, academic institutions, etc., administered perhaps by the designating agency, such as the AAA, at various locations throughout the country. Such training should be updated periodically and be required of all mediators and arbitrators.

Training in the conduct of mediation and arbitration could be provided by a mentoring program with experienced panelists.

Successful completion of such training would be reflected in the resume or panel cards of the arbitrators supplied to the parties for their selection process.

3. Panel Selection

Upon request of the parties, the designating agency should utilize a list procedure such as that of the AAA or select a panel composed of an odd number of mediators and arbitrators from its roster or pool. The panel cards for such individuals should be submitted to the parties for their perusal prior to alternate striking of the names on the list, resulting in the designation of the remaining mediator and/or arbitrator.

The selection process could empower the designating agency to appoint a mediator and/or arbitrator if the striking procedure is unacceptable or unsuccessful. As noted above, subject to the consent of the parties, the designating agency should provide the names of the parties and their representatives in recent cases decided by the listed arbitrators.

4. Conflicts of Interest

The mediator and arbitrator for a case has a duty to disclose any relationship which might reasonably constitute or be perceived as a conflict of interest. The designated mediator and/or arbitrator should be required to sign an oath provided by the designating agency, if any, affirming the absence of such present or preexisting ties.

5. Authority of the Arbitrator

The arbitrator should be bound by applicable agreements, statutes, regulations and rules of procedure of the designating agency, including the authority to determine the time and place of the hearing, permit reasonable discovery, issue subpoenas, decide arbitrability issues, preserve order and privacy in the hearings, rule on evidentiary matters, determine the close of the hearing and procedures for post-hearing submissions, and issue an award resolving the submitted dispute.

The arbitrator should be empowered to award whatever relief would be available in court under the law. The arbitrator should issue an opinion and award setting forth a summary of the issues, including the type(s) of dispute(s), the damages and/or other relief requested and awarded, a statement of any other issues resolved, and a statement regarding the disposition of any statutory claim(s).

6. Compensation of the Mediator and Arbitrator

Impartiality is best assured by the parties sharing the fees and expenses of the mediator and arbitrator. In cases where the economic condition of a party does not permit equal sharing, the parties should make mutually acceptable arrangements to achieve that goal if at all possible. In the absence of such agreement, the arbitrator should determine allocation of fees. The designating agency, by negotiating the parties share of costs and collecting such fees, might be able to reduce the bias potential of disparate contributions by forwarding payment to the mediator and/or arbitrator without disclosing the parties share therein.

## D. Scope of Review

The arbitrator's award should be final and binding and the scope of review should be limited.

Dated: May 9, 1995

Christopher A. Barreca, Co–Chair

Partner, Paul, Hastings, Janofsky & Walker; Rep., Council of Labor & Employment Section, American Bar Association

Max Zimny, Co–Chair

General Counsel, International Ladies' Garment Workers' Union Association; Rep., Council of Labor & Employment Section, American Bar Association

Arnold Zack, Co–Chair

President, Nat. Academy of Arbitrators

Carl E. VerBeek

Partner, Varnum Riddering Schmidt & Howlett; Management Co–Chair, Arbitration Committee of Labor & Employment Section, ABA

Robert D. Manning

Angoff, Goldman, Manning, Pyle, Wanger & Hiatt, P.C.; Union Co–Chair, Arbitration Committee of Labor & Employment Section, ABA

Charles F. Ipavec

Arbitrator; Neutral Co–Chair, Arbitration Committee of Labor & Employment Section, ABA

George H. Friedman

Senior Vice President, American Arbitration Association

Michael F. Hoellering

General Counsel, American Arbitration Association

W. Bruce Newman

Rep., Society of Professionals in Dispute Resolution

Wilma Liebman

Special Assistant to the Director, Federal Mediation & Conciliation Service

Joseph Garrison

President, National Employment Lawyers Association

Lewis Maltby

Director, Workplace Rights Project, American Civil Liberties Union

# INDEX

**References are to Pages**

**AD HOC ARBITRATOR**
See Types, Ad hoc arbitrator

**ADVISORY ARBITRATION**
See Types, Advisory

**ADVOCATES**
 In general, 34–35

**AGREED CASES**
See Awards, "Agreed"

**AIRLINES**
 In general, 94–97

**AMERICAN ARBITRATION ASSOCIATION**
 In general, 8
Excelleration Program
 Text, Appendix D
 Cited, 56, 59–60
Expedited Labor Arbitration Rules
 Text, Appendix B
 Cited, 49, 56, 59, 262, 265–66
Forms, Appendix E
Labor Arbitration Rules,
 Cited, 48–50, 222, 246, 262, 264–65
 Text, Appendix A
National Rules for the Resolution of Employment Disputes
 Text, Appendix

## AMERICAN ARBITRATION ASSOCIATION—Cont'd
National Rules for the Resolution of Employment Disputes
—Cont'd
Cited, 49–50, 100, 261–62, 267, 272, 275
Publication of awards, 268–29

## APPOINTMENT
See Arbitrators, Appointment

## ARBITRABILITY
In general, 115–18, 133–47
After expiration of the contract, 140–43, 186–87
Prerequisite for strike injunction, 124–29
Procedural, 118, 133–34, 146–47, 299–304
Substantive, 118, 133–46, 293–99
    Arbitral determinations, 138–40, 293–99
    Judicial determinations, 134–38
Successorship, effect of, See Successorship

## ARBITRATION ACT OF 1888
See Federal Laws, Railway disputes

## ARBITRATION CLAUSE
See also Arbitrability; Interpretation of contracts, Arbitration clause
As limitation on arbitrator's authority, 186–87
Broad form, 116
Content, 13–15
Definition, 13
Enforcement, see Section 301, In general; Section 301, Injunctions under Exclusions, 116–17, 134, 136–38
Expiration, Effect of, 140–43, 186–87
Standard, 116, 136

## ARBITRATORS
Appointment,
    AAA Appointment Form, Appendix E, Form 4
    In general, 33–34
Arbitration profession, 23–25
Authority, terminating
    Completion of award (Functus Officio), 50, 270–72
    Other reasons, 269–71
Awards, 31–33
Biographical data, 31
Ethics, See Code of Professional Responsibility
Learning about, 28–33
Panels, 264–65

## ARBITRATORS—Cont'd
Professionalization, 7–9
Qualifications, 29–33
Ratings, 33
Selection of, 23–35

## ARBITRATOR'S BILL
See also Costs of Arbitration
AAA Form, Appendix E, Form 9

## ARBITRATOR'S OATH
AAA Form, Appendix E, Form 4

## ATHLETICS
See Professional sports

## AWARDS (INCLUDING OPINIONS)
AAA Form, Appendix E, Form 8
Administrative and judicial review
    In general, 180–216
    Arbitral partiality, 191–93
    "Draws its essence" test, 119–20, 181, 183–85
    Gross error or irrationality, 196–97
    Incompleteness, ambiguity, or inconsistency, 206–08
    Individual employment arbitration awards, See Individual employment arbitration, judicial review of
    Lack of arbitral jurisdiction, 119–20, 185–90
    "Own brand of industrial justice" test, 119–20, 189
    Party misconduct, 191
    Procedural unfairness, 193–95
    Public policy, violation of, 197–206
    Public sector, 86–88, 214–16
"Agreed," 235–37
Conflict with law, 197–206, 308–09
Consent, See "Agreed," in this topic
Enforcement of, 118–20, 272–74
Finality, 39–51, 209–11
Form of, 261–62
Incomplete, ambiguous or inconsistent, 206–08, 261–62
Individual challenges to, 208–12
Interpretation, modification or correction by arbitrator, 271–72
Publication of, 31–33, 267–69
Time of, 49, 262–64, 269–70
Vacation or modification of by court, 50–51, 118–20, 272–74

## BOARDS
See Types, Tripartite boards

# INDEX
**References are to Pages**

**BRIEFS**
Post-hearing, 48–49

**CIVIL SERVICE REFORM ACT**
See Federal Laws, Civil Service Reform Act

**CLAYTON ANTI-TRUST ACT**
See Federal Laws, Clayton Anti-Trust Act

**CODE OF PROFESSIONAL RESPONSIBILITY**
    Text, Appendix I
Origin, 8–9
Use, 221–22, 265, 267–69, 271

**COLLECTIVE BARGAINING AGREEMENTS**
Effect of expiration, 140–43, 186–87
Enforceability, see Section 301, Damages; Section 301, Injunctions under

**COMPULSORY ARBITRATION**
See Types, Compulsory

**CONFRONTATION**
See Due Process, Confrontation and cross-examination

**CONSTITUTIONAL PROTECTIONS**
See Due Process

**CONTRACTUAL REQUIREMENTS**
See Procedure, Contractual requirements

**COSTS OF ARBITRATION**
    In general, 51–54

**CROSS–EXAMINATION**
See Due Process, Confrontation and cross-examination

**DAMAGES**
See Remedies; Section 301, Damages for breach of collective bargaining agreement

**DEFERRAL**
Courts to arbitration
    In general, 111–21, 164–79
    Arbitration awards, 114–15, 118–20
    Arbitration process, 111–118
    Criticism of, 120–21
    Labor cases, 113–21, 164–65
    Statutory cases

**DEFERRAL**—Cont'd
Courts to arbitration—Cont'd
   Statutory cases—Cont'd
      Collective bargaining context, 165–70, 178–79
      Individual employment context, 171–79
         Consent, 175–76
         EEOC opposition, 176–77
      Prerequisites, 174–75
      Weight given to awards, 168–70
NLRB to arbitration,
   In general, 156–63
   Court approval, 159–61
   Post-award, 158–61
   Pre-award, 161–63

## DEFINITIONS
Arbitrability, 133
Arbitration, 1, 4
Grievance arbitration, 1
Individual employment arbitration, 2
Interest arbitration, 1
Labor arbitration, 1
Seniority, 324–25
Submission agreement, 12

## DEMAND AND REPLY
Demand,
   AAA Form, Appendix E, Form 1
   Content, 16–17
Reply, 17–18

## DISCIPLINE AND DISCHARGE
   In general, 314–22
See also Just cause standard
Aggravating and mitigating factors, 320–21
"Fundamental understanding," 317–18
Off-duty conduct, 321–22
"Progressive" or "corrective" discipline, 319–20
Requirements, 319–21
Reasons, 319–21
"Seven tests," 315–17

## DISCOVERY
See Due Process, Discovery

## DUE PROCESS
   In general, 205–06, 217–37

## INDEX
**References are to Pages**

**DUE PROCESS**—Cont'd
"Agreed" awards, see Awards, "Agreed"
Confrontation and cross-examination, 229–30
Discovery, 38–41
Evidentiary rulings, 193–95
    See also Evidence
Ex parte hearings, 234–35
Notice, 219–21
Procedural unfairness, 193–95
Search and seizure, 226–29
Self-incrimination, 224–26
Separate representation and intervention, 221–24
Surprise, 231–34

**DUTY OF FAIR REPRESENTATION**
See Fair representation, duty of

**EDUCATION**
See Higher education

**ENFORCEMENT**
See Awards, Enforcement of; Section 301, Damages; Section 301,
    Injunctions under

**EQUITY PRINCIPLES**
Prerequisites for strike injunction, 123–24

**ERDMAN ACT OF 1898**
See Federal Laws, Railway disputes

**ETHICS**
See Code of Professional Responsibility

**EVIDENCE**
    In general, 242–61
Applicability of rules, 242–44
Discovery, 38–41
Hearsay, 229, 245–46
Medical evidence, 259–61
Parol, 247
Past employee conduct, 255–59
Past practice, 250–55
    Creating, 250–52
    Terminating, 254–55
    Using, 252–54
Plain meaning rule and extrinsic evidence, 246–49, 305—06
Precedent, See Interpretation of contracts, Precedent

**EVIDENCE**—Cont'd
Preparation, 41–42
Surprise, 232–33

**EX PARTE HEARINGS**
See Due Process, Ex parte hearings

**EXCLUSIONS**
See Arbitration clause, Exclusions; Interpretation of contracts, Arbitration clause

**EXPEDITED ARBITRATION**
  In general, 55–60
AAA Expedited Arbitration Rules, see American Arbitration Association
AAA Excelleration Program, See American Arbitration Association
Experiments, 56–59
FMCS Rules, see Federal Mediation and Conciliation Service
Steel industry, 56–57
United States Postal Service, 57–59

**EXPERIMENTAL NEGOTIATING AGREEMENT**
See Types, Interest, Steel industry

**EXPIRATION**
See Arbitrability, After expiration of the contract; Arbitration clause, Expiration, Effect of; Collective bargaining agreements, Effect of expiration

**EXTERNAL LAW**
Use by arbitrators
  In general, 147–55
  Application of theories, 154–55
  Theories, 151–53

**FACT–FINDING**
See Types, Fact–Finding

**FAIR REPRESENTATION, DUTY OF**
  In general, 208–12
Allocation of damages for breach, 211–12
Standard of fairness, 208–11
Use of, 221–22

**FEDERAL GOVERNMENT**
See Public Sector, Federal government

## FEDERAL LABOR RELATIONS AUTHORITY (FLRA)
In general, 86–87

## FEDERAL LAWS
See also Section 301
Age Discrimination in Employment Act (ADEA), 171–73, 176
Airline disputes, 94
Civil Service Reform Act (CSRA), 64, 84–85, 214–15
Clayton Anti–Trust Act, 121
Federal Arbitration Act (FAA), 50–51, 105–07, 109, 175, 182, 190–93
   Text, Appendix J.
Labor Management Relations Act (Taft–Hartley Act or LMRA), 73, 108, 342–43
National Labor Relations Act (Wagner Act or NLRA), 64, 190
Norris–LaGuardia Act, 73, 112, 121–24, 126–28
Postal Reorganization Act (PRA), 64
Railway disputes, 63, 104–05
Title VII (of the Civil Rights Act of 1964), 166–70, 173–74, 176–77
War-time, 6, 8, 61–63

## FEDERAL MEDIATION AND CONCILIATION SERVICE (FMCS)
In general, 8
Expedited Arbitration Rules
   Text, Appendix G
   Cited, 49, 56, 60,
Forms, Appendix H
Procedures for Arbitration Services
   Text, Appendix F
   Cited, 49, 262–63
Publication of awards, 268–69

## FEDERAL POLICY
See also Deferral
Criticism, 120–21
Favoring arbitration, 110–32, 134–38

## FEDERAL SERVICES IMPASSES PANEL (FSIP)
In general, 84

## FINAL–OFFER ARBITRATION
See Types, Interest, Final offer

## FINALITY
See Award, Finality

## FRINGE BENEFITS
In general, 331–35
Holidays, 331–33
Sick leave, 334–35
Vacations, 333–34

## FUNCTUS OFFICIO
See Arbitrators, Authority, Terminating

## GRIEVANCE PROCEDURE
In general, 35–38
Contractual requirements, 10–12, 36–38
Steps, 36–37
Union control, 37
Time limitations, 38

## HAYS, PAUL
Criticism of arbitration, 120–21

## HEARING
In general, 42–47
Notice,
    AAA Form, Appendix E, Form 5
    Employees right to notice of hearing, 219–21
Order of presentation, 44–47
Record, 43
Reopening, 48–49, 233
Site visits, 47
Swearing of witnesses, 43–44
Time and place, 42–43

## HEARSAY
See Evidence, Hearsay

## HIGHER EDUCATION
In general, 89–91

## HISTORY
Ancient, 3
Nineteenth Century, 4–5
Twentieth Century, 5–7, 101–110

## HOLIDAYS
See Fringe benefits, Holidays

## HOURS DISPUTES
See Wages and hours disputes

## INDIVIDUAL EMPLOYMENT ARBITRATION
In general, 7, 97–100, 171–79
AAA Rules, text, Appendix C
Court deferral to, See Deferral, Courts to arbitration, Statutory cases
Criticisms of, 176–78
Due Process Protocol,
  In general, 99–100
  Text, Appendix L
  Cited, 275
Judicial review of, 212–14
Minimum standards, 177

## INDIVIDUAL RIGHTS
See also Awards; Due Process; Section 301

## INJUNCTIONS
See Section 301, Injunctions under

## INTEREST ARBITRATION
See Types, Interest

## INTERPRETATION OF CONTRACTS
In general, 284–313
See also Arbitrability; Arbitration clause
Arbitration clause, 293–403
Conflict with law, 308–09
Implied covenant of good faith and fair dealing, 307–08
Past practice, 250–55, 306–07
  See also Evidence, Past practice
Plain meaning rule, 246–49, 305–06
Precedent, 285–93
Principles of, 304–313
Reserved rights doctrine, 307–08

## JUDICIAL REVIEW
See Awards, Administrative and judicial review

## JUST CAUSE STANDARD
In general, 205–06, 218, 220–21, 314–22
"Fundamental understanding," 317–18
Off-duty conduct, 321–22
Requirements, 319–21
"Seven tests," 315–17

## LABOR–MANAGEMENT RELATIONS ACT (TAFT–HARTLEY OR LMRA)
See Federal Laws, Labor–Management Relations Act

## LEGAL STATUS
At common law, 101–103
Under early statutes, 103–07
Under modern state statutes, 107–110
Under Section 301, see Section 301

## MANAGEMENT RIGHTS
In general, 323–24
Reserved rights doctrine, 307–08, 323

## MED–ARB
See Types, Med–Arb

## MERIT SYSTEMS PROTECTION BOARD (MSPB)
In general, 214–15

## MODEL EMPLOYMENT TERMINATION ACT
In general, 109–10

## MODIFICATION OF ARBITRATION AWARDS
See Awards, Interpretation, modification or correction by arbitrator; Awards, Vacation or modification of by court

## NATIONAL ACADEMY OF ARBITRATORS (NAA)
Founding, 8–9
Publication of awards, 269

## NATIONAL LABOR RELATIONS ACT (WAGNER ACT OR NLRA)
See Federal laws, National Labor Relations Act

## NATIONAL LABOR RELATIONS BOARD (NLRB)
See also, Federal Laws, National Labor Relations Act; Deferral, NLRB to arbitration
Relationship with arbitration, 156–63

## NATIONAL RAILWAY ADJUSTMENT ACT
See Federal Laws, Railway disputes

## NATIONAL WAR LABOR BOARD
See Federal Laws, Wartime

## NEWLANDS ACT OF 1913
See Federal Laws, Railway disputes

## NORRIS–LAGUARDIA ACT
See Federal Laws, Norris–LaGuardia Act

## NO–STRIKE AGREEMENTS
See also Section 301, Damages; Section 301, Injunctions under
Implied, 124–25
Specific enforcement, 72–74

## NOTICE
See Due Process, Notice

## OCCUPATIONAL SAFETY AND HEALTH
In general, 340–43

## OFF–DUTY CONDUCT
See Discipline and discharge, Off-duty conduct; Just cause standard, Off-duty conduct

## OPINIONS
See Awards

## ORDER OF PRESENTATION
See Hearing, Order of Presentation

## OVERTIME
See Wages and hours disputes

## PANELS
See Arbitrators, Panels; Types, Permanent panels

## PAROL EVIDENCE
See Evidence, Plain meaning rule

## PAST PRACTICE
See Evidence, Past practice

## PERMANENT PANELS
See Types, Permanent panels

## POSTAL REORGANIZATION ACT (PRA)
See Federal Laws, Postal Reorganization Act

## PRECEDENT
See Interpretation of contracts, Precedent

## PREEMPTION
See Section 301, Preemptive effect; State Laws, Preemption of

## PREPARATION
See also Evidence, Preparation; Grievance Procedure; Stipulations
In general, 35–42
Witnesses, 42

## PROCEDURAL ARBITRABILITY
See Arbitrability, Procedural

## PROCEDURE
See also Demand and Reply; Due Process; Grievance Procedure; Hearing; Individual Rights
In general, 10–54
Contractual requirements,
In general, 10–15
Arbitration Clause, 13–15
Submission agreement, 12, 186
Initiating arbitration
Demand for arbitration, 16–17
Reply, 17–18
Post-hearing, 48–52

## PROFESSIONAL SPORTS
In general, 91–94

## PROOF
Burden of
In general, 237–42
Producing evidence, 238–29
Persuasion, 239–40
Quantum, 240–42

## PROTOCOL
See Individual Employment Arbitration, Due Process Protocol

## PUBLIC POLICY
See Awards, Administrative and judicial review, Public policy; Federal policy

## PUBLIC SECTOR
Federal government, 83–87
Administrative and judicial review, 85–87, 214–16
State and local governments, 74–75, 87–89

## RAILROADS
See Federal Laws, Railway disputes

# INDEX

**References are to Pages**

**RAILWAY LABOR ACT**
See Federal laws, Railway disputes

**RECORD**
See Hearing, Record

**REINSTATEMENT**
See Remedies, Discharge cases

**REMEDIES**
    In general, 274–83
*De minimis* breaches, 282–83
Discharge cases, 276–81
Interest, 280
Limitations on arbitrator's authority, 186–87
Mitigation, 279
Monetary, 277–82
Punitive, 281–82
Statutory claims, 275

**REMOVAL**
See Section 301, Removal to federal courts

**REPLY**
See Demand and Reply, Reply

**SEARCH AND SEIZURE**
See Due process, Search and seizure

**SECTION 301**
See also Deferral, Courts to arbitration
    In general, 40, 110–32, 263
Damages for breach of collective bargaining agreement, 129
Duty of fair representation, See Fair representation, duty of
Effects, 111
Individual suits under, See Awards, Individual challenges to
Injunctions under, 72–74, 111–32
Interest arbitration, application to, 72–74
Judicial interpretation, 111–32
Jurisdiction of state courts, 113, 122–23
Meaning, 40
Preemptive effect, 129–32
Removal to federal courts, 123
Substantive law, creation of, 111–12
Text, 110–11

## SECURITIES INDUSTRY ARBITRATION
See Deferral, Courts to arbitration, Statutory cases; Individual employment arbitration, In general

## SELECTION
See Arbitrators, Selection of

## SELF–INCRIMINATION
See Due Process, Self-incrimination

## SENIORITY
In general, 324–27
Definition, 324–25
In airline disputes, 96

## SEXUAL HARASSMENT
See Awards, Administrative and judicial review, Public policy

## SPORTS
See Professional sports

## STATE AND LOCAL GOVERNMENTS
See Public Sector, State and local governments

## STATE LAWS
Early, 103–07
Modern, 107–10
Preemption of, 63–64, 122, 129–32

## STATUTORY ISSUES, ARBITRATION OF
See Deferral, Courts to arbitration, Statutory cases; Individual employment arbitration

## STIPULATIONS
AAA Form, Appendix E, Form 7

## STEELWORKERS TRILOGY
See also Deferral, Courts to arbitration
In general, 113–21

## STRIKES, INJUNCTION OF
See Section 301, Injunctions under; Sympathy strikes, Injunction of

## SUBCONTRACTING
In general, 335–37

## SUBMISSION AGREEMENT
In general, 12

## INDEX

**References are to Pages**

**SUBMISSION AGREEMENT**—Cont'd
AAA Form, Appendix E, Form 2
As limitation on arbitrator's authority, 186

**SUBPOENAS**
AAA Form, Appendix E, Form 6
Arbitral authority to issue, 40–41

**SUBSTANTIVE ARBITRABILITY**
See Arbitrability, Substantive

**SUCCESSORSHIP**
In general, 143–46

**SYMPATHY STRIKES**
Injunction of, 125–26, 128–29

**TAFT–HARTLEY ACT**
See Federal Laws, Labor–Management Relations Act

**TERMINATION**
See Collective Bargaining Agreements, Effect of expiration

**TIME LIMITATIONS**
See Arbitrability, Procedural; Grievance procedure, Contractual requirements

**TITLE VII**
See Deferral, Courts to arbitration, Statutory cases; Federal laws, Title VII

**TRANSPORTATION ACT OF 1920**
See Federal laws, Railway disputes

**TRIPARTITE BOARDS**
See Types, Tripartite Boards

**TYPES**
Ad hoc arbitrator, 22–23
Advisory, 65–66
Compulsory, 60–65
Expedited, See Expedited Arbitration
Fact–Finding, 65–68
Individual employment arbitration, See Deferral, Courts to arbitration, statutory cases; Individual employment arbitration
Interest
  In general, 68–82
  Criteria, 75–79, 93

## INDEX

**References are to Pages**

**TYPES**—Cont'd
Interest—Cont'd
    Enforcement of interest arbitration agreements, 72–73
    Final–Offer, 79–82, 92–93
    Private sector, 69–74
Public sector, 74–75, 84
    Steel industry, 71–72, 73
Med–Arb, 81
Permanent panels, 21
Single permanent arbitrator, 18–19
Temporary arbitrator, 22–23
Tripartite boards, 19–21, 95
Umpires, 18–19

**UMPIRES**
See Types, Umpires

**UNIFORM ARBITRATION ACT**
    Text, Appendix K
Cited, 50–51, 107–09, 182, 190, 261–62, 264, 271–72, 275

**UNION SECURITY**
    In general, 337–40

**UNIONS**
See Fair representation, duty of; Section 301

**UNITED STATES ARBITRATION ACT**
See Federal Laws, Federal Arbitration Act

**VACATION DISPUTES**
See Fringe benefits, Vacations

**VACATION OF ARBITRATION AWARDS**
See Awards, Vacation or modification of by court

**WAGES AND HOURS DISPUTES**
    In general, 327–331
Hours disputes, 330–31
Shift premium, 327, 333
Wage disputes, 327–30

**WAR LABOR BOARD**
See also Federal Laws, Wartime
    In general, 61–62

**WITNESSES**
See also Preparation; Subpoenas
Swearing, 43–44